AS GOD IS MY WITNESS
THE LIFE AND DEATH OF MY
BELOVED FAMILY MEMBERS

I0532943

AUTHOR
Leolah Muhammad

As God is my Witness

Editor :	**Leolah Muhammad**
Consulting Editor :	**Kelsey Brown**
Book Design/Consultant :	**Andrew Richardson**
Publisher :	**Evident Books L.L.C**

Published by:

www.evidentbooks.com

ISBN:

Paperback: 979-8-218-48738-6

Ebook: 979-8-218-44734-2

Printed in the United States of America

For more information, or to book an event, contact :

leolahbm@evidentbooks.com

arrich@evidentbooks.com

As God is my Witness

TABLE OF CONTENTS

As God is my Witness

TABLE OF CONTENTS

Continued

As God is my Witness

AKNOWLEDGEMENTS

I must give All Praise and thanks to the Almighty living God-Allah, for every single thing He has ever done for me since I have entered in this world. I will forever be grateful and indebted to Him. I also Thank Him for sending His Man and Servant, The Honorable Minister Louis Farrakhan. A Man who God and His Messenger, The Most Honorable Elijah Muhammad, both, sent into this world for the redemption of All of God's people, wherever we may be in the world. I Thank this divine Man Farrakhan from the bottom of my heart, and I am forever grateful for His coming, and being right here, right now in the world today.

I also thank The Honorable Minister Louis Farrakhan for reminding me to always be respectful, humble, and kind to every human being in this universe, regardless of a person's race, creed, color, religion, or decision. Thank You So Much beloved Minister Farrakhan, for giving your life in this wicked world, for the mission of Allah-God's. May Allah forever hold You in His bosom. I also thank and dedicate this book to my children and grandchildren for being so strong and having patience with me writing this book for this world. I believe I have the strongest and Most humble Sons in this universe. I could not have done this without my Kings! May Allah-God continue to bless both of You tremendously, as you both so well deserve to continue being BLESSED! May God bless you all to always do what is right in this world fearing nothing or no one. I don't want to say their names to expose my children, they know who they are, all of them.

As God is my Witness

I want to give special thanks to my son **Kelsey Brown** whom provided me with critical information in relation to Bobby Krissy because they were extremely close, as well as technical help in putting some of the other information in the book together. I will always love you my son!

I like to thank my manager **AR Rich**, of AR Rich Entertainment for coming aboard and helping me with this project as well. Thank you for your honesty, loyalty, and patience with me and the long process of helping this whole project come together. I believe we will always have with each other's back no matter what. I know it was a lot of work, but it was well worth it.

I'd like to recognize and thank Pastor **George Bruce**, a man of God's who stuck by me throughout it all and has always been right there with open arms and with so much understanding in all that I had to go through to complete this project. George, without ever judging me, you have always been right there playing a huge big role in helping me with this altogether, and I thank God Almighty for you! You have always been there in my life and in my corner, and I understand you to be my angel that God has sent to me and I am forever grateful for you, and will always be here for you as well. May the God of your understanding continue to bless you! Oh man of God, George Bruce! I could never thank you enough!

I'd like to thank **Cassandra Williams** from WETPR, for all the encouraging telephone conversations

As God is my Witness

Larry (Sky life) Powell, for all his help with my book project. You made my days so much better when I couldn't hold myself up you were there to hold me up and I thank you! Thank you, Larry!

I also want to thank my brother Daouad Shariff for all he has done to help as well. We all have our own part in making this a better world. May we all grow closer to God more and more each day and fully awake to realize that we are all here to do His (God's) work each day that God allows us to be here.

If you are reading these words, you are now reminded to do your part in this world, as God has given us all our own. You are also reminded to fear nothing but God and to always do right in the world from this point on while fearing absolutely nothing but God and Him alone.

As God is my Witness: (*The Life & Death of my Beloved Family*) is a non/fictional autobiography book detailing the life of myself, Leolah Muhammad aka, Leolah Brown) with my brother entertainer, Boddy Brown, my sister Whitney Houston Brown, my Bobbi Kristina Brown, and my nephew, Bobby Brown Jr.

PEACE............

As God is my Witness

PEACE BE UNTO YOU!

Before You Read This Book

Reader, I wish God's peace on your life today as you read this book. I am so grateful to God that I can finally deliver this book to you, and you can now finally read this journey of my life. By the way, and while you are here, if you are alive today after all that has taken place in this world with the pandemic and all, I believe that it can only mean that God has given you, like me, another chance to fix whatever it is that is broken with us. Everyone in this world needs to focus on being a better person, regardless of who we are, how much money we have or what decisions we have made in our lives. All of us who are living today, we stand to be corrected and need to come to God before it is too late.

There has been many people waiting for this book release, because deep down inside of any intelligent person's heart, we all know that the death of Whitney Houston, her daughter, and my nephew Bobby Brown Jr., (which are all Bobby Brown's immediate family), have all been killed in the worse way. And it is so sadly looking like no one else but me is concerned with bringing them any justice. The way it all went down was so very sad and unheard of. We all know that something is very wrong with the picture of losing them all the way we did. Never have we ever heard of a mother and a daughter dying the same way as the both of them did. It is a lie and they know it is a big lie told, but I am here to tell this world the absolute truth. It made no sense that they came in there and saw her body like that and just reported it an accident.

As God is my Witness

That is a serious disrespect to my family and those who loved Whitney Houston and my niece, Bobbi Kristina. It's a crying shame that they would even do that and take her death so lightly and disregard the truth and then continue to keep it suppressed for all these years. On top of it all, it tells anyone in their right mind that there is something very wrong with the so-called law system that we as tax payers are always demanded to pay. Nowhere in the history of this life or any other, has a mother and a daughter both keep coming up in a bathtub. This thing happened way too many times for it to be an accident. And regardless to what anyone says, we are talking about individuals who have not indulged in drugs by their own will. The drugs were forced on my niece and Whitney DID NOT DO DRUGS ANYMORE.

Their deaths also proved that there is someone out there in this world who seemed to have it out for my brother, Bobby Brown. My brother hasn't done anything to anyone for someone to want to come after his wife and children and kill them. When God shows this world that He did not sleep on any of this, we will all be shocked at what we will finally witness as justice for all of them. I not only believe this, but I am also 100% certain and I know that it will come to pass and fairly settle soon by the God that I believe in.

Their untimely deaths were surely not in any way some accident caused by themselves, as the media has been falsely reporting. It is also one of the reasons why this book has been necessary for me to write to this entire world. It is despicably sad that they have lost their lives in the way that they all did. Which was only because of another person's evil and demonic ways and their very selfish desires. They were killed because of others who literally plotted on them and took their lives unremorsefully.

As God is my Witness

This book has been a long time coming, and I am extremely relieved and happy to finally deliver this to you so that you will have the absolute truth regarding what really happened, and what exactly "went down" with Whitney Houston, her daughter Bobbi Kristina Brown, and my nephew Bobby Brown Jr. And if you have asked the question of why I have decided to write this memoir book, please allow me to explain it to you straight from my own mouth.

First, I am the biological blood sister of entertainer, singer and actor, Bobby Brown. I am also the sister-n-law of Whitney Houston. I have so many experiences and memories of being with them, along with my niece, Bobbi Kristina Brown, and my nephew, Bobby Brown Jr. Also, I lived with them both for a long time and was also employed by them both, also having legal court ordered custody of my niece, their daughter, Bobbi Kristina Brown.

I know a whole lot about all of them, period. One of my main reasons for writing this book is simply because I am a witness that they have all been cold bloodedly murdered. Everything written in this book is the absolute truth, and to the best of my knowledge, based on my individual experiences, and what I know to be the absolute truth resulting from what I have investigated and found in all their cases.

There has been nothing but lies on top of other lies that have been put out here by the media, as to what really happened to all of them, and I am here to set the record straight and just very simply tell you the truth. I will without a doubt, explain and prove to you that they did not just pass away by drug overdose, drowning, or by any accident that were caused by engaging themselves in drug use. With that said, know and understand that their untimely deaths are what led me to write this book today.

As God is my Witness

It may even shock you that, even though I know, and I am 100% certain, that they have all been set up and deliberately murdered, I have sincerely in my heart forgiven all of my brothers and sisters, whom I believe to be guilty of some or all of it. I have to forgive in order to please God, and also as a help for my own soul. If I did not have the knowledge, wisdom, and understanding that I have today regarding God, it may have been harder for me to forgive them for what they have done to my family members. Yet, I thank God that I can tell the world that I have honestly forgiven them. But, because I forgave them, does not mean that I should allow the truth of what happened to them, remain suppressed and away from the public, who are so deserving to hear this truth. Meanwhile, the media will continue to report the bogus and made up lies concerning them and how they died and left here so suddenly. Regardless of what I say or have always said, I expect them to do their jobs, as I am obligated to do mine.

Of course, I do not know exactly whose hand killed Whitney, but what I do know and what I am so very sure of is the fact that Whitney was beaten to death. This is something that we (my family and close friends) all know far beyond any shadow of doubt. In the case of Nick Gordon, yes indeed, he intended to kill my niece, Bobbi Kristina Brown, by beating her near to death, and then leaving her to die in her own bathtub. Yet, technically, he is not guilty of murdering her, only because she came out of that trauma, after being rushed to the hospital and fighting so hard to live. And she fought hard and did come out of that and lived! It was not until Pat and Cissy Houston both, who are the two main people who are responsible for the death of my niece. I wish I could say it another way but I can't because it's that truth. And I will prove all of this to you, far beyond a shadow of a doubt in this book right here and now.

As God is my Witness

In the case of my nephew, Bobby Jr, it was obvious to anyone with the least intelligence who took his life. The person we believe is responsible was still right there in the bedroom with him when my brother Bobby came in and found his son dead. From what I was told by family members, this girl said she knew nothing of him being dead and yet, he had been lying there dead right there next to her for who knows how long before his father came there and found him deceased. She was right there with him while no one else was. I and others are witnesses that my nephew was very clean and had not done any drugs on his own, meaning by his own hands, when he was found. I will explain this as well. Every one of their deaths are open and shut cases that have not been given the proper attention needed to just very simply close their cases with guilty parties being charged.

It is not impossible to figure it all out and break it all down as to who did what. These deaths are actually very easy to solve, but to this day they have not been solved properly. There is only a limited number of people who were around all of them. Therefore, it is very easy and can be narrowed down right away if those in authority would just simply pay the proper attention to their cases. As of today, I believe it is going to take A FEDERAL INVESTIGATION TO DO THE JOB. One undeniable fact about Whitney Houston that we all know is that she always had 24-hour security, especially whenever she went out of town. The ugly thing about all of this is, that someone did not just take Whitney's life, but they literally "beat" her to death in that hotel room. And the way her body was found, there had to be a lot of noise coming out of that room. I am sure someone heard 'something' at some point in time, but I believe they are just not saying anything.

As God is my Witness

When her body was found in that Hotel, anyone looking at her face and her entire body knew and was sure that there was indeed foul play. By the way…. Did you know that my niece, Bobbi Kristina was also found in the Beverly Hilton hotel bathtub the day before her mother, Whitney? Some people know this, while a lot of other people have never heard it. This is something that was never mentioned when the first person decided to speak out on a camera to talk about Whitney Houston and her body being found in that hotel. I am speaking of those who were present at that hotel with Whitney and her daughter, and saw it fit to give their statements to the media after learning Whitney was pronounced dead.

They first said that it was Ray J, who found Whitney, and then they changed it and said it was Ray, Whitney's security guy who found her. I heard about 4 or 5 stories altogether when it comes to who found her body first. I saw something in the media where Ray J's publicist stated that it was Ray J himself, who had initially found Whitney. Everyone believed her statement because of the caliber of person she is. Then she or perhaps another person, retracted that statement and said, no, it was Ray, Whitney's security guy, who found Whitney first.

I have always believed that out of all of what I have heard, some of these people were just trying to cover for whomever they were trying to protect at that time. There are so many people that supposedly found her, and so many lies that were told, and I believe none of them. There is no telling what the truth is and who really found Whitney first. It appears to me that people have not been honest at all. Let me also tell you something that you may not have ever heard. The coroner "Ed Winters", who examined Whitney, stated in his coroner's report, he got a phone call the day before Whitney Houston's body came up dead.

As God is my Witness

He said the caller on the other end said, quote; "Be prepared to pick up a body at the Beverly Hilton Hotel today!" After the person on the other end of that phone said that they just hung up! The coroner said, "I waited to get the call again to pick up a body at that hotel, but no call came in until that next day, and it was Whitney Houston's body that came up dead that next day. THE FEDS NEED TO OBTAIN THOSE PHONE RECORDS...NOW!

Now, let's go back to the day before at this Beverly Hilton Hotel, which was February 10, 2012. My niece, Bobbi Kristina, had woken up in her hotel bathtub, throwing up water from her lungs this day. This is why the caller called in the first place. The crazy part about this was "my niece had no idea what happened to her." I believe someone spiked her food and/or her drink; to try to kill her this day but was unsuccessful and it was the reason that coroner did not have to go to that hotel to pick up a deceased body on that day after-all. Now, my belief is that this was "PLAN A" and they planned to kill my niece first and then wanted to kill Whitney after, so that they could say she committed suicide after finding her daughter in the bathtub.

Yet, it did not work out that way because my niece came up out of that tub of water, she jumped up and ran to her mother's (Whitney's) room right then and there. Now, this was something a lot of you knew nothing about, but I will explain. According to my niece, she told us, she had eaten breakfast and lunch that day without going out of her hotel room. She remembered feeling sleepy after eating lunch and got up to lock the deadbolt on her hotel door and that was all she remembered before waking up in her hotel bathtub naked. **(This told me someone spiked her food or drink)**.

As God is my Witness

She said, when she woke up there were several hotel security guards standing over her looking at her and watching her jump up out of that water as if they saw a ghost! Not one of them tried to help her up out of the water, she said. My niece said, after she jumped out of that water, she realized she was naked, and of course ran to find her clothes but could not find anything, and not even her suitcases! She now realizes that someone has taken her suitcases out of her room "that quick!" She said, she went to step down out of that bathtub and onto her rug, and her hotel room rugs were soaked with water all the way to her hotel door! (I want you to remember this with Whitney's case). When Whitney was found, the water was heavy in this same room as well, if you understand where I am going with this. This means that Whitney was found in Krissy's room and she was not in her own room when she was beaten to death. This also let me know that it was Nick Gordon present, but with who else I do not know. See, Nick Gordon's room was adjoined to Krissy's.

Plus, Nick Gordon made the statement that "He saved Pat Houston with Whitney's death!" He gave it up by saying what he said. So, it is a matter of who was in that room where the wet rugs were with Nick Gordon? I believe it was Gary Houston and perhaps Ray J. Now, I will say that I am not sure if Ray J was in that room right at that time, but I am positively certain he was in that hotel that day. How and why all of that water got all the way out of that hotel bathroom and ran all the way into that room is a mystery, but then again, my guess has been that they were trying to let the water run to make the lie appear real and say that she passed out after running a bath and accidently drowning herself.

As God is my Witness

In any event, their plot did not work because my niece awoke in that bathtub, and she ran down to her mother's room after she jumped up out of the bath water (naked without any clothes on). Which means that someone took all her clothes out of that hotel, and someone did indeed take her clothes out of that room that day. Which means, as soon as she locked that deadbolt door, she passed out! Someone quickly removed her clothing after that, and that fast, thinking that she was not going to get up.

Now, it would help to know who was in her room with her this day. And we can very easily guess just by knowing who was there at the hotel during this time. Whitney and Krissy did not hang around random people for starters. They were both very private and had limited company. It would be between Ray Whitney's security, Pat and Gary Houston, Nick Gordon, Ray J, and Brandi Burnside. Raffles Van Excel was also around this day as well. We will get to all of them including Raffles Van Axel a little later in this book, but all of them were indeed present this day at the Beverly Hilton for sure, because we saw them all on video.

Anyone who knows Whitney knows that she was very private and hard to get to. The first person who came to my mind when my niece could not find her clothes was Pat and Gary Houston. These two people came directly to my mind, as if God was giving me this whole picture as it took place in real time. I felt a strong sense that came over me almost immediately when I first heard this. I said, yeah, Pat and Gary had to take her clothes out of that room. Yet, I could be wrong, and it could be Nick Gordon or someone else. In any event, Krissy ran to her mother's room naked after jumping out of that water.

As God is my Witness

After this, Whitney was furious calling around looking for everyone so that they could explain to her about how or why her child woke up in that bathtub and then had no clothes to put on. Reader, please stop here for a moment and think! I want you to remember this as you remember when Pat Houston sat on Oprah saying, "she did not answer Whitney's phone calls all that day." The whole world heard her say that on Oprah. I had to find the truth in all of this. I believed her when she said, Whitney tried calling her, but she just would not answer any of her calls that day. I was determined to find out just why she would do that. I knew it was a reason why Pat wasn't answering. When I heard what happened to my niece, I said BINGO! We all know in our family that Whitney hardly ever speaks to Pat. From right there, and after hearing that, I began investigating with a fine-tooth comb because we knew in our hearts that something very sinister was wrong with that statement and this whole thing.

I also remembered and kept in mind that Ray J also said that same thing, "he regretted the missed phone calls from Whitney as well." Therefore, in my mind, they did not answer their phones because they knew what exactly Whitney wanted with them both. I am sure Whitney was calling everyone who she thought may have been around her daughter and involved with trying to kill her daughter in that hotel that day. There was no way my niece almost drowned herself in that bathtub. Nor did she remove her clothing out of her hotel room. She had clothes on when she walked to her door to lock it. Now, keep in mind, this is all happening at the "Beverly Hilton Hotel" and before my niece was found in Atlanta after finally being beaten by Nick Gordon and then later killed by Pat Houston. Please stay with me because there is so much for you to remember and understand here.

As God is my Witness

The fact that she had no clothes on when she awoke in that bathtub (at this hotel in Los Angeles), and no clothes any longer available to her, when she jumped up out of that water and was spitting it out of her lungs; "it let me know that they were moving fast to expedite their murders." Someone was moving real fast to do this! We later see Whitney after her death, on a video, experiencing being hot and running into a pool of water to cool off. After watching Whitney stand in front of Clive Davis, Monica and Brandy Norwood being wet, it told me that perhaps Ray J gave Whitney something to make her hot as well. Reason I say this is simply because, my niece Krissy, she went through this same thing with Ray J (after Witney died). Stay with me, and I will explain.

Again, after seeing Whitney like this, I knew that Whitney and her daughter were both experiencing and going through the same thing, because of when Ray J, offered my niece Krissy this pill after Whitney was found deceased! I said, BINGO! Here it is right here! I said, Oh my God! He must have given Whitney the same thing and it was why Whitney was also looking for Ray J! SHE WAS HOT! SHE NEEDED WATER! IT MAKES SENSE! It makes sense to us, because after Whitney dies, my nephew literally witnessed Ray J literally forcing my niece to take this pill that was to make her stop crying and mourning her mother. After my niece takes it, she GETS REAL HOT and she goes into a seizure and is rushed off to a hospital by ambulance. Then I hear Ray J say in the media that he too was regretful of the missed phone calls that Whitney was putting out to him, but he wasn't answering! All these people were doing sneaky things and running around this hotel trying to get rid of my sister and her daughter and no one can tell me different.

As God is my Witness

This is why Whitney's niece Aleah got those phone calls in New Jersey, that someone was doing fishy things to Whitney. It was all adding up and I saw it for myself. I strongly believe that Whitney knew that Ray J was trying to kill her, and it was why she felt HOT, and it is why we see her with Krissy approaching Brandy Norwood, as she sat with Monica and Clive Davis in that live setting, (which is all over social media today).

I told everyone, Whitney could not reach Ray J, Pat, Gary, or even her security Ray, I believe that she took it upon herself to take Krissy's hand, and go and interrupt that live meeting, with Clive Davis, Monica, and Brandy Norwood, as they sat there together. I am speaking of the video where Whitney passed Brandy that "mystery note." I still to this day believe that note was for Brandy to give to her brother Ray J, hands down.

What other reason would she give that to Ray J's sister, we all said. See, we knew Whitney, unlike many other people who had no clue as to what she was doing that day. The moment I saw that, I said to myself and those sitting with me, yeah, that was for Ray J. I read Whitney's body language as well, which also told me she was upset about something, right at that time. In fact, I looked at everything with this whole case, and I came to a sane and logical conclusion without involving my emotions. Yes because, as she walked up on Clive, Monica, and Brandy; Monica says, "Oh your wet again Whitney?" Go and see it for yourself, it is right there. This told me that someone tried spiking her food or drink more than once while she was at that hotel. I believe I figured this out and it makes all the sense in the world to me and others who feel the same way.

As God is my Witness

This also made me think that this is why someone wanted her to be there two weeks prior to the Clive Davis event. In my mind, they needed this time to do away with her and knew it may be hard, so they needed those days. God has given me this information, whether anyone wishes to believe it or not it is my story and what I believe. After Krissy ran to her mother's room wet and naked, Whitney had time to talk with her daughter and question her about who was in her room that day. Who knows, my niece may have told her that the people who were in her room were Ray J, Brandi Burnside, Nick, Pat, and Gary; it sure sounds about right to me? We don't know all of what her and Whitney's conversation was while she laid in that room with her mother. But in my mind, and what I strongly believe, is that all the evidence is right there of Whitney walking up to them and handing her that note. And Whitney is keeping her daughter close to her at that time, to protect her.

It all makes sense to me and everyone else who knows this story, and we all believe it for so many reasons, and especially because of that note that Whitney was so determined to hand to Brandy that day. We believe that is why Brandy will not allow anyone to know what is written in that note. It was not anything good is why she doesn't want anyone to see it. I believe it would incriminate her brother. One thing is for certain, they were all right there after Whitney's body came up deceased. Isn't that something? And none of them were around when Whitney was looking for them! No, they were not answering their phones when Whitney was calling all of them, but now suddenly out of nowhere, they all strangely appear when she came up dead this day. As they say, "I have receipts" on Ray J literally forcing my niece to take a pill that she did not want to take that ended up making her hot and throwing her into that seizure.

As God is my Witness

All of this with Krissy and Ray J happened "after" Whitney's death. I said, well look at this, now Whitney's gone, and now they all feel like it's an easy thing to deal with Krissy. Krissy was crying hysterically after she found out her mother was dead. She was in the hotel hallway crying and then in the hotel room crying. Ray J is right there as well at this time, and now he says, "Here Krissy, why don't you take this pill, it will make you feel better and calm you down! My nephew told me that Krissy told him, "No", so many times, and yet, he (Ray J) would not take no for an answer. Now, this part is all according to what my nephew Jerod Brown Carter and another person who witnessed Ray J doing this has said. He stood right there and witnessed Ray J doing this, so I am not making this up.

My nephew stated that Krissy finally took it after Ray J insisted too many times. And by this time, Krissy is in the hotel room bathroom with Ray J, and she for some reason takes this pill he keeps asking her to take. Immediately after Krissy takes this pill, she comes running out of the bathroom throwing her shirt off and screaming, "Ray J, what did you give me, what is in that pill, I am HOT!" She begins crying and screaming at the same time, and she goes directly into a seizure, right there! They called an ambulance, and she is rushed off to the hospital by ambulance "because of what Ray J insisted she take from him. "And while I'm here, this is what I saw all of them doing to my niece, by trying to get her to do drugs so that she will be set up to be unfit to be over her mother's estate after Whitney is gone. I am telling you; I strongly believe this is their whole motive for doing all of this. Yet, Krissy came out of that ordeal, and they continued to come after her until their mission was accomplished. This is why I kept doing my best and trying to "get to my niece!" I kept telling my niece to please contact me so that we could sit down and go somewhere to talk.

As God is my Witness

You will hear the rest in this book about how I tried getting to her. I even called my brother Bobby begging him to get her because I felt it in my gut that she was next. I feel this heavy in my heart, and in my mind, this is none other than Pat and Gary Houston orchestrating all of this. I believe, at this time, they were throwing these rocks by telling them to do this and hiding their hands as if they had nothing to do with this. Either that or they were all getting orders from someone else to do it. Either way, all their hands were right there on deck. I will not ever believe that all of them present had nothing to do with their demise by having this kind of behavior coming from Ray J, Nick Gordon and Brandi Burnside. Stay with me and let me explain more

Now, my niece, Krissy gets to the hospital by ambulance from having a seizure from what Ray J gave her, and she calls my son, Kel-Rock, or he calls her, whichever way it went down, they both spoke during this time. The two of them are on the phone after Krissy is taken by ambulance to this LA hospital. Meanwhile there is someone in the background right there with my niece, telling the doctor or nurse that they should 5150 my niece! According to what my son told me, the doctors were finished with Krissy, and said that she was just mourning her mother and would be OK, and that she just needed rest. I am sure had they checked her for poison, they would have found something in that pill that Ray J gave her, I strongly believe this.

My son knows exactly what 5150 meant as Brandi Burnside and her mother were both trying to convince this nurse or doctor to 5150 Krissy. He hears them very clearly, and so he immediately asks Krissy, "Who is that with you Krissy, that keeps telling the doctor that they need to 5150 you!?" Krissy, not even knowing what 5150 means, she says out of her own mouth, "Oh that's Brandi Burnside and her mother Kelsey, why, what is 5150?"

As God is my Witness

She doesn't even realize that these people have set her up, Kelsey said, and now they want the doctor to send her to a mental institution after Ray J has talked her into taking this pill! No one can tell me that this wasn't a sinister act, and that this was not deliberately done, to set my niece up. I have never seen anyone do such a foolish thing. Nowhere in this country or any other country have I ever heard of anyone that would have the nerve to even entertain such thoughts of suggesting that to a hospital official, after someone's mother dies! They did this knowing that my niece was not the type of person Pat tried to make her out to be on that "Reality Show." I said, See, I told you all, and it had to come from Pat and Gary Houston, I said. I had already told all of my friends and my family members that Pat and Gary both, were going to try to do this to my niece after Whitney was gone. I also predicted that Pat Houston would try to place Krissy before a judge and try making that judge believe that my niece was not sane, and in any shape to be over her own "ESTATE!"

Everything that happened, I had already predicted it to happen. I had already told everyone this news, before it happened, because I felt that it was God Himself, who was giving me all of this information that had already been downloading in my head before it all happened. I could just feel the set up and the plotting against Whitney and my niece going on. We all know that Ray J and Brandi Burnside are good friends and have been hanging out with each other. According to Whitney, she told us that this girl Brandi Burnside, had been trying to get on with any network, to be on any show that would have her. Whitney said, "She was trying to use her (Whitney's) name out in the streets, to get people to believe that Whitney was her godmother. Whitney told us, she goes around telling people that she was Whitney Houston's goddaughter all the time to gain fans of some sort. I asked Whitney one day, is she, her godmother?

As God is my Witness

Whitney said, "That girl met my husband and wanted Bobby to be her godfather so badly, and she just put me in it, but I am not her d*#m godmother!" After a while, Whitney did not like her going around saying that. Whitney said she found out that they did a lot of lying and she wanted nothing at all to do with Brandi Burnside and her mother. That lie about Whitney being her godmother has probably opened a lot of doors for her out here in these streets. I just hope that she has let go of that lie and is older now, and not found still doing that because enough has been enough already, and we all know the truth of all of this. Especially after what she was caught trying to do with my niece's life. She knows that had Whitney been alive, she would have been dealt with seriously by Whitney for doing such a thing, her and her mother. I didn't know all of this until it was over and haven't seen Brandi after the fact. Whitney said a lot of things that just didn't sit well with me about this girl Brandi and her mother.

The amazing thing is, I told everyone one day, I said, "I would BET any amount of money that her and Ray J, both will be on some show together after all this smoke clears with Whitney's death." When "Love and Hip-Hop" ever came on with the two of them on it, I said, "There you have it, and it's just as I said it would be!" I predicted it, because I felt it directly in my heart and gut that they were going there. I could literally feel it in my guts that someone offered them a place on a show because of what they did to Whitney for them. Who that person is, I cannot call it, but I believe it's all in cahoots with Pat and Gary Houston along with Mama Cissy Houston who stands in the far back so that she isn't noticed. After all that I have heard about everyone, they are nothing more than handlers to me. I told everyone to mark my words, and all of them who heard me say it, they said, "Leolah, you were absolutely right!" They are both now on a show together just as you said they would be.

As God is my Witness

" I said, "I told you so, I cannot be fooled by anyone." On top of it, I am not stupid, and I knew what the deal was all along. I believe they all have something to do with the demise of Whitney and my niece because of the way they were all acting and moving out here. People give themselves up by what they have said and their actions which are easy for a trained woman like me to see through so easily. One of the things that I determined and concluded after doing my own investigation in this case is, I believe their aim was to "first" kill my niece, Bobbi Kristina, and then kill Whitney. They were unsuccessful on the first attempt with the bathtub thing.

Then they tried the car accident, by sticking a knife into a tire of the car my niece was forced to drive in Atlanta. I am sure there were many other attempts, they just did not succeed in those beforehand. Joshua, who was Krissy's friend, told us how they plotted that out and failed at that as well. The way I see it and understood it all, somebody was very angry that Krissy hadn't been taken out sooner. I feel like they were becoming impatient with Nick Gordon because he was literally planted there to help with Whitney and Krissy's murders.

The people out here in this world believe that Nick was innocent and didn't do anything, but it is most definitely the total opposite of who he was and what his job was given to him for. I am 100% sure and I also 100% "know" that he was a handler person who was sent in. Of course he is, because he did not come into Whitney and Krissy's life until "AFTER" Bobby and Whitney's divorce. I have told this world that I have lived with Bobby and Whitney, and had custody of Krissy, and I never once met Nick Gordon, period. Furthermore, I am 100% certain that he did not live with them all his young childhood life, No Way.

As God is my Witness

That was a big lie told for whatever purpose they saw fit. I just can't understand how they thought we would lay low on this and not reveal the truth about Nick Gordon. The media told this world that because it is what Pat Houston gave them to say. No one in our family ever met Nick Gordon. Trust us when we say that he was nothing more than a handler for Pat Houston. See, I never forgot Whitney telling us, whenever we see things out here that don't look or sound right, know that it is Pat Houston out here perpetrating a fraud by lying to the media to benefit whatever it is she has going on in Whitney's name. Whitney said that Pat had friends in the media. It is all done fraudulently, hands down. He beat my niece down in her living room home in Atlanta, and the way he did that, it told me and everyone else that he was angry and frustrated so much, that he did everything he did to her that day. When I ever read that police report, I said, "My God, if we could have walked in that house at that time and got our hands on him, I am certain that we would have been carried off to jail. That is the very sad part of all of this. This boy got away with doing what he did to my niece, and had we been there, we would have been arrested for protecting her.

We love our sister, my niece, and my nephew just like anyone else loves their family members. We are certain that all their deaths were premeditated murders, hands down. They had been plotting this whole thing out, and the reason it took so long to get my niece after Whitney was gone, is because they had nothing planned for my niece after Whitney's death and had to get it together. Plan A had failed them, so they had to come up with something else and it took them awhile. That is why there was a three-year gap before they got to Krissy. Every attempt to take her out failed them and so it just took them that long to get her, but believe me, they were trying time after time.

As God is my Witness

I am sure they tried multiple times, and only God knows how many attempts they failed at it. I have strong reasons to believe that they wanted Krissy dead first so that they could possibly bate Whitney into committing suicide, and then they could report the incident as that when she would have found her daughter in the Beverly Hilton hotel bathtub. However, Bobbi Kristina Brown came up out of that bathtub water and did not die that day. This is the reason the coroner got that phone call that day. They thought Krissy was really going to die. In my investigations alone, I concluded very easily what happened with each case and believe it wholeheartedly without the slightest doubt. When it comes to my niece, Krissy, my family members, and myself, we all know unequivocally who literally and boldly took her life. By the permission of Mama Cissy, Pat Houston is that one person who literally killed Bobbi Kristina, and I will "PROVE IT" so very far beyond a shadow of a doubt right here in this book. What people do not know or understand is that her case is no different than Whitney's case. The very same people that were present, you will hear the facts as you read what exactly happened to Bobbi Kristina and Whitney altogether.

Just keep reading.... I thank God that Bobby Jr was not beaten to death like Whitney and Krissy were. The person who beat Whitney had to have a hate for her, and I believe I know whose hands were there and are guilty of it, as you will hear in this book. None of these cases are hard to solve at all, and I pray that after this book I have written, the rightful people of God will stand up to help bring some kind of justice to every single one of them. This is my prayer at the end of the day, and I pray that God grants them their justice for this world to see. No one person is more special than the next person.

As God is my Witness

And at the end of the day, we all are human, and we bleed the same color blood, and we all deserve to have equal justice under the laws of God first, and then the laws of this land. Whitney deserves to have her justice for her and her daughter, especially when you have done as much as she has done to give back to this society and this world.

I am sure that anyone reading this book would not agree with any of their loved ones being murdered and nothing positive happening behind their wrongful deaths. We all feel the same way whenever we lose someone close to our hearts. Therefore, we should all be able to understand just what my family and I are feeling and going through. No one can imagine how the Brown's feel behind everything that has transpired thus far. Those who call themselves Whitney's family are fine because they got what they wanted. The Browns have suffered these losses more than any one of us when it comes to our families. My children have suffered the most out of all the younger people in our families, I believe. My oldest son has been seriously traumatized in a way where he needs special counseling and therapy, and it is far more serious than anyone can possibly imagine today. As I write these words, he is still suffering and going through so much today.

Some people can understand it while others have never given it any thought at all. All my family member's deaths have taken a hard toll on my immediate family. My sons and I have suffered so much since the deaths of my family members. If anyone knew what we had to suffer altogether, most people would more than likely not be able to bear it and still stand strong. There are a lot of things I can't even say because it is too painful right now.

As God is my Witness

I personally have been tested and tried so many times by the most ignorant and harsh people in this world, and yet I thank God that I have overcome and stood strong amid my suffering. I know and I fully understand that what does not kill me, will always make me so much stronger. Regardless to what I am or have suffered, my job is to remain humble while knowing that God has this and He will indeed repay everyone back for what they all did, regardless to what it is they.

With all due respect, I am wise enough to understand that the most important thing in any trial is to come out much stronger and stand without bitterness. This is another reason why I have forgiven my brothers and sisters." I must forgive in my heart because that is a part of believing in God; and when you say that you are a believer, you must bear a lot of things that you may not be willing to or ready for. Especially if you are not educated as to who we really are and why we are here altogether. It is my obligation to be as strong as God would want me to be, especially for my children. If not, how could I be a good example of one who says they believe in God. Yes, it is hard to do sometimes, I must admit it as an honest human being. Yet, it must be done, and more importantly, it has finally been done. I had to have peace within myself so that I could remain in tune with God. That is something that so many of us do not know how to do when the time comes to do it.

When we have problems and issues, we will run to anything, even a person or just people in general, before we will just simply go to the God of our own understanding first. He is the answer, if we would only be patient with Him and have more faith in Him, He is the answer to it all for us. God is not a liar when He says, come to Him and He will make His yoke easy for us.

As God is my Witness

Most of us do not have enough sense to know and understand how God works, and how He will always have open arms whenever we need Him. A lot of us believe we are not worthy of praying to Him, but you are! There is nothing that you can do that God will not forgive you for. He will judge you by your heart, and you must humble yourself before Him in that rightful spirit and He will hear you regardless of how you think or believe that He won't. We must do better in treating other people better in this world. You must treat people exactly how you wish and desire to be treated. And as life has it, we need to understand that there is a cut and an end time to everything under this Sun. We would be wise to stay in tune with God and get to know Him.

When we finally leave here, we had better make sure that we have carried no weight in with us. All of us must make sure that our good outweighs our bad in this world, otherwise we have a problem. We all need to flee to God right now and not waste another moment because the time is critical. When we are looking for answers, comfort, or peace, He should be that only one we move towards. Otherwise, we will finally learn one day after much pain and suffering that it is only Him who we should depend on. When we reach for a source or something outside of Him, it is why we do not ever find it and become satisfied.

At the end of every day, it is God who always sits with open arms waiting for us to just simply look to Him for "all" of our needs. I am striving so hard to become an example and the person I entered this world to be, rather than one who lacks being herself without a purpose. The one thing that I desire to inspire and instill in every reader of this book is forgiveness.

As God is my Witness

We must forgive our very own brothers and sisters for what they have done to us in this world, regardless of who they are or what they have done. I believe that I have passed this test, but it makes me no better than the next person. I am still striving to be that righteous person. There is a reason that the Bible tells us to forgive our brother and sister many times over. It is something that God will not compromise with us. He does not think like us, and He is not an emotional God like we are. The Bible says, the mind of this world is foolishness with God, and it is! That's why it is Him at the end of the day that I look to.

He is that Man who is the judge of us all, and it is He who will judge "all" of our hearts. Whether we like it or not, or believe it or not, what we do today, we will face Him tomorrow on. Even those of us who think we got away with wrongdoing. There is a price to pay for everything done in the dark as well as the light. None of us are getting a pass, we will willingly bow to the proper God of this universe and time, be it by force or willingness, it will indeed be done.

I am sure that most of us know that none of us are without sin nor are any of us perfect. And it is only God who knows every one of our hearts, and what we are really made of with that said, and with all of my own imperfections, I pray and hope that all of my trials are met, faced, passed and overcome with flying colors, and I am an example of what we all should be, when it comes to forgiving my very own people, as we are told to do. What's also detrimentally important is, when we know the truth, there should not ever be anything under this sun that we fear or shy away from when it comes time to speaking it. Especially when we know in our hearts that our loved ones have been murdered.

As God is my Witness

We should always, without any fear whatsoever, speak up and out into this universe with the absolute truth regardless of who likes it or not. And never fear losing people if you do stand for truth. If they will not support you for liking the truth, you will have to make up your mind, and seriously think about this one. If that person is worthy of being your friend, you will know it because they won't judge you and they will respect your wishes at the end of the day. It is detrimental that we all get closer to God in this hour of time today and make Him (God) sufficient for us in everything we do. It is in fact, an emergency, believe it or not. He should be the focus of everyone's day. I and we, owe no one else anything, but God.

When it calls for you to do so, simply stand and speak the truth for your loved ones. We should always do the right thing and help bring our loved one's justice especially if someone takes their life. You should not ever be afraid of anything under this Sun when you know you should speak the truth. Place yourself in someone else's shoes because you would want the very same thing for yourself; and keep that faith in God that you are supposed to have. No one is more important than God. The Bible even teaches us to not be afraid of anyone or anything but do fear Him who has power over your SOUL. Nobody would want to lose someone close to them by murder, and then try to go to sleep on those thoughts every single night that God allows you to be here, knowing your people were killed for foolish reasons where they did nothing to anyone.

I knew and understood this as my test and my trial by God, and that I must do the right thing before God. I knew that I had to because of all the evidence that was placed before me. The things that I was witnessing, learning and experiencing right before my own eyes was telling me that God wanted me to see all of this for a reason.

As God is my Witness

He placed me in a position to not turn my heels and walk away from knowing what I know when people are taken from their loved ones so viciously, that of course, is enough and it makes it harder to deal with. And yes, of course, I know that we all must go and leave this world someday, but it is "how" we go that makes all the difference. It is very sad to know that my own people have been so cruel and evil and so wicked to have done such a vicious thing to my family members. They have done some of the worst inhumane things to Whitney, Krissy and Bobby Jr. And yes, I do believe there are others involved, but they were not right there striking the blows, and they are those whom I have no knowledge of Therefore, I can only speak on what I know to be the truth of what went down and happened here.

There are even many people who want me to say that Clive Davis has something to do with this. Well, you are going to have to write your own book and put Clive in it if you have information on Clive. I cannot do that because I would be lying on Clive if I said I had information on Clive Davis. I do not have anything on Clive Davis regarding the murder of Whitney or anyone else. But what I do have is what is in this book that I am 100 percent certain of Yes, I think, and I strongly believe it is bigger than the people mentioned here. But again, I have no knowledge of anyone else but the people who have made themselves known to me and other people that did see them. And while I'm here, black people in this country should not ever allow anyone else to bribe you into doing your own people wrong for financial gains.

What is wrong with us that we have become so gravely evil and are willing to do this kind of evil to our own, and so much wrong, and so easily to each other? We should not even have it in our hearts to do this kind of thing to our own people or any other people just because someone may offer us money or something we think we want or need. If it's money you need, you can go and make your own money without harming anyone. We are going to have to change the way we think in this world.

It is God that you must answer to whether you believe in Him or not. And just because a person doesn't believe in Him, it does not hold any weight whatsoever against the realness of Him being who He is. Trust me, He will eventually make you a believer in Him before it's all over. We should not be the people who want vain and material things in this world, and then we would sacrifice our own just to get it. That alone is so insane to me and so evil to even think about. By doing this, you have placed yourself in such a dark position and it is very important that you repent with God before it's too late. If there is any remorse in your heart, you should do the right thing and simply repent for all your wrongdoing and do it NOW before it's too late, I can't stress it enough. People who go around killing others for financial gain and what they have, have placed themselves in a terrible position by doing this.

We have all lived in this world long enough to know and understand the consequences of sin and what happens when we sin against others. I have lost no love for any one of them, of course not, because they are my own people. I pray that God delivers anyone who has an ill heart and loves him and sincerely desires to come back to Him. I am saddened because I know, and I am fully aware that it is us as black people in this country who need to stand together in "UNITY" and without allowing anyone to 'whisper into our ears about bringing harm or murdering our own people. Every race of people in this world other than the black man and woman, stick together and help each other, whenever they are called to do so.

As God is my Witness

Every other race of people looks out for one another. What we do not understand is the fact that, God is going to hold us accountable for everything we do to each other, whether we like it or not, or whether we believe it or not. We will not be able to say, "The devil made me do it." We will not be able to blame anyone but our own self for what we do. We know right from wrong today, so we cannot fool God. We know what we are doing, and it is sad that some of us just do not care enough to want to do better. How have we lost the desire to want to do better while we live? We must make it better for the next generation of people who are coming up after us.

Yes, there are many of us in the world today who are really trying to do right and striving to make a difference. Yet, there is still that fear missing that I can still see in a lot of leaders out here. The fear is still there even though we are appearing as if we are trying to do right. There are so many people hiding behind their holy books thinking they are doing right, when they are clearly doing wrong. As a people, we should be standing together in UNITY in this world and doing things to get ahead with our own nation.

Another great and important thing that we need to be focused on and do and be very serious about it is, we must get out of the idea of worrying about what someone else is going to say just because we start respecting and loving our own people and caring about our own nation. We have got to know and understand that there is nothing wrong with loving yourself and embracing your own people. We can do this without hating anyone else or doing wrong to someone else. We can also do it without worrying about what another person will say. We should never allow anyone to place us in a position of guilt because we are doing a good deed to each other. Where is there wrong in that? We will get to the rest of this part at another time.

As God is my Witness

Now, back to the deaths of my family members. It has been so painful for me to accept what happened to my family members. There are so many people who know this truth and are aware of the Whitney Houston death case. There are others who still believe and go by whatever the media decides to spin in the air, by saying Whitney Houston died of a drug overdose and then her daughter the same way three years later. It's OK with me, because people are entitled to believe what they will. At the end of the day, we all have our own opinions and beliefs. God knows that I will always respect any man's decisions they may make. But, if you choose to believe what they're saying in the media, you need to know that it is only being said to take us away from the reality of what really happened to my family members. Please keep in mind that drugs are not an issue at all in Whitney's case.

THERE WERE NO DRUGS IN WHITNEY HOUSTON'S BODY, PERIOD. Please do not forget that the coroner stated she had no drugs in her system from day one. He said it was only a "minute" amount in her system, which basically means none. As I have told people before, they are suppressing the truth of this whole thing. And they can do what they will. We know the truth, and I also know that, even if it were drugs, I know drug users who were way worse off and placed themselves in the biggest bathtubs and pools, and they still did not ever drown themselves. Fortunately, people who do not do drugs, and never have, will not ever understand what I am saying. Those who did drugs, they know, when a person does Cocaine, it awakes and alerts them even more. I would never believe that a person doing crack, or any form of cocaine would ever drown themselves in a bathtub, I don't care how high they were. It is believable about a person who would use heroin though.

As God is my Witness

It is far more understandable, because when you do heroin, you can fall asleep and nod off First, cocaine or any other street drug was not found in her body according to that coroner who examined Whitney. Furthermore, cocaine will not ever make someone as intelligent as Whitney drown herself, if she did have anything in her body. No, we can scratch that off because it is something that just doesn't exist in this case, not even in the biggest pool of water would she drown herself after using cocaine. they may do as they please. No, Whitney did not drown like that, trust me when I tell you.

Besides, also keep in mind that Whitney did not get into hotel bathtubs. The statement that Pat Houston made sitting in front of Oprah and whoever else regarding this person Mary, who supposedly told Whitney to take a bath, this too is nothing more than another lie, to cover up the truth. Trust me, she was NOT asked to take a bath by Mary. We know Whitney, and what we all know about Whitney is, she would never hold a one-minute conversation with Mary. Mary was a person attached to Pat Houston; therefore, Whitney did not even speak to this person when I last checked. Furthermore, I don't even believe that Whitney even knew that all these people were coming to LA, when she was there.

I believe they stalked her and that was how they ended up in that same hotel with her. I believe it was done to carry out the murder scheme they had planned to take Whitney and my niece out. I believe that Pat made up all those lies, which were just words being said to pass the time, because Pat Houston knew that there would be no investigation into this case, which is so sad. They know that Whitney Houston was murdered. And because they desired her estate and to take over everything she built in her life; they are pleased that she is not here.

As God is my Witness

Do not believe for a moment that her daughter hurt herself either. These murders were planned and carried out by people who wanted her legacy and estate, so that She was indeed painfully beaten and murdered and then placed in that hotel bathtub just like her daughter was beaten and placed in one after her death. I shall prove to you in this book that it is nothing more than a bunch of made-up lies. I am only here to tell you the absolute truth and prove to this world that an injustice was done to my family members. If you don't believe in what I am saying, I am not upset with you, nor does it make me feel any ill type of way towards you, because I am sure of what I am saying. Whenever I tell the truth, I am comfortable because I know it's the truth, and so there is no need for me to be upset at anyone, it is your right to believe what you will.

The only person I am trying to please today, is God. As I do not belong to anyone but Him. Therefore, my loyalty is with Him at the end of the day. Unfortunately, me and my friends and family members have all been forced to believe that there are people out here who were paid off, to keep quiet and say nothing. I am not sure what led them all to believe that we, the real family of Whitney, Krissy, and Bobby Jr., would follow them and keep quiet, and not reveal this truth, but here I am after the long wait for this book to arrive, I told God that I would go. So, here I am, God has sent me.

CHAPTER 1
MY LIFE WITH BOBBY & WHITNEY

My brother, Mr. Bobby Brown, called me on January 1, 1991. I was living in California. He called to wish me a happy new year! In that same breath, he said, "I want you and the boys to move to Atlanta with me!" I am saying to myself, "Are you out of your mind, Bobby I am doing well in California!" Immediately I said, no way. He tells me he will put me in the studio so that I can finally do my long-awaited album. He said that he would also put the right producers with me to make this thing happen for me. I was in LA and had already moved there from Boston to finish where we had started from the beginning. What I mean by that is, my brother Bobby and I used to sing as solo artists back home in Boston when we were younger. Long story short, I suddenly ran away from home and Bobby kept going. The rest is history of how his and my life ended up. I got up and ran away forgetting about all my dreams as a singer and solo artist in Boston. It was real, I was the very first sibling out of all my mother's children to be a singer, dancer, and solo artist. Bobby came after me and like I said, the rest is history.

I unfortunately took to the streets and Bobby kept on pursuing his dream as a solo artist. By the divine hand of God and my mother's determination, I came out of the streets and moved to Los Angeles with Bobby and my parents, and never looked back since then. At this time in my life while living with my brother and family in LA, I wanted to make sure I paid my very own way as much as I could. I wanted to earn my way and not have Bobby paying anything for me at that time. I got a vocal coach (Ira Lee Studios) in LA and took vocal lessons to make a strong comeback with my vocals.

As God is my Witness

I was doing things every day in LA to further my career without the help of my brother. When Bobby called me that day, he knew that a studio would make my eyes big because it was something I needed. He went on to say that he would put me in his studio to do my work if I moved to Atlanta with him. He also said he would buy me and my boys a new home and I would have no worries. It sounded good because that was my main concern. I must keep a roof over me and my children's heads, especially if I move to another state, and know nothing about it. I am thinking to myself, "Bobby, why call me all of a sudden like this, and want to do this for me out of the blue?" A nice new home for my children and a new environment sounded good though. I thought about how I could make a good life for my boys and myself as a new business owner.

Atlanta is a place known for a lot of black entrepreneurs. My children, and their well-being have always been my top priority, so I was thinking about them. I first said "no," without trying to hurt his feelings. I had just got off the phone with Don King and asked him to manage my singing career; and he said, "yes sure!" I was happier than a kid at Disney World after Don said yes, Bobby asking me to move to Atlanta with him out of nowhere did not sound right. This was right after I got Don King's word that he was now going to be my manager and help me with my singing career. I was going bananas at this time.

I did not know it then, but Mommy called Bobby and told him about what me and Don had planned. That is why they were trying to get me out of Los Angeles, little did I know at the time. They have now both found a way to get me out of California to keep me from obtaining a record deal, and they did it in a slick way, but I was blinded by this fact at that time.

As God is my Witness

After I told Bobby, no, a few times, Bobby hung up the phone from me and did the thing that everyone in the Brown family does when they want something. "We all called on our mother, Ma Brown." Mommy had a way of convincing us to give in to whatever it was we had planned. It did not matter what it was, you would indeed allow her to have her way every single time; depending on whose side she was on. Mommy called me and said, "Lele, go ahead and go to Atlanta you are going to hurt your brother's feelings if you do not. He wants to buy you and the boys a brand- new house in Atlanta, and you will have the studio! The boys will be in a nice new environment; Atlanta is nice, so just go ahead! I replied, "But Mommy, I just spoke with Don, and he is going to manage my singing career, so I have to stay!" In my head I was thinking "I am now finally getting ready to do my album here in California!" On top of that, I felt like Don, and I was like father and daughter; and I did not want to let him down, and just leave like that. I used to date Mike Tyson and Don King always treated me like his own daughter.

I believe Don favored me over all the other women Mike had ever dated at that time. I just knew that Don would take good care of me as my manager and see to it that my career took off If I leave, I am going to miss out on that and not further my career, Plus, I love it in California so much because it was that sun that had my skin looking so flawless, I thought. I was living like a princess doing well in LA and living a nice peaceful life. I had just gotten a new job working at a travel agency and had a nice home with an iron gate. I had an apple, lemon, and banana tree in my backyard that grew fresh fruit all the time. I was comfortable living in nice California weather and did not want to go away from it. Life was pretty good for me at this time.

As God is my Witness

However, after much convincing, Mommy persuades me to give in as always. Mommy's thing was, she always wanted her children together wherever we decided to all be. She loved the idea of us all always being in one place. Well, I finally gave in and now I am on my way to Atlanta! Bobby called me to confirm my flight information and car shipping info. In just two days (Jan 2, 1991) my Jaguar was being shipped that day from California to Atlanta.

I arrived in Atlanta on January 3, 1991. I and my two sons, nicknamed, Flawless and Kel Rock, were on a plane headed for Atlanta to start a new life. We have now arrived in Atlanta, Georgia, and made it our new home, which didn't take me long at all because I was now determined to move. My children were happy because we had a bigger house that was brand new, and we were the first owners of it. We were living around my family again. All I wanted to do was work in the studio on my singing career. I did it for a while but then things went left for some strange reason.

At the beginning of living in Atlanta, there were always family gatherings and great times at Bobby's mansion. I was always available to cook for family and friends and just be there whenever they needed me. I helped Mommy out a great deal with whatever she needed at the mansion. She did not need me to do too much because she had hired a whole crew of people to remodel Bobby's new mansion. Some of the working crew members robbed Mommy as they worked on Bobby's mansion. These guys were robbing Mommy blind, and she did not know it right away. I remember Mommy saying the main person was our "father's other son by another woman." Mommy's heart was crushed because she hired folks and gave them a chance when they did not deserve her kindness.

As God is my Witness

In the end, it was Bobby who lost the most because it was his bank account that these thieves were robbing. Mommy was hired by Bobby to do all the remodeling at his mansion. She did a great job decorating and making his mansion beautiful. I remember Mommy saying, that one of the other guys that were working for her had gotten hit by a huge Mack truck and died at the end of the project. Mommy got a lot of compliments and made a lot of celebrity friends while decorating the mansion. Mommy was good friends with retired NBA basketball player, Dominique Wilkin's mother back then. Her buddy was the British singer, Mr. Elton John, who was amazed at her work and told her he wanted Mommy to help him with his home when she was done. Elton John was so impressed with how Mommy did all that glamour, he told Mommy, he would like her to decorate his home.

I do not know if anything ever came of it, but Mommy was sure interested in being a part of making his home just as beautiful as Bobby's home. Some of Mommy's other friends, just to name a few, were Joe Jackson, Janet and Michael Jackson's dad, Toni Braxton's Mom, Evelyn Braxton, Jamie Brown from Sister to Sister Magazine, and a few other celebrities. Mommy did not mess with a lot of people and was very private. She did not believe in friends in the music business, but if she messed with you, she liked you and you were worth it. But, if you crossed her, that was it! You can stick a pin in it and know that you will not ever get another chance with her. Ma Brown took nothing at all from anyone at any time. She was a praying mother who was all about her children and a no-nonsense person.

CHAPTER 2
BOBBY & WHITNEY IN LOVE!

Guess who is in love and talking about marriage during that time? Yes indeed, it is my iconic king of stage, bad-to-the-bone entertaining brother, Mr. Bobby Brown, and the iconic glass-breaking, angelic singing bird, Ms. Whitney Houston! I was, of course, extremely happy for both of them. I have always loved Bobby and Whitney's voices.

Of course, my brother has always been my favorite male artist and Whitney my favorite female artist, hands down. My vocal coach (Ira Lee) back in LA, taught me my voice lessons. My first day in his studio, he told me to go home and sing my favorite songs and just simply practice all the songs every day at home. I immediately went home and sang all of Whitney's songs throughout the house daily. I stayed in the mirror practicing and singing her songs until I sounded just like her. I remember singing one of Whitney's songs at a friend of the family's funeral in Atlanta. I sang "I will always love you" and Gary Houston (Whitneys play Brother) said "if nobody was looking at you, we would have sworn it was Whitney on that stage." He went home and told Whitney how much I sounded just like her at the funeral. I had been rehearsing Whitney's songs way before Whitney and Bobby met each other.

When the two of them did meet, I was so shocked for several reasons. All I knew prior was that Bobby was dating Janet Jackson back then, and the two seemed to be in love with one another. Of course, I loved Janet as well who did not if you were a music lover.

As God is my Witness

She has always been a very talented individual and came from a very talented family of course. Bobby and Janet hid their relationship very well for a while without ever letting the world know that they were dating. Now, this is the part I never understood about the two of them.

I could not understand why they seemed to like each other so much but would not let the world know about them. Then, I saw Bobby's movie, which told me more, and things I did not know. Yet, it depicted another Janet that I was not familiar with, nor could I believe what was being said about her. I just saw it a different way and thought that someone was lying about Janet, to be honest. I did not know my brother was going through all of that with her. I loved the idea of my brother dating Janet

Jackson back then. I mean, what sister would not be happy about her brother dating Janet Jackson? But now that Whitney is in the picture, we all knew it was over for Janet or anyone else now. This is what I was saying in my head at the time.

It was clear from the beginning Whitney Houston loved her some Bobby Brown, and she made it known that she was not going anywhere anytime soon! Bobby loved him some Whitney as well, and little did I know, he stopped seeing Janet anymore. Besides, Bobby and Janet were so secretive about their relationship. I remembered them being together a lot when we lived in Los Angeles. Now that were in Atlanta, it seemed as if Bobby had stopped taking Janet's calls altogether, but only Bobby knows why. I remember feeling sorry for Janet at one time. I had to lie to her several times when she called the mansion for Bobby. I would always be the one to tell Janet that he was not home, or that he was asleep.

I had to because Bobby would tell me to say that to her if she called. She kept calling for him and I kept telling her the same thing until I did not have to do it anymore, and I felt kind of bad because of that. The last time I spoke to Janet, she sounded so sad over the phone asking for him. I guess Bobby got tired of her and wanted out of that relationship, I eventually came to believe. Bobby seemed to be upset with her about something and I would never dare ask him what it was. Bobby has always been the type of man who just does not like you in his business, therefore, I never bothered to discuss his and Janet's relationship.

It seemed to me like it took her a while to finally get it and move on. Whitney was now in the picture, and the two of them seemed very happy with one another. He and Whitney were together all the time, and I knew he did not make or have time for anyone else because Whitney was always right there with him. She was so in love with Bobby and even told me then that she was going to be in our family forever! I loved Janet for my brother when he was with her. She was a sweet soul and a beautiful sister. However, when Whitney came into our family it was so much different. It was like she really belonged with us and had been with us for a long time already because in my eyes at that time "Whitney and Bobby were extremely perfect for each other"

She was a perfect fit right into our family as if it was destined from above long ago. When I saw them together it reminded me of a Bible verse that says, "What God hath joined together, let no man put asunder" (Matthew 19:6). I believe to this day that God has and still is going to chastise anyone who worked to separate Bobby and Whitney. When the creator brings two people together it is for his special purpose.

As God is my Witness

Of course, the public and people who were jealous of Bobby and Whitney's relationship were not going to ever get the chance to experience and see what we have seen and witnessed with the two of them. We always knew this, and it is why anyone's opinion of them never bothered us. People's perception about the two of them have never been so far from the truth when it came to who they both were, their union and marriage with one another. The public's words or opinions did not bother any of us because we were right there and saw them both. There were far too many people seriously jealous of them both, and it made no sense at all. They were such a perfect match that if the world would have left them alone, they most likely would have been a very successful married couple that could have been a great example for so many of our young brothers and sisters who would get married today.

I really believed that they would have grown old and stayed together forever. I had admiration for both Whitney and Janet for my brother. Yet, it was no one else's choice to make except for Bobby. Both women are two of my favorite female artists and more than anything they are my sisters. Whenever Whitney sang, she made anyone cry automatically and Janet made me dance. I always wanted the chance to tell Whitney just how much she changed my life with her music. Her songs did a lot for me at a certain time in my life that I will not ever forget. One day, I finally got the chance to sit down and talk with Whitney and tell her just how much she had changed my life with her music. I loved her voice, and she eventually loved mine when she finally got to hear me sing. Her songs were more emotional for me than I had ever been able to explain to anyone. I went through a lot at one time, and so, it was a dream that came true for me, and even more so because she is now officially my sister-in-law during this time.

As God is my Witness

Whitney was always there with us spending time, so we were used to her coming around a lot. Overall, we had a lot of good times together as one big family. I must mention that Whitney loved the Brown family so much. Even after her and Bobby's divorce, she came to our mother's funeral and let everybody know how she felt as she stood on that podium. She was pointing to Mommy's casket and said, "This here is my mother once a Brown always a Brown!" Whitney wanted everyone to know that our mother was still her mother even though she and Bobby had divorced. Everyone clapped for her and thought it was such a nice thing she said. Whitney loved our mother as if she were her mother, and Mommy loved her like a real daughter as well. I always said, that if Mommy was alive when they murdered Whitney, Mommy would have died right after her of a broken heart.

I believe God took Mommy first because He knew that Mommy would not have been able to handle Whitney's death. And then again, she may have because Mommy was a beast! She would have been fighting for Whitney until justice came to us.

She and Whitney were "that" close! Mommy passed in 2011 and Whitney passed the year after (2012). Then, right after we lost Whitney, we lost Daddy. Our sister Bethy was the first in the immediate family to transition. Before Bethy passed, it had been a long time since we lost anyone in our family. After Whitney was Bobbi Kristina and then Bobby Jr. Our family has been through a lot! There is a lot that this world does not know about Whitney before she left this world. One thing was certain, if you are a Whitney fan and you have been following her when she was alive, you know, like me and my family, she was very private with a small circle of people surrounding her. She was never the type to have a lot of people around her.

As God is my Witness

To be even more candid, some of the people that were around her were not there by her choice. From what I saw and witnessed, being around Whitney, she did not possess complete control over her "own" life like people normally would. Mama Cissy would not leave her alone when it came to her choosing the people that "she" wanted to work for her. Mama Cissy always seemed to come directly behind Whitney with her input and decisions. Mama Cissy has always tried to make decisions for Whitney without Whitney's consent or full agreement.

Whitney was a person who was very intelligent and very business-minded and could make her own decisions. However, in my opinion, and with all due respect, Mama Cissy treated Whitney as if she was not her own woman and a person who could not even think for herself. The way I always saw it was that Mama Cissy was always right there to make sure that things went her way and not Whitney's way. I believe that when my brother came into the picture, Mama Cissy kind of panicked, and it was why she could not explain how or why she felt like she did towards Bobby. Nobody could understand where the hate was coming from, but I figured it out after Whitney's death, everything was clear to me.

I remember our mother and Mama Cissy arguing a lot about Bobby and Whitney back then. And if anyone wishes to ever understand why she disliked my brother Bobby so much, trust me, I honestly believe it was because of how much Whitney loved him and the protection of Whitney's new family is what it was. This is the only thing I can see. I am not saying this to talk down on Mama Cissy at all because I am a big, huge respecter of my elders. I am just speaking the truth on what I believe and saw altogether. From the start, Bobby was not liked by Mama Cissy.

As God is my Witness

And if anyone notices today, Mama Cissy seems to be OK with him now, since Whitney is gone in her grave. I saw where she had mentioned it in an interview. She said something to the nature of not having anything against him anymore.

After hearing her say that my belief was that it was because Whitney was no longer with us, and so, Mama Cissy did not have to look at Bobby anymore being with her. I said this before that Bobby was a security blanket for Whitney, and I meant it. That is why Whitney loved him so much because he was that man that she had been looking for all her life. My honest belief is that she wanted someone strong enough to just take her away from her family. I can even relate to that, because it is not a secret that a lot of women feel that way when they get a man. Any woman loves a strong man who would protect her and be willing to fight for her. No one is perfect, but Bobby has always been respectful and just not ever been someone that you can just walk all over and disrespect. And I think for that reason she loved that in Bobby.

Also, Whitney knew we had a strong foundation as a family, period, and we would protect her with everything we had in us. There was not a time that something happened to her on our watch. Bobby seemed to be a threat for Mama Cissy for some reason, since Whitney was married to him, they would not have the control they held over her head anymore. Please know that I am not speaking on this trying to lash out at Mama Cissy or be disrespectful. As God is my witness, I am just speaking facts on how I honestly and sincerely felt and what I understood and witnessed overall. I am just trying to keep this real and true to every single letter here. This is the sole reason why my niece is not here today as well.

As God is my Witness

I hate to say this, but, with everything in me, I believe that there was not ever a time that anyone had any true love for my niece, because they have showed very little for her mother Whitney while she lived and in her death.

Therefore, in my eyes, when she was gone, there would be no love for my niece that she left behind. "A child who could be in the way of that estate money!" An estate that was given to her as her mother's child. It was not until Whitney left this world that Mama Cissy said, she no longer had anything against Bobby anymore. I saw this for what I believe it was. Not to mention all the times that she and Mommy argued about Bobby and Whitney. What I saw was, after the death of Whitney, the next thing in their mind to do was to snatch that estate and to get rid of my niece, who would have full control over Whitney's money and estate.

They fought my brother in a courtroom, for his daughter's estate while she was laying up in the hospital. Whitney said on several occasions that she did not want them, or desire them to be over her estate. Her "WILL" speaks for itself if the world could see the original WILL of Whitney's. I also believe that was tampered with.

This is a very sad story that only almighty God can help me explain. After Whitney's death, I began to think about how everything went down when she first came into our family, how Mama Cissy was, what she was doing to Whitney, and how people in Whitney's family were treating her altogether. Everything that is in my head today makes so much sense to me as to why she is not here anymore. "Her life was not in any way nearly like many people in this world may have imagined!"

As God is my Witness

What I mean by that is, in my most honest opinion, "Whitney was treated as if she was just a slave trophy and someone who just worked solely for her family, and like a slave, if you will. They all depended on her to bring home the bread and none of them had jobs outside of their homes or outside of Whitney."

To the best of my knowledge, none of Whitney's brothers or their wives worked outside of their home with jobs outside of Whitney, and not everyone was on her payroll either which was really weird. And to be more honest, I do not believe that Pat Houston was ever on Whitney's payroll at all. If she was, it had to be because of Mama Cissy who they say literally pushed her in there. Whitney did not like talking to Pat nor dealing with her for anything, she did not like being around Pat, and she did not want anything to do with Pat, period.

She did not even like the idea of Pat being in her family nor visiting her home. As long as Bobby and Whitney have been married, I had never once seen Pat in their home. I had never seen Pat outside their home. It was not until Pat came to Whitney's home to bum rush her was, she in that house. She stood there with Whitney's attorney again, Mama Cissy is the person whom we all believe pointed her in the direction of her son Gary. "I believe Mama Cissy did that to make sure that she had someone other than her sons to help her with watching Whitney and keeping an eye on her and Bobby's marriage!" That is my opinion that I will go to my grave believing. This is what I saw for myself being around Bobby and Whitney for years.

See, people in the world saw Mama Cissy as being a caring mother who really cared about Whitney when it came to Bobby, and that is totally the wrong idea and even Whitney knew it.

As God is my Witness

As God is my witness, I believe it was to spy on Whitney, and to keep up and have information about every small or great thing she did with her husband. Whitney was a grown woman, and I hate to say it, but she seemed to be held with a leash by Mama Cissy. I am not saying this to upset anyone, nor do I mean to sound harsh. I am just telling the truth as to what I witnessed and what has always been in my head since I have been around watching how they dealt with Whitney. Furthermore, I am not the only person who thinks or believes this. There are many people who can and will bear witness to this.

As much as I have always loved my brother, Gary, yet, after learning a lot of things, he is not Whitney's biological brother. They are not related by blood. What I mean by that is, Gary Houston was conceived by Mama Cissy, and her sister Annie's husband, Moss. It is a story behind their relationship that I won't get into because that is none of my business. It is said that Mama Cissy went behind her sister Annie's back, and slept with her husband, Moss, and conceived Gary. Now, let me stop right there for a moment and explain something important to me. I do not want anyone to think this is gossip talk about Mama Cissy or Gary. That is not why I have said this. I am saying this simply because we need to understand Whitney's life in its entirety, and why things were as they were, and why everything turned out the way it did for Whitney.

This world is extremely blinded to who Whitney Houston really and truly was, who her so-called family were and how she dealt with it. Now, I am not looking at Mama Cissy in a bad way nor am I judging her at all. I do not know all the circumstances of her and Moss's relationship and what she had to go through in her life. Therefore, I do not judge her because I do not know the full story of her personal relationships with men.

52

As God is my Witness

I have not ever disrespected her nor spoken ill about Mama Cissy, and I have asked that people please do not do that. I just know that "it is what it is" and the truth must be told in order to understand Whitney's full picture is "why" I am speaking this truth. I also know that Gary was born a Garland, and he changed his name to Houston for a strange reason to me. Today, I understand it as a set up to get Whitney's estate money. He and Whitney did not get along well, nor do they share the same father or mother, which means that Gary and Whitney have no blood ties at all.

They argued and fought a lot, and Whitney did not like his wife, Pat, because of all the stealing Whitney has accused them both of, and they all know this is true. Both are two people who are walking around with Whitney's name, her wedding ring that my brother brought his wife Whitney. I also believe that they are also illegally over Whitney's estate today. We all know that it is the very last thing that Whitney would ever want. Yet, her family will not bother to help Whitney and put a stop to all that's going on.

I have been told by several family members, and people who grew up with them that Gary was so jealous of Whitney and that he was only out to get her money is why he changed his name to Houston, and that was the real reason he took on her last name. I had asked myself long ago, with Gary doing that and changing his birth and rightful name, could it be because he wanted in on Whitney's estate once she left this world? And today it seems to me that they planned her death. As much as I love my brother Gary, I have to speak up for Whitney and my niece because I feel like they literally killed them solely for Whitney's money and estate, regardless to what anyone may say. It very seriously makes all the sense in this world to me, as an intelligent person.

As God is my Witness

From what I gathered in 2022 through 2023, I came to find out and believe that there is not any blood whatsoever between Gary and Whitney. "I say that because I also believe that there is a possibility that Mama Cissy is not Whitney's biological mother either. In fact, I "know" that Mama Cissy is not Whitney's biological mother" Yes, of course, Mama Cissy raised her for all of Whitney's life. Yet, the things she has done to Whitney as a child according to Whitney, Mama Cissy is not her mother. Furthermore, it is a possibility that Whitney could have lived a better life had she had the chance to be raised by her biological mother, whom I know to be the late, Teresa Graves.

Why do I believe this? I researched, investigated and read a lot in the media regarding seeing a lot of things in the media concerning Poppa John, Whitney's father, and this woman Teresa Graves. It is said that he slept with Teresa Graves when she was just 15 years old and because she was so young and probably just could not take care of Whitney, Poppa John took her and brought her home to Mama Cissy.

My guess was that he asked Mama Cissy to deal with it, because he dealt with her cheating with Moss and having Gary. I am not sure if Whitney ever felt comfortable with Mama Cissy growing up, but I have witnessed from being around Whitney that she was so sadly limited in what she could do for herself and her daughter, with her own money that she worked so hard for. After all that she did and built for herself and her child, she did not enjoy the fruits of her labor as many in this world probably imagined her to. My brother Bobby always took very good care of Whitney and his family period, when it came to finances. Bobby Brown is known to be one of the best providers in the world and he gets it from our father.

As God is my Witness

Bobby has always taken good care of his family, including us as his siblings, to be even more honest. He and Whitney have done a lot for our family, and I am grateful for them and will always be grateful for whatever my brother has done for us in the past. It was a very sad thing to have witnessed with my sister, Whitney. She had to deal with a lot when it came to what she always wanted for her life. Whitney was a very talented and famous icon who was very serious about her life and her business. She wanted a better life without anyone else's ideas all the time because she had a mind of her own and wanted to be respected for that.

There was something huge in her way that was hindering her from really being herself. To be more honest, she was not happy with how her life was cut out for her no matter what anyone else has said in the public to this day. I saw with my own eyes, and I witnessed Mama Cissy directing Whitney's life to where "she" wanted Whitney's life to go, rather than allowing Whitney the respect she so well deserved. Anyone telling you anything different is lying or they just do not wish to talk about it, but it has not ever been a secret in any of our families. I know for a fact that my sister lived a miserable life outside of her marriage when it came to her Houston family.

Gary Houston said it best. Whitney's cousin Micky Drinkard, (God rest her soul) told me that Mama Cissy invited Pat and Gary to her house after Whitney was found. Mama Cissy asked the question to Gary and Pat, "What happened to Whitney in that hotel and how did she die?" Micky said that Pat and Gary jumped up from the table and said to Mama Cissy, "Oh that's what you called us here for, you knew she didn't want to be here anymore!" In my mind, this told me that Gary and Pat were going to use this as an excuse for Whitney dying.

As God is my Witness

They did not seem to care about Whitney dying and being found in that hotel because in my mind they did it. Why would they say such a thing to someone's mother after they have been found in a hotel, I am asking myself? And why did they feel comfortable to say that to Mama Cissy?

After hearing this, I said to Micky, "So, this is what they had planned and wanted to tell everyone in the world!" Of course, Micky agreed with me. She said some horrible things about Pat after that. I said, Yeah, and this was why Bobbi Kristina came up in that bathtub first, at the hotel. I said that is what they were going to tell the world. They were going to say that Whitney committed suicide when she found her daughter in that bathtub, but Krissy came up out of that water and they had to say something else. Pat didn't know what to say while Oprah interviewed her. It forced them to get a plan B, I said. I thought this even more after hearing Micky tell me that. I cannot wrap my mind around how and why they would both feel so comfortable to even say that to Mama Cissy at that moment.

My reason for feeling suspicious of Pat and Gary is simply because "my nephew stood in that hallway of the Beverly Hilton hotel and watched with his own eyes, Pat and Gary rushing in and out of that room where Whitney's body laid, and they both were taking things in and out, and moving quickly to stage this room before the police and/or authorities got there!"

They did this back and forth while my nephew was consoling Bobbi Kristina as she cried for her mother, after coming down that hallway and finding out her mother was gone. My nephew said they did this so freely as if they had the authority to do it.

As God is my Witness

The only thing I can say to this is that they basically "staged" that room before the authorities got there, because they figured they were not going to be checked on it. What else could I say or believe at this point? Whenever someone dies, you are not supposed to touch anything, anywhere at any time before those in authority get there. This is not something that anyone does.

It just does not happen, especially when you are innocent. Then to allow the media to continue saying she died of an accidental drowning due to a drug overdose, when the coroner clearly stated that she did not die of a drug overdose, it makes it even worse. The coroner stated that she only had a "minute" amount in her body which was basically nothing! If anyone was paying attention, Whitney looked so good the night of the Kelly Price event. It told anyone that she was clean, hands down. I urge anyone reading this book to go back and look at Whitney Houston's pictures at the Kelly Price event, the night before she was found.

Whitney's death was planned long ago trust me. In my mind, everyone in her family knows that Whitney was murdered, and they seem to be OK with Pat and Gary Houston doing things against Whitney's desires and wishes, which also tells me they also orchestrated her death. Now, that is my belief, and I am entitled to what I believe. On top of it, I feel it in my gut that Pat and Gary Houston both did this with the help of Ray J, along with Nick Gordon, who is now deceased. People have always talked about my brother Bobby and what he did and did not do, but Bobby was that security blanket for Whitney and nothing like this would have ever happened had Bobby been there. Nothing has ever happened to Whitney on Bobby's watch when they were married.

As God is my Witness

The people who are speaking ill of my brother or have ever spoken ill of him in the media have not a clue as to what went on with them. I am a living witness to the fact that Whitney Houston appeared a certain way to the public, but her life was "so far different" than what anyone could ever imagine it to be. And it is so unfair to her as a human being, and it had "absolutely nothing" to do with Bobby. Besides, people should use their heads when thinking about Bobby and Whitney.

There were too many people jealous and upset with their marriage, and all will pay a heavy price with God for ever interfering with their marriage. I believe that People were jealous because Whitney loved him so much. Whitney was not some young girl who was a fool with her heart. If Bobby was so bad, Whitney would not have been in love with him for over 15 years, think about it. She was not desperate for any man, she just very sincerely loved Bobby for who he truly was as a man and a husband to her; and he loved her for the woman she was, which was first no one's business.

Many people in this world have never been so far from the truth when looking at someone's life. Bobby was good to Whitney as well as Whitney to him. No, they were not perfect and neither has anyone else in this world ever been perfect in their own relationships. Her father, Poppa John, he loved the idea of my brother for his daughter. He knew that Bobby was a good man and a very good security blanket for his daughter, Whitney. Poppa John talked about his love for his son-n-law on many occasions with us, and anyone else who had the opportunity to see him around Bobby and Whitney. Poppa John hated it when people talked down on his son-in-law, Bobby. He would argue you until the sun went down about Bobby.

As God is my Witness

DOES JANET JACKSON HAVE MY NIECE OR NEPHEW? OK, back to my life with them. As time went on after I got to Atlanta, it was always said that Janet Jackson had given birth to children and was hiding them. I am hearing people talk about this, and it became overwhelming for me. I saw this in the tabloids and the media later, after she and Bobby's secret relationship. I always wondered if it was just a rumor or if it was true that she had given birth to children, and if so, could they be related to me?

I wondered more so, after a visit to my doctor's office while I was residing in Tarzana California during this time. I was living with Bobby, and we were neighbors to Janet's brother Michael Jackson. We were only a few blocks away from Michael Jackson's Hayven Hurst home during this time. We lived in Tarzana and Michael lived in Encino. But as I said, we were only a few blocks away from each other. At this time, I was pregnant with my son Flawless and going to my pre-natal doctor in Tarzana. Of course, I chose a prenatal doctor in the area that was close to us. I remembered the doctor's name and all.

Also, during this time, I had good reason and did not fully trust the doctors in L.A. (to deliver my baby) because of an experience my younger sister Carole had with her son, Antwon. Therefore, when it was time for me to deliver, I flew back to Boston to give birth to my son, "Flawless" to ensure his life, safety and wellbeing. When I finally gave birth to him, I went back to LA and raised him in that same house in Tarzana. As he began to grow everyone called him Lil Mike Tyson Jr. Amazingly, he looked like he could be me and Mike's child when he was a young boy. Even his body structure and build were like Mike's.

As God is my Witness

A few people did at one time actually think that Mike Tyson was his father, since we were together at that time. Surprisingly today, my son is also a boxer just like Mike. He is also a great street fighter and has a lot of experience in both fields and is one of the best at it. On top of it all, he is drug-free, pays close attention to his health, really takes good care of himself as an adult, is very handsome and so very humble today. If you did not know him, one could easily think he is a passive guy, but he is not, at all. He just carries himself so well and he is a respectable young man to anyone he crosses paths with.

Now, back to Janet and what I experienced while pregnant with my son Flawless. One day, I walked into my prenatal doctor's office and got mistaken for Janet Jackson. I never forgot how this woman looked at me when she said, "Hi Janet!" She said it as if she thought I was Janet. At that very moment, I guessed that she knew Janet who came to that same clinic. I looked at her and said, my name is Leolah, not Janet (and just for the record, Bobby used to say that I looked like Janet back then). So, when he was upset with Janet, he would look at me sometimes and say, "Get outta here... you look too much like Janet!" LOL! Janet Jackson has always been so beautiful to me; so of course, that was a compliment without argument.

Now, this woman in the doctor's office could have just walked away and simply gone back to work after I told her that I was not Janet. At this point, I did not know which Janet this woman was referring to. But now, she makes her way back over to me and whispers in my ear, "my God, you look like Janet Jackson!" Then she says, "And please do not ever say anything, but yeah, 'I saw, Janet Jackson' here as well and that is why I thought you were her." I said, Oh really? She said," Yeah, but please just don't ever say anything please, I'd be in deep trouble!" I smiled and said, "Yeah, I get that a lot!" I am also saying to myself, "You do not have to tell me more than once, I wasn't going to say anything anyways. But why did I experienced that, I'm thinking. Of course, I am not going to say anything to anyone because it could easily start something. For the record, I never did say a word to my brother Bobby or anyone else about it until now. I held this to myself for many years.

I did not want to start anything that caused negative energy between the two and put their relationship at odds with each other. It blew my mind to keep hearing it repeatedly in the tabloids that Janet had secret babies and was hiding them away from the public. I honestly never believed it, knowing how much the media can print lies all the time. I just always thought to myself, there may not be any truth to this whatsoever.

Yet, it startled me and had me worried because I knew in my heart that she and Bobby were seeing each other heavily at that time, and anything is possible. So, can you imagine what I had been feeling when I first heard this news or rumor? No one has any idea how this has been on my mind all these years, and I have held it in until now. I am not saying it is true, and that she has my niece or nephew. I do not know if it is true, but I can honestly say that this indeed happened for sure at this doctor's office, and the big question is "Why would any woman visit a prenatal clinic in the first place if they're not having a baby?" I am just saying, it doesn't make sense to me. This Doctors office is hidden away too, so it made me think. As the years came and went, I have been thinking about this more often. I cannot imagine any woman having children and hiding them for so many years without allowing the father of that child to know the truth about their own child's birth, I'm thinking to myself.

As God is my Witness

This was another reason why I guess I did not say anything to anyone. I just cannot see Janet doing something like that but then again, I have seen worse in the industry. Now, Bobby has been in the business for over 40 years, so if I really and truly believed it, I would have said something long ago. I had to think about myself and what I would like done if it were me.

I would never want to just react to something that someone said without any proof This is the reason I will not accuse anyone of anything unless I am 100% certain of it. We must always be careful of what we think, what we believe, and what we say and accuse people of as my Daddy used to say, "Everything that shines ain't necessarily gold!" Everything that seems real is not always real, no matter how real it may seem and vice versa. I say this with all due respect to my sister Janet. I always wanted to be able to ask Janet myself, if there was any truth to it at all that she and my brother shared a child together. I cannot imagine a mother hiding their children from this world, and more important, from their father all their child's life.

On another note, I said to myself, as a Jehovah's Witness, I am sure that Janet and her family do not believe in abortions, so she very well could have had a baby and did not wish to let my brother know. It could have been a situation where her parents may have not been so pleased with her choice of men as my brother explained in his movie. I wondered if her parents just forced her to keep the child, and keep it a secret and have the child, and then, hide the child from the world to protect her image, perhaps since they don't believe in abortions. This was just something I thought about in my mind because I was dealing with the fact that that woman seriously thought I was Janet Jackson inside that pre- natal clinic.

As God is my Witness

I was wondering if there is any truth to what Bobby's movie said about Janet, (which I did not ever witness her being like) treating him in a certain way and all because of her mother. Now, I do remember her father Joe Jackson talking with my mother a lot on the phone back then. Mommy and Joe Jackson became very close and would always be in conversation on the phone.

I said to myself, it would make a lot of sense as to why she did it, if she really did get pregnant and hide a baby. I also know how people could allow someone strong in their families to guide them in their steps and make important decisions for them when it comes to certain situations like this. Mama Catherine Jackson could have very well been that influence to tell Janet to not have an abortion because it is against their religion. As I write this book I am praying and hoping that if there is any truth to it, Janet would turn to God and ask His forgiveness for hiding my niece or nephew away from us. If not,

I apologize for even mentioning it, and shame on the people who are responsible for spreading such a lie regarding her name and character in the media in the first place and accusing her of such a thing. I would be the first person to apologize for thinking that it was a possibility. At the same time, I am only human, and we just do not know the absolute truth because we just do not know.

The only person who does know is Janet and God Himself. And if there is any truth there, so be it. It will be between Janet and the God at the end of the day. No matter what we think, hear, what we believe, or what we do in this world, we will all have to answer to God's face and be judged by our hearts on that day. Furthermore, none of us are without sin in this world and are in no place whatsoever to try to judge another person at any time regardless of what it is.

As God is my Witness

I will love my sister Janet Jackson no less either way. Mommy and I used to talk about Bobby and Janet all the time. We heard wedding bells back when they were dating. We honestly thought they would never separate. Janet seemed to seriously care for Bobby, as far as my mother and I were concerned. I was actually shocked to see how they depicted her in Bobby's movie. I did not see the person they were calling Janet Jackson, and that person they portrayed in Bobby's movie. I felt like something was just not quite right with them describing her character.

Of course, I did not know everything about her and Bobby's relationship. In the end of it all, I do know and remember Bobby not being happy with her anymore. I did not know why exactly, and never asked. I just remember him telling me to always say that he was not there whenever she would call him. We thought that Janet would not ever allow Bobby to leave her. That was the Janet we remembered, and we judged it based on how she would act or behave every time she laid eyes on Bobby. She would always have that bubbly spirit, like that young teenage love.

I remember a time when my family members were all going to an event, (if my memory serves me correctly) MCA records was having for Bobby. When we walked in, the cameras were all on us. They were focusing on Bobby of course because we had just walked in the door where they were waiting for him to arrive. Janet was sitting with her family eating at their dinner table. I believe her ex- boyfriend Rene was also sitting there with them at this time. When she saw Bobby walk in, she jumped straight up out of her seat and ran over to Bobby, and she was smiling from ear to ear. She did not hesitate at all, she just rushed over to Bobby! I guess she forgot that her boyfriend Rene, was sitting right there with her at that moment.

As God is my Witness

I think this was either before or in the beginning stages of their relationship. Cameras were flashing and they got nice pictures of Bobby and Janet together. She placed herself in those pictures with Bobby. I was right there to witness this and thought it was so cute when it was happening, so I always knew how much she liked Bobby. We thought that they were going to settle down, get married, and have lots of children together. I had no idea it was over with them at this time since we were now in Atlanta. But at this time, I did question myself on how their relationship would work since he decided to move to Atlanta without her.

I wondered if Bobby had even asked her to move to Atlanta with him. A lot of people ask me, was your brother really with Janet Jackson? Of course, he was, and if you saw them together, you too would have thought that they were two inseparable people who were seriously in love with one another back then. Bobby has always been a man who could have any woman he wanted, and still to this day, he can. In any event, he eventually left Janet and ended up with Whitney. When Whitney entered the picture, all bets were off with anyone else. Whitney was that Queen who sincerely loved Bobby with all that she had in her. I remember saying, oh well, the show is over for all other women now. Because it was clear that Whitney was on board with my brother, and she said that she was in it for a lifetime. She was not shy to let people know just how much she loved him.

It showed every time you saw them together. I had never seen a woman's face glow so much seeing them two together. I knew of many women in the music industry who were either fascinated with my brother, dating him, or just talking to him as a friend and potential lover.

As God is my Witness

Bobby was no different from any other man out here who gets attention from women when a man is good-looking and has money, whether famous or not. This world judged him on that women's stuff so badly that they gave him a bad name in the media. Yet, Bobby has always been strong and dealt with it as any man should. I thought that was very unfair to spin such nasty words in the media about someone they knew nothing of They have not seen how a lot of women threw themselves on my brother without him doing anything to initiate it.

I have seen it with my very own eyes all over the world and everywhere he went. I was there and saw how some women had forced themselves on both of my brother's, and my father as well. I can also name a lot of women that I know for a fact, which have either been with my brother, literally chased him down, or catered to me, his sister, trying to get to him. I have seen it all with women and my brother. It is not always the man coming on to women either. Back in LA, I remembered a lot of famous women being huge fans of Bobby.

I will keep their names a secret at this time because it is not necessary to tell all their business in this book. Some women are probably married now, and who knows what they may have told their husbands. I would not want to be the reason for any arguments, fights, or break-ups. It has

Never been a secret that Bobby Brown is that man that a lot of women just love even to this day. I know a lot of females that are in love with both of my brothers. Well, Whitney was with him at this point, and she said to me back then that she was in it for a lifetime!

CHAPTER 3

<u>MIKE TYSON</u>

During this time when Bobby and Whitney were starting to blossom together, I was missing Mike Tyson a whole lot. I was dating him while I was back in LA, and one day, I just got up and left out of the blue. We weren't together anymore when I left. Yet, I did always wonder what he was going to think if he did not see me anymore in Los Angeles. I knew he was going to wonder where I was, plus miss me as I was missing him back then. I was now sick over the fact that he had no idea that I had left LA. I'm thinking, I just got up and moved away out of nowhere without him knowing where I was or why I left. I did not bother to call him because, first, I was sure that he was seeing someone else, and I was also seeing someone else by that time. Overall, Mike had no idea that it was Bobby's idea alone to get me out of Los Angeles.

I kept saying to myself," if anyone is to blame it is Bobby for forcing me out of California" and if Mike finds out I'm gone, and has a problem with it, it is Bobby's fault, I'm saying to myself I was going through a lot around this time and trying to move on without him in my life anymore. It had been hard for me, but I had to remain strong for my two sons that I was raising as a single mother. Bobby seemed to be upset and seriously angry with me, because I wasn't with Mike Tyson anymore. I believe he always held that against me for some reason. It was like he hated the fact that me and Mike were not together anymore. Bobby seemed to take it harder than anyone in my eyes. And the truth is, I always thought it would always be just Me, Mike, our children, Don King and his woman, and their children after all the smoke cleared; regardless of who came and went in both of our lives.

As God is my Witness

In my mind, no matter who came and went, I was there to stay. I was in love with Mike Tyson and that is how I saw myself with him. He was in love with me as well. Even though we are not together today, Mike and I have a bond and we will always be loyal friends because we both genuinely love each other as such. Speaking of Mike Tyson, I have been wanting to speak out for him for a long time, regarding that so-called rape he spent time in jail for. I honestly do not believe he raped that girl. This world has no idea that they did not get the chance to bring all the evidence into that courtroom that I believe would have cleared Mike Tyson all the way home.

There was a young white boy who wanted to come into that courthouse on behalf of Mike to prove to the judge that this same girl also accused him of rape and yet, it was consensual all along. Mike's limo driver told me they would not allow that evidence into that courtroom, and of course, it would have helped Mike tremendously and probably sent him home altogether. I thought that was so unfair and that they just wanted him to go to jail because he was a black man that they were afraid of; and so, any chance they had to break him, it was a done deal. I thought that was one of the saddest cases of an innocent black man to ever enter a court room.

I do not care how long ago it was, even today, I feel obligated to talk about it today because, to the best of my knowledge, it has never been corrected and they sent an innocent man to jail. I know Mike Tyson, and to know him is to love him regardless of how many people are afraid of him. It has nothing to do with who he really is. If anyone ever says they know him, they better have love for him to go along with it because he's a good person, period.

As God is my Witness

Mike Tyson may be the kind of person who scares a lot of people in this world, mainly because he is a great fighter. He is honestly just a really good person with a big, humongous heart and spirit that many people just do not have chance to get to know in this world. He is a person who has been through a lot and to appreciate him, you have to know where he came from. You have to understand where he came from and his struggles in life before his life now. And his story is not like everybody else's. He really and very seriously went through a lot of things.

You can never imagine the real man behind all of what you do see, if you understand me at all. In other words, he is much stronger and has had to deal with so much more than you can ever imagine. The worst thing that Mike hates is a phony person. He appreciates realness and a person who is not hiding themselves. He loves loyalty and is all of that and that is why he despises it. I am not saying he is a perfect man because no man is perfect. But to accuse him of things that does not belong to him and just don't fit him is just a sad case. You have to understand where he came from and what he suffered coming up to appreciate him at the end of the day.

Mike Tyson went through a whole lot that this world just does not know about. He has a hard time trusting people because of the way people have done him in the past. When he gives you his heart, he expects you to give yours the same. That was why I was always so real with him because I imagined people doing him wrong a lot and basically turning him into the monster many people witnessed him to be whenever he fought someone. He suffered a lot as a young boy and he went through a lot coming up, period. The things he went through not many people could handle, seriously.

As God is my Witness

What was always important to me was the fact that I personally experienced really getting to know him. I know him and what he is capable of doing. Raping a woman is not something that Mike Tyson would ever do. Now, he can make a female feel uncomfortable if he doesn't like her or he feels like you are being other than your better self with him, if you understand me at all. In other words, you can't play games with him and think it will fly well with him because it won't. He just does not like fake and phony women that act a certain way. If you do, he can make someone feel uncomfortable to be around. You will just not be as important to him anymore once he finds you out. But raping a woman is not something I will ever believe he did.

My life was so hard back then. I always believed and felt in my gut that Mike was an innocent man who got sent to jail for something he did not ever do. I did then, and I still to this day really do believe that he is an innocent man, and he will always be innocent of that as far as I am concerned. I was out on the road touring with Bobby and Whitney back then when he was locked up. Me, Bobby, Whitney, and Daddy went up to see Mike in jail, after I saw Spike Lee, in our hotel lobby, and he told me that Mike asked him to tell me hi, if he saw me.

Spike Lee just walked right up to me and asked me was I Bobby's sister? I said, "Yes I am." Spike said, Mike Tyson asked me to say Hi for him if I saw you. I felt so good knowing he was thinking about me, but I wanted to see him and be there for him in any way that I could. So, I gathered Bobby, Whitney, and Daddy together and we all went up to see him. When Mike came out and saw us there to see him, we left Daddy, Bobby, and Whitney sitting right there, and me and Mike went to a comer to spend the whole visit by ourselves.

We took pictures and sat down to talk for that whole visit alone without them in our faces. That was one day that I was not able to bear to leave him after our visit was over. I have never felt so lonely and terrible that he was not leaving with me. This was a hard day for me, and I did everything I could in my power to stay strong leaving him there without crying. I had to smile and pretend it was nothing for me to do, but it was so hard going back on the road touring, knowing he was in jail and could not come home. I was so sad at this time and in that moment after seeing him locked down like that. I cannot explain the feelings I got, but after that ordeal, I was ready for a major change in my life. It was a very stressful time for me, but I got through it. I was craving a big change in my life at this time.

MY BROTHER, MR. TOMMY BROWN

Speaking of change, my brother Tommy has changed a lot today. Whenever you hear the name Tommy Brown, you should always take your hat off to salute my brother and even more towards my mother. The two of them have worked very hard to make Bobby's career possible. They are both responsible for who Bobby Brown is today. Of course, we are to praise no one but God Himself for any and every success that we experience, witness or ever have in our lives. After God, is of course Bobby himself because God gave us our talents first of all, and you cannot get anywhere without talents. Bobby has always been an entertainer to his heart. Tommy and our mother both worked super hard to make Bobby Brown a huge success and who he is today. Before Bobby started in the music industry, Tommy was going to college for journalism and left school his career to take care of Bobby with his career. He just dropped out and dropped everything and was right there with Bobby throughout every single thing Bobby had to do and go through in this industry.

As God is my Witness

It breaks my heart because my brother Tommy is no longer Bobby's manager today, as he should be. The one thing that I always believed in was giving a man his respect, flowers and due diligence while he lives. More importantly, I believe in giving flowers while they are alive and never forgetting where you came from and who helped you along the way is so very important for us all to remember. Especially if you have worked as hard as Tommy and Mommy has. Of course, it is God we should always so selfishly praise! He is the main man who is indeed responsible for any man's success. God is and has always been right there guiding my mother and Tommy when it came to Bobby's career altogether, because our mother was a praying mother.

Tommy has always been the backbone of the Brown family and has an outstanding record of his work with Bobby and his career. Many people call me the matriarch of the family, and I have to say that I do agree with everyone. However, Tommy is the one who has worked his fingers to the bone for Bobby and the rest of this family out of all of us siblings. "Tommy would die and go to hell in a gasoline jacket a million times for his baby brother, Bobby, please believe it!" He and Bobby have always had a wonderful history and life together and should not ever depart from each other; regardless of who comes and goes. I am one who is big on loyalty and believes in it wholeheartedly. Make no mistake about it, Tommy Brown started this whole thing with Bobby Brown and deserves to be with his baby brother today.

Tommy was not just any manager, he was always known as the "wise shrewd businessman in Hollywood doing a lot of good things for his baby brother, being good with numbers, knowing contracts, and knowing how to close deals for Bobby.

As God is my Witness

He was the perfect manager for Bobby and has even done some things for Whitney as well. Tommy was always there and has always helped our mother make the right decisions for Bobby to see to it that he was a huge success. Tommy will protect Bobby with his life at any given time and cost. That is what I love the most about him because we share that same heart at the end of the day. He was even going to manage Whitney at one time, but Whitney's father is the only one who's ever managed her. After Papa John managed his daughter, Whitney, she said that she did not ever need another manager nor would she ever have a manager, and she did in fact leave this world without one.

Speaking of Whitney and Tommy with management. The lie that Pat Houston talked about being Whitney's manager was the first red flag for me in knowing that somebody had done a terrible thing to Whitney. It was one of the reasons why I immediately spoke out against Pat Houston. I could not sit back and allow all that was maliciously happening and going on to continue on my watch. Pat who now calls herself a Houston, was sitting on the Oprah Show, literally looking Oprah in the face and lying to Oprah after Whitney was found in that hotel dead. I and a lot of other people already knew for a fact that she is not and was not ever Whitney Houston's manager.

Mama Cissy and the rest of the Houston family, they all know that this is "not" true, but, of course, even they will not say anything to go against Pat, because Pat is doing them all a favor with helping Mama Cissy obtain everything of Whitney's estate. They are all working together now, and they sold just about everything of Whitney's after her death. They did not waste time getting rid of all of the things that were important to Whitney. It is so sad the way they have done her.

As God is my Witness

It is as if they had a very serious hate for her, in my eyes. It was like they hit the ground running to sell Whitney's catalog and everything else right after her death. It seemed to me that they could not wait to get their hands on Whitney's money and her estate. Whitney told me and some of our family that she would never do "any" such things with Pat. That woman has never been accepted by Whitney to be over anything of hers. It proves to me that Mama Cissy did not care about Whitney's wishes and Desires.

None of them respected her in any way whatsoever. I am not the only one that knows this. It's a lot of us who know about Whitney's personal business and what she will and will not do under any circumstances. I don't believe that Oprah even believed Pat as she was interviewing her because Oprah is no fool. It seemed to me as if Oprah was looking at Pat during that interview knowing that she was not being honest about that whole story, while she was talking to her. If Oprah did believe her, she sure fooled me, because Oprah looked like she was going to shut Pat down at any moment while she was talking to her.

CHAPTER 4
THE REAL DEAL ABOUT
"NEW EDITION"

Now I must speak the truth of what went down with that whole New Edition separation ordeal. I do not believe New Edition knows what actually went down even to this day. The media and the public have it all wrong and they have been saying a lot of things that hold no truth regarding my brother and New Edition altogether. I feel like they don't give Bobby his props properly and truthfully. Now, I would agree that some things just do not need to be mentioned, So, I am not going to say a lot of things. However, where it is necessary, I will speak up because it will set the record straight and knock out all the lies that are continuously being told to this world when it comes to the real story of New Edition.

First and foremost, with all due respect, Bobby was the one single person who originated and/or started the New Edition group. I remember this clearly as if it were yesterday. The both of us were single solo artists at that time. I am Bobby's elder sister too, so don't forget I was there and a bit older than them all. The Strand Theatre was giving a talent show and wanted groups only. I had a group and was the lead vocalist and had two backup dancers. We called ourselves the "OP Girls." Bobby was always a solo artist and loved to entertain. Long story short, Bobby and I wanted to do this at the Strand this day. However, he had no group and neither did I at that moment. The Strand was not taking any solo artist, you had to have a solid group. Bobby goes to get Ralph, Michael and Ricky.

As God is my Witness

He told them they could win a recording contract with "Street Wise Records", if they did this show together. They did the show, and I stood down and did not gather my girls for the talent show. Of course, I was there with Mommy when they performed and won, 1st place, and a record contract with "Street Wise!" They won that night and Bobby was so excited! When they announced the winners, Mommy and I screamed with so much joy! After they won there was always so much practicing and rehearsals in our home.

Afterwards, and after so much hard work and success, the boys got together and decided they wanted to vote Bobby out of his own group that he created. None of us could believe what was really going on with them. My and everyone else's opinion back then was that it was because the other boys were so very jealous of Bobby being who he was as an entertainer. Bobby would rock that crowd while jumping on speakers and tables to entertain the people. Please, let us get this straight and always remember, I am not talking about them to speak down on any of them. I am just simply speaking the truth here. We are all much older today and can handle the truth. There are no hard feelings today from me towards any of them, I am just telling it like it honestly was, if people will respect it and simply bear witness to the truth.

Yes, they were young, and I am sure so much more mature today, and I do not want them to feel bad for what I am about to say because it is just the truth if anyone would keep it all the way one hundred. Bobby just simply always had high energy and could always rock the crowd more than any of them and he would force his audience to scream with the dances he performed on stage all the time. Everyone knew and experienced the audience when Bobby would do his thing on stage.

As God is my Witness

They would scream more for Bobby than anyone else all the time. Bobby was young and more energetic than they were, and I believe this made some of the boys even more jealous. Everyone saw this and had these thoughts as well as our family back then. With all due respect, some of these boys were so jealous of Bobby that they would do things and say things to break Bobby's heart, and I didn't like that, neither did our mother. I am just speaking the truth to tell the actual story as I remember it. My brother Bobby knows this is true, yet he may not want me to say this, I am sure. I am not talking about this to cause anyone any embarrassment or anything of the nature. If this world does not have the truth, it would never be known, and people will continue on acting as if things were different with them and it wasn't. It seems as if they have always tried to make it seem as if Bobby was making trouble and hard to get along with; but no one wants to face the facts of what was really going on with these boys back then.

I and my family remember it clearly as if it happened yesterday, and it's the truth. Bobby was just more energetic, and the other boys were shy, and they took that out on Bobby. He had to suffer for them being shy and having insecure issues and it's not fair to my brother. It's always good to speak the truth in case anyone has an agenda to propagate something intentional or unintentional. People will sometimes unconsciously try to cover up lies to make others believe a certain thing that does not exist or even go as far to do movies without depicting what is real and true. The person being left out is Bobby who knows the truth, while other people get to walk around acting like another person while the real persons are hidden, and I do not like that as his sister.

As God is my Witness

I have no clue as to who they really are today in all reality. Today, I am trying so hard to be an example of what we are all supposed to be, and at the same time speak the truth since I witness people having issues with doing so. It is hard when you have to speak negatively to get the true story out. It would be nice if we could all live in a world where people would not lie so much and simply speak the truth where it is important to do that.

We have a lot to learn about treating people properly in this world. Especially folks you grew up with and supposedly known all your life. So many times, we overlook how we treat one another and then we become surprised when someone reveals the truth of what has really gone on. And I noticed how some people will live in the past, and oftentimes continue on hurting the person whom everyone is used to hurting throughout their life; while that hurt person is still being so damaged and bruised in such a severe way. We should always at least strive to live to make others feel good or even better, especially when there are people who are so deserving of it.

When you've done wrong to a person, and you are not willing to make it right, and you are not so much concerned with change, and willing to make their lives better by just simply being better and treating others right, it builds unnecessary animosity.

So many people are walking around not allowing themselves to become better people when it is not such a hard thing to do. When we tell lies, it goes on for so many years, and sometimes people forget, and they start believing the lie because it was told for so long that they begin to believe it as truth. It can also bring on more lies on top of more lies to cover the last lie, and then worse, people often believe the lies, and then the media and critics, among others have been exposed to this lie and then the process begins of perpetrating a fraud without correction and worse, adding onto it. When Bobby got on stage with New Edition dancing and entertaining, he would always jump up on huge speakers, he would go off stage, walk into the crowd, and get close to his fans while doing his dances. I remember these boys complaining about that and having a problem with Bobby being himself. Mommy used to say they were just jealous because they did not have the heart and energy that Bobby had.

He has always been a real true entertainer to the heart. Bobby is a born entertainer who loved to sing, dance and simply entertain. When it comes to instruments, you name it, Bobby can play just about anything, and he did not ever go to school for any of his talents he's learned over the years of being in the business. Bobby is who he is, and he will always be his own man as an entertainer. Some people cannot handle you being yourself and it is what he has had to always face being around them, if you ask me. When all the boys were young, they were not as energetic as Bobby and so, a lot of other people believe it caused all the commotion and jealousy issues with them, and it made them unnecessarily bitter towards him. Ralph and Johnny in my eyes was always two of those in the group that seemed to be closer to Bobby and always seemed to be genuinely friends with him. Johnny came later, and of course can sing very well, but we all accepted him as if he was our brother and he did the same. Ralph sang like a bird as well as Bobby and Johnny, and in my and others' opinion, all three of them together were the greatest singers out of all of them.

As God is my Witness

They all sing well today of course, because practice has made every one of them even much better, of course. From the beginning but a bit late, Ronnie was placed in the group by his uncle who was hired as the choreographer. That is how I remember Ronnie coming into the group. Originally, it was just Bobby, Ralph, Ricky, and Michael. I of course love them all because they are all my brothers, but I must tell this story exactly how it was for the sake of truth being told. It is what it is at the end of the day, and no one should ever be ashamed of the truth being told, especially when things happened years ago, and they were younger. I remember it like it was yesterday. I know from experience in life that people do not like to talk about certain things like this and I get it.

They are all older now and it is probably embarrassing to even talk about, but it's OK. Bobby went through a whole lot of things with them, and things that none of them will probably ever dare talk about amongst them today. My family remembers all that happened with most of them teasing and laughing at Bobby back then. Bobby went through a lot, and he may not desire to tell it all himself, but it was something that always bothered me as his sister coming up around them and witnessing it happening to him. I was angry a lot of times he would come home and tell us what they did to him. On top of it, they had no idea what he suffered at home as a little boy. My brother has really been through a lot of things he may not ever talk about with anyone. I know that the boys have more than likely grew out of all of the child-like ways by now, but it did exist with some of them. Like I said, it was my brother Bobby who started New Edition from the beginning, and for some reason someone doesn't want to give that credit to Bobby, it seems to me.

As God is my Witness

This is why we all felt that it was a total disrespect to Bobby and my family for them to all get together and vote Bobby out after all in the beginning. It was long ago, and all is forgiving but they have to tell the truth how they treated Bobby, and I did not see that in the movie that someone decided to do on them.

After going through a lot of things back then, Mommy said people were calling her phone telling her that, voting him out of that group was just a trick to get the rest of the boys to do that so that they could get Bobby by himself and blow him up as a solo artist. In other words, what the rest of New Edition thought was bad for Bobby was not at all bad but better for him. Overall, it was a much better deal for him, and Bobby became successful on his own. Bobby's heart was broken but only for a little while. I do not know why Bobby has never talked about it, but they gave him hell back then. What they wanted bad for him turned out good for him because he had God on his side. "God had another plan for Bobby, little did they or anyone else know."

I am sure they all know this by now because they have seen what God has done for my brother's career. The thing is, when it all happened, they were all invited out to a restaurant to sign this "vote out" contract against Bobby. While they were all sitting in this restaurant, they were all told to meet at, they did not know that Mommy was directly across the street, at another restaurant at the very same time chopping it up with someone about Bobby's solo career. Mommy said, "Oh they thought they were going to count my son out but oh no they aren't and watch this!" They met with Mommy and signed Bobby to a solo contract "without" New Edition, at the same time.

As God is my Witness

If my memory serves me correctly, they did it in a way where New Edition had no idea of what was going on, and so, the joke was on them after all. I also remember how Michael Jackson, Stevie Wonder, and Marvin Gaye, they all called and spoke with Mommy telling her not to worry about them doing that to Bobby because they going to make sure that Bobby succeeded in anything he did from there on. Several celebrities felt bad for Bobby and reached out to let him know that they had his back.

Especially Michael Jackson, who took it hard because of the way they had treated Bobby back then. Marvin Gaye took it hard as well. He was talking to Mommy almost every single day of the week back then. I clearly remember the conversations because I and my sister Tina were joking around and playing in the living room about how we were going to act and what we were going to say when we met Marvin Gaye in person. We had the fake microphones (hairbrush) in our hands, pretending to be interviewed by some media person questioning us about all kinds of stuff We were practicing how we would speak and answer questions once we met Marvin, Michael, and Stevie Wonder. Then BOOM! We heard the news that Marvin Gaye was dead! This made us all feel so terrible for Marvin and his family. Now, we will never get to meet him in person, we said to each other! Marvin Gaye and Bobby Brown's meeting would have been nice.

They had planned to do some things together and we were excited and ready to see what they would do together. Tina and I cried so hard after they announced his death. When I moved to LA, which was long afterward, I met Marvin's daughter Nona Gaye, and we got the chance to hang out together back then. My brother Tommy had the idea of Nona and I being a girl group, but Nona was so shy. LOL! As beautiful as Nona Gaye is, she was so shy.

As God is my Witness

She was the perfect person to get along with and I called her my friend. After seeing her in her movies, I had never been so shocked! I was very happy but just so surprised that she would go into doing movies as shy as I always thought she was. Today, she is one of the best actors out there! OK, back to the "New Edition." Above all, none of the boys understood the assignment that God had placed before them while they were hating on Bobby back then. None of them understood that they were all under trial, and they were all being tested at that time.

Yes, they were young, but we all must learn that God will still try you even when you are young because it tells people what is in you. Life's lessons start somewhere at a young age, because the sooner you learn the better your life is supposed to be. After they voted Bobby out, Mommy and Tommy both paid close attention to Bobby's contracts from then on. Mommy fought like hell to make sure they did not do her son wrong.

And she did it without any fear whatsoever. In fact, she was the matriarch mother of all the boys that were in the group. Therefore, as a mother who handled the business with New Edition, she gave advice and made all final decisions when it came to making decisions as a whole and for the group. Mommy always felt that she was more knowledgeable of the industry stuff along with the contracts because she also had Tommy helping her with that, and so they together led the group pretty much. Everyone looked to Mommy for all the answers because the other mothers were not as versed in the music industry at that time in hindsight.

As God is my Witness

I clearly remember all of the other mother's looking to my mother to make the final decisions whenever it came to the New Edition group, but they did not depict her image properly in the movie at all. In fact, that or any other movie regarding the new Edition or Bobby has not in any way told the truthful story in my opinion. A good story can be told if only the truth can ever be told right. Mommy was the type of mother that was a strong leader, and she would not have it any other way. Without taking anything from the other mothers, when it came to the contracts they looked to Mommy and Tommy for guidance back then. Mommy talked a lot about New Edition and how they treated her son, and she did not like it at all.

She always felt like Bobby was being teased by the boys for just being himself, which was a real entertainer at the end of the day. She took it real hard and thought they were trying to seriously play her son's talents down and discourage him from being who he was after all. It took a while, but Michael finally came to apologize for voting Bobby out, she said. She went on to say that "the rest of them never came back to apologize." Mommy went through a lot with the business for the boys during those times. It was a lot that went down back then. At one time, I clearly remember Mommy having conversations with someone representing MCA records regarding Bobby's career. She would be yelling and screaming through her phone. This day, I remember someone telling Mommy that they loved Bobby. I am not sure who was on the other end of that phone, but Mommy screamed to the top of her lungs! She said, "You do not love my son Got-Dam It and don't you ever try to insult my intelligence by telling me that! I love him, I am his mother, so do not give me that Ish!" Do not ever say that to me again because I am not a fool!"

As God is my Witness

Mommy did not play games with anyone at any time when it came to her children that she brought into this world. There are many people reading this book and know exactly what I am talking about when I speak on Momma Brown. She did not like anyone playing games with her children. She would fight you to her death about us. Pop Brown, our father, was the very same way. Many people who came from where we come from, always knew both our parents and understood how it was for us growing up. Mommy was the type of mother that, whenever the police officers were beating a black man in front of her house (which happened often), she would tell us all, "Come on yawl, get your shoes on now, we are going down there to get these police off this brother!"

Mommy hated it when the police put their hands on anyone because she had sons herself. She would jump in the fight regardless of knowing the situation or caring about her personal safety. She would throw them hands and talk later. Whenever she started it, the whole neighborhood came behind her and all was up in smoke!

Mommy had our whole family and neighborhood fighting with these officers all the time because they were always chasing and beating black men in our neighborhood. She always said that we had to fight them off regardless of who it was. She did this to let them know that they cannot come into our neighborhoods jumping on our black men for basically nothing, and without a fair fight. She felt this way because she had sons to raise in one of the worst hoods in this country. When I think about these encounters, we had with the police it is funny now because the police always called for backup whenever they were trying to handcuff Mommy and get her in their car. She never made it easy for them. It took them a long time to get her hand cuffed and into a police car.

As God is my Witness

There were only two things you just did not do with Mrs. Brown. You don't mess with her children, and you do not mess with her children, period. She had a huge heart for her children regardless of how old we would ever become. The same for Tommy, and I used to tell everybody that Tommy only had two spaces in his heart. One for Mommy and the other for his baby brother, Bobby. There is no mountain in this world that he would not climb nor any ocean he would not swim across about his mother and his baby brother, Bobby. He has always loved his baby brother with all his heart and would kill a brick about him, as Daddy would say about us all. Bobby is the reason Tommy worked so hard for Bobby and New Edition in the beginning of their rise to fame.

I am happy that Bobby became the solo artist that he should have been from the beginning. I think he would have suffered a lot more had he stayed with those boys back then and remained a group. It was a blessing from God and much better for him that he had his own contract and was always doing his own thing. Bobby Brown is a pure entertainer and his own man at the end of the day. Trying to play him down and forcing him to not entertain and not be himself is something that would not ever happen with him. Bobby is going to be himself once he is on that stage regardless of who likes it or not. Besides, you have to really like to entertain when you're in that business because a lot comes with it.

But at the same time, you have to appreciate other people and their talents as well because we all complement each other and there is no need for jealousy and envy. We as a people in this country, need to accept people for who they are without being biased or envious of another man's talents. God has blessed us all with our own talents. I say this with all due respect.

As God is my Witness

This is a very important issue that was never talked about and never dealt with amongst New Edition, I believe. And when you don't deal with an issue as serious as this one was, it continues to go one because people go unseen. People are hidden and others become confused as to why things go the way they do.

I never liked jealousy and envious people. It makes my spirit feel so terrible. I have had to deal with a lot of that myself If nothing is ever done about it, it can become seriously dangerous because it ends up being a way of life for individuals. And before you know it, they become so used to how they act and treat others, that it seems fair seeming to them when it is clearly wrong. And now their wrong appears to be their right to them and other things happen, and excuses are made for folk's ill actions, if you understand me.

A person who is jealous of you can plot your death and people have to know this. Jealousy and envy can lead to a lot of ugly things if we are not careful and attentive to people by watching them and distancing ourselves from such individuals. God is always there, of course. He says, "I will sit your enemies at your footstool." And He will indeed do it we better know this. Especially when a man's heart is good. Bobby has always had his hands out to help people and his heart has always been right there in it. And no, none of us are perfect, but as long as our good outweighs our bad in this world, and be far better than bad, at the end of the day, were in that realm with Him. If enough people believed in God period, we could get so much further along in life. Bobby has always had bigger dreams about becoming who he desired to become in this world. He is an entertainer to the heart.

As God is my Witness

I am happy that my brother has people like me who are alive today and keeping up prayers for him because he has so many demons following him today. Demons that are trying so hard to snatch him into that fire that God has set for them and not Bobby. The bottom line and the absolute truth that none of them dare talk about is, Bobby has always desired for all of them to be successful as a group, and the boys never took it seriously whenever Bobby said something about them "making it big" as they would say back then. God has always been right there whenever people let you down in this world, and that was the lesson for all of them to learn. Bobby always told them that they would be big, and they laughed at him. They do not dare talk about this because I am sure it is embarrassing for the ones that were laughing back then. I remember the countless hours of my mother and my brother Tommy working, and all the headaches they got dealing with people and Bobby's business.

I don't care who it is, Bobby will never have anyone working for or with him who will love him and be more concerned for his life and well-being other than his brother Tommy Brown, who would literally die for him and has already put in a tremendous amount of time, energy and work for him. There is not a soul out there in this world that has Bobby's back like his brother Tommy.

With all due respect, since the death of Whitney, I believe they have focused in on dividing and conquering the Bobby Brown family which includes me. They took my brother Tommy out of the picture with Bobby to keep him away so they can do what it is they desire to do with him. They killed Bobby's wife, his daughter, and first-born son, Bobby Brown Jr., and did this to obtain my brother and sister's estates.

As God is my Witness

I believe they feel like when and if anything happens to my brother, Bobby, his daughter and son would not be in the way of the estate monies. This is my belief, and I will go to my grave believing this fact. I know that my family members were all murdered in cold blood and for their own money and estates, and no one can bring me a better story. I am one hundred percent certain of this because of how they did what they did by killing all of them. You would have to be seriously ignorant and just so unintelligent to not see this as the reason. Mommy always said, you better not ever think that you have friends in this kind of business.

I honestly wish that Bobby would at least look at everyone for who they really are and just simply face facts because, I believe even his life is at stake now, and I do not believe he is safe. In any event, I am certain that God has his back at the end of the day of course. The one thing that sinners do not ever think about is the fact of facing God.

I always thought that people were foolish to think they would not ever have to look God in the face and deal with every single thing they have done of evil in this world. And for people to not know what it is like on the other side is another scary thing. Either they don't believe, or they do not care. If it is the latter, I feel so sorry for them that they will face a powerful God one day.

When Bobbi Kristina was in hospice, they had the audacity and nerve to bring in men who posed as security right in her room and near her door. They were security men that were not there for Bobby or his daughter. They were security for Pat Houston. We all looked in wonder and questioned why she felt she needed security in a hospice center where my niece was?

As God is my Witness

Nobody knows her and she is not a celebrity everyone said, so why the security guy all the sudden everyone was asking? These were not guys who were there to see to it that we had peace while were mourning as a family. It was like Pat had things focused on her while my niece is in this hospice center needing our (the Brown's) care. We did not need Pat or any other Houston there disrupting our last days with our niece, and they did not care even a little bit.

I cannot even begin to explain the sad things that my family had to suffer and endure as my niece laid in this hospice center. We did everything in our power to keep the peace and act civilized under so much unnecessary and intentional arrogance. When I tell you that there are a lot of people who have a lot of things to answer to God for behind what went on in that hospice center by all who were present and doing the things they have done to my niece and our family, you have no idea what I am saying.

Thing is, it was so unnecessary for all of these people walking around in hospice with attitudes, lurking around my niece's bed, waiting for the first chance they can get to do something to her, and they did do something to her believe it or not. It was so obvious what people were there for because they had no problem with showing you who they were. They were "that" bold! I do not know who told them that it was OK to do such evil to a human being.

They literally starved my niece until she shut her eyes and died from whatever they did to put her to sleep plus the starvation. Now, I do not understand how this hospice center was able to do this, but it was done. It was done because that nurse who was impersonating did something to Krissy while she was there.

As God is my Witness

My niece died a horrific, cruel and wicked death, and in a way that was so unheard of It was also so very sad how all of these unknown people who placed themselves in that hospice center while she laid in there. I cannot make this up, this is real.

They murdered my niece and literally starved my niece to death as well! *"YES, THEY LITERALLY DID THIS! THEY DID NOT FEED MY NIECE FOR WEEKS NOR DID THEY GIVE HER EVEN WATER!!! SHE DIED OF STARVATION AND HAD NO FOOD GOING INTO HER BODY, NOT EVEN A DRINK OF WATER!"*

We dealt with knowing that and then we have evil spirits walking around my niece all day every day waiting for her to shut her eyes so that they can get that estate and go on about their merry way. These people who were there making noise were so disrespectful, and they did this right in front of my niece while she laid there.

You cannot ever imagine the trauma that Bobbi Kristina was going through listening to all of this right at her door. When I say they did not care about my niece and her well-being it was on a level that is so unimaginable that they did not care. They disrespected my family on a level that I cannot even begin to explain. Some of the security men, who did not need to be there for starters, were THERE STARTING TROUBLE WITH MY BROTHER Bobby and Tommy. I could not believe the things that were going on. There are some wicked and evil people in this world that will have God to deal with them. I cannot understand how a person can be so ugly and evil to do such things to a family who have already lost people and are now losing their baby girl.

As God is my Witness

When I say they have some terrible days coming by God you have no idea. I say that because there is no way that God is going to allow them to go untouched for all the evil things that they have done to us. A whole lot of repenting has to take place and I feel sorry for them. Now, first of all, a lot of people had questions they wanted Pat Houston to answer. One of the questions were, "why would Pat continue to go into Krissy's room alone after her father told everyone to not go anywhere near her room without a second person in there with her?" Pat constantly violated and disrespected my brother's wishes regarding this and entered Krissy's room "alone" and when my brother was not there. Of course, I and everyone else believe she was being malicious as she went into that room with my niece, make no mistake about it.

I believe 100% that she did something to my niece, and she did it when there was not anybody looking at her to see her. God saw every single thing and every single spirit as it came into that hospice center, and they are all granted back whatever it was they dished out.

This was a time of devastation at its highest level for my niece. My brother Tommy comes to my house and tells me one day that this white man jumps up in my brother's Tommy's and Bobby's face and yells, "Tell your sister (meaning me) to shut up!" They were upset that I was speaking out on my social media outlet about Pat Houston having something to do with Whitney's death. My brother Tommy told me that he jumped right back in this man's face to say, "Hell no, she doesn't have to shut up she's a grown woman!" Bobby as well said something to him. Bobby and Tommy, both told him, "My sister doesn't have to shut her mouth and told him that he needed to mind his business and stay out of our family business!"

As God is my Witness

I could not believe the things that these people who were strangers to us, did as they came up in hospice! It was seriously unbelievable! They did things that people just do not do. And they did all of this while my niece laid right there in hospice. They did not care, not even a little bit; to have respect for us as a family while we went through all of that with my niece. Back to Tommy Brown.

Tommy had been working with his brother since the beginning of time, and was not only going to school as a journalist, but he was also a great boxer and fought and won every fight he was ever in. He had a serious career and was really good at what he did and enjoyed doing it. Then he finally left boxing alone to pursue Bobby's career for him. He made sacrifices with his entire life to change his whole life for his baby brother, and now he is standing on the side today, and not so much with his brother like he should be anymore. His entire life has always been devoted to his baby brother, Bobby. Today, my prayers are that Bobby awakes and doesn't allow people to rule and run his life like they want it to be instead of what he wants for himself.

I pray that he stands up as a man and a believer in God and just simply let it all go and make his greatest sacrifice before God, putting all of his faith in Him who indeed has all the power that he needs. They have taken just about everything from my brother and it's time now for him to say, no more! If Whitney was alive, I believe her and Bobby both would be living a happily married life, and Tommy would have his job back. Whitney would see to it that Tommy had employment with Bobby and was his manager because she cared about family.

As God is my Witness

Speaking of my sister Whitney again, her father, Poppa John, he was the only one who had ever managed Whitney. After Poppa John managed Whitney, she went through some things and did not think it was ever necessary again to ever have a manager anymore. Therefore, she managed herself up until the day she left this world. She said she left this world without anyone being her manager. If anyone should ever see her signature anywhere on a piece of paper with someone else's name posing as her manager, especially Pat Houston, "know" and be assured that it is a fraudulent and forged document. I am positively 100% certain of this. Whitney never signed any papers as Pat Houston being her manager. This is an absolute fact, and my brother Bobby is even a witness to it.

As time passed, Whitney became pregnant with Krissy and was also in another state filming her new movie. We were all excited around this time and was even touring with Bobby while she was pregnant. A lot was going on for both Bobby and Whitney and they were doing so well together. While she was away filming every chance she got, she would call Bobby back at the mansion, and of course, it was me again who answered the phone.

I was extremely excited that she is filming this movie with Kevin Costner, titled, "The Bodyguard." Kevin Costner has always been one of my favorite actors. Therefore, out of curiosity, I immediately asked Whitney, if she was having fun filming with him? She immediately said "Oh, no girl, I hate it! I cannot wait to get home away from all of this and be with my man, Bobby!" I could not believe it! I just knew she was having the time of her life filming this movie with Kevin Costner. I asked why she didn't like it and she said it was because she did not like Kevin Costner's smell, and that it was making her sick to her stomach to have to keep smelling him.

As God is my Witness

Yes, as God is my witness this is what Whitney said to me. I am only telling the truth so that you know the real deal. I could understand and relate to what she was saying because she was also pregnant at the time and your senses are through the roof when you are pregnant, I should know because I was pregnant and experienced something of that nature at times with people. Any woman who's had children know where this is coming from. But long story very short, Whitney did not like filming that movie with Kevin Costner for that one specific reason that she told me out of her own mouth. Trust me when I tell you that she did not like Kevin Costner at all while she was doing that movie. There is absolutely no interest there at all coming from Whitney when it comes to that man. Whitney talked about how turned off she was with him in filming that movie and she was so tired of doing it she said.

If anyone thinks or believes that there was something there, they have never been so far from the truth, because I certainly have the truth of what it was like for her because she told me straight out of her mouth. She said that she was miserable making that entire movie with him. I said, Aww Whitney, that's not nice, and she said, I don't like the smell of white men, I can't stand it! I said, oh, well that's different, OK, well I heard you loud and clear my sister! As God is my witness, that is what she said to me. I guess that is why she never dated any white men. I'm not sure but she surely said that to me. Overall, and at that time, she was missing Bobby so much, and thinking about him every single day that she was there. Furthermore, she said that she almost walked off and left the scene of that whole thing one day almost giving it all up and throwing it away for good because of a problem she had the whole time she was filming.

As God is my Witness

And trust me there was no faking it. It was "that" serious and Whitney very much so, wanted to come home more than anything else at that time, but she hung in there to the end. When Whitney arrived home, she showed extreme happiness! The glow in her eyes indicated nothing but pure love! This is where I was convinced that she and Bobby both were so seriously in love with each other. We all knew that nothing could take their love away from each other because of how they were with one another. Now it was even more valid in my eyes, and I was sure of their love. I remember being so happy to see my brother finally happy with a woman who loved him just as he loved her. It gave my heart so much joy to be around them both and witness the real love between them. It was always fun, and we did a lot of family outings together. Anyone around Bobby and Whitney had to feel their love for one another.

CHAPTERS 5
BOBBY & WHITNEY'S WEDDING

Me, being Whitney's biggest fan, I was even happier. It was just like we had all grown up together and had known each other all our lives as each day would go by. Before she even went to shoot that movie, when we got the news that she was pregnant, I had never seen a woman so joyful in my life to have a baby! Whitney was beaming and looking so beautiful the whole time she was carrying Bobbi Kristina. She wanted a boy in the beginning because she always wanted another Bobby, she said. I believe this was why they named her Bobbi. But of course, everyone was happy whether it was a boy or a girl. I think my sister Tina named her Bobbi Girl.

At the time of their wedding, yes, it was true that Whitney handpicked all the women who were close and dear to her heart for her wedding, and she started with "her family" first. She picked me and my younger sister Carole as her bride's maids. She then chose all her close friends and just those that she cared about and loved. Speaking of family, we all know that Whitney did not care who you were, she had to like and trust you to be one of her bridesmaids or her maid of honor, family or no family. That was her most precious day! I asked her the question, "Why did she not have Donna Houston or Pat Houston, who was her brothers Michael and Gary's wives, as a bridesmaid?

We all knew that Pat was that one particular person that Whitney would not ever choose to be in anything that she was orchestrating or having because it was not ever a secret how Whitney felt about Pat, Gary's wife.

As God is my Witness

Whitney liked Monique Houston a lot, but things did not turn out with Gary and Monique Houston. Anything that was of importance to Whitney, you can bet Pat Houston was nowhere in, around, or near it. And I say that with all due respect. As a matter of fact, as I am writing this, I do not at all remember seeing Pat at my brother and sister's wedding or their home at all that day.

And, for those of you who are out here in this world following Pat Houston, you have to ask yourself, (if you choose to continue believing Pat when she makes statements out in the media regarding her and Whitney's relationship). Ask yourself, "Why did Whitney "not" include her in special moments like her wedding? I am not saying this proudly either, but you have to know what is going on here in order to see this picture for what it truly is. Pat also sat on Oprah telling the world how close she and Whitney were. It would be a beautiful thing if they were, please do not get me wrong. I am not pleased to witness sisters who don't like each other.

But I cannot allow her to continue lying to this world out here while she does all the evil things that she has been and still is doing to Whitney. Whitney Houston just simply did not mess with Pat Houston like that. I don't feel good saying this, but it is what it is. Pat Houston has done a lot of things to Whitney and is responsible for how Whitney felt about her. You have no idea how many days I prayed and asked God to please calm Whitney down as she dealt with Pat, so trust me, I do not hate Pat, nor would I ever have ill feelings about two sisters "not" getting along with each other. In this case, Whitney just did not like this woman she said, because of all the sneaky things that Whitney said she was always doing to her. Under no circumstances did Whitney ever want Pat Houston around us, and I never seen Pat in my brother and sister's home.

As God is my Witness

I lived with Bobby and Whitney for a long time, so I know the real deal. It is not something I always liked or agreed with back then, but I fully understand it today as I should have yesterday. I was always the one trying to stop Whitney from what she was doing to Pat by cussing her out all the time, calling her names and such. Little did I know or understand that the decisions that Whitney was trying to make for herself back then, were for her benefit. I am just trying to tell the truth here so that you can see for yourself the kind of person that Pat is, so that you can take a closer look at her with Whitney's life and death, and figure things out for yourself by looking at how she is handling Whitney's estate and all of Whitney's business. Right after Whitney's death, Pat Houston ran to sell all of Whitney's things. We are talking "Catalog" and other important stuff here.

Things that Whitney would never do had she been alive. Pat Houston placed my niece on that "Reality Show" right after Whitney's death, and I believe she did it to make my niece look horrible to this world. Yes, I believe it was done deliberately to make my niece look bad in the event they had to fight her for her mother's estate. I knew it was a set up for Krissy and encouraged her "not" to do it. Why did Whitney "not" choose her for her wedding? See, it does not matter what people say, at the end of the day because $1+1=2$, and that cannot be debated at any time. I did not realize that Whitney was right in everything she was saying about Pat until Whitney was gone and I found out the real deal about Pat, and Gary too.

Bottom line is, there was always a good reason for Whitney's behavior towards any of them, which we knew nothing of back then, to say the least. Overall, I was so happy when she told me that she wanted me to actually be in her wedding as a bride's maid.

As God is my Witness

It was the first wedding that I had participated in as a bridesmaid and the first wedding that I had ever attended period. We had to all come to the mansion in New Jersey and stay at the house to prepare for the wedding. When it was time to get our hair and makeup done, I remember the male makeup artist who kept a smile on my face. He was racing back and forth trying to get me and CeCe Winan's makeup on properly and within a reasonable time. As he was standing in front of me playing with my hair, he yelled for the other makeup artist that was doing my eyebrows, to go very lightly on my face so that when he was ready for me it wasn't much makeup on me. He said that I did not need that much makeup and he adored my look without it. He kept talking about how pretty my face was naturally. I got all dolled up and had never felt so good! My sons both also looked so cute with their young man suits on. I was just so happy to be in this wedding.

My oldest son Kelsey was Whitney's ring bearer and was so handsome walking down the aisle carrying Whitney's ring. The wedding itself was so emotional, I could not stop crying from being so happy for the both of them. We had a good time before the wedding took place, during the wedding and after. We had a ball at the after-party and danced all night long! I had never seen Whitney and Bobby so happy! They both were ready to go and be married. Whitney seemed to be glowing so beautifully! It was her special day so whatever she wanted, she got without any problems or issues.

Just like any human being would do, Whitney thought about those who were dearest to her heart for this special occasion. Many people asked me the question, "Why" Whitney did not include Pat and Donna Houston in her wedding as her bride's maids?

As God is my Witness

The simple answer is, Whitney said out of her mouth that she did not like Pat and did not want her anywhere near her, and was not fond of either of them, nor did she ever trust Pat and just did not want Donna in it, period. I am saying this because this world needs to know how important this was for Whitney that this woman Pat is not in her business the way she is today in her death, and it is serious.

At this time, I want you to think reader, and use your common sense here. Any woman that is the only girl in her family, and supposedly has two brothers, is going to pick her sisters-in-law with her brother's first to be in her wedding if they are liked, wouldn't you say so? When I asked her about this, she came right out to tell me. She always saw Pat as a very conning and sneaky individual, she said. Several people said that Whitney always knew that Pat was Mama Cissy's puppet and was there to expedite whatever it was that Mama Cissy had her there for. I eventually came to bear witness to that part and could not believe Mama Cissy and Pat's relationship with each other after watching them two.

It was very strange to me how they communicated with one another. Now that I look back, I honestly feel and believe that the both of them had been conspiring against Whitney altogether and they did it for so many years right under our noses. I also believe that Whitney knew and was sure of this. Many people thought automatically that Whitney would include them, especially since she knew Donna before she knew any of Bobby's sisters. A lot of people overlook this situation without giving it thought where we should in this case.

As God is my Witness

There is a very serious reason why Whitney left both of these women out of her marriage and on her most special day. I promised everyone who asked me and requested that I talk about this in this book, and so, here it is. I can only tell you exactly what my sister told me and what I saw and realized to be the truth after being in this family for so long.

Speaking of the Wedding, right before Whitney was killed, it had been revealed that Whitney and Bobby were getting married again! Yes, they were now back together and planning their 2nd wedding right before the Clive Davis event in Los Angeles. I believe that certain people found out about this because they had her phone tapped and were watching her so much at this time. I came to believe that they were not going to let that happen because, her getting back with Bobby meant that she would be farther away from them, and they did not like nor want that.

I also believe that they wanted her estate and wanted her gone now so that they could have their way with all of her money. I also believe it is why they killed my niece as well, because they did not want her daughter to have that estate either and it is why they were all there at hospice to attack Krissy and make sure she did not leave that hospital alive. And yes, this is the bottom line to this whole entire book. It made even more sense after learning that my niece was now down in the hospital from the same thing just like her mother.

There is no way that that is just a coincidence that two people found in the same way is an accident. Anyone who believes this has to be either insanely unintelligent, brainless and extremely ignorant or just blinded to truth.

As God is my Witness

Everyone knows that Mama Cissy is the one and only person who brought Pat into that Houston family to marry her son Gary. And I believe she catered to Pat because she needed her as a watchdog and a spy for Whitney. I also believe that she wanted Pat to marry her son Gary to keep him somewhat grounded. I do not believe that Mama Cissy could handle her sons and needed them to have wives to handle things with them that she could not. She needed someone there in that family at her beck and call and for her personal purposes, just like she has Donna working for her and not Whitney. I heard this a lot coming from several Houston's and now as things have played out, I can see just why Mamma Cissy did everything she did, just like I understand why Whitney did everything she did.

It has always been told to me that Pat was working her way into the Houston family to marry Gary with the permission and force of Mama Cissy. Mama Cissy seemed to be playing a dangerous game by taking Pat in little did we know at the time. I am sure Whitney knew, now that I look back and see everything. Yet, I did not understand it all as it really was or believe what I had heard and was actually seeing at the same time.

It now not only seems so real and valid to me where I can understand it all, but it is so very real and so real that I cannot ever deny it even if I wanted to. I believe 100% that Mama Cissy "purposely placed Pat inside" of her family for the sole purpose of doing everything she has done and is doing today with Whitney's estate today. I used to hear this "a lot" and not understand just why Mama Cissy saw this as a necessity for her. I used to say to myself, "why does she treat Whitney the way she does and vice versa?"

As God is my Witness

There were a lot of questions I had because of the things that I saw within this family that had me thinking. I could not understand why a lot of things were going on with Whitney and why Whitney had such a hard time dealing with everyone when it came to her own hard-earned money. One of the main things that I witnessed Whitney having problems with was her very own money. It seemed to me like Mama Cissy and Donna, were in control over Whitney's bank, and both were closer than Mama Cissy and Whitney were. Now that Whitney is gone, I can now see so very clearly why things were the way they were. Everything adds up now and is so evident to me. Now, Donna was married to Whitney's brother Michael and had been in that family before we even met Whitney.

Whitney went to school with Donna and had known her for some time. However, Whitney still did not pick Donna to be in her wedding on her special day, and there is a reason for that. Now, we are talking about a woman who has "NO" sisters. Keep this in mind as you follow me with this story. Today, after looking back at Whitney's life, I am not certain if Whitney even agreed to have Donna work in her foundation. It seems to me like Mama Cissy hired Donna to work for her (Mama Cissy) personally. Whitney seemed to always be upset and always have issues with her family when it came to her own money. It was like Whitney had no control over her own money and her mother had it all and there was not anything Whitney could do.

One day, someone asked me, "Have you seen Donna's home?" I said, "Yes, I have, why?" They said, "Well, she has far more expensive things in her home than Whitney ever had!" They believed that Donna Houston was stealing a lot of money from Whitney and that was why her home was the home of a celebrity, while Whitney's home was not.

As God is my Witness

Now keep in mind that Mama Cissy is the head to all of this going on since the beginning of Whitney's career. From my understanding and what I believe, Mama Cissy placed Whitney in the music business at a very young age, just to obtain a rich lifestyle. I feel like she set things up "back then" and while Whitney was too young to sign anything for herself, and so that she (Mama Cissy) could be the head of everything without a fight "today", if you understand me at all. I also believe this is why they never wanted Whitney to marry anyone. This is what I wholeheartedly believe hands down. Whitney may not have known exactly what she had signed at a young age.

Something tells me that there was something in Whitney's contract that could not ever be fixed or changed because of the way it was originally set from the beginning and by her supposedly mother, Mama Cissy, and it is why her life was like it was. Whitney Houston was miserable the way her life was with her Houston family. And it is why Gary said what he said at Mama Cissy's table when he and Pat was invited over there to explain to Mama Cissy what happened to Whitney. Whitney cousin Micky Drinkard, she told me that Mama Cissy told her that Gary and Pat were invited to Mama Cissy's home for dinner after Whitney was found dead. Mama Cissy said that they both came in and she asked them, "What happened to Whitney at that hotel?" Gary and Pat both jumps up and shouts, "Oh, you knew she didn't want to be here anymore!" They really got upset and left Micky said. Micky said, Lele, I wanted to rip Pat's throat out of her neck! Micky did not like Pat not even a little bit. See, all of the Houston's know and understands just what I am saying here.

As God is my Witness

With all due respect, I have to be honest as I possibly can and speak the truth of what is in my heart and mind today. Today, and as I write this book, I see and look at Whitney Houston just as I would see a person who was a product of "human trafficking" if you really want the truth from me. It appears to be like this with her because of who she is and how she was treated by all of the Houston's, meaning all of them including the in laws because Mama Cissy had them on her team. She made all of them to know to obey her above all and not Whitney because they worked for her.

I strongly believe that they all know how Whitney came into that family, and it was revealed to Pat and Donna after being there for so long. Michael and Gary been known that Cissy was not Whitney's mother. But the in- laws, I believe they found out later. I could be wrong, and maybe they all knew. I know that Whitney hardly ever made any decisions for herself when it came to those being hired to work in her business, etc. She could not get her hands on her own money when she wanted to, and the beat goes on and on. Something or someone had a strong grip on her business, and it was unlike anything I had ever witnessed with anyone else before. You don't see people in Whitney's position getting treated the way she was while she was alive and while she is gone. I knew something was so very wrong with that picture and I have it now.

Now, you may ask me, why do I believe all of this? Because again, a whole lot has happened and transpired in this family, for one. Second, she was young when her career started, and she took the advice of her mother (Mama Cissy) without knowing or understanding the seriousness in those decisions back then, or the consequences of those choices she made, which would lead to how it would be for her in the future, like a lot of celebrities.

As God is my Witness

I believe Mama Cissy signed Whitney's life away because Whitney was too young to make decisions for herself. I believe that Mama Cissy took and used Whitney as a "slave trophy" for herself and family finances. And because she did not come from Mama Cissy and Poppa John together, there was no real love for Whitney, and Whitney felt this all the days of her life in that Houston home. As God is my witness, I say this with all due respect to any Houston family member. I can only judge things by what I personally witnessed, seen for myself, what I feel and believe altogether. In my heart this is just the simple truth of it all as far as I am concerned. Whitney had been through a lot with her family, and it was why she acted the way she did with Pat and her mother. I had never seen her treat Donna like she did Pat, but Whitney surely frowned whenever you mentioned Donna's name after a while.

At the same time, I knew that Whitney was not a mean or bad person and had to have good reasons for doing anything she ever did when it came to them. In my book and from my experiences, Whitney was the sweetest person you ever wanted to meet in your life. She had a strong soul and a good heart that loved God.

I can just imagine how happy she was when she got married to my brother Bobby and coming out of that family. Now, I see why she loved our family so much! I guess she never felt comfortable with all the stuff going on in her family. Let me be clear, my family aren't all that either. We have a lot of things that have happened in our family that we are ashamed of as well. Many black people's homes unfortunately suffer and go through some of the worst things in this country to be honest. On another note, and back to their wedding. During their wedding,

As God is my Witness

I had never had so much fun with people from all walks of life at their wedding. It was seriously like a movie playing out. My family invited most of our friends from back home and the people we grew up with, and it was mixed with celebrities and just all types of people. I think that everybody that attended Bobby and Whitney's wedding had the time of their life! To see everyone enjoying themselves and just having a good time was so enlightening for me and my children to witness it! I love to see people happy, smiling, and enjoying themselves.

It honestly gives my heart so much joy to see it! I remembered being so happy and feeling so good and taking pictures and talking to so many people, including celebrities that I had always wanted to meet. I talked with Malcolm Jamal Warner a few times that evening, my boy Johnny Gill and I were dancing and having a ball! There were people everywhere all over the place talking, dancing, drinking and just having so much fun meeting others. The one thing that stuck out in my mind at Bobby and Whitney's wedding that evening was, that I saw a man who is famous in the music industry (I won't mention his name here) who kept trying to get Whitney's attention to flirt with her.

I sat and literally watched this man as he was trying to flirt with her and give her the eye. When he finally got her to look at him, he winked at her as if to say, hey baby, I got my eye on you! But Whitney looked the other way so quickly and as if to say, I am not interested buddy! I said to myself, "good for you Whitney, stay down with Bobby Brown! Do not give him the satisfaction of disrespecting my brother like that." One day I will tell Bobby, but I never mentioned it because Whitney handled him well, and Bobby would have moved him out of there with a lot of noise. My brother Bobby ain't no punk either! He can fight and always kicked behinds when he had to.

As God is my Witness

Ten minutes later, I saw him all up in Bobby's face smiling right after he did that to Whitney. I was just so glad that Whitney paid him no mind at all. It puts a bad taste in my mouth to see this kind of sneakiness going on with people you expect to respect you. I don't like it when people will go after somebody else's wife or husband like that. In any event, I continued to enjoy myself that evening and dared not inform my brother because we were all having such a good time. It is amazing the things God will allow you to see with people.

Some people may think it's unimportant and petty to mention, but I believe it is very important to know how people are and how they act when you cannot see them, which is two different things because you can call people your friends, and allow them to smile in your face pretending to be such, and not even know their true motives and intentions, which can lead to a lot of other bigger and darker things down the line. Overall, it was the best and greatest wedding ever! After leaving from outside where the wedding took place. I proceeded to walk into the mansion because my feet were hurting from walking and dancing in heels all night. I finally took my shoes off and walked into the house limping. As soon as I entered the mansion, I looked over into the comer of this dark room and saw Robyn Crawford sitting in a chair in the dark by herself. She first appeared to be crying to me, but as I got closer, she was just so sad. I said to myself, wow, this is kind of spooky the way she was sitting there all by herself in the dark.

The look on her face told me that she was not at all happy with what had just taken place at this wedding. She looked as if she had lost her best friend and was upset. At this same time, I am saying to myself, "Now Robyn, you just told me that you were happy that Bobby and Whitney were getting married!" Are you sure you are happy for her or are you really sad and angry?

As God is my Witness

I am now trying to figure out what Robyn's problem is because she just told me that she was happy that Whitney was getting married. Please do not get me wrong, because I sincerely like Robyn a whole lot. It is just that, prior to this wedding night, we were in New York at an event that I believe MCA was giving for Bobby. Most of the Brown and Houston families were all out there together with Bobby and Whitney at this event. I remember BeBe Winan amongst a host of other celebrities who were also there this evening.

I remember personally talking with BeBe Winan that night while everyone was standing around and having a good time speaking to one another. Robyn walked over to me out of nowhere and asked me if I would walk with her down the street to the store. I didn't get it then, but it came to me later, just why she did that by asking me to walk her to that store. When she asked me, I remembered Whitney looking over at us with a surprised look on her face as if to say, why are you asking my sister to walk with you, Robyn? As Robyn and I proceeded to walk away from the event...Robyn began talking to me about Whitney.

She was asking me questions about how I felt about my new sister and so on. Then out of nowhere, she said "well I'm glad she's marrying your brother because "I am tired" of sleeping with her!" As soon as she said it, I knew what she was trying to do, but I kept saying to myself, "I am not feeding into this!" I was so shocked that she would even go there and say that to me. I am a realist and I do not like biting my tongue, I just get straight to it. After giving that thought, I said to myself, "She's acting as if she is so seriously jealous that they are getting married!" More than anything, I believe that she wanted me to take that back to Bobby and/or Whitney, but I didn't. I thought that was very sneaky of her.

As God is my Witness

Now today, she wrote a book about Whitney, and I don't believe she would have done it with Whitney alive. At that time, I said to myself, "I am not going to come between my brother and his wife with any news like that, it's not right." They did not deserve or need to hear that kind of talk. Furthermore, in my mind, I am saying to myself, that is not something that you say to anyone's sister after learning her brother is getting married, how sneaky and ugly that is.

We call it dry snitching where I come from, if it held any truth at all, which I do not know to this very day. I never saw Whitney in a bedroom with anyone other than my brother and so I always left it right there at that. Also, it was not my place to repeat or spread that and so, I didn't. I also had to keep in mind that she could have just been saying that to start something between them because she was not happy that they were getting married. I just kept it to myself all this time, because I am not going to run back too quick with stuff to start confusion with anyone. Besides, it may have been false that Whitney was ever in a bed with her or any other woman. The fact that she said that was a lot though. Of course, my brother will know now because it is here in this book. If he does read this book, I am sure he will not let it bother him knowing Bobby and the man he is. He's got bigger fish to fry today, and this is the last thing on his mind. On the other hand, I wish Robyn the best with her life.

I sincerely believe in my heart that she is a nice person, but she should not have done that to Whitney, because Whitney did not deserve that. It seemed to me like, after Whitney died, any and every person that had something against her came out either telling lies about her or they made up things to make her look bad. Yet, they would not do that if she was alive. And I'm the type of person who believes in being yourself at all times.

As God is my Witness

If you say you are someone's friend, then stand up and be that friend and do for that friend in their death that which you would normally do if that person was alive. In my eyes that is not a good friend to do something like that, I will just keep it real. And I love and respect Robyn, but I must speak truth. I have to look at it and place myself in both people's shoes. I am the type of person that would never do that to anyone because it's not a good thing to do.

ROBYN CRAWFORD

Speaking of Robyn, I wanted to talk with her regarding how she handles my brother's name out in public. Now, I understand she wants this world to believe that she was with Whitney or was working with her for a long time before Bobby came along. But as a woman and one who knows truth and knows how to respect others and place my feet in their shoes. I believe that she is a person who is and has always been one who is just real jealous of Bobby and Whitney's relationship. And I say this with all due respect to Robyn. She seemed to always have a problem with Whitney and Bobby's relationship.

Maybe because she was not wanted around them after they got married. I can understand Whitney and Bobby not wanting her around them anymore. You cannot ask a woman or a man to stand down and allow their EX to come around (if she was Whitney's EX) and remain in the presence of them and then alone with his wife, whether he was there or not. I feel and believe that it is just so disrespectful to even come around and try to place yourself in their space, knowing that they are now married, and knowing what's in your mental. You have to give respect where it is due, regardless of how you feel about a person. Bobby did not want Robyn around his wife and who can blame him?

As God is my Witness

No one can blame him because he is within all of his rights as a man, as his wife's husband and as a human being first. You cannot blame him for being that person who will not allow you to come around his wife, after knowing that you have some type of feelings for his wife, he is a man. Whitney loved him and he loved her and they wanted their space, period. And when you love someone or respect someone, you give them their space out of that love and respect, I think.

Now, I am not saying that what Robyn has said about her, and Whitney are true either, because I do not know, and Whitney never told me anything about her and Robyn. But I do know that Bobby and Whitney were a married couple that loved each other unconditionally and at the same time, they did not need anyone like that around them, because I do believe she had feelings for Whitney. If he or she felt uncomfortable or some type of way, then he had a valid reason to ask her to not come around his wife anymore. He did not have to explain why because he is the man in their home. A lot of women have problems with respecting a real man, I think. Robyn had no right to question my brother's decision because again, he is a man, and he is her husband. Bobby is a man who was protecting his wife and his marriage, if you ask me.

And as much as I like Robyn, I have to let her know that she was wrong and will always be wrong as long as she has those desires in her heart. You cannot ask a man to stand down and allow you to come in his space and flirt or even delve up some kind of feelings for Whitney while in their presence. It is wrong and I agree with Bobby that Robyn should have stayed away from Whitney and him and just respectfully allowed them to enjoy their marriage to each other. God don't even like that when anyone comes between marriages.

As God is my Witness

Life is real and you have to ask yourself, if you would have felt some type of way had the tables been turned and your mate wanted to always welcome their Ex? I seriously dislike seeing people get disrespected all because someone isn't finished in their feelings about a person. It's not right and it is just too bad that they feel that way, but life goes on and their lives had already moved on. You cannot do that and expect a man to say, OK, I'm with it, you can come in our space and on top of that, I trust that I can turn my back on you and allow you to spend time with my wife. No, nobody's going to do that for anyone.

No, life is just not like that, and does not go that way because the flesh is far too weak in this day and time, as it is already written in our holy books. Furthermore, some people are not civilized enough to respect other people's relationships. I really think that Robyn owes my brother Bobby an apology for how she has always acted towards him and treated him.

My brother was not ever wrong to not want Robyn around his wife, I must be honest in saying this. You have to always respect a married couple regardless to what relationship you thought you may have had with her. Even if it was true, it's over at that point and so you have to wake up and move on is all I can honestly say to this.

Regardless to how much you like her and believe how close you or she was with you, it is not right in the eyes of God and for that reason. On top of it all, too many people have expected my brother to react a certain way and stand down and take what they wanted to dish out for him, and he just remain humble while others disrespected him and his wife all the time. Bobby was already catching hell from Mama Cissy and God knows who all the time.

As God is my Witness

And then they always wanted control over Whitney's money and estate, and did not want her to marry any man I believe, or have any children. They treated my brother so unfairly because of their greed and sick hearts. A lot of people have God to answer to when it comes to Bobby and Whitney trust me. A lot of people have kept their noses in their business unjustly.

To think about how they plotted to get rid of her and my niece is something we have to take in and accept so painfully today. No human being should ever suffer what Whitney and her daughter did. And to know it was all because of someone having a love for her money so much is ungodly. It is crazy, insane and so evil to do what has been done to her and them as a family. And people can say what they will, I was there, and I saw them live with one another and seen their love for each other. They had a better relationship than most people I know in this world. They were two human beings that God brought together for good, but far too many people were in the way of their relationship to make sure they had chaos and trouble so that they would get a divorce and be no more.

Whitney is gone now, but I am here to tell all of the people in this world who have something to do with her and her daughter's demise, along with helping to make sure she got that divorced, they have God to deal with. He did not like the way too many people were interfering in their marriage and doing their best to break them up. Wherever these people are in this world trust me, God is dealing with them because it is so wrong to do. These are or were two people who deserved to have their peace and loved each other. On top of it they had so much to live for and deserved to be happy in their lives without all of that.

As God is my Witness

Regardless to what Whitney did, she found true love and wanted to live a normal life that God had given her for once in her life, and everywhere she turned there were demons right there to swallow her up again. I am pissed to know how her life really went after all. No one can imagine how I feel and what I have to deal with on a daily basis after learning what I know today about everything and every person. Getting this book ready and putting it out here for the world to hear this truth has been so hard to do because it's a hell of a story to tell. And then, not everything is in here either, just a few things. I could never do it all in one book.

It is no secret with me today on how and why Whitney's family followed her so much and why everything turned out the way it did. It seemed like everyone was around her to see to it that she fell, and they betrayed her while she was down, and they are so sadly betraying her in her death. There are far too many people doing too many things that they know Whitney would not ever do if she was alive today. It's wrong, the way a lot of people have treated my brother. He did not deserve to be treated the way people have always treated him. We have to place ourselves in other people's shoes even if it's uncomfortable to do. I am a right is right and wrong is wrong person, regardless to who it is or whatever the situation is, right is right and wrong will always be wrong I don't care who's doing it. You have to think, what if it was you going through what he had to endure and take from people? I would bet that so many people would not accept that kind of disrespect they dish out to others.

Again, I think Robyn owes my brother an apology, because Bobby owed Robyn absolutely nothing at the end of the day. He was trying to live his life with his wife, and no one had any business to come between them.

As God is my Witness

People were upset with him because he wasn't allowing anyone coming into their life to play games. Who knows, it could have very well been a case where Robyn felt she had a chance or there was a possibility where she may have felt that she was able to sway Whitney back over to her side, who knows? One thing for sure, no man is going to take that chance and allow that for him and his wife, regardless to how anyone feels. It is not your place to disrupt their home whether they were happy or not. Their business was no one else's business but there's alone. Their marriage was not so terrible that they needed anyone to try to step in and do anything.

I believe had they been left alone they could have lived out their life as they were striving to do. My belief is that all of everyone who were in or around Whitney's circle, had one thing or another to do with her life being unhappy and then her life as it ended in death. Now I know that this is why they tried to point the finger at the Brown's so much! They were worried about the Houston's being exposed! WOW! Whitney's death was horrific and too horrific for her and her daughter to have had to bear. Whitney just could not catch a break from all these people who surrounded her and swore they loved her. Meanwhile, they were only there to get what they had wanted all along.

It was all a game to too many people that were around her. And I am not saying that Robyn had anything at all to do with her demise, but my thing is, why write a book and say things you already know that Whitney would not agree with, had she been alive. I do not believe Robyn would have written that book nor done the interviews that she did had Whitney been alive. I just like and believe in treating people the same way in their death as I would when they are alive and right here with me.

As God is my Witness

I love a loyal person and the whole idea of being loyal. Everyone should ask the question, if it were you, and someone did you that way, how would you feel? Yes, I know many will say, there is no feeling because Whiney is gone and she doesn't know. But it is the principle for me at the end of the day. It is the loyalty for me that I am concerned with. You can spend a lifetime doing well by a person and treating them right and as family. You may even give them a fortune while you're alive thinking they are your loyal friend. And then when you leave here and are gone, that person you placed all your trust in has betrayed you and done the one thing you didn't like or did a thing they would never do in your presence. What are your thoughts right now if it were you? See, this is what a lot of people "don't" do. They won't place themselves in someone else's shoes.

When will we all grow up and become the civilized adults and human beings that we are supposed to be? Why can't we be seriously loyal to each other and just simply do whatever is right? It feels good to do righteous things, it really does. I do not like this world because it has too many materialistic people in it that focuses on all the wrong things in this life. Another thing that bothers my soul. I watch how people will scream and shout about a TV ball game being on, but will not do everything in their power to do that for God, if someone asked them to just sit to hear God's word. I watch how people will look to others for answers that only God can give them, instead of placing their "faith" in the God that they supposedly believe in. Life can really be simpler than what we think it is, we just make it complicated by the decisions we make I think. There are people who just will not place their faith in God. We have to start being whom God desires for us to be because this old and wicked world is going out and it is going to take down a lot of people with it if we are not mindful of what we are supposed to be doing here.

As God is my Witness

So many people were trying to rule Whitney's life and she was just struggling hard trying to be a woman of her own. What people didn't understand was, Whitney wanted, more than anything in her life, to just live her life with Bobby.

It pains me to know that, she couldn't even get that, even after living her life for others, nor was she even granted that in her death, which I think was really wicked of a lot of people who claimed to love her. When you really love someone, you will be happy to respect who they love and then respect them all the time, not just sometimes. And real talk, it's one of the reasons why I fight so hard for Whitney. It is because I know and I am sure that she deserved so much more because of what I seen her give to others and what she gave to this entire world while she lived. That's why I am careful today how I treat people. While alive, I want people to treat me the same when I go. It matters because people are watching even when you think no one sees you.

Overall, I like Robyn Crawford and I respect her as well. I just don't like the way she has always treated my brother. I am sure it would have hurt Whitney to know how everyone treated her husband when she left here. And yes, I say husband because as God is my witness, Whitney literally begged Bobby to please remarry her again. She was very sorry for divorcing him and she told him it'll never happen again. Bobby said no so many times before he finally said, yes!

CHAPTER 6 BOBBY'S
"HUMPIN AROUND WORLD TOUR!"

We were all happy getting ready to prepare for this new wedding again and they took her out of here. The devils are always lurking and people have to stay on their toes out here. I wish I could have been with Whitney because I believe she would still be alive today had I been with her. Nobody has a clue as to how God made these two people for each other. They really belonged together and could have been so happy had people left them alone.

This is the time in my life where Whitney and I got extremely close. We are now rehearsing for "The Humpin Around World Tour!" I was so happy that I passed the audition to go on tour with my brother. I felt like I could finally fulfill my dreams! No one knew how much this all meant to me for real. Mommy knew it, and it was why she told me to go down to that rehearsal hall and tell Danny Lamelle (Bobby's musical director), that she said, for him to allow me in there, so that I could rehearse for Bobby's tour.

I said, "No Mommy, Bobby may not let me, I may not be good enough to sing on his tour." She said, "Oh no, Lele, your voice is beautiful baby, and Bobby knows it and you will pass the audition, II already spoke to Bobby." She said, "I know how much it means to you baby, so, called your brother, you're going on that tour, just go on down there!" I was a bit nervous but overall, I had all the balls in the world to do it, and so I did, and the rest is history.

As God is my Witness

It was a lot more to it but now is not the time to tell it all, but I was there, and I did a world tour singing as my brother's back-up singer and did a world tour and we start overseas. The first date was Australia, and we were off in the air! And yes indeed, I did have to audition to possibly become my brother's backup singer. Upon walking into that rehearsal hall, I could tell it made a few people extremely uncomfortable that I was there.

Certain people were acting as if I was not worthy of singing for my brother. If the world could have been the fly on the wall to see the faces cutting me with their eyes when I walked into that rehearsal hall. Wow! I am saying to myself, they just do not understand just how important this is for me to be on this tour with my brother at this specific time in my life. I am not "just" Bobby Brown's sister, I can sing, and I have always sung well, little did they know. I also have talents and dreams just like anyone else who does. None of them had any idea that I used to sing as well. I was a lead singer who later started a group and was "the first" person of my siblings to sing and dance.

I was known for my singing and dancing and to be honest, I was doing it before Bobby was. I am older than Bobby so of course I started out before him, little did they know. Even he knows that it was always a real dream of mine that finally came true for me. At this time, Mommy was ready to fight anyone in our way because she knew how much this meant to me to finally be in this space. Mommy used to sing herself with her brother, our uncle Bobby whom my brother Bobby is named after. Mommy and her brother Bobby were a singing group way back in the day. With me looking so much like my mother out of all her children, I believe that my brother Bobby and I reminded my mother of her and her brother Bobby.

As God is my Witness

It may have been the real reason she sent me into that rehearsal hall like that. In any event, God knows I was ready to finally do what meant so much to me, but not for the bad energy that came with it at this time. Despite it all, I was one humble dove at this time. I was being so nice to everyone, smiling and giving the best energy I possibly could. I had never felt so grateful to God in my life that my brother allowed me to finally fulfill my dreams and go on the road with him. I was so determined to be the best backup singer that I could possibly be for Bobby. I made sure that I made it to all my rehearsals, I was always kind to everyone who was there. I did my very best to respect every single person in his entourage to the utmost. I made sure that there was nothing that anyone could say bad about me. I followed all the rules without any problems, and so on.

I wanted to be extra nice to people because I did not want anyone to think that just because I was Bobby's sister, that I was to get special privileges or anything of that nature. I never entertained that idea a at any time whatsoever. Yet, I could feel that it was on several people's mind based upon their actions towards me. I never understood how people could feel so intimidated so easily. I would have never imagined the things that I went through as my brother's backup singer. At this time, it was very important for me to do what I always wanted to do, which was sing and just stay focused on that. I kept telling myself to just stay focused because I knew that God had me there fulfilling my dream at the end of the day.

I took a lot and I suffered much, and I also kept that smile on my face, treating everyone as I wished to be treated at all times. I did not mind the suffering, but what bothered me more than anything at this time was that I had to suffer the insecurities of others who became intimidated by me being there, and because of their insecurities.

As God is my Witness

There was absolutely nothing that I did wrong to anyone. Some people kept saying that there were certain people on this tour jealous of me because I was Bobby's sister. I kept saying to myself, "I am on this tour to sing as his backup singer because I can sing, period." I believed that certain people did not expect me to be as good as I was on this tour. I did not say this, but others were saying this to me, and I must admit, I did feel the vibes all the time coming from certain people.

As time went on, word was getting around quickly because of the actions of others and how they were treating me, which everyone started to witness for themselves. I did not know how to take it at first, because I do not like jealousy and envy, especially when it is directed at me. I am a very nice and respectable person to anyone I cross paths with. For a person to continuously deal with so much, on so many different occasions, one eventually gets tired. We should know and understand that God blesses us all in so many ways, and we are to appreciate that and be grateful for whatever we have, and when He allows us to meet others who have that same beauty, and talent, along with a good spirit we are supposed to appreciate that as well, because it is meant to compliment you when you witness it.

I am the kind of person who, when I see a pretty girl walk in the room as if she owns it, it makes me feel good! It should tell every other girl or woman in the room who she is! I do not judge her, and I think positively and allow her that space. There is no need to be jealous of anyone because we think someone else may look better or have more than us. See, that's what makes other girls jealous, when they see a girl who looks better than them, they become jealous. I also think it's sad when we can't just love each other and get along for the sole sake of God, whom we will all swear we love and believe in.

As God is my Witness

The words of Jesus are, "Love Ye One Another As I Have Loved You!" We all know this verse very well, yet it is so hard for people to do. Many people will say that they believe in God and believe in Jesus, but we will not strive just a little bit for them or in their name. We are all beautiful, smart, intelligent, and strong people that reflect and complement one another, and we have to look at it just like that. We have so much to learn when it comes to loving ourselves and our very own people; and just simply respecting one another. Well, Whitney is now out on the road with us. She saw for herself without me saying a word to anyone how certain people were treating me. Whitney was prepared and watching just like others who reported it. This was a time when things were getting really bad with the way I was being treated. And make no mistake about it, I'm not a punk in any way whatsoever, and anyone who knows me, they know that about me.

I just do not like pettiness and so I ignored a lot of stuff when I could have very easily done differently. Above all, I was trying to keep the peace for the sake of my brother because this was his business and his livelihood, and I was trying to protect him at the end of the day. Also, at this point in my life, I am just trying to work without any smoke coming behind me for once. I am busy keeping my focus on doing my job well. Instead of spending time with bad-energy people, I just tried hard to stay out of their way, remaining positive, and enjoying the opportunity that I was given. I was sincerely grateful to God that my brother allowed me to come out with him and sing. Even unto this day I still say how grateful I was for my brother allowing me the opportunity. I dislike having this conversation and giving this energy at this very moment by talking about it, but I have to in order to tell this story.

As God is my Witness

I want others to know just how Whitney and I began to get close to each other. This day, Whitney saw how certain folks were dealing with me and how peaceful I was in dealing with them in return. She did not like it and wanted to talk with me regarding it. She said, this kind of stuff was not anything for anybody to continue to take lightly and continue overlooking. She snapped and went off like she was ready to literally fight for me after she saw how they kept treating me. I had never seen Whitney get so upset! Overall, I did well on Bobby's tour. At the end of his tour, Bobby's musical director, Danny Lemelle brought me this huge hallmark card and had everyone sign it for me. In the card, he wrote that I was the most advanced person on that whole Tour and told me how proud he was of me. I thanked God for such a successful tour. I was really happy that I contributed to making my brother's tour a success.

During this tour, Whitney and I sat down to talk because she felt like I reminded her of her and Aretha, the way I was being so kind after people were treating me so ugly she said. She told me the story of her and Aretha Franklin and what she suffered as a young woman just from being around her. She began telling me that I had to stop making it a point to prove to people that I was who I was, if you understand me. I was always basically going out of my way to be nice to sum it up. She said, "Leolah, no matter what you do, they are not going to care!" She told me that she went through something like that with Aretha Franklin, where she continued to be nice to Aretha but no matter what she did, Aretha had always treated her as if she did not like her, while Whitney was always being respectful, smiling, and treating Aretha kindly she said. Whitney said, every single time that Mama Cissy would turn her back or was not around her, Aretha treated her terribly.

CHAPTER 7
<u>WHITNEY & ARETHA</u>

Whitney said, she could not think of any other reason why Aretha was treating her the way she was and could not understand where all the bad treatment was coming from, until she realized in her mind that she was just jealous of her. Those were Whitney's exact words to me, as God is my witness. Now, I have always loved Aretha Franklin's music and of course, her as my sister without knowing anything else about her. I felt so bad for Whitney, and of course I was shocked listening to this as she was telling me. I always said that she and Whitney were my top two favorite female singing artist. I am only mentioning this because I am very seriously trying to get us to think about how we treat each other and do my part in trying to help make a difference in this world of ours. It is no secret that a lot of people go through this and have to suffer this kind of thing all the time.

I would feel so much better if we would treat each other better and at least try to be considerate of other people's feelings and try placing ourselves in their shoes whenever we are dealing with each other. I can't stand it when we hate on each other for reasons that are not meaningful. After all we've been through, we should want to do better by treating our own people properly. We do that by first, facing the truth, and peacefully talking about it, and then find solutions to be more positive altogether. We need to make sure that this does not keep happening over and over again with us because people are hurt by it, and this had weighed heavily on Whitney's heart, little did anyone know.

As God is my Witness

I knew the kind of person Whitney was which a lot of people did not get to understand about her, and so, I could relate to what she had suffered and how she felt. Furthermore, I also experienced things like this on so many different occasions in my life. And I am not one of those who like sweeping things under a rug just because we can. We must face facts even if it hurts regardless of how painful it is. I would like for us as a people to have more love for ourselves and one another.

I would love to see us in unity, respecting one another and pouring all the love that God has equipped us with, into ourselves, and our brothers and sisters. I know that it is hard because of what we have all been through with one another, trust me I know, and I understand much. But this thing is going on all over this world and has gone on for so long without anyone of us ever properly checking ourselves on this issue and it's very important whether we will believe it or not. It has become a way of life for so many people who call themselves God fearing people. Especially those of us who have been placed in positions where we think we are better than others. Regardless to how much money we may ever have or how much one believes they are more important than the next man or woman.

In God's eyes we are all deserving of respect whether rich or poor. None of us are perfect and we will never be in such a world. We will have our days of falling short of God's glory, as they say. But when we do, we must get up and continue that path we set out to do by calling ourselves making a difference in this world. What I am trying to say is, many people in this world, whether rich, poor or in between. We sometimes stand to be accused of unnecessarily treating our sister or brother so wrong upon meeting them and not knowing much about them.

As God is my Witness

In other words, we will be so very petty with one another by envy, jealousy for some of the most petty, ridiculous and unexplained reasons, and we think it is OK to be this way because we are not checked on it often enough, I think. We can be so cruel to one another and then turn right around and be so sweet to everyone else, when we should care and respect every man and woman, we ever cross paths with regardless to who they are, what color they are or what decisions they have made in life, everyone is due their respect.

We know how painful it is to be treated a certain way for nothing we've done to deserve it. I have even had times where I have had to check myself on things that I was not doing so right when it comes to others as well, and today I am mindful, and I am a better person. I am mindful because I know and understand how important it is to treat your brothers and sisters kindly and anyone else for that matter. Also, when and where I see a need for myself and us to change as a people, I feel obligated to speak on it. I am always open minded to see myself first and how I treat others, and then I am quick to apologize if I am ever checked and found wrong or feel myself that I have wronged someone. I am aware of who's really in charge and who holds the keys to my salvation and soul. There are so many people out here today who have gone through or are going through a lot of things today, and maybe even things of this nature. This is one of those things where I strongly believe that it needs to be recognized and dealt with head on but in a peaceful way.

We have got to bring ourselves up to higher level and become spiritually involved in being better if we are going to ever make it as a people and leave the next generation of people coming behind us more civilized than ourselves. Otherwise, I feel like our lives have been lived in vain.

As God is my Witness

If we cannot or will not do it for ourselves, then why won't we just try for the sake of God, since He has asked us to be this way? Overall and the bottom line here is that we have got to learn to respect and love our own people, period. We have a bad habit of loving everybody else in this world but ourselves, and we don't have to hate anyone else outside of our race, to just simply love ourselves. Loving ourselves, and our people is a very important thing with God, and it has nothing to do with any other race of people but our own. We already treat others right so there's no question there. It is an inevitable thing that we must do with each other before we depart this world, and we had better do it cheerfully.

Another very important thing that we must remember, and understand is, when God blesses us, it is also a test to see what we will do with that blessing. We even have too much jealousy with our sisters and brothers who have come right out the same womb as us. It is going on all over the world today and it needs to stop. I would sincerely love to see us all change from such a condition. As black people in this country, we all have been through so much just because of the color of our skin. And we know what that feels like to be hated for no apparent reason. Out of all the people in this world, we have suffered more than any other persons on this planet. Therefore, we should be more understanding of one another, and consider the time, where we have been, and where we are going from here.

We should have more love and respect for one another, like any other race of people, and do something about these ill feelings when they come up in us. Some of us see it as a small and petty issue, but I beg to differ. We need to ask ourselves; do we want this for our children that's coming behind us?

As God is my Witness

The next generation of people need us to be so much better than us and the only way that will happen is if we lead by example now. We also need serious solutions on how we will get over all of this. Black people have a lot to learn period about healing and loving one another. Nobody is going to do it for us, and we have to do it ourselves, and it has to start with us like yesterday. We know this deep inside, but it seems as if we do not ever want to talk about it or begin the journey. I got a feeling that if we don't start now, God is going to help us in a way where we will wish we had of started sooner. I am a person that does not want us to just talk about it and do nothing. It is like going to Church on Sunday shouting and clapping with joy, and then we leave the Church and go right back out into the world doing the same things that we know are wrong. We cannot afford to keep doing this and then laying down forgetting. This is an appointment that we do not want to miss either.

I know that Whitney loved many people dearly in her heart, and she had an enormous amount of respect for Aretha Franklin. From a young age, she said that she loved and adored her. She had to grow up not understanding just why she was being treated in a certain way, and it bothered her more than anyone knows. She went through some things psychologically that stayed with her for very a long time. It really messed her up because of how she looked up to Aretha.

I understand what that must have been like for Whitney now that I was able to make sense of most of her life. Whitney has been through so much in her life! believe it is the main reason why she has sung so well. Her life was already hard from a little girl growing up in the home with Mama Cissy. Whitney had done a lot of praying in her lifetime as a young girl.

As God is my Witness

She prayed a lot because she suffered a lot, and that is where I believe her voice came from at the end of the day. Yes, she practiced a lot, because Mama Cissy placed her in the Church to sing at a very young age. It went a lot deeper than what others may have imagined it. Whitney had a connection with God that I believe they knew nothing of as we talked, I could say that I understood because I used to talk with God in private when I was young as well. I had my own secret relationship with Him at a very early age. It broke my heart to hear things coming out of her mouth all the time. It was always easy for me and Whitney to communicate with each other and talk. Yet, I did not know the depths or fully understand everything as it really was and the pain she was in. We sat up many nights and talked about a lot of things. It seemed like, everything I told her I went through, she said she went through the very same things too or similar.

She and I share nearly the same birthday as well. We are born in the same month and just a few days a part. She would talk to me about a lot of different things that happened in her life. I would be looking at her almost in tears as she was trying to get it all out. Whitney was brokenhearted for a very long time before she met Bobby, and that is "why" she was on drugs for so long way before Bobby came into her picture. By the way. I am sure we all know by now that my brother did not introduce her to drugs. Whitney's brother Michael opened up on Oprah and told the world that he was responsible for introducing Whitney to drugs, not Bobby Brown. That was thrown out the window when her brother Michael sat on Oprah and told the story of him being responsible for that. Bobby was never given an apology either.

As God is my Witness

Many people in this world have always had it wrong when it came to Whitney Houston and Bobby Brown's life. I hate that I must be the one to talk about this, but I am doing it because somebody has to do it. And let me be clear here, "there is no love lost for Aretha Franklin." I believe that she was struggling herself with things she too was dealing with. Therefore, I understand and respect her as a human being and as my sister. I am just not afraid to talk about things that many people are afraid to mention and discuss. We are all human and we should never feel like someone is too good or too big to respectfully talk about.

Again, we all go through things in this life. All I am saying at the end of the day is that we must do better with treating each other better and kindlier. We must have patience with one another, and more importantly, be willing to make a difference in our lives while we live. I have always thought to myself that maybe Aretha just had some insecurities herself and/or just issues that she was dealing with that she never got the chance to talk about with anyone. Perhaps she needed help and was also going through something that she could not deal with on her own as well.

Trauma and pain are a thing that, whether physical, mental, or emotional, it has and will affect us to the point of hurting others without us even knowing it at times. Aretha was well known for having such a great and beautiful voice, but she was also human just like anyone else. We do not know why everyone called her Whitney's godmother. I read somewhere where it was said that Aretha never saw Whitney as her goddaughter. Whether it was true or not I have no idea. For Whitney to hold all of that in for so long, and not say anything to anyone for so many years is another thing. I would have never guessed that that was the real deal and a situation at hand with them.

As God is my Witness

Some may ask, why did she not talk to her mother about that? I am not sure if she ever has, but if not, it could be that she did not feel comfortable? If you ask me, I believe that Whitney did not say anything to Mama Cissy simply because she felt that not only coming from Aretha, but she also felt it coming from those who were close to her and supposedly family as well. Now, both women (Whitney and Aretha) are gone today, and I am left with trying to clean this all up for us so that it does not continue to happen with us as a people anymore.

I was so sad to learn that Aretha was not going to make it to Whitney's funeral. Many people did not know that Aretha didn't show up for Whitney's funeral. Her name was called, of course. She was on the obituary to come up and sing for "her godchild's" funeral but was a no show. As I sat there looking at her name on the obituary, I was saying in my mind, "Aretha please do not do this to Whitney, they have already done so much to her in her death, please be here for Whitney!" But she never graced that stage with her beautiful voice to sing a song for Whitney that day, and I was so shocked. I am not sure if Mama Cissy knew she was not coming, but if she did know, she surely made me believe that she didn't. This is what made me cry even more at Whitney's funeral, little did people know. I was crying for Whitney because I felt like everyone was letting her down that should have been there for her. I sat there and witnessed a lot that day. I could not hold my tears back, but God was with me. There was a man sitting right next to me who was comforting me and hugging me trying to get me to stop crying for my sister. I could not hold back the tears no matter how much I tried to.

As God is my Witness

My sister suffered a whole lot of things that this world just does not know about, and that is what was on my mind. This world does not know the magnitude nor the depths of her troubled life as a singer and an Icon. I do not know anyone in the music industry who has lived and endured what Whitney has. But I am sure there are people out there with a similar story, I just don't know them. My brother Bobby has a sad story himself, and he has been through a lot too. Yes, many of us have gone through things and we all have a story. The saddest of all is that there will be many people reading this book, yet there will not be that many or enough that will read it and really understand it for what it really and truly is. As light as I have trodden in explaining her story, I am probably the only one that has or will ever have the balls to just simply do it. Yet, I could never tell the whole story because I really just do not know it all, and I thank God almighty and I am happy that I can't. It has been too painful enough to know what I do know. You have no idea how this has taken a toll on my heart and my life, to get through this book and explain this to you. Whitney's life was so hard and painful to have lived. Now that I look back on the things she used to do and how she did it and how she moved and just her whole life that played out for me to witness and see for myself, it is amazingly hard for me.

Then, after her death, I had to sit down and very seriously think about the things I had witnessed, and it reminded me that our meeting was divinely orchestrated by God Himself. It hit me and I had finally understood just why Whitney kept looking at me and saying, "You are my angel!" She knew something about me that I didn't even know myself I didn't even understand what was really going on at that time. For her, to be whom she was, and as strong as she was, it taught me a lot about strength.

As God is my Witness

And just to think, that she woke up every day of her life, and carried on so strong, it told me a lot about her strength as a woman. You can't imagine what was thrown at her to eat and swallow on a daily basis. My niece was born into a darkness that she was not given a chance to prepare for and that's another thing that upsets me. It was so unfair for her, and she was so innocent and had a beautiful heart and did not deserve all that evil that happened to her. I hope that the people who have done this are somewhere "very sincerely" asking God for His forgiveness. I really hope that they have all very seriously repented because I do not believe that they are acquainted with the God that I know.

I'm not sure that they even know what they did and who they did it to. They have to let go of that ghosts and strive harder to make their way to God. It needs to be done NOW, because there is not much time left, God is here to give tickets out baby. There are far too many of us walking around today worshipping the wrong things, and then turning right around doing things to others that they know are wrong. Time is at hand now and God has made Himself known to us all so there is no excuses anymore. It is extremely late and detrimentally important to all of our lives that we all strive harder to get on that rightful path and do unto others as you wish is done to you, regardless to who you are, where you come from, how much money you have or what you believe. Nothing can save you from the hand of God if He has found you wrong out here. He has come to remove all evil from this earth and universe, and regardless to who you are or what you say you believe in, there is nothing under this Sun that has the power to stop God.

CHAPTER 8
THE TRUTH ABOUT
<u>WHITNEY & EDDIE MURPHY</u>

He will complete His mission, period. As I mentioned before, Whitney and I sat up a lot of late nights and just talked. We would talk about a lot of things. On this night, we were talking about boyfriends, and she told me that she did in fact "talk to Jermaine Jackson." She said that she had never slept with Jermaine Jackson, and all they did was talk. All of the rumors can stop now. I did not understand the narrative when it was being played out in a movie, but Whitney told me this straight from her own mouth and I believed her. This is exactly why I can say that the movie they produced and directed, talking about Whitney and Jermaine sleeping together, is not at all the absolute truth of what Whitney told me. I believed Whitney when she said she never slept with Jermaine Jackson, so it should not be repeated by anyone at any time, especially not in a movie.

When it comes to Eddie Murphy, with all due respect to Eddie, I always knew this whole story. I am choosing not to speak on all of it simply because it is not necessary as far as I am concerned. A lot of what she said is not anything nice to hear. This whole world by now has heard the Whitney Houston and Eddie Murphy story, I am sure. However, what they have not heard is the truth as to the details of what really happened, and what really went on with the two of them. The relationship was a short one, from what Whitney told me. Furthermore, she said that she was never happy dating him from the beginning. She never trusted him and did not feel right being with him altogether.

As God is my Witness

If you hear anything other than what I am saying, you can count it as another lie, which they are used to telling anyway. But the story went like this when I asked her. Whitney specifically said she was lying in bed with him one day when her house phone rang. My guess was that Eddie gave her home phone number out and back then there were no cell phones yet, I believe. According to Whitney, he proceeded to walk out of the room, while thinking that she was asleep. He walked out to answer it away from her. Now, we all know that if a person must go away from you when they are talking on the phone, nine times out of ten, it usually means it is something that they do not want you to hear them say. She became curious when he walked out so she leaned over and picked up the other end of that line and it was a man on the other end of that phone.

The man on the other end of the phone said, "Baby I miss you, are you still there with her, you got to come home now!" Whitney said that Eddie was asking for more time ... and blah, blah, blah. The man on the other end said some other things that Whitney did not like. Eddie was still trying to buy time, and the other man kept yelling at Eddie telling him to just get out of there and come on home now! Whitney said she became furious at his voice on that other end, and she heard everything they were saying. Of course, no woman is going to be pleased after hearing what she heard.

When Eddie came back into her room, she looked at him and said, "Pack your dam bags and get the hell out of my house now Eddie!" They of course argued a bit, but on that day, Whitney said, it was over from that point. She said she never looked back at Eddie after that. She made it clear that he was history, gone and gladly forgotten about. Whitney said it was not a hard thing for her to do because there was no love there with her and Eddie.

As God is my Witness

She said that she was never in love with him and telling him to leave was not hard when she left him. When Robin Crawford mentioned in an interview that Whitney phoned Eddie or was going to call Eddie during the time when her and Bobby were getting married or was already married, I will not ever believe it in this lifetime. The Whitney I know would not ever contact Eddie for absolutely anything that had to do with her and the man she loved more than anything in this world. I honestly believe that Robyn just said that to make my brother upset and there was not any truth to that whatsoever.

When she said that I said, wow, she must really hate my brother because I know that Whitney would never call Eddie for nothing! I will never believe that Whitney considered calling Eddie for anything. Sorry, wrong guy ...wrong girl. I am sure even that my brother Bobby knows his wife and had to laugh if he heard her say that. We know Whitney a whole lot more than Robyn, I think. Furthermore, Whitney Houston was not the old Nippy anymore. She had changed so much and was a better woman altogether. knows how Whitney felt about Eddie. Their relationship was a thing of the past and one of those things where she did not ever desire to remember ever happening. She was just shocked at what she found out about him and how she found out.

Whitney was a wise woman who was not about any foolishness or games when it came to her personal life. You may think you were fooling her, but she was very smart and always observing. Of course, she was because she had been through a lot in her life already. She was extremely happy that God saved her from that relationship with Eddie she said.

As God is my Witness

Overall, she was just happy that she was now married to my brother, Bobby. Furthermore, she said that she had never had a man like Bobby, nor had she ever loved a man like she loved Bobby. Their life pretty much went for what it said if you knew them and were ever around them. Bobby and Whitney were two people who were very seriously in love with each other and more than anything they were made for each other; little did a lot of people know or understand. It did not matter what people thought of them, especially those who did not know them. They just wanted others on the outside who did not like the idea of them being together, to stay far away from them so that they could live their lives the way they wanted to.

They could have gone further in their marriage and stayed together until death departed them at an old age, had people left them alone. Whitney did not care for any other man except Bobby Brown, hands down. She also told me this again when I asked her about Ray J. Because, for a moment I thought she was messing with him, so, of course, I asked her. I knew deep down inside that even Ray J was not in any way whatsoever her type of man. In fact, a lot of people knew this without even going there. She had been in the media seen with him, so I had to ask her about Ray J. She said to me, "Aww hell Naw!" Ray J!? Aww Hell No Dog! He ain't got nothing that interest or excite me, she said! I believed my sister, because at least I felt I knew when she was telling the truth.

She said that she never in her life saw Ray J as an attractive boy, and that he was nothing more than a runner boy! I said, "With all due respect Nip, I am with you on that one, hell to the Naw!" And the moment "hell to the Naw" was coming out of my mouth, she said it again at the same time I was saying it. We both started laughing out loud together!

As God is my Witness

With all due respect, in all honesty, to even think about her and Ray J, is really nothing more than an insult and a joke. Just because people are seen together does not mean anything is going on. Whitney had no hard feelings, but he just was not her type at all. Ray J ended up around Whitney for whatever purposes he was serving at the time, but I do not believe anything intimate was going on with the two of them, at all. Ray J was a young man that would be the very last man on this planet that Whitney Houston would have ever considered a relationship with. Trust me, I know my sister and he was not in any way her type. Besides, the look on her face that she gave me when I asked her about him was very convincing to me. Therefore, I had no reason whatsoever to ever think otherwise. Let me tell you about my sister Whitney, and this is for those of you who do not know her. She did not care what the world thought when it came to whatever she wanted or desired in her heart. Whatever the purpose was for Ray J being around her, so it was, but I do not believe the two of them were intimate in any way whatsoever.

All these rumors going around out here about Ray J and Whitney are false and I have never had a reason to doubt Whitney's words. The rumors are nothing more than the ideas of those who do not know my sister well. I could not ever imagine her with Ray J, and so I will not ever give it any more energy than it deserves. Let's go on.... Whitney offered me a job while I was living with her and Bobby. She asked me out of the blue one day if I would work for her. At first, I said "no way!" because I wanted her to know that "you don't have to pay me nothing Nip!" She was so sweet she was trying to pay

CHAPTER 9
WHITNEY'S DEVASTATING
BANK TRIP

me far more than I had ever expected. I said, No Whitney, you do not have to do that keep your money sis! In all honesty, I said this to her because I knew Mama Cissy, Donna, and whoever was over her money, and I felt like they were going to have her upset and arguing with them about her own money. And just as sure as I thought, the moment she contacted them about me being her new assistant, they gave her smoke! As she was on her phone arguing with someone, I was sitting there shaking my head with disgust.

She hung up that phone and said, "no I am going to make sure that you are OK, and that you are taken care of and paid Leolah!" I was already there taking good care of her and Krissy. She just wanted to put me on the payroll, because I was spending all my time with them and was working less time on my projects. She had such a beautiful heart and wanted the best for everybody she loved. I did not even care if the checks came in, but they surprisingly did every week without missing a beat. I was happy that she asked me to move in with them and then to offer me a job was just the ultimate high for me at that time. I had a job that I loved so very much plus I was getting paid, so I could not be any happier! She was so happy that I said yes! I do not know who was on the other end of that prior call, but if I had to guess, I would say it was her accountant or attorneys as well as her mother or Donna if anyone else.

As God is my Witness

I am not certain, but whoever it was, they put her on hold, added someone else to their call, and gave her hell. I can still see Whitney's facial expression right now as she spoke to them. They were not pleased with her hiring me and wanting to pay me what she wanted to pay me. Whitney went on yelling and arguing with them. I am saying to myself, who argues with someone about their own money, and how and why are they even challenging her or able to have a word to say about who she wants to hire for herself? I knew it was about me being Bobby's sister, but I didn't say anything because I already knew how they act when it comes to a Brown.

Whitney was a very smart businesswoman who managed herself all by herself for many years. She did not need anyone to tell her what to do with her business of being an entertainer, she was well-versed and had many years of experience. That was one of the things I noticed about her. It was the one thing Mama Cissy could not do with Whitney. She allowed her father to manage her at one time, but that was as far as anyone was ever going to get with her. Whitney made sure nobody else would ever manage her, and Pat Houston surely would be the very last person if Whitney would ever allow anyone to manage her and Pat knows this. Besides, Whitney always knew all the ins and outs of the business so there was no need for her to ever entertain the idea of a manager coming on board for her.

She taught me a lot about the business that I didn't even know, so she was very much capable of managing herself and she did for many years except when her father managed her. Pat Houston just wish she could have managed Whitney, but she knows that would never happen under Whitney's watch and it never did. Whitney went through some things with her father, yes, but I do not believe that whatever happened was his fault.

As God is my Witness

I think Whitney eventually found that out late though. I felt bad that they even went through what they went through because she didn't even go to Poppa Johns funeral. She stayed in the house that day, I remember clearly. I kept asking her was she going to just get up and go but she said no! She did not want to go.

Some people you must allow them to mourn the way they see fit for themselves without judging them, and that is exactly what I did for her. I was just there as a support system for her when Poppa John passed. I knew she loved her father, and she had nothing to prove to anyone. Whitney and I would go out sometimes shopping or just do spa stuff on this day at this bank, Whitney and I ended up there because Whitney wanted us to have a girl's day out this day and go and get pedicures and massages for both of us. I offered to pay but she insisted that she pay it. We got to the bank, and because there are no regular parking spots available, she parked in the handicapped spot. I stayed in her car to watch for the authorities in case they said something about us parking where we were without a handicap sticker. I could see Whitney through the glass window as if she were yelling at the banker!

I got out of the car and walked inside only to find Whitney almost in tears! She was screaming to the top of her lungs at the same time! She said, "You mean to tell me I have nothing in my bank account?" The banker kept apologizing to her, but Whitney was still screaming, but how? Me and everyone else is looking at her in shock because everyone knew who Whitney Houston was. I was immediately embarrassed for her because I knew how that felt and how hard it must have been for Whitney Houston to walk into a bank, and then be told that she had no money in her account.

As God is my Witness

Second, the people looking at this and witnessing this at this moment in time are all in shock as well. They know what is going on and of course, it does not sound right even to their ears. Meanwhile, I am ready to go to war for Whitney, and now I am upset with how they did her with her own money. What do you mean you don't have any money in your account, I'm asking her?

My spirit was so vexed at this point because it just did not make any sense! I turned to Whitney and asked her why, and who would do that to you Whitney? She then said, quote: "It's Donna and my mother that did this!" I had never seen Whitney's heart so broken! She was devastated to the point of looking as if she was ready to die. She looked so hurt in the face and so embarrassed that everyone was looking at her and she was going through this in that bank. We finally left to go, and as were driving down the street she was on the phone with someone in her so-called family. I assumed it to be either Donna or her mother, Mama Cissy. One thing for sure, she was extremely angry that day and it messed our whole day up!

I got so tired of seeing her suffer about her own money. Bobby took good care of her and Krissy and did not care about Whitney's money. I want to say that she eventually got her money, but it was just always things she had to go through to get it, and "THAT" I just could not understand. Bobby was not there with us at this time, I think he may have been filming "Being Bobby Brown" on that day, I believe it was around that time. Speaking of that; there are some people who think that Whitney was made to look bad while filming that show with my brother. Let me tell you that that reality show was for my brother Bobby, period. When they made that deal it was told to Whitney that the show was about Bobby and was for him. Bobby did not want her in that show at all.

As God is my Witness

I was a witness that Whitney placed herself in it and came on the set without them knowing when they began filming. She did not like to be away from Bobby at any time. Therefore, no, it was not Bobby's fault that she looked or appeared bad to anyone doing that show. If anyone had any thoughts coming from their mind, then those thoughts belonged to them alone.

Whitney was always known for handling her own business so this is why I could not understand why it was so hard for her to get her hands on her own money. However, after she left this world it all came to a head for me. I kept saying to myself, Mama Cissy must have signed Whitney's contracts a long time ago to have power over Whitney's stuff all of her life. I could not understand why they had the control over her money as they did. And then, to think about how they always said in the media, how we the Brown's, were using Whitney for her money, was such a crazy, ugly and insane statement to make about us because we knew the real deal.

We have always been sure who it was stealing Whitney's money and doing all kinds of things to make sure she did not stay here for that long. In other words, I believe Whitney's demise had been long planned out a long time ago and there were people who just made sure she did not live that long. But I also want to tell them that they too have to fall into that same ditch they plotted out for her because they did it in a day and time where God has come for His children. They did it in a time where they should have been focused on repenting to a God who has so much more power than they could ever imagine. See, the thing that many people make the mistake at is this.

As God is my Witness

They really don't believe in God because they cannot physically "see" Him according to their mentality. A lot of read the Bible but we have no clue as to what we are reading overall. There are some people who think that because they have money or are offered money and they love this world and the things that are in it, they do not think that what they do of evil is going to follow them. They are not thinking about the consequences that they will have after deciding to murder someone for what that person has accomplished in their lifetime. They have no problem with cheating in this life and being so wicked that they don't even think about God's word.

They do this without thinking about God and what they will have to deal with because they really just do not either believe in God or they believe they will be excused and don't know Him altogether. But I would urge these very people to surf the internet and look at YouTube in particular and listen to the voices of those who have left here for a moment and then came back to tell how it was if they were doing evil.

They have no idea what they will suffer for just a small thing such as a trinket in this life that cannot do anything for you after you leave here and while you continue to be here. It depends on God how He will deal with whom He wishes and desires to do so with. But one thing is for sure, and you can count on it regardless to what you think, believe in your head or wherever the wind may blow you after you read these words. You will surely suffer many times over for all of the deaths and blood that are on your hands and mark my words as God is my witness. And the sole reason for their suffering is because they took Whitney, Bobbi Kristina and my nephew Bobby Jr so gruesomely cold and so brutally ugly.

As God is my Witness

They had no goodness whatsoever in their hearts as they beat Whitney and Bobbi Kristina down and did all of what they did to them so proud and boldly. They did it all out of hate and greed of another person's own belongings. And instead of just making their deaths go quickly, these people we call humans, they desired for them to die a very slow and very painful death, which makes them even the more so wicked. These are people who also have children, and some grandchildren themselves.

These are people who have people they love dearly and have people themselves that they care about. They would do such a cold and malicious thing to another human being that has done absolutely nothing to them to deserve such treatment. We are talking about them harming people who have not ever done a single thing that they deserved all that was plotted out for them. The only one thing that I am certain of in this life is that, no matter where you are or what plans you have made from this day on, the God that I believe in will surely pin point you out from wherever you are and He will indeed reward you 10 times over for what you have done to some of the most beautifully spirited people that have walked this earth. I assure you that wherever you are in this entire universe, for you is a huge mountain of rewards that you so surprisingly have coming. Just like my niece, my nephew and my sister had no idea, and they were so innocent, so shall it be. Nothing or no one will get by the God of this universe and time without answering properly.

If this world only knew and understood exactly what you have done and how you have done it. It is not something you can easily take in and swallow without becoming sick to just think about. All of your work has been cleverly done and so quietly done where my sister did not see it coming so soon.

As God is my Witness

For, her and her child were so good hearted that they had no idea it was in the heart of those who was supposed to at least respect them and at least be grateful for how Whitney had been treating them and keeping them safe out here in the world. In return she got nothing but plotting on her life, tricks and hardship that led her to do every evil she eventually indulged in that was detrimental to her own health and wellbeing. Whitney Houston was surrounded by a bunch of demons who were out to gain all that she had ever accomplished of good in this world. And when she was down and deceased, they wasted no time at all selling and getting rid of all of her items, her personal goods and lifetime achievements.

I sat back quietly and very patiently to reveal it all for her. No, she will not go down and out and in vain either, because it is God who will take it from here. I am just a little vessel, and one who is so glad and so grateful to God that I was able to see and be that vessel for them and Him to just simply tell her story that she could never tell. Yes, I am her angel and she saw me and pointed me out way before I even knew who I was myself I was a silent fly on the wall on many occasions and today I look back with much intelligence today. I finally put it all together and said, OMG!

I got it now, and I now understand why they were and are still today doing all that they are doing in the name of Whitney Houston. They have made every effort in the past and in the media, to point the finger at the Brown's for being money hungry. They did this for many years trying to keep that bright light off of them. They are and have always been the only ones who have always been right there up around Whitney to get what they could get, and whatever they could not get while she was alive, they were willing to kill anything in front of them to take it in her death including my niece Bobbi Kristina Brown.

As God is my Witness

And that is where they made their biggest and worse mistake at. On top of it all, they went for my nephew Bobby Brown Jr. Now, I am not certain if they did it to throw everyone off, but he is now gone as well. I am not sure who they think or believe we are as people or as a family. But I can assure them that I am not who they think I am, and I do not stand alone, ever.

I can see so clearly today. I really got it when I heard Whitney tell me one day that my sister Tina's actions towards her was nothing compared to what her family did to her. OK, let me tell this story because it's necessary right now. Especially with all that's transpired out here in the media, I must tell this story so that people do not get the wrong ideas. OK listen. Do you remember when that "Bathroom Picture" that was supposedly Whitney's bathroom picture that surfaced on the internet? It was a picture of a bathroom filled with a bunch of trash that looked like someone had got high in it and was just throwing trash anywhere they could after using drugs.

It appeared to everyone that it was Whitney's things, but I spoke with a reliable source who was present those days talked about, and they said that Whitney had absolutely nothing at all to do with whatever was in that bathroom in that picture, and she was in fact, out of town when that was taken place. I had to be reminded because I was even there that day they said.

Now, my sister Tina was the one who placed that picture out there for people to look at and see as Whitney's stuff in her bathroom. However, Whitney was out of town and so it could not be her trash or her drugs that were used in that bathroom picture. My sister and Whitney were both feuding with one another at the time of this picture arising out of thin air.

As God is my Witness

Tina deliberately did this to Whitney, so that she would be seen as this terrible druggy who had all this trash in her bathroom. During this time, I and everyone else I and my family knew, and was so upset, and we all thought it was so horribly degrading of my sister Tina to do such a thing. Both of my sons, Flawless and Kel Rock were angry with their Aunt Tina as well. It was a horrific and very traumatic time for us all because it made Bobby Brown's family look bad. What my sister did not realize was that we all look bad whenever we do something like this. I don't even want to discuss how my brother Bobby must have felt.

I don't believe either of my sons, to this day, has forgiven my sister for doing this either. Now, on the other hand, you may have thought that Whitney out of everyone was the most upset, at Tina, but she really wasn't as God is my witness. She was a for a moment, but Whitney was actually one of the first people to forgive Tina for doing that, and I am a witness that Whitney did forgive her fully and thought no more about it, and I will explain why right here. It was a situation where I was like the go between for Whitney and Tina during that time. Whitney and I were both on the phone this day talking, and Tina calls on the other line of my phone. I told Whitney to hold on that it was Tina on the other line and to hang on. I answered Tina and told her I was on the phone with Whitney right now and she had to call me back. She immediately said, "Well that's why I'm calling, can you ask Whitney to please forgive me for putting that picture out there and I want to talk to her. I go back to the phone to tell Whitney that Tina is asking her forgiveness and wants to talk with her. Whitney says, No, right away! I am not going to lie; I was glad and agreed with Whitney because I was still so upset with her myself I did not want Whitney to go back to being friends with Tina, because I did not trust her anymore.

As God is my Witness

Whitney was not ready then, and I was so glad she wasn't. Everything I am saying right now, Tina already knew because I discussed it with her and told her face to face that I was disappointed in what she did, and I did not want Whitney speaking to her so quickly again because I was still angry at what she did to our family. However, I love my sister and always will. I honestly said to Whitney, "the hell with Tina, she shouldn't have done that to you Nip, what the hell is wrong with her!" Again, I have told my sister Tina this, so she knows I am being honest right now because she has heard this story a hundred times. At that time I was still angry that my sister Tina brought all this shame on our family, and so, yes,

I admit that I told Whitney not to trust her again. I am sure that God saw me doing a wrongful thing by telling Whitney to not forgive and befriend our own sister right away because of the betrayal we all were experiencing as a family. Whitney wasn't ready herself, to speak with Tina, and so, Whitney and I just ignored Tina and continued to talk on the phone that day without her.

Later, Whitney decides to speak to Tina and forgets about what she did to her. I was still angry and did not want to accept the fact that Whitney forgave Tina too quickly. I spoke to Whitney about it and asked her why she was speaking to Tina again, and to please be careful of her because I didn't trust Tina anymore. Whitney's words to me were, "Sis, it's OK because what Tina did to me is nothing compared to what my mother and my other family have done and are still doing to me to this day!" She said, "She's our sister, Leolah, so, yes, I forgave her. I believe she said something like, "We have bigger fish to fry. When she said it, I kind of looked at her like she was crazy! But at the same time, I understood where Whitney was coming from.

As God is my Witness

I can still see the look on Whitney's face right now, as she was saying this to me. Whitney loved tina, and she literally meant every word she was saying, and with every ounce of her being. What Whitney was saying altogether was that her family does so many bigger things to her that are so bad and so terrible, that what Tina did to her was really nothing. It was just another drop in the bucket for Whitney.

After Whitney's death, I saw how her family treated her death and funeral, and where they had her funeral at and how they treated her during her funeral. It told me that none of them cared even just a little bit for Whitney. I told those close to us that they really and truly had to despise Whitney. There is no way a mother or any family members would allow her funeral to go down in the place they had it at, unless they seriously didn't like her and didn't care at all. I'm saying to myself, now I see what Whitney was talking about when she said she forgave Tina. I now see why she forgave Tina so quickly and said that Tina could never do to her, what her family have done and been doing to her. I had finally got it and I had never cried so much thinking about how Whitney would have felt knowing they were doing this to her at her funeral.

It's one thing to come from another family and be raised in a family where they place you up to be famous just to gain money and fame. You give them everything they want for a lot of years, and you keep them propped up and make even them famous because of your name, and they treat you like a stepchild and someone they have no respect for. They won't even send you away properly and just give you your last respects. I know a lot of people who are adopted and been raised by other people they have come to find out is not their real parents. Some or perhaps most of them are good for the most part.

As God is my Witness

Of course, not all are happy, and no home is perfect. But I never met anyone who was treated like Whitney. I never met people who treated anyone so ugly and were so arrogantly proud about how they did things out in the open either. Yes, there are many stories out there of people going through a lot of things in life, of course, we all know what's in this world. But what I am saying is, Whitney was not loved at all! There was not a level of respect that was given to her when those cameras were off, and she was used in such a cold way where none of them even cared to hide their hatred for her. It was so obvious to me that, in my mind, I was saying, either people were straight up jealous of Whitney, or they just hated her guts that bad that they did not care who knew it, or it was both. And me, walking around with this on my mind, knowing that I am right by what I am saying, and knowing this and what I know, and me being able to see it and actually know who these people are is so painfully ugly, and I'm not speaking of physical looks.

I have to miss my family members that I believe they have something to do with their deaths, and I just cannot believe the actions of Whitney's so called family members as they pretend out here in the media to have her back after she is gone. I know all the things they did to get rid of my niece right under our noses. I see how they move after Whitney died and how they even treated my niece Bobbi Kristina when she was alive, and even worse after her mother was gone, they just taunted her, and they just took over and destroyed a beautiful young girls' life and they got away with it with the law! I sit back and watched how Pat and Cissy Houston both went and retained an attorney to fight my brother in a court of law to be over his daughter's estate just so they could kill her and have rights to her estate!

As God is my Witness

They did all of this knowing that Whitney would not ever in a million years allow them anywhere near her estate had she been alive. This is not anything that is easy to sleep well on if you do not have God with you at the end of the day. I just wish I could have saved my niece from the vultures who lurked around her until they saw her gone away from here.

I am not sure if my brother Bobby even knows what I know, but I do know that he knew his wife far more than I or anyone else did, and I would hope that he would shake off the chains of these demons and fear absolutely no man on this planet but God! I pray that my brother is still wise and that he does not fear anyone but God and that he will wake up now! It does not take anything other than FAITH to make it out of any situation in this world. I know this because I have tried God on many occasions. God cannot PROVE to you that He is God unless you try Him. Or should I say that people will not fully believe unless they try Him, because it is not God, it's the people who do not have that faith at the end of the day. He loves to show up for us it is simply that we just do not have "faith" in Him enough. It is written that even a small grain of a mustard seed of faith is going to move any big, huge mountain! There is a reason that that is written for us to take heed to.

Many ofus have heard that, we've seen that written in our holy books, but how many of us really believe it? Only those of us who really believe and understand it, do we go out here on that faith worrying not about anything but God. He works for all and any who will simply believe. It is not a hard thing to do we just have to get to it and DO IT! Did we know that when we place it all with God, He loves that!?

He loves it when we allow Him to do His thing with us. God will be your protector and be there for you as long as you make none other than Him your God and just simply believe in Him. Because we have been lied to so many times and so many people have let us down, we think in the back of our minds that God does not hear us and He will not be there for us when we need Him, but that is not at all true. God is not like the people that have lied to you. He is not going to ever let us down after placing all of our fear and trust in His hands. I am a person who wishes and desires to be an example for you.

TINA, WHITNEY & BATHROOM PIC

Even in all of my imperfections, I will try my best to be that example for people. Nobody was funnier than these two people whenever they were hanging together. They had fun together, always laughed and got high together and were just in their own world whenever they were together. Tina and Whitney were very close and had been close and were doing things together. Tina became upset at Whitney for whatever reasons. What people didn't know was that Tina is the type of person, when she's mad or real angry with you she will say the worse just to hurt you; and she doesn't care if she goes way far beneath the belt.

Doesn't matter to her when she's upset. Her and Whitney, they loved each other in real life. When that bathroom picture surfaced, I was in between the two of them asking Tina why she did it to Whitney. Tina told me that Whitney she had accused Whitney of doing something to her. I honestly could not see Whitney doing what Tina had accused her of, and so, I told Tina, I did not believe that Whitney would do that.

As God is my Witness

Tina didn't want to hear anything I had to say and she was still mad and upset. Next thing we knew the picture was out in the media of this bathroom. The world ate that up and really thought it was Whitney's stuff in that bathroom but it was not. Whitney was out of town when that stuff was in that bathroom, and so, all the excitement that others got from just looking at that and thinking it was Whitney's was all for nothing. Kanye West went in his pocket and pulled out $85K to license that picture for the cover of Pusha T's new album Daytona and I never laughed so hard! I wasn't laughing "at" Kanye, because God knows I love him, he is my beloved brother.

I was laughing at how easy was to fall for something like that and believe so quickly. No, that picture had nothing to do with Whitney, The things in that bathroom did not belong to her. My son had to remind me that his aunt was out of town. Later Tina laughed and said, it wasn't the deal and that she made a mistake accusing Whitney of it. By this time, this picture is really out here making Whitney look bad. They made up and are friends again and that was it altogether. It went no other way. Whitney forgave her and they were back at it like it never happened before. Whitney forgave Tina so quickly because she knew that the Brown's love was a lot more genuine than the Houston's, trust me when I tell you because Whitney told me from her mouth anyways.

She loved our family so much because she knew we really loved her and that was just it. For the most part, my children and I had a lot of wonderful memories of living with Bobby and Whitney. I always had my own home, of course. Yes, Bobby brought me a brand-new brick house at the beginning of my being in Atlanta. It was his choice to move me out of Los Angeles and to Atlanta. Just like it was his choice to buy me a house in Atlanta.

As God is my Witness

However, I moved out of the home Bobby purchased for me, and I eventually purchased my own house on my own and with my own money. I actually brought my first home in Atlanta. I put myself through "Business and Law School" and raised my children as a single parent in Atlanta and have done well for myself and on my own without asking Bobby for anything. I have been told many times that I have done extremely well as a single mother who raised two boys.

Both of my sons graduated from high school with flying colors and have continued their education and are successful at whatever they do to this day. I managed alone to place them in a private Islamic school, and they have always even unto this day done well for themselves. We come from a family that has a 100% success rate on my father's and mother's side. Every single person, from the grandparents down to the last cousins, all graduated, went to college, have their own homes, their own cars, businesses and plenty of money on my father's side of our family. Not one of them has a police record or has ever been to jail, and they have always done well for themselves. Some are law enforcement. We have attorney's, police officers, judges, architects and some in our family. And were talking about a lot of people.

We have a huge family in the South on our father's side. We have a large family in the South, up North, East Coast, West Coast, you name it, we have family, and they are all doing exceptionally well. All of them are very successful people that live their lives. We have more than a few millionaires on both sides of our family. There are some people who would love to place lies in the media about the Brown's but really do not know much about us.

As God is my Witness

Bobby has been in the music industry for over 40 years, and you have never seen me trying to ever get in the media to say anything about anything until the murder of our family members. No, I am not a troublemaker, nor do I try to find something to say about anyone. I just simply speak truth. It was not until then that I stood up and said anything. When all the lies being told about my sister, Whitney began, that is when I stood up to tell the truth. Enough is enough, and I am here to set this record straight, once and for all.

We have a huge family, and a whole lot of close friends all over this world who love us dearly, and who also know the truth of what's really going on. And anyone who knows me, they know that I am not going to stand up and speak lies about anyone. They know and understand and have major respect for us. What these people need to understand and know is the fact that, not all people will sit down and allow the horrible, treacherous, and erratic things to continue going on with silence. Just because Whitney's family have decided to not say anything, does not mean I will follow them. Far too much has gone on with the evil that they have been doing to my family members. They have done this without anyone doing anything to them to deserve to have their lives taken. And whether or not they can see themselves has nothing at all to do with me or us.

CHAPTER 10
WHITNEY, CLIVE
&
TERESA GRAVES

God is with my family today and they need to know that. Like it or not, believe it or not, He is right here After Whitney passed, I kept thinking about our late-night talks and how she told me, Mama Cissy sent her away to Los Angeles at the beginning of her career. Whitney was about 17 years old when she first went to Los Angeles with Clive Davis. She said she was sent out there all alone and all by herself. Son or daughter, I would not ever send my child alone anywhere in "Hollywood." I happen to let my son go with my brother Bobby on tour when he was a young boy, and since all of this madness I hear about Hollywood and everything that happens I would not do it today.

My God, it's a lot of scary things that go on, and parents don't understand the risk you're taking, by allowing your child to go anywhere away from you without you being able to see them and make sure they remain safe, because you just simply do not ever know. When it comes to Whitney, my thing is, "what kind of contract did Mama Cissy do for her" is what I would like to know? The things that happened to Whitney when she got there, let me know that she was alone, and no one was there to protect her at such a young age. She said, she almost got into prostitution because she met a pimp who tried to tum her out and pimp her! Yes, Whitney told me this. I could not believe what I was hearing.

As God is my Witness

She should have never been in LA alone and on her own and by herself. I just felt so bad for her listening to her stories of when she was young and got her deal with Clive Davis. Another Houston told me that Mama Cissy had Whitney 'just" for Clive. Those were the "exact" words of a Houston family member to me. They strongly believe and always have believed that Mama Cissy literally had Whitney just to give her to Clive Davis, and I now believe it and believe I know how it all went down and happened. I didn't really understand it until I was done analyzing and looking into certain things regarding Whitney's life. Mama Cissy raised her, but she is not her biological mother, and that is why it was so easy for her to give Whitney to Clive. Whitney told me herself that Mama Cissy sent her there with Clive at that young age to become a "super star" -if you will, with Clive Davis.

I am sure that Whitney has a hell of a story and a life with Clive. She and I just honestly never talked about it a lot. As I write today, I believe that she probably went through some things that she just doesn't wish to remember maybe. Whenever Clive's name came up Whitney would sound frustrated and agitated and didn't want to talk about him. Her sentences would be very short. Whitney was an innocent child coming into the Houston family and she probably has a lot of bad memories of being treated badly.

She has been through a lot and was so very strong to endure it all and hang in there all the way until someone ended her life. She had to learn a lot of stuff early on her own. After her death, I knew why she kept calling me her angel. Whitney knew that I was going to be the one to write this book for her, and I am not even saying anything bad about anyone. Just some of the things that she discussed with me are enough, trust me.

As God is my Witness

You would be surprised to learn that she had to endure much at a young age just like many other young black girls in this country, including myself when you are out there alone. My thing was I left home on my own as well. Whitney and I have a lot in common. First, our birthdays are close to each other. We were both born in the month of August and are just a few days apart from each other. One year apart and a few days in the same month.

We would sometimes celebrate our birthdays together. I guess it was why we got along and understood each other so much. She was always there for me, and I was always there for her. On top of it, we have been through some of the same things in life. A lot of people will say that she was a slave for Clive Davis, and of course, I agree with that narrative. However, we cannot leave out Mama Cissy, who gave her to him. And it is clear to me today why Mama Cissy did it. She was sent to Clive as a teenager and went all the way to California from New Jersey at 17 years old, don't forget. We are talking about a mother who was in the music industry and/or business and had been in the business for a very long time. So, she knew what went down and how it went if anyone did.

A person who I believe loves money and the finer things in life but did not make it to where she desired to while living in that lifestyle, from what I understand and heard from some family members. I could see her training and molding Whitney for that industry just like it showed in that "Whitney Houston Movie" in the very beginning of the movie. It meant money and she (Mama Cissy) did not have to get up and go to work for herself. Now, there is nothing wrong with liking the finer things in life and desiring to have all the money you possibly can in this life. It is something that even God wants for His people.

As God is my Witness

It is just "how" we get the things that we desire that I have a problem with. It makes me feel terrible to know that some people will be willing to even take a human life to get that money. Mama Cissy had been out there long before she sent her daughter there, so she was aware of the things that could go on and happen regardless of what anyone says. She was backup a singing for Elvis Presley at one time, which was, I believe, the beginning of her career in the industry. I believe she even sang for Aretha Franklin. I am sure that Mama Cissy went through some things with Elvis Presley that she would probably never talk about with anyone. She knew the business and those who were in it and what they did.

I am almost certain that she sent Whitney on her way hoping she would become who she became. It is the thing that some parents will do, in order for their child to become the people they wish to be or have the money they wish to have. Especially when the child did not come from your womb, the love needed is not there. There is nothing wrong with singing or becoming an entertainer and fulfilling your dreams in this world either. But the things we know and the things we will do on top of it, to become successful, is where I have a huge problem at. When you will gamble like that on a human life, knowing what this lifestyle can bring and/or what could happen in that process is just a whole other thing, and mind blowing to me.

Furthermore, Mama Cissy considers herself a very intelligent person. It would be disrespectful for anyone to consider entertaining the idea of her being so foolish and believing that Clive would not pull something over her head. Of course, they all have those contracts you have to be aware of signing. People in the music industry is hard to trust, in my experience over time.

As God is my Witness

Therefore, Mama Cissy, she is a woman who demands respect from any and every person she crosses paths with. You may get cussed out for thinking that anyone is even smarter or wiser than her. It has been said that she believes she is the queen of matriarchs and wiser than a lot of women in that industry. I say all that to say, with all due respect, I am going to give her the flowers that she is always expecting everyone to give her. I am certain and I think it's safe to say that she knew exactly what she was doing when she sent Whitney to Los Angeles to be with Clive and I will leave it like that.

Now, I must be completely honest and tell the truth here. Whitney has never discussed any terrible news or told me anything bad that Clive did to her personally while she was there or ever. If anything happened to her, I do not know about it. Now, she has talked a little about his personal life to a lot of us in the family, which has nothing to do with me or anything to do with her death. She just said that anytime Clive invited her over to his home, she had to expect to see men dressed down sometimes in funny clothing and sometimes even without clothing on.

That was all I heard and not any other thing, honestly. Whitney was sent there alone when she was young, and I believe it was mainly because she was not Mama Cissy's real daughter is why it was so easy for Mama Cissy to do everything she did with Whitney. What I mean by that is this, the motherly love that was expected to be there was not there, if you understand me. Some people reading this will not believe this and think that I am storytelling, but I just happen know in my heart, and feel it in my gut that Whitney came through Teresa Graves, and I am so sure today. I don't care what anyone says, I believe that Teresa Graves is Whitney Houston's biological mother.

As God is my Witness

I mean, there is no crime committed in that so I don't see why it would be a problem for anyone to admit after so many years. Whitney and Teresa Graves are now both deceased. I believe that Teresa was young (15 yrs.) when all this happened, and I just think that Poppa John was messing with her and didn't want to go to jail after anyone learned that truth of him sleeping with Teresa at a young age. So much of that has happened in this country and all parties are deceased now, so what could happen? Nothing if you ask me.

It is said that Poppa John dated the late and beautiful Teresa Graves at one time. I used to watch her shows as a little girl, and always loved her as an actress. Word is that Teresa Graves had a child in the year that Whitney was born (1963). It is said that she was only 15 years old, and could not care for her child, so that child was taken from her. This is a story that is so believable to me for so many reasons. I read where it said that Poppa John took Whitney home to Mama Cissy, for her to take care of Whitney when she was a baby. He was married to Mama Cissy at the time that this baby (Whitney) was allegedly conceived with Teresa. Again, it is believable for many reasons in my mind. For one, in those days that is just what people did that were in the business. To keep the noise down and to keep people out of your business, you would do what you had to do to keep secrets like this.

When I heard this, I of course had to believe my ears because I was looking at a spitting image of Whitney first of all, as I examined Teresa Grave's picture. As I am looking, I am saying to myself, who would not believe that these two are related as much as they look alike? You would be considered a blind person to say that it was otherwise. And I am a person who will not sweep anything up under the rug just because others decide to.

As God is my Witness

Teresa Graves is gone, and I do not know anyone who knows her and can tell her story, but it is so real to me. Yes, indeed, I believe that Poppa John was seeing this woman, and that she is the biological mother of Whitney. It has put all the pieces of Whitney's puzzle together and answered all the questions that I and a lot of other people have in mind.

One thing for certain, it makes a lot of sense as to why Whitney's life was the way it really was, altogether. From this day on, I am left with no other choice but to believe that this is her real mother. It makes a lot of sense when I think about why she was treated like she was by everyone in the Houston family. I believe in my heart she was treated like a stepchild. It all makes sense to me as to how they dealt with her. Even up to her dying and how they have decided to treat her death. It tells me that Whitney was not loved as a child should be loved, it tells me that she was not loved as a sister or friend would love her and treat her situation. No one that is supposed to, or was expected to care for her, seemed to even care for her. Everything has come to surface in its rightful place and just really makes more sense now that Whitney is gone. As I looked at Teresa Graves, I took a deep breath and said to myself, yes, this has got to be the reason why everything is everything. The only people that I believe really loved Whitney was, Whitney's Aunt Bey and her family.

Now, on the other hand, what makes me believe it even more. And I say this with all due respect to Mama Cissy. It is no secret that Mama Cissy was with her sister Annie's husband, Moss. Mama Cissy and Mr. Moss were together and conceived Gary, Whitney's so-called brother. His birth name is Gary Garland. He changed his name to Gary Houston for some strange reason that I believe know, and he and Whitney are not even blood related.

As God is my Witness

I am picturing this whole thing, and saying to myself, OK, so, Poppa John brought Whitney home to his wife, Mama Cissy, because perhaps he was paying her back for cheating on him, and saying in his mind that she cheated on him and had a baby with Moss, her sister's husband, and so, in his mind, she will have to deal with the fact that he slept with Teresa Graves as well, and conceived a baby girl named Whitney. Now, I could be as wrong as the two left shoes, but I doubt it. I believe that I am directly on it.

Poppa John may have felt this way, and it may be why he did not care that he had a baby. It was payback time for him, is why he brought Whitney home for Mama Cissy to help him raise. Teresa was young, and I believe they said she was only 15 years old. Therefore, back in those days, she could not keep Whitney. It may have sent him to jail if the word got out, and into the wrong ears, if you understand. On top of it, Teresa was doing some acting and singing and wanted her career more than she wanted anything else at that time. It all makes sense to me, as to why Mama Cissy would agree to raise Whitney, if she had thoughts in her mind to raise her the way she wanted which was as a benefit to her. If this is so, now they both are even and can move on with their lives as a married couple, and they did. They did not separate; they remained together and raised the children they had in and out of their marriage.

My mom and dad were like that too; and regardless to what daddy did, mommy was right there staying married to him. A lot of black mothers are strong like that. Third, it answers all questions and makes so much sense to all that has been in my head all these years regarding Whitney and the Houston family. Nothing could sound better or make more sense to me right now. This answers why she went through what she did every Christmas too.

As God is my Witness

I was told by a member of the Houston family that every Christmas, Whitney was so very sad, and did not wish to even be around Mama Cissy. It was said to me that Whitney had to deal with Mama Cissy comparing Christmas gifts every year that Whitney gave her father, and not her mother (Mama Cissy). They said this would make Mama Cissy say something to Whitney and it would place her in a terrible mood on Christmas day, always leaving Whitney sad. I felt so bad for Whitney when I heard this.

I could not understand the things I heard that happened in that family, but I could believe it because it didn't sound farfetched to me. On top of it all, I have witnessed things that I needed answers to. Like her and Mama Cissy's relationship altogether. As an intelligent black woman who has been through a lot in this world and knows the difference when I see it. The idea of Teresa Graves answers it all for me.

People don't know what I mean when I say that. See, this world sees Whitney in her interviews and people may think that she and her mom (Mama Cissy) were close. That is how Mama Cissy wanted this world to think. Yet, she and Whitney were so distant and apart from each other. I always said it was something wrong there, and I always felt it was always something missing there. I just could not place my finger on it, and today I believe it is this. I believe we hit that hammer on the proper nail with this one. Who would admit it though? I don't believe there is anyone alive who will ever admit this. I am convinced so far beyond a shadow of a doubt, and if I am wrong then it will be between me and my God, but I do not believe that I am. I also believe that Whitney knew this and was aware that she had another mother who was her biological mother. I also believe she knew her mother was Teresa Graves.

As God is my Witness

I thought back to when I saw Robyn Crawford on a certain show, being interviewed and talking about Whitney. She said that Whitney always wanted to re-do the movie, "Get Christie Love!" Teresa Graves played Christie Love, and I used to adore her playing that role and remember it clearly. When I heard Robyn say that it told me that yes, Whitney knew who her mother was indeed. On top of it all, I believe she had known a long time ago, because Whitney was also wearing wigs like her mother, all the time. I guess she was trying to look like her.

If you examine Teresa Graves and look at Whitney, both of them are twins. In my mind, Whitney wanted to look like her mother. Why would Whitney want to re-do that movie out of all the movies there are to do out here? On top of it she dressed like her mother and wore the same hairstyles. Her and Mama Cissy had an altercation in the house one day. As I continue to think back on that, I kept seeing Whitney's face in my head, when I asked her not to disrespect Mama Cissy, the day that Mama Cissy came to that house to throw Whitney in that drug program.

The expression on Whitney's face, I will not ever forget it. Her facial expression was telling me that, No! That is not my mother! That is exactly what I saw as I look back and remember that incident between the two of them. I am just grateful to God that I was able to witness things like this, because otherwise, I do not know how I would have found out to tell this story for Whitney. God had me to see a lot of things that I had to stand on for Whitney in telling her story. This is one of those things where you have to go with your gut feeling and spirit that God provides for you.

As God is my Witness

To know the other things that I know today, I am going to my grave believing that Teresa Graves is Whitney Houston's biological mother. I think that whatever Whitney seems to have of Mama Cissy, when it comes to features or body structure, it is just a coincidence because she raised her and has been around her for so long. But Whitney looks nothing like Mama Cissy to me. I say that with all due respect, and I hope that no one is angry at what I am saying. I am not saying this as a lash out against Mama Cissy either, because God knows that I love her dearly, and respect her as my elder mother. It is just simply my opinion that I am entitled to as a human being.

As far as Clive Davis goes, I am sure he has a lot of enemies out there who speak down on his name because of Whitney and other artists. I see it on social media all the time. Yes, I can believe that Clive is guilty of a lot of things. However, the things that I know about Clive have nothing to do with anyone but himself, which is none of my business. I don't know what Clive's hands have done literally, and so I cannot speak about what I do not know. When you watch a person's actions, after a while you will have your answers about the type of person they are. But I am never going to talk about something that I do not know, regardless of what's going on or who says what. And sweeping things under a rug is not something I like to do, so, ifI knew something I would surely say it here and now, but I really don't. I don't think Whitney told anyone anything about Clive.

I am also a firm believer that if we are going to create solutions for any problems, we must go all the way to the root of the problem first. Therefore, we must look at our parents whenever we are dealing with someone going into the industry as a child, and the way that Whitney went in. Especially with a parent who was there long before their child and is well educated on what goes on in that industry.

As God is my Witness

I say that to say, I was told by a family member of Whitney's that, it was very serious when Mama Cissy intentionally and deliberately placed Whitney with Clive for the purposes of her making money for her (Mama Cissy). Like I said, they said she was "given to Clive." It was said that Mama Cissy did this by way of human trafficking, no joke. And as God is my witness, that is exactly what I saw being around Whitney and the Houston's. It was like money was that sole reason that she was there for in my opinion, hands down.

Now, my brother Bobby was in the music industry as a child. Yet, there is a huge difference here in parenthood. My father nor mother were not in the industry to know and understand all that goes on behind closed doors. Yet, she knew it was a lot of backstabbing going on because she was up in there to see it for herself, and it being done to her son. I am positive that my brother went through a lot of things, because Bobby has been in it for a long time.

Bobby is the type of person who will go to his grave with whatever he has been through, whatever he endured, and whatever he knows of that industry. That is just how Bobby is, he will never tell a soul everything that he goes through with people. You can stick a pin in that. Even the bad things, Bobby will never tell anyone. He is another loyal person who knows how to hold on to secrets. And I will not ever dare ask him anything, because I already know he will never speak up about anything.

Again, I do not know anything about Clive Davis doing anything terrible at all to Whitney. Now, Whitney has said some things that Clive has done, and she was laughing in the process of telling us. However, it is not anything that I desire to talk about.

As God is my Witness

It is Clive's very own personal business, and it had nothing to do with her as a person and was solely his business. If anything, ever happened with Clive and Whitney, I surely do not know anything about it. All her trauma seems to come from her immediate family and her brother's wives. God knows, I wish that I could put this another way, but it is just strictly impossible for me to do. The only thing that Whitney has ever said to me regarding Clive Davis was that he invites her over to his home and when she gets there, he's always got a lot of weird male company who dresses funny, and that was it.

Do I believe that Clive had something to do with Whitney's death? Yes, I do believe that it is possible that he was involved, meaning he could have sent someone to do it because that is what people do unfortunately. However, I have no concrete proof that he has done anything. Therefore, I cannot make up stuff about him. That would not be fair or right to do to anyone. But what I can do is talk about what I know and the facts of what has taken place and what Pat and Gary Houston HAS DONE. What I do know is that my own people have done things to my sister. It is a sad day in this hell that we live in that I must talk about it.

The truth is the truth regardless of where it is at. Yes, it is no secret what the white man has always done to us and still is doing to us to this day. And I get that everyone believes that Clive Davis has something to do with Whitney's death and a lot of people really believe this. I cannot prove it and then still say yes, he sent someone to kill Whitney because I really do not know. Even if that were true, the fact of the matter would still remain the same. I have no proof of him doing anything to Whitney BUT I KNOW WHAT PAT AND GARY HOUSTON HAS DONE.

Also, what I do know is that Ray J, Pat and Gary Houston, Nick Gordon, Raffles Van Excel and Brandi Burnside and her mother as well, they are those who I know for a fact, were at that hotel. I also believe that they all know for a fact what happened with Whitney because every one of them that I just named had one thing and/or another against Whitney! Every single one of them was not all the way 100 with Whitney and they are all found together at this hotel the night my sister comes up dead. Something is not right with this picture.

The thing is, Pat and Gary were both the closer people to my sister and niece during the time of their deaths, and so they are the main ones that I look to and blame as the main culprits and guilty parties, along with orchestrating this whole thing.

Nobody likes talking about us and what we do to each other, but the truth is the truth no matter where it is standing or coming from. No, I do not feel-good talking about us, but what I am not going to do is sweep what I know up under a rug, just because it is my very own brothers and sisters. I cannot and will not do that and then think that I am doing something good. My main thing here is that I just pray they are all willing to ask God for His forgiveness for what they all did because they are all out here in this world walking around as if they did nothing wrong, and they all did.

They all know what they did wrong, and they all need to change their way of thinking altogether, repent with God and just simply do better. Hopefully, this book will wake up people so that we can be stronger people and begin to heal, and love, and respect our own people just like we respect other people. We cannot continue to do things like this and think we're going to keep getting away with it.

As God is my Witness

We cannot let anyone bribe us either, or make us do harm to our own sisters and brothers. And I am not saying that they listened to anyone by doing what they did to Whitney, because I don't know if anyone did bribe them. It appears they did this on their own, the way they followed Whitney and stalked her out all the time. And yes, indeed I have proof on this. A part of me believes it's someone even bigger than all of them, and then another part of me believes that no, it's just Pat and Gary Houston are the only ones who orchestrated this whole thing all by themselves, and did what they wanted to with Whitney's estate afterwards. I cannot pinpoint it all to anyone else as the main people. I just know who did the most.

What they all need to know is that we are all living in a time where, we must be willing to change our thinking and our ways or we are in trouble with God. He wants us to come together in unity and stop and think about what we are doing to our very own people out here. As the Honorable Minister Louis Farrakhan has always taught us. Karma is something else and it can get really bad for people with such evil in their heart. When we look at our brother's and sister's we are looking at God, but how many people can seriously take that in and believe that?

I am sure that is hard for some people to take in and comprehend, but one day we will all someday really understand it and wish and pray that we had of listened to this Man of God, who has come to us with this divine spirit of God to bring us the truth about ourselves and God. We are so quick to kill our brothers and sisters and especially for that green paper. You may or may not enjoy it today, but tomorrow will be so much harder for you when you do such sinister things like this and 'you will' have to pay back whatever you owe this universe.

As God is my Witness

Why do we feel good doing wrong to our own people? And then how can we sleep at night knowing a person's life was taken for all the wrong reasons, and they did not do anything to deserve it? How can we be OK with taking innocent lives? Do we really think or believe that God is not going to make sure that justice is served? You have to seriously be a fool if you believe that God is not going to do anything after someone does wrong like that. Do we really believe in God because that is a better question. People need to know that absolutely nothing gets by God and He does not sleep on anyone or anything.

What bothers me is, we are already a people who have suffered so much in this country. And for us to keep doing things to each other is crazy! We have made our own brothers and sisters are enemies when we should unite and love and respect one another. We forget that we are the remainder of those who survived the holocaust of our people. Yes, that is who we really are. After all our people have been through and is still going through, we should wise up and pick up our strength and unite within one another and act like we have some sense left in us for once.

Do we know and understand who we really are, and the fact that we have come in on the backs of our ancestor who fought, bled and so painfully died for us to be here today. We are always talking about what other people do to us, and we are doing even worse to ourselves today. And I hate to say this, but God will also blame a lot of leaders out here for holding back from helping us in our communities and speaking the truth out here. They know the truth of the holy book but will not tell it or speak it and we are out here as a lost people.

As God is my Witness

Well, those of us who are not students of Minister Farrakhan. Then, when The Honorable Minister Louis Farrakhan is out here doing God's work and doing what He is supposed to be doing for God, and helping the people of God, they want to talk about Him because they are just straight up jealous and envious of Him, and the fact that He is doing the rightful thing by God and they aren't. They just simply cannot handle the truth.

They "know" that He got the right message and some people will still deny the God He represents, knowing that they are wrong. And we wonder why other nations of people look at us and shake their heads even to this very day. They do that because they know how foolish and weak we are when it comes to how we treat each other which is how we treat ourselves at the end of the day. Then we have people who know the message that Minister Farrakhan is teaching is right and exact but won't bust a grape to just simply fall in. And what I mean that that is exactly what I plainly just said, if you understand me.

We have a lot to learn and very little time to get it right and together now. We must face the facts in this life we live, and then be willing to change the way we think out here and better ourselves so that the next generation of people coming behind us will not go through and suffer the same things we have, and they will be a better people who love and respect each other and God. If you are a person who says you don't care about our next generation of people coming behind us, then I feel so sorry for you, because it could only mean that you are not in tune with God, and it can also mean that you have no idea the reason for your own existence in this world today.

As God is my Witness

Which also means that you do not know who you really are. What really startles me is, I cannot ever understand why a lot of people just really do not care for God anymore. Too many of us act like we don't care what He thinks and what He wants for us and from us all. I do understand why a lot of people are confused and discouraged out here, because of all the fake and phony pastors, ministers and leaders out here in this world, who have been perpetrating a fraud, by teaching falsehood, and using people in their congregations for their own personal gain and personal desires. These leaders who are leading God's people to the slaughter, who are all caught up in all the vanities of this world, while taking many straight to hell with them, they have got to know that they have it coming with God, because they still know wrong from right.

We can blame what we will on who we will, but God has placed in every human being's heart, common sense. And by this, we know right from wrong and so, we will not be able to stand and face God and say that we did not know, and the devil made us do it. And we just killed our own brothers and sisters for our own selfish reasons. We will not be able to blame anyone for our wrongdoing of murdering our own people. At the end of the day, regardless of what we have been taught, it does not mean that we do not have our own minds where we cannot discern right from wrong as intelligent human beings, we know better.

You cannot do wrong, by killing your own brothers and sisters, and then think that you will get away with it, just because you have not been checked and brought to justice in this world. Money and fame have some people blinded to where they cannot see the actual time we are living in. There is a God who indeed sees absolutely every single thing that we do and every single thing that goes down.

As God is my Witness

He is who you and I will have to face whether you believe there is a God or not. No one will be able to give back what they put out into this universe. Whatever we do in this world, this universe is obligated to return it to its sender. Most of us have no idea what sin really is to God or how much of it that we have done. It has always been said that the mind of this world is foolishness with God, so that is something to think about right there. It is something that not a lot of people really get or understand. God is going to hold every man accountable for the decisions they have made with our heart, whether you believe in Him or not, and no one will be able to say the devil made them do anything.

There is no devil outside of yourself that can make or force you to do anything, and again, we know right from wrong. Every one that says they fear God and believe in Him will have to really show up today and be just that. Many people who think they stand with God stand with no one but the devil (self) because of their actions and this is why the Bible states that many will say, "God didn't I serve you? God is going to say, "No, depart from me, you workers of iniquity. Mathew 7:23: Did you know that everything we do is written down and we all have two angels who are always watching us, one who report our good and the other who reports our bad to God? If you think you got away, you didn't. Ifwe are remorseful and want to repent, then we should not waste any more time and rush to our knees and ask God for forgiveness. We have to do that and be sincere in our prayer in asking.

I urge anyone, who has something to do with the death of my sister, Whitney Houston, my niece, Bobbi Kristina Brown, and my nephew, Bobby Brown Jr., to ask the God of your understanding for forgiveness "NOW" if you are sincerely sorry for what you did.

As God is my Witness

You don't have to say to it me, but I urge you to hurry and make peace with God and don't wait because you have no idea of the time. If I ever wrong anyone today, and I know and I am aware that I have, I very quickly apologize today because it is the rightful thing to do. I apologize to the person, and I also ask God for His forgiveness. Some people just do not believe in God and so, they don't think they have to do that but it's the wrong way to think.

I personally have The Honorable Minister Louis Farrakhan to thank, for Him teaching me when I didn't know. I thank Him for standing up first being an example and giving His life for this entire world, and teaching this world the true knowledge of God.

His entire life is dedicated to God's mission, never make no mistake about that. Meaning, He is no longer living a life like you and I, having worldly desires, if you understand me. In other words, The Honorable Minister Louis Farrakhan, gave His other life up when He began His work that God chose Him to do. We would call it a regular life. Yes, He gave it up, to do the work that He knew that God had cut out for Him to do. He solely focused on what God wanted Him to do to help Him in His mission of raising up all the dead from our graves (mentally dead) of ignorance. Meaning, ignorance of not knowing and understanding the truth of who we are and who our God really is AND WHY WE ARE REALLY HERE. He has the hardest job of any man in this world AND NO OTHER MAN WAS READY LIKE He was to do the work, is why God chose Him for the special mission. On top of it, He is hated by those who do not like the truth.

As God is my Witness

Why do you think that these other preachers and pastors out here are not hated like they hate Farrakhan? It is because they are not a threat like Farrakhan is, that's the only reason why.

None of these pastors or preachers (whatever you wish to call them) compare to Farrakhan when it comes to teaching God's true word and doing the works of God, and they know this. None of them are really speaking that truth that God desires them to speak. That is why none of those who rule care or even bother them. It is because they know that those men and/or woman are doing nothing compared to what Farrakhan is doing. And that's just the plain truth. The white man looks at them smiling while saying, "Good job now keep going! It's because they ain't saying nothing. And see, God don't like that because they read and study that Bible and I am sure that by now they see the difference from what Farrakhan is teaching and THEY KNOW and THEY UNDERSTAND that they are not being honest with the people and teaching God's rightful words.

Minister Farrakhan's job is a heavy job because His job requires Him to be badly spoken of and accused of things that He is not guilty of He was chosen out of all the other men in this world by God and His Messenger (Jesus: Malachi 4, Bible), The Most Honorable Elijah Muhammad, simply because they both saw something in Him that would help Him (God) in His mission, and something that will also help all of the people in this world, who desired to come to THE REAL AND TRUE GOD OF THIS UNIVERSE AND TIME. He is a GREAT example for us as black people in this country to learn how we are to be in order to come back to God Minister Louis Farrakhan is not only a great example, but He is THE BEST example of what every man and woman can be, regardless of our race in this world, did you know that?

As God is my Witness

Any man who would have the same heart, they too would be capable of doing the same thing. But they are afraid of a man that breaths and bleeds just like them and they know it. They are afraid of what may happen if they did speak the truth to the people in this world. They even dislike Farrakhan because he is bold enough to speak God's words, and He looks so much better and younger than them, and He is older than most of them. Not all but some of them are so jealous of Him. They dislike Him for so many other reasons including jealousy.

How can any people be upset with a Man who had nothing to do with God choosing Him? People are upset with God in reality and not Louis Farrakhan. Also, Minister Farrakhan did not write the Bible or Holy Quran. So, why would people want to take it out on Him, what is already written and had been before He was even born? I cannot understand how people can be so upset with such a divine Man of God for speaking nothing but the truth and is just helping His people by the demand of God. And NO, He IS NOT like those other ministers, preachers and pastors. He is so far away from them and stand-alone all by himself.

They try to say that He hates Jews and white people, and they know in their hearts, that is ludicrous and so ridiculous to say. He does not hate anyone. In fact, He teaches us to 'not ever hate' anyone and to RESPECT ALL people in this world. As a matter of fact, He has a whole lot of white followers as well as Jews, WHO LIKE, RESPECT & FOLLOW HIM. Yes, indeed He does, and all nations of people follow Him, but see, some people don't know that because they're too busy hating on Him. Some people just assume and think without knowing the truth. I urge you reader, to go to a "Saviors' Day Event" one day and you will see every nation of people standing in one spot together worshipping Allah-God in one place together and in PEACE.

As God is my Witness

On February 26th of every year, we have Saviors' Day. And yes, Allah only means God (in Arabic). If you'd like to know more just go to www.noi.org and you will see that it is a lot of things you can learn. You will be able to read and get all the information you're seeking.

There is not a man out here in this world that I met or ever cross paths with, that has a heart more beautiful than The Honorable Minister Louis Farrakhan, hands down. To call Him a hater is to straight up LIE on Him in one of the worse ways. Another thing, people should be very careful when lying on someone, and especially a Man of God like Farrakhan, because to accuse Him like that is a terrible habit to have.

Also, it is already written what they would say about Him. The Bible is a book for all of us living in this world today. If the Bible were for another people, it would have left with them when they passed. But it is for us who are in this world right now today. It would not make sense if it were for a people who lived yesterday and before us, because it would mean that we have someone else's book and we would be in this world without our own book, and stand in need of one ourselves! This is our book and the prophets saw us today and where we are right now. It clearly describes us and everything we do in the world today.

People have to wake up and judge Farrakhan by the enemies He has. The only people that don't like Farrakhan are people who are not of God. His enemies are those who rule God's people unjustly and so inhumane. Farrakhan does not hate them, but some of them do hate Farrakhan without a just cause.

As God is my Witness

What does that tell anyone? God does not hate any people. He only hates THE EVIL things that people do and that is all Farrakhan is saying at the end of the day. You yourself would hate any evil actions done by a person that "you" deem doing evil. But, what do you deem evil is what the question is. You have to be careful in what your calling evil. There is a BIG HUGE difference here. For someone to speak truth only means they're simply speaking the truth. You can't call it evil and ungodly because GOD IS ONLY ABOUT THE TRUTH.

Minister Farrakhan is a person who has not physically harmed anyone in all His life, and has not hurt anyone but has only spoken the truth, and so, that is not what evil means and it is not what hate means. When a Man of God stands to speak truth, it is just what it is, the truth being spoken, as it has to be. He has never lied about anything he has ever said. Nor has He ever hung people on trees and done anything close to or near what the white man has done to us black people in this country. He talks about it because it's true! It is the same with God; anyone in their rightful mind is not going to feel good about evil being done. Especially when it is towards another race of people. It is wrong and it is not a good feeling when it is someone suffering.

Any intelligent person is not going to say anything negative about Minister Farrakhan. The wise KNOW HE IS NOT EVIL AND THEY KNOW THAT HE DOES NOT HATE ANYONE. The haters only say that because it is nothing else to say when they cannot handle the truth of what is being said about a Man of God whom they despise and are jealous of. And then, I never understood how people would think that just because they heard something He spoke about that they never heard before, they think it's a lie or made up.

As God is my Witness

They only believe whatever it is they have always known or what they have been taught in this land. They think it is the gospel truth. They don't stop to think for a moment that perhaps the knowledge they have or always believed, IS NOT THE ABSOLUTE TRUTH AFTERALL. The question is, "Who taught you what you know?" That is a question they should ask themselves. And who's to say that what you know is the absolute truth?

How did you weigh it out and why do you believe that you know it is true? There is no excuse today because everyone in this entire world knows today the truth about our slave masters and those who taught us everything we knew before The Most Honorable Elijah Muhammad brought Islam and the whole TRUTH to us all. And the Bible has continued to tell us that THE TRUTH WILL SET US FREE. Has anyone thought about that part? Evidently the Prophets "knew" that we were going to be lied to, for them to write that in our Bible, "The truth will set you free." They knew that we were lied to and/or going to be lied to is "why" that was written. And so, now we have that truth today and no one can say it isn't so.

When people learn the TRUE HISTORY of everything in this world, they will finally get it, and then there are some who may not ever get it and that's OK. IT IS IMPOSSIBLE FOR SUCH PEOPLE AS A SLAVE MASTER TO TEACH YOU RIGHT THAT HAS NOT TREATED YOU RIGHT. It would defeat their purpose to teach anything right. Anyone in their rightful mind knows that this is true and it is something that we have to keep up front when believing them instead of God's Man.

As God is my Witness

Of course, a slave master is not going to teach you the truth about who you are, because if we knew that part we would wake up and be free of their slavery. I mean, for a people to brush this off and not take something like this very seriously, something is very wrong with the people, in my mind. Minister Farrakhan is a great example of what every man can be in this world. I am sure that God is pleased with Him.

What's happened to us that we do not even feel it when we murder our brother or sister for nothing at all they did? The life that we live when we are out here doing wrong, it will eventually catch up to you and trust me it will indeed. And like my father always told us, if you don't stop doing wrong, it will stop you eventually. Life is like school, and we live and we learn as we make decisions out here every day and according to what we decide it will always determine our status in this life. After we make decisions, we are tested and scored on everything we have done in this world. Here is a good story that I will explain to you which is similar, and how serious it is right now with us all.

And I say this because A Man of God is calling us all to the table today trying to get us prepared for God "who has COME AND IS HERE AND HAS ALREADY ENTERED THIS WORLD AND DECREED WHAT HE WILL DO. HIS DECISION IS ALREADY MADE AND NOW WE HAVE TO COME TO THAT TABLE &/OR GET OUT OF THE WAY OF GOD'S WRATH. And it's likened to "Noah's Ark", which is written in the Bible. It goes like this.

Noah is calling everyone to that boat and giving us all the opportunity to come in and get safe away from the rest of the world, because today is that last day and that "FINAL CALL."

As God is my Witness

Some people don't even believe in God, or even believe in a story such as "Noah" telling them that He (God) is approaching your door. You are asked to get in this Ark because you may get caught out there when God comes through to flood the cities of the people. Many are being hardheaded and not listening, and it's mainly because, a lot of other people are nothing more than followers in the world, who are just simply not listening or do not care. Most people of this world choose to follow what they call normal people. These so-called normal/worldly people are telling them that Noah is not of God and His whole idea is a hoax, and it's nothing more than lies, and that Noah is a hater of certain people and should not be followed.

These people are saying, Noah isn't a real Man of God's, He is speaking evil, and He hates certain people, Etc. Some people are foolish enough to follow the rest of the world and believe what those in the world are doing because they are used to it and feel more comfortable staying the way they are. It's also because Noah is a different kind of Man in the world and the people are not ready for God, and it is why they choose to ignore Noah's voice. Noah is not of the world so, of course He is different than others in and of the world. He's not indulging in things that the rest of the world is. Some people cannot see Noah for who He truly is yet because the blinders are still on the people. And we are talking about people who consider themselves wise, smart and intelligent people.

They do not realize or even know that they do not know and are so lost and confused. Yet, they believe they are wise and they really believe that they are making the right decisions. Meanwhile, the big and powerful evil doers who rule and govern this world have not ever taught, shown nor given any of the people, the real truth about God in the first place.

As God is my Witness

They have always taught them wrong and evil since the beginning, which is all their lives of being in the land. Yet, the people still follow the world and see Noah as a strange Man. The people have not woken up yet many years later. Those in power do all they can to whitewash and bad-mouth Noah because they do not want God's people to go with Noah, which means go to God and be safe and out of harms way. They work night and day to keep God's people away from Noah by saying all kinds of wicked things about Noah. These people are more worried about what others will think rather than pleasing God, so they stay away from Noah.

Those in power have systematically kept God's people blinded and they have orchestrated this intentionally and deliberately just to keep the people blinded to the truth of God, and who they (slave masters) really are themselves. You would think the people are smart and wise enough to see through all of this, after being so afflicted and so oppressed for so many years, and it is so ridiculously easy to see who these slave masters really are, but the people still do not get it. And while I'm here, again, it is another reason why the Bible says, "The Truth Will Set You Free!" And the Bible also states in "Deuteronomy," God told Abraham, "Tell His children NOT TO FORGET HIM once we got over here in this strange foreign land. He specifically told us to NOT SERVE THEIR GOD AND FORGET OUR OWN GOD. And the people are doing just that.

The Honorable Minister Louis Farrakhan told us that EVERY BLACK PERSON WAS INDEED A MUSLIM when we arrived here in this country off of that boat. None of us had ever heard the word Christian until our slave masters beat us into submitting to their God which they always called themselves Christian.

As God is my Witness

There is nothing wrong with being a Christian as long as a person lives up to what they believe in their Bible, and the same for a Muslim as well. To be a Christian means, one who submits their will to God; and it mean exactly the same to be a Muslim also. They both mean the same exact thing. Therefore, I see myself as both because they both mean the same exact thing, just one who believes in God and does the "WILL" of God, period.

God knew what our people would do out of fear for our slave masters, but today there is absolutely NOTHING TO FEAR ANYMORE, because GOD IS NOW HERE. There is no need to fear anyone or anything because YOUR FAITH in God will protect you today. Your trust and faith in God will grant you the ultimate protection today. We just have to have it and we have got to place that trust and faith with our Father without hesitation or fear of anything else in our hearts. How are we going to KNOW THAT God really works if we do not TRY HIM? Try Him and you will see that HE REALLY DOES WORK. You will not be disappointed in the least when you trust Him and His word, period.

The prophets knew that we were going to be LIED to, and then the day would come when someone, which is indeed a Man born of a woman (The Honorable Minister Louis Farrakhan), sent by God Himself, and carrying the divine spirit of God, He would be in this world telling the whole truth, and He would tell us everything we need to know about who we really are and who our God "really" is and why we are really here right now.

When a Man of God is here to speak and teach the truth and you have guilty people who do not like that truth because they know that they have done so much wrong and evil to God's people, they will do any and every single thing in their power to suppress that truth and do their best to 'try" to make the truth speaker look bad, even if it means to LIE again to the world by telling the world that this divine Man of God, is hating on them. It's all they could say. One thing for certain, they never called Him a liar. No, they can't do that because Farrakhan, OOPS I mean Noah, has come with all the receipts He needs. That is the one thing He is not.

If you notice, they would not ever say that He has lied about anything, because they know that is impossible for them to do because we have experienced and live with everything that He has told us and so it is impossible for them to do. Common sense is the only thing that is needed in something like this. It is why the Bible tells us, "The truth will be so plain that even a fool would find it hard to error." See, not even a fool can deny the truth that Louis Farrakhan teaches today. It is because everything is already with us meaning we have gone through everything He teaches so no lies are being told at all, and every single thing that comes out of His mouth makes all the sense in the world if we are listening.

We are already told in the beginning of our Bible, NOT to forget our God- and we have done that by accepting their God and their way of life since our beginning coming over here to this land. Yes, we were forced into whatever it is we believe today because our people felt they had no choice. But the truth has come now and so, we can go back to who we were and take back our way of life and our God, turning our hearts back to our family as it is written we would do after Elijah came to teach us (Malachi 4). No, we are not forgetting our God whose proper name is indeed Allah, the real and true God of our ancestors. God did not want us to come here, and be over here for over 400 years, and then forget that He is our God.

Yet, it is exactly what happened to us, and it is "why" He had to wake up our brother Farrakhan to teach us after Elijah has taught Him. If we study these real Men of God, we will find our history and proudly stand and take our places in this universe. We fell asleep a long time ago and forgot so much that if anyone even mentions anything about our God today, it sounds so foreign to us. It has been over 400 years and that is a long time, and so, it is only when we take the time to study and pay attention, that we will we finally get it and realize Jesus was amongst us all this time AS IT IS WRITTEN HE WILL BE!

We have to make sure that we are reading our Bibles properly to even be able to recognize Jesus, our brother and God's Man for the hour of time. We should already know Him by the description given to us, and what God said He would do when He came before us. The Most Honorable Elijah Muhammad turned our hearts back to our parents and brothers and sisters alike. He did everything written of Him while He was amongst us right here in this United States of America. The Honorable Minister Louis Farrakhan, both fit the description to a T, if we will only understand what we are reading in our Bibles. If I can see it clearly and understand it, being a fool, and one who was out here not even in my rightful mind, I am certain that those who were more intelligent can as well.

Are we as a people sure that we are the real and true believers in God and Jesus as we say we are, or are we hypocrites who are here in this world today fulfilling what is already written in the scriptures regarding hypocrites and what they will say and do when He does appear in the world?

As God is my Witness

We have to be sure that we are not those people who will not believe, only because it's not coming from the slave master's mouth who enslaved us and taught us what they wanted us to know, only to keep us down deeper in our graves, while they continue to laugh at us who call themselves believers in God and Jesus. I am 100% certain that I am a believer in God and Jesus today, make no mistake about it.

The enemies of God work diligently each and every day to keep us afflicted and oppressed while continuing to sit back and laugh as they are treating us worse and worser every single day. On top of it all, certain folks act as if we are not wise enough to understand what is going on here. In fact, most of us are so dead (mentally) and so far down in our graves that we do not even desire to come up out of there because we have gotten so comfortable and are afraid to move on away from there....

Today there is a Man called Farrakhan who (along with Master Fard Muhammad and The Most Honorable Elijah Muhammad) fits the description in our holy books. As Go and His Man who sits at His right side. Farrakhan has come into this world to call us out of this world, and to come on back to God now. He is that perfect representation of Jesus the Christ. A Man born of a woman who comes to crush the wickedness that is going on in the world. That is what "Jesus the Christ" means at the end of the day. Yes, I said it, the Jesus this whole world has been looking for, if we understand our books that we are reading. That Jesus is none other than The Most Honorable Elijah Muhammad.

If I wrote this book and did not place those words in it, I would not be myself and speak as I know to speak. Therefore, I must tell you that No, I am not crazy, nor am I a fool anymore and yes, my brain has been washed from the garbage that the rulers of this world has placed in my educational system that I was used to going along with.

It was written that Elijah would come and turn our hearts back to each other, AND ELIJAH MUHAMMAD DID THAT WHILE HE WAS IN OUR FACES. God is here to gather His people, if we would pay attention and understand. He stands today and is calling us out of this world to come back to Him through our brother Farrakhan and we can take it or let it alone, but either way, it will continue to stand and be THE ABSOLUTE TRUTH today. He 1s that perfect representation of the Jesus this whole world has been looking for all this time, take it or let it alone.

See, what a lot of people don't understand about Farrakhan is, Elijah and Master Fard Muhammad both sent Him into this world to continue in the mission of God. Yes, I said Master, because He mastered this whole universe and did every single thing that the Bible said He would come and do. We are not saying that He is the God who created everyone from the beginning. There is a lot more to learn if we are interested in knowing the truth. These are facts that no man can argue nor defeat.

We can start at "NOI.ORG." and learn so much by going on there and ordering the books that The Honorable Minister Louis Farrakhan has on there (which are very inexpensive) to educate us. Furthermore, we can see and listen to Him on YouTube as well. The true story of Master Fard Muhammad is book in itself and can be found on www.noi.org website as well.

As God is my Witness

The duty of God's Messenger and every believer in God, is to call God's lost children first, because we are the ones who have been so lost and so far in the grave (mental death), and the ones who needs God's true and rightful teaching first. Then He is to gather the whole world and invite all the people of God to come into obedience with the true and rightful God of this universe and time today. The Honorable Minister Louis Farrakhan has been mistaken for so many other things and other than who He truly is. They have called Him just about every name in the book of evil. They did this "knowing" that He has never been anything even close to what they have shouted out in this world. He is a Man of God, whom God chose Himself for His mission. And because of the sickness that is in just about every man's heart in this wicked world; so many of us have made excuses as to why we do not desire to take heed in what He teaches.

The saddest part of all of this is, The Honorable Minister Louis Farrakhan is literally the best friend that any person could ever have today in this wicked world. He is in fact the calm before the great storm of God's. A storm that is at the door of every man alive today. He is a divine Man of God who has stood in the doorway holding back the WINDS OF GOD WHICH WILL EVENTUALLY DESTROY THIS WORLD and us if we do not get our lives together.

I am just a little tiny small warner of God's. We say we know the mercy of God, but we have absolutely no idea the mercy that has already been given to us through Farrakhan! No, we do not get it, and No, we do not understand His being right here in front of us today and right NOW as you are reading these words! Farrakhan is that last Man that we will get before that great and Dreadful storm that is on its way to this country. We can believe it or not believe it, but it will still stand as TRUTH either way it goes.

As God is my Witness

With all due respect, many people have been following the wrong path in this world, and they have been given the wrong ideas about God, when we should have our own mind, and be sure that you are on the right path. And so, "Noah's Ark" is like running out into the streets to party with people just because we see everyone else out there partying. We have run out of the house and gone into the party to join the sinners of this world, simply because everyone else is doing it, and it is "the norm" as they say.

See, this is the part that people are taking for granted. They think because Farrakhan has been speaking for so long, and it seems to them (because of their mentality) that God wasn't going to ever show up in the land where they can physically see Him. They did not realize they were looking right at their own brother who was representing God right before their eyes! They thought it was a hoax, but it was only God giving them so much time to just come to Him. THAT IS WHAT MERCY IS! Yes, He is such a Merciful God. Now, no man nor any woman can get upset and say that they were not given time to get it together. In the coming hour, everyone will bow and bear witness that Allah is God and He did have SO MUCH MERCY on His people. Those who took heed will be with Him and those who refused and did not take heed, they went down in that pit of hell fire that wasn't even made for them. They chose that fire that could not be stopped by their friends who taught them.

We are living in a dangerous hour and Minister Farrakhan has told us this so many times, but who is listening to Him? Who really believes in what He is saying and why He is here? I don't care what anyone says, all of these people in power know and they are sure of the time and who He is. They just want black people and all nations of people including white people to continue ignoring Him.

193

As God is my Witness

They don't want people to follow this Man Farrakhan, because they know who He is. And I am not trying to convert anyone by writing this in my book. I am just a little vessel of God's trying to do my part and speak the truth, is all.

Has anyone ever grave it real thought as to why the government doesn't bother with any of the other pastors or preachers in this world? They even give them money to help them stay propped up! It is very simple, and it is because so many of them are not even preaching the true and rightful words of God, so they don't care, they are not a threat, and on top of it they ARE HELPING TO KEEP THE MASSES BLINDED BY THEIR SPEECH.

Of course, they are no threat because they are not speaking the true words of God, and so, those hire ups care not that they are not speaking God's true word and for that they are not in any trouble with them, as they see it. If they are not speaking what Farrakhan is speaking, they are not speaking God's true word, period. They are doing this government a favor by not doing right by God. Many of the leaders are afraid to even go there, and they don't want to lose their congregation, so they keep quiet and say nothing leading their sheep into the fire with them. CAN WE NOT SEE THAT THIS IS WHAT IT'S MEANT IN OUR BIBLES ABOUT THE SHEPHARDS LEADING THE SHEEP ASTRAY AND INTO THE FIRE?

We think it's something that we can go to Church and hear a good sweet song sung by a Church member who can sing their heart out! God don't care nothing about singing a good song. That song can't help His people come out of the graves they been in for so long. Besides, they are no sweat and no problem for those in power.

As God is my Witness

They get taking care of with funding that come into their Church to make them look pretty and well propped up. Many of them are building more and more facilities around their Church, but are doing nothing to help God's people where it matters most at. They have nice green grass, beautifying their buildings and all kinds of fake programs that say they are helping people, and yet, this world is getting worse. I cannot see the help coming to our youth who are out here today searching for God. Some are now turning our youth away because in reality, the plan was never to help them anyways. It has never been about that with some, not all churches. I do know a lot of pastors who are good and who really love God and are doing the work and have good intentions. But, the majority of places that call themselves the house of God are out here faking it hard.

Also, not one of them are doing more than Farrakhan, nor will they give Him the respect of coming into the true knowledge they are now learning about their Bibles. We have to give thanks and respect where it is due. If it were not for The Most Honorable Elijah Muhammad and The Honorable Minister Louis Farrakhan waking everyone up, they would not be in the positions they are in today having more knowledge about our Holy books.

Elijah did a great thing before He left from amongst us, and He is not dead either, trust me! Oh yes, He is very much alive, and we will all bear witness to that one day soon. We have to speak up out here and speak those true words of God and come out of that fear and make all the greatest sacrifices that we came into this world to make so we can change the condition of our people a lot sooner. If we will do that, all we have to do from there is watch God take over. It has to go down regardless of who is trying to delay the process.

As God is my Witness

It matters NOT with Allah-God because any time given is indeed His mercy for His ELECT SAKE, please don't forget it. Minister Farrakhan has that "Final Call." Whenever you see our brothers on the comer in your city selling that final call newspaper, know that it is just what it says beloved. That is exactly what it is, the final call from God. We are either going to come out of this world and get in THE ARK and get the real teachings of God or be left out. No stress, it's just a call and you have the choice of going wherever you like. God is not going to twist your arm and force anyone to come to Him. If you're going through things and it's hard for you, that is a sign that God is trying to talk to you to save you. You have to know the difference. God just wants us to get it right WHEREVER WE ARE IN THIS WORLD, AND DO UNTO OTHERS AS YOU WOULD HAVE THEM DO UNTO YOU. WE HAVE GOT TO STOP THE KILLING OF OURSELVES AND COME BACK TO GOD, PERIOD.

He has given every man the freedom of choice to do what you will, so if you are not going through anything I would worry if I were you, honestly and just straight talk. God gives His most adored soldiers the hardest trials. The more you are suffering today the bigger and greater your blessings will eventually be. If you aren't going through anything and you got it made, oh well, I guess you ain't got no worries today, but tomorrow will come for you. Noah's Ark is certainly real baby, and we should know this. Oh yes, it is, and it exist with Minister Farrakhan, and you do not have to be a Muslim to get to God. No, you have a choice to be and stay wherever you are in this world. As long as you are treating others as you wish to be treated and you are not out here doing wrong and your good is surely outweighing your bad, you are OK. Minister Farrakhan said, that's all that God is interested in at the end of the day.

As God is my Witness

He will check our "hearts" to make sure they are what they are supposed to be. And whether we like it or not the test is on now, and the more that you say, "You believe in God", the more you will be under trials. God will test us, and it is not a bad idea. I once heard Minister Farrakhan say, "The Best Religion is treating people like you wish and desire to be treated, and as long as you are doing good in the earth, God has no problem with you or your religion or how you choose to worship Him. As long as you are not harming others and you are living properly and righteously in His world, you are good. And overall, that is my message here.

I have an obligation as a believer in Him to spread this word to you. We have to repent from all wrongdoing and do better in this life of ours and stop walking around forgetting who owns your soul. We have to get it together because the time is running out. It really is out I don't want to scare anyone, but you have no idea of the time now. That is why I have said, I forgive those of my brothers and sisters, whom I believe to have something to do with my family member's demise. I am striving to clean up my act as well. I am not perfect by any means. I stand to be corrected as well and will never think that I am perfect!

You nor I are the author of another human being's life, nor do we have the authority to take it away from them. Therefore, we do not have the right to take another man or woman's life, and so if you did, you had better humble yourself NOW and run fast to that gate of God because He is approaching every man and woman's doors as I speak. We have to come to our senses in this universe and awake from what we have done to others and come to God and repent so that your soul is saved, and you have peace now. Either that or you will have to suffer the consequences of your actions with God.

As God is my Witness

It does not matter who we are or what we believe, or how much money we have, it will not save your soul. The bottom line with God is, right is right and wrong is wrong and we all know the difference, period. If we do not have the desire to change the way we think and DO out here, well, I feel so sorry for you. A rude awakening is destined to come and it WILL come for you.

God is calling all of us who desire to be with Him. And we don't have a lot of time as someone has lied and told us we do. Common sense tells us, we will not get younger; we will only get older the longer we are allowed by God to stay here. But time is of the essence right now, and it is at hand now. God is here and, in this world, right now and many people reading this can relate to what I am saying without argument; while others will laugh and think it's funny and such a bold thing for me to do. But there is nothing funny about what I am saying here. I am not a saint by any means nor am I holier than thou. No, I am not, and more than anything, I am one who does not care what anyone thinks of me, I will always speak the truth regardless to whom or what.

None of us are perfect, and we can never be perfect in a world so full of sin and a world that is not perfect itself This world has become unbalanced and it was made like that because of the people who forced I to be that way. But what we can be in this unbalanced world is simply a person striving to be right by treating others properly and just simply strive to do right in this world, for the sake of God, AND THAT WILL BALANCE IT BACK TO PERFECT. A lot of things that happen in this world doesn't have to. A lot of us just do evil because we been so used to it. Today it's called wrong and evil in the wrong hour of time. Just because a baby is helpless does not mean its right to do what you want to do to that baby, or to that child.

As God is my Witness

God will hold you to every single thought in your mind that you carry out. He is not playing right now, God has come for His children, and He cannot be defeated regardless to what you think, what you heard or what you believe today, I promise you, He will not lose. And by the time you read this, one or many of you will bear witness to what I am saying overall. God is indeed that powerful. He will make believers out of those who do not believe. Regardless to what color we are, what our religion is or what decisions we have made out here. You can always come to God any kind of way that you are, I say it all the time. He will accept you whatever you have done or any kind of way you come to Him.

But WE CANNOT REMAIN THAT WAY AND STAY IN THE FAVOR OF GOD! NO WAY IT WILL NOT HAPPEN! GOD IS NOT THAT MILK TOAST GOD WE HAVE BEEN TAUGHT HE IS. WE MUST CHANGE AND BE WILLING TO COME OUT OF THIS WORLD ALTOGETHER. AND, WE HAVE TO KNOW, if we do not give up our sick, ill and evil life of treating people badly, and doing all the wrong things that we all know that we are doing wrong, we will go down in the fire that is prepared for those who do not desire to simply do right and come to God. He is here to let everyone know that He is not playing with anyone anymore.

By the way, serving God has always been very easy to do. I don't see what all the fuss is about and why people are so afraid to do right. People have been so afraid and so scared to try Him, is what I learned. His yoke has always been very easy, as it is written it is. People that are afraid or think they are not ready are just people who have not bothered to experience it to tell everyone else how good and easy it is! IT IS A BEAUTIFUL THING STRIVING TO SERVE GOD.

As God is my Witness

And you don't have to be perfect! No, God has never asked us to be perfect! All He asked of us is to just simply STRIVE to be right that's all! And I can honestly say that I have, and it is why I am here writing this in this book, and calling people to repent and leave this world of sin that they are indulging in today.

Wherever we may be in this world, we should strive to be a better person, period. And yes, it is possible, I don't care who you are or how bad you think you have done; YOU CAN BE SAVED AND YOU CAN CHANGE! YES GOD WANTS YOU! Think for yourself, and come out of this world my people, that you be not partakers of this world and the sins you are committing. IT CAN BE DONE AND YOU WILL FEEL SO MUCH BETTER, I PROMISE YOU!

Minister Farrakhan has told us all, "No, you have not done anything "THAT BAD" that God won't forgive you for." You can come to GOD any way you are, but we just cannot remain in that same way. And I must say for those of you who think it is not important to respect and listen to Him, I feel so very sorry for you, because a day is coming real soon where you will see and fully understand without the slightest doubt in your mind, exactly why I have said that. You may walk around proud today and unwilling, but as God is my witness, I promise you that will change. You will know that HE IS GOD'S TRUE AND RIGHTFUL MAN WHO HAS BEEN SENT TO US IN THIS WORLD BY GOD. The day is approaching where every person left alive in this world will indeed bow down and bear witness and confess with their own tongue that Allah is the God. A day is coming where we will all appreciate and understand the words of His Servant, Farrakhan.

As God is my Witness

I have been out here in this world for a very long time and have just about done it all, and I am a witness that it is a beautiful and easy thing to do on this side of the mountain. I am in love with God, and I am so proud to say it. You have no idea where I have been nor any idea where I have come from and that is something that is irrelevant right now. The important thing is, is that someone very sinful lied to a lot of our people and discouraged them from coming to God and wanting to do for God what He desires. I am a living witness that it is not bad at all! In fact, I would not ever want to be anywhere else in this world if I cannot be with God and do what He ask of me. I do not have a greater desire today. Wake up people and save yourselves because the clock is ticking...

CHAPTER ll
BOBBY, WHITNEY & THE DRUGS

The first thing I want to say is that I never ever saw Bobby or Whitney put a pipe to their mouths! The media has pumped this and the world has thought this way for a long time, but it is not true at all! People who don't even know them have said this for forever, and IT IS A BIG LIE! The media and tabloids have always labeled Bobby and Whitney as crack smokers AND THEY HAVE LIED TO THE PUBLIC. Where that came from and started at is another story, but right now, it doesn't even matter, because it's wrong and it has always been a big lie being told about them and that's why Bobby is always silent and never says anything about it. When a person is not guilty of a thing, they are usually quiet about it. I am always praying that God gives my brother the strength he needs to overcome whatever comes in his path anyways.

I have always thanked God that none of the rumors bothered them as others may have believed it did. My brother Bobby is a strong man and has always stood on all ten toes regardless to what was ever thrown at him, and me, being his ELDER sister, I have always been so proud of him for that. But it does not mean that he doesn't have his days where he is overwhelmed with the evils of this world. None of us are perfect, but I can tell you this, when it is all weighed out in front of God, I strongly believe that my brother's good will outweigh his bad in this world. Regardless to what anyone thinks or says about him. He is not perfect, but he also is not the man that a lot of people have always thought he was. My brother has done "A WHOLE LOT OF THINGS THAT HAS MADE GOD VERY HAPPY AN PROUD OF HIM FOR."

202

As God is my Witness

Bobby has taken care of a lot of people over the years of him being in the business he's in. He has had a heart of Gold and done some things that others would dare do. Bobby is not one to bother people and he has always minded his own business. He's the type that likes to live and let live. For some reason, trouble has always come to his door, and God has always held him up through it all! All trials are allowed for God's children by God, as a test for us all. And none of us pass our test all the time, and we may fall short of the glory sometimes, but we get back up and move on with the strength we are equipped with. But this drug thing that this world has tried it's best to break my brother down with has been enough now. Enough is and has been enough for far too long.

As his sister, I have even gotten so sick of it. It's obvious that this is what they like to do to tear you down once you have been brought all the way up to that top. I just pray that my brother is talking to God on a daily basis in secret and when he is away from everyone and everything that tries to get in his way of being who he came here to be. If he is reading this, please Bobby talk to your Father, God, each and every single day that you awake baby, and establish a serious and personal relationship with Him, because He wants to show you something!!! Let Him use you as a witness so that you have a story to tell the world. God will sit every enemy that is plotting on you and trying to bring you harm in a fire so HOT they won't even understand what dimension we are in. When God says that your enemies will be His, He means just that, and it goes for anyone you are not feeling comfortable with.

As God is my Witness

Always stay with Him in secret Bobby telling NO ONE about your relationship with Him, because I promise you, GOD WILL SHOW YOU SOME THINGS BABY! He will show up when you need Him the most, and prove to you that He is with you when you have that faith in Him. YES! Be straight crazy with it and I promise you, He will be there my brother.

I am sure you already have, but just in case, very seriously establish an un-withering faith and trust relationship and bond with Him AND WATCH WHAT HE DOES FROM THERE! He comes through right before your eyes! He'll go after all the fake and phony people right before your eyes and chastise them right in front of you, so that you can see that it is Him who is on your side.

I remember we sat in a meeting a long time ago, and someone told you Bobby, "All you need is God! Do you remember, Bobby? Yes, He is all you need! And You have no idea how much He can show you! It will amaze you; and you will see for yourself once you place that trust and faith in Him who has POWER OVER ALL THINGS IN THIS WORLD! Anyone who turns to God, and places their trust fully in His hands and walks around with assurance of His love, His protection and His will power, you are already covered! All you have to do is have the "faith' of a lil tiny mustard seed to receive His protection, and you will see Him work for you. I love talking about God and anyone who knows me, will tell you, I have been this way all my life. No, reader, I am not perfect, and I did a lot of sinning in my life in case you are sitting there reading this with that devil's spirit in you so unhappy that I even wrote a book like this and talking like this. Yet, overall,

As God is my Witness

I believe that my good will outweighs my bad and God knows my heart, and so, it is why I can feel His love and experience His loyalty to His children that really love Him at the end of the day. Oh yes, I love God because He has always been there with me throughout my entire life and brought me through the toughest times in my life, where I could have been gone so many times, but He was right there to see me safe and home free. His love and His power are the reason why I am who I am today. It is why I exist as strong as I am today.

When I was in the world sitting in bars drinking back in the day, I brought my Father's name up and loved talking about Him and what He wanted for His children all the time. I did it so much that some people hated when I talked about God while I was even drinking, but I never cared not even a little bit, nor did I allow someone else's fear to interfere with my faith and love in my Father. And I did that when I knew nothing of Him, it was just what I was feeling in my heart, my spirit and my soul that had me talking. And don't be afraid to tell people, "I am certain that God has me." You have to seriously feel it and cheerfully wake up every single day and "know" with everything that you have in you that He has you! He will be right there with you and help you fight all of your battles, my brother.

Anyways, Bobby and Whitney both were two functioning people who did drugs. And I say that to say, a whole lot of people in this world has done the same thing, it was nothing new. People did it before they were born, and hopefully they will NOT do it anymore when we all leave here. Overall, I am so glad that they did not allow the media to do what they thought they were going to do with them by always throwing up drugs as the narrative whenever they spoke their name. It is a part that goes along with being in the music business.

As God is my Witness

They will never say anything good or never focus on anything POSITIVE! Whitney and Bobby have done a lot of good things but you will never hear about it unless someone who really cares about them will tell you. It is what the media gets paid to do altogether. They have to make people look bad it's part of their job. I used to believe that it was because others would come along and give the media information about a person. But the media are people who can make up what they will about a person too, in my opinion. But besides that, right now, and with all due respect, if I were anyone who worked in media, I would tread lightly in this hour of time.

God is very angry at a lot of people, especially people who think they can get away with things in this world. KATT WILLIAMS SAID IT BEST! IT'S UP FOR ALL THIS SEASON! GOD HAS HIS EYES ON FOLKS AND HE IS NOT PLAYING WITH ANYONE IN THIS HOUR. I must humbly say this, "All of those who have disregarded the God of this universe, and done the evil that He hates such as taking lives, your days are coming mark my words." And I am not making any threats to anyone, oh, trust me, God knows I am not. I am just simply telling it like it has to be told and if anyone is WISE, they will ease up off of the people of God and focus on themselves. Because see, that is the problem in this world.

There has always been way too much JUDGING going on with "other people" and the very people doing all the judging, they somehow forgot about THEMSELVES. They forgot that anything can fall down that pipe for any one of us, including them. With all due respect, you cannot be a person who spit lies about people out into this universe, and then think that nothing will come of it FOR YOU. It's a new day today and the Sun has come out to protect all of God's children now.

As God is my Witness

Bobby and Whitney are not guilty of a lot of things that has been being said about them in the media with drugs. They always knew it, and it is why they just ignored the rumors of crack. I lived with them, and I watched them and how they did their thing with drugs. They have not ever once put a pipe in their mouths! I LIVED WITH THEM AND NEVER SEEN A PIPE OWN BY THEM INTHEIR HOME! This was always THE BIG LIE TALKED ABOUT THEM. It was always said by people who did not have a clue about who they really were as people, and what they were really doing with drugs. Overall, it was someone feeding the media all along. Whitney always told us that she knew it was none other than Pat Houston, who was telling the media all of these lies about her, and so whenever we heard anything, Whitney told us, "Know that it was Pat" having her friends in the media to do that. My thoughts have always been that Pat Houston was angry that Whitney wanted no parts of her, and that was why she always went to the media with lies about Whitney.

With all due respect, the way I saw it was, Pat has always wanted to work with Whitney, and she always wanted to be seen with her, and Whitney wasn't having it. Mama Cissy again, was placing Pat up there and forcing her in that door with Whitney and she did everything in her power to have Pat around Whitney. Whitney just saw something in this woman Pat that was not in any way genuine to Whitney. Today and now that I see Whitney gone, I fully and completely understand just why now. She always said that Pat made friends with people like this in the media because she had sold her soul to the devil a very long time ago. I never knew what Whitney really meant when she said that until after Whitney passed and another Houston told me.

As God is my Witness

I was told by another Houston that Pat practices "witchcraft" and she was raised by a white family who taught it to her. Of course, I do not believe in any witchy persons doing anything to me, I don't care what they know or how strong they believe they are-MY FAITH and MY BELIEF is ALWAYS with MY GOD ALLAH and HE IS THE POWER OVER ALL THINGS IN THIS EARTH so it never bothered me, not even a little bit.

Now, I did not know nor did I have any knowledge about any of this until this certain Houston told me this. I didn't even know about her being raised with another family other than her real parents. However, many people have wrote me concerned with the way she looks in he face. A lot of people say that they can easily see that something evil is going on with her whole demeanor and character, and I agree with it. In any event, there is absolutely NOTHING in this world that anyone would ever have to fear when you have ALMIGHTY GOD ALLAH WITH YOU! And that is it! No need to even think about such things. When God is with you NOTHING OR NO ONE can come near you to do anything.

Furthermore, anything we do, we better know that there is a God right there and the angels adding up all of your faults and sins. There is not a soul walking this earth today that will get away with anything in this universe. We may believe otherwise and think we know, but that means absolutely nothing to the God of this universe and those who believe in Him. It does not matter who don't believe in God, because it is destined for all to know Him eventually. And I don't care what you're doing today because tomorrow every knee will bow and every TONGUE will indeed confess that Allah IS THE GOD.

As God is my Witness

Not one person ever had proof of Bobby and Whitney ever doing crack, and yet, the media still took that and ran with it. People lie without ever having any knowledge or truth about the person they are lying on. They just assume it in their own mind or mental that, that is what they do. Meanwhile, Bobby and Whitney would not ever touch crack, and as Whitney said it long ago to Dianne Sawyer, it's Whack! I am not saying this to try to cover up anything for them or try to say that they were angels. Nobody is perfect in this world, of course. I am only saying this because it is the truth about them both. I have been a witness for them and lived with them and know how they did their thing with drugs.

They walked around their home hiding from no one except Bobbi Kristina. I never once witnessed Bobbi Kristina ever seeing them do anything either. Bobbi Kristina was always in her bed asleep while they partied and did their thing, or she was not in the house altogether and was at her friend's home sleeping over whenever they would be in the home drinking and doing drugs. And they took very good care of their daughter. I know some other people that never touched a drug in their life but did not raise their children nearly as good as Bobby and Whitney raised theirs, so a lot of people can't even talk about what they don't know of them.

I can remember a time when Bobby and Whitney were on their phone talking to someone about drugs. A person who went on a run for them, a runner boy if you will. They were on the phone with the person because the person had gotten to the destination but could not find what they were looking for. The person told them that where they were at right at that moment, they did not have what they were looking for at that time except crack or hard rock as I think he mentioned.

Bobby and Whitney both immediately went off on him and told him to never insult their intelligence and offer that to them! They immediately hung the phone up in his face! They really hated that stuff They were upset that the man would even offer "crack" to them. They both said, "Aww hell Naw! You can keep that!" They hated for anyone to tell them that they had anything other than pure uncooked POWDER cocaine. They used pure powdered cocaine and sprinkled it on their weed. THAT IS THE ONLY WAY, I EVER SAW THEM GET HIGH.

Now am I saying, that them doing pure power cocaine is any better? Absolutely not, but what I am saying is that I NEVER saw them smoke anything in a pipe. I only knew them to take pure uncut cocaine, sprinkle it in some weed, and smoke their weed and/or hemp that way. AND THAT WAS IT.

I never ever seen them with a pipe in their hand, or do it any other way, and neither did the people who are claiming they were crack smokers out here in the world. I used to clean their house up, and I never ever ran into a pipe of any sort that belonged to them. The public or media has not ever seen Bobby or Whitney do any drugs, so they need to stop spreading lies about something they know nothing of BOBBY NEEDS TO START SUING PEOPLE WHO REPORT THESE KIND OF LIES TOO!

Another thing that had me upset was when they made Whitney look bad as she performed at the Michael Jackson tribute. Where they had her looking like a skeleton trying to make people believe that she was so strung out and so thin that she was dying! I am not sure of the person who was responsible for that picture, but I do not believe it was Whitney 100%. NOWAY!

As God is my Witness

I believe her look was altered and the whole picture was compromised to make her look as skinny as it did. Oh yeah, I so strongly belee that that picture was altered like that to make her look THAT BAD! And, the reason I say this, is very simply because, I was around her often back then and during that same time, and she did not look that thin when I had seen her! When I saw that appearance on TV, I immediately said, OH NO SOMEONE DID THAT DELIBERATELY! I said that to everyone who was sitting there watching that TV with me at that time. I said, I cannot believe that was the real Whitney, I believe they altered that of Whitney! Oh, I was furious at that time. We all know that Whitney has always been a very thin girl all her life, (which of course, made it that much easier for anyone to alter a camera or picture of her).

As soon as I saw that video, I said right then and there, I believe someone did that to purposely make her look that skinny and that bad to this world. It had only been a few days since I had seen her before that event, and she did not look like that when I saw her. I think she knew that someone had set her up for the media to believe that and run with it. She said then that it was Pat Houston's job to make her look bad and take her down, and it was actually THE BEGINNING of them taking her down. She said then that Pat Houston hated her "that" much and we had no idea the things that she was capable of doing. Now that Whitney is gone, we all can easily see it and believe it for ourselves.

THE TAPE JONATHON HOUSTON EXPOSED OF PAT HOUSTON After hearing that tape that Jonathon Houston, (Gary and Monique Houston's son), released on social media, regarding Pat Houston called, "The Grinch Who Stole Krissy!" Everyone I know has listened to that on YouTube and said, Whitney was correct.

As God is my Witness

People were upset everywhere and they did not like Pat after hearing that. You can hear her talk about Whitney in a way where she thinks or so sadly believes that she is so much better than Whitney. And Jonathon Houston produced that tape right after Whitney's funeral, which everyone thought was so sad of Pat to even say after Whitney was now dead and gone. It made everyone believe that there was no one who cared about Whitney on that side of her family because they did not stop this woman, Pat who was married to Gary, and who today we know has NO BLOOD AT ALL OF WHITNEY'S RUNNNG THROUGH HIS VEINS!

Now, we can see why they treat Whitney like that. Which means that not even Pat and Gary's child is related to Whitney Houston. They are not blood related at all. Jonathon Houston was one of the first people to pull me to the side and tell me that he knew who killed his Aunty Whitney and he knew who did that to Krissy and had Nick Gordon beat her down in her living room. I said, who, Jonathon? He said, "My stepmother, Pat (Houston) and my father, Gary (Houston)! Their own son, Jonathon Houston told me and my son that he knew for absolute sure it was the both of them! He said that he also had other videos of them and also had them on other recorders, and oof course, I believed him. I said, I know Jonathon, I been known who they were!

He said, no, Aunty Lele, but I am serious! I said, I am too Jonathon! And yes, I know who they are!! Every time I said yes, Jonathon I know, he seemed to have to say it again, and as if l didn't hear him clearly enough. He kept saying, Aunty Lele, I am sure because I been watching them, and I know they did it! I said, baby, let me tell you something, I know as well, otherwise I would never talk as I am about them like that if I didn't know.

As God is my Witness

I would never accuse someone of something I was not sure of So, you see, I know what I am saying and so does Jonathon, of course. The only thing is today, I don't believe he is willing to let the public hear anymore. I believe they scared him into not going further with it and letting the world hear the other stuff he has on them. Jonathon just wants to live his life and not be bothered with any drama I am guessing. They have been aggressive with him and I believe it frightened him for the most part. But see, this is what I mean when I tell people, God will look at you and how you allow others to place fear in your heart rather than faith in God. When you believe in God there is no room for fear of another person, regardless if it is your father, mother or whoever. Because meanwhile, Whitney and Krissy are laying in their graves without justice.

If I was Jonathon, I would not dare even give it thought to quit and not bring justice to my loved one. I would not care what someone else thought. They should not have done what they did to Whitney! Furthermore, if you love your family member so much, you help bring them the justice they deserve, period. God is holding every person responsible for holding back the truth as well as those who did it. People don't realize, it is God at the end of the day that we all have to face. I would never allow someone to force me to have a bad record with God at the end of the day. Now all of Whitney and Krissy's blood is on all of their hands because the whole truth is still not out here and people have it to give but won't.

Overall, I believe that he has seriously been traumatized just like my sons have been when it comes to the deaths of our family members but that should make him "want to" report them even more. I just can't understand people and their fear sometimes. We say we believe in God but we fear man far more than we fear God, and God

Himself will confront us about that. I know that if it were my child, I would tell them to do what is right in the sight of God at the end of the day, because your relationship with God is far more important than it is with any man or woman in this world at the end of the day. No soul, and especially not a good one, is worth sacrificing against God for in my eyes. I would not care what they thought of me, I would just simply do what is right "for God" so that when I meet my Father, He is pleased with me. I could care less about what a man or woman (who has brought their ticket into hell anyways) would say or do, neither of them is more important.

These people don't realize how many hearts they broke by killing my family members like that. I believe they scared Jonathon into not giving that information up and just keeping it suppressed and hidden today. It seems as if everyone is afraid to speak the truth for Whitney and Krissy. This is another reason why I knew I couldn't quit and give up on them. I did not want to be that person who did not speak the truth for them.

When we know things, we are responsible for what we know. God brings things before us as a test of our faith in Him and we are to focus on nothing else but that test. On top of it, I could never let God down because my loyalty is with my Father at the end of the day, and I will never EVER walk this earth in fear of anyone but God.

We have to know that God Himself does not agree with us NOT doing our best and trying to bring justice to our people, and we should not ever place anyone before Him, and be so afraid that we don't tell the truth. Especially when we know it will help with their case, and also for this world to know the truth. I honestly wish Jonathon was a lot stronger for God.

As God is my Witness

I feel so sorry for him because I don't think he understands what is really happening, and I honestly thought he was stronger than that. They have now brought him into their realm of sin by not giving up that evidence that could help Whitney Houston's case altogether. These people are heartless to do what they did to Whitney and my niece.

Nick Gordon panicked after he beat Krissy down in her own living room. After the ambulance rushed her to a Gwinnett hospital, Nick thought that she was not going to make it. He was scared that he was going to go to jail for murdering her. The thing was, Krissy did not die from what he did to her. She was so strong, and she came through so quickly and was healing and almost home!

The doctors had just told us that she would be fine, and we would take her home and that after just six months she would be doing so much better. And while I'm here let me clearly tell you that no, my niece was not in a 'coma" anymore. She had been out of that coma and came out in the first hospital she was in. After that, she was awake every single time I came in her room. I never saw her eyes closed and I always saw her with her eyes open and watching TV after she came out of that coma, which was right way and after being brought to that "first" hospital.

My guess is that my niece was afraid to go to sleep knowing the Houston's were surrounding her bedside coming in and doing what they wanted to do to her, and it was not fair. If a person doesn't want a certain person or people around their hospital bedside it is not fair to have them around especially if they are as evil as the Houston's were. They did not want my niece to live and they saw to it that she didn't and we all know it!

As God is my Witness

There is no other way to put this **THIS IS REAL AND IT HAS TO BE KNOWN REGARDLESS OF WHO LIKES IT OR NOT. IT'S NOT ANYONE ELSE'S FAULT THAT THESE PEOPLE ARE LIKE THIS AND THEY DON'T NEED TO GET AWAY WITH WHAT THEY DID ALTOGETHER, NO THIS IS NOT RIGHT. AS GOD IS MY WITNESS, HE KNOWS I AM TELLING THE ABSOLUTE TRUTH HERE.**

Remember, she was brought to at least three (3) to four (4) hospitals altogether before she even killed. And that was because they were waiting for the right time to get her and do something to her. Then this impersonating nurse is sent in. THE FEDS NEED TO RE-OPEN THIS CASE AND CHARGE THESE PEOPLE WITH MURDERING WHITNEY, BOBBI KRISTINA AND MY NEPHEW, BOBBY JR! THEY DID NOT ALL JUST DIE FROM THEM CAUSING THEIR OWN DEATHS. My niece went through A WHOLE LOT before she left this world. And then for her to NOT be dead and her body placed in a morgue and STILL BE WARM TO THE CORE IS INSANELY BRUTAL FOR HER! AND I WILL NEVER FORGET THIS!

I want everyone to know that no, she did not die from what Nick Gordon did to her, and we were way past that part. It was Pat Houston who killed my niece. After Krissy was rushed to the hospital, she awoke from that coma so fast! Nick got out of town and was hiding, and then not long after that he was found dead in Florida somewhere, I heard. They said it was some kind of an overdose, but I and everyone else believe it's the same ole thing as usual. Someone came in and forced drugs into his arm just like he did my niece Krissy, and then threw her into a bathtub. It was that he was drugged up intentionally and some kind of way unknown to us all.

As God is my Witness

People began saying, oh, it'll happen again to the next person whom they decide to kill to shut them up. They think they don't have any weaker links out there, but people talk all the time, and especially the people they decided to trust to be a part of this whole killing spree thing with them. God is a mysterious Man who's full of surprises, and just as sure as I am saying it here, trust me HE WILL GRANT JUSTICE TO MY FAMILY SOON.

I am not worrying about it anymore because I know He has it. The next person that speaks will probably go more in depth about everything that transpired. Pat has already gone out there and made people see her guilt. Therefore, she herself is a weak link as far as everyone is concerned. We all believe that she gave up the first suspect which is herself, because she's not a good actor as she believes she is. Everyone I have spoken to and then those on social media that has seen her all on social media somewhere, they have said that she is surely guilty of doing all of this to Whitney and Krissy. People are not stupid, and they can see it straight in her eyes as she's talking. It is too evident what happened and transpired with them all. The death of Whitney Houston and her daughter, and my nephew, none of them will go down in vain, I am here to tell you.

The truth will be exposed to this world and the God that I believe in will do it just wait and this world will see because an awful lot has gone down and been done with them and the authorities have not granted them justice, they all know they so well deserve and it is not sitting well with God I am here to tell you. The mistakes that people made will finally be exposed and come to pass real soon...Pat Houston has also been seen speaking out and talking about Bobby and Whitney's relationship, and at the same time, she forgets who she is married to.

As God is my Witness

All the things she's done AFTER the fact of Whitney not being here anymore it speaks for itself Whitney would NEVER do the things that she has chosen to do. On top of it all she was busted "speaking so ill of Whitney right after Whitney's death!" That alone GAVE PAT HOUSTON AWAY! Everyone we know has said, Pat married Gary Houston while "knowing" he was on drugs and had been on drugs for many years and far more years than my brother Bobby had ever did drugs altogether, so, what does that tell anyone about this woman Pat Houston. She is that type of woman that would make such a decision to marry such a man. It is because she saw the bigger picture with Whitney is why. She saw money ($$$$$) signs, is all. You cannot throw stones in a glass house if you live in a crystal clear one.

Everyone saw her as trying to ridicule Whitney for being on drugs, and then someone sent me a mug- shot photo on Facebook saying it was Pat Houston in a Florida prison, and they said that she was allegedly there for being on drugs. I believe they said that she had gotten some jail time back in the day, but to be honest, I honestly did not think it looked like her as I examined it. For a minute I thought it was her, and then I said, well, I'm not sure. My friends told me, yeah that's her, she just looks different is all. They actually wanted me to expose it to this world, but I did no such thing, because I am not interested in exposing anything or anyone unless I am 100% certain of it so, I passed.

What was strange to me and everyone else is, if Pat Houston hated drugs so much, why did she marry a man, who had been on them for all his life? Gary Houston had been on drugs far longer than Whitney because he is older than Whitney and Pat knew this. So, what does this say about her?

As God is my Witness

What she did to Whitney by talking about her, she did nothing but show the world who she is as a person, in my eyes. Jonathon Houston wanted the world to hear that tape so that we all got the real Pat Houston and not the person she tries to act like in the media whenever she is being interviewed and talking about Whitney pretending and acting as if she and Whitney were so close. I am a witness that there was not in any way a healthy relationship with her and Whitney ever and as long as I have known my sister Whitney Houston there was not ever anything there it is all a hoax between Pat and Whitney. I believe wholeheartedly that MAMA CISSY DOESN'T CARE BECAUSE PAT HOUSTON WAS A HANDLER FOR HER AND THAT IS WHY

NOBODY CARES OR IS DOING ANYTHING AT ALL ABOUT PAT DOING ALL OF WHAT SHE IS DOING WITH WHITNEY'S ESTATE. Whitney in my opinion did drugs because they forced her into doing drugs and made sure to keep them around her. I believe IT WAS ALL A BIG GAME THEY ALL PLAYED WITH WHITNEY'S LIFE ALL THIS TIME. Now that Whitney is gone, all I can see is Gary hanging around when he did come around, and even he was feeding Whitney these drugs. WE ALL ALREADY SAW MICHAEL HOUSTON ON OPRAH WHEN HE TOLD THE WORLD THAT HE WAS RESPONSIBLE FOR WHITNEY'S DRUGS. HE ALREADY SAID, WHEN THEY WERE YOUNGER, HE INTRODUCED WHITNEY TO DRUGS, AND I BELIEVE THEY TOOK IT FROM THERE AND MADE SURE SHE HAD THEM ALL THE TIME.

As God is my Witness

ALL OF THESE YEARS AND NO ONE EVER TRIED TO STOP HER? WHY? I BELIEVE I KNOW WHY. MY BELIEF IS THAT THEY WANTED IT THAT WAY. TOO MUCH HAPPENED TO WHITNEY AS A CHILD IN THAT HOME, AND IT WENT DOWN IN SECRET BECAUSE WHITNEY WAS BEING MOLDED INTO THE PERSON CISSY WANTED FOR CLIVE DAVIS AND THAT INDUSTRY, IS MY BELIEF AT THE END OF THE DAY. WHEN IT GOT WORSE, CLIVE STEPPED IN AND DEMANDED WAY TOO MUCH OF

WHITNEY, AND IT WAS TOO LATE. WHITNEY WANTED OUT! SHE WANTED TO LIVE HER LIFE THE WAY SHE WANTED TO WITHOUT BEING TOLD WHAT TO DO ALL THE TIME...AND I THINK, THEM, BEING USED TO HER SUBMITTING TO THEIR WILL, THEY DID NOT WANT THAT AND SO THEY SAW IT FIT TO MURDER HER AND MAKE MORE MONEY OFF OF HER DEATH BECAUSE THEY WANTED THAT FREEDOM "OF SPENDING HER MONEY WITHOUT HER AROUND, HANDS DOWN!" NOW, THAT IS THE WHITNEY HOUSTON STORY IN ALL TRUTH TO ME! I FEEL THIS, I BELIEVE THIS IN MY SOUL THAT THE HOUSTON'S WANTED HER DEAD SO THEY COULD HAVE THEIR WAY WITH HER MONEY, PERIOD.

I cannot see this any other way. The same thing goes for Pat Houston. In my eyes and what I witnessed is that she is a person who was there with her husband making sure he was doing what she and Mama Cissy was expecting him to do with Whitney, and she was his watch person making sure he was keeping Whitney on these drugs as well, and whenever he could get them for her.

As God is my Witness

Their problem was, Whitney woke up to all of them and didn't want drugs anymore and was really trying to live a good life for once. She was getting Bobby back and wanted her life back. I don't care what anyone says, THEY DID NOT LIKE THIS. Now, today, I am not certain, but it seems as if for the first time in the history of Gary's life, he is now today drug free. After all these years of him using drugs, I noticed him in a video someone sent to me, and he seemed sober. The first thing that came to my mind was, "Oh, well now Whitney is gone, so they got rid of her, and so now Pat forced him to stop using since there was no need for the drugs anymore."

BUT NO ONE STOPPED GARY OR WHITNEY IN THEIR EARLY AGES, WHY? BECAUSE IT WAS PART OF THE PLAN, I BELIEVE. I will always believe his job was to see to it that Whitney used and now that she's gone, Pat made him quit because she did not like Gary while he was using plus it was causing her the embarrassment. His excuse while Whitney was alive, was that it gave him the urge to 'keep' using as he was being that supplier for her for a long time. Something is telling me this, and it is what's in my mind today as I reflect back and remember things with all of them, and I see him lurking around Whitney back then. I believe that Ray J was put on her at some point and he did his job until Whitney would not be bothered with him anymore. All of what everyone has seen with Whitney Houston was all PLANNED AND PLOTTED OUT FOR THE DOWNFALL OF WHITNEY IN MY EYES. AND I CAN NOW SEE EVERY SINGLE PERSON FOR WHO THEY WERE AND THE PART THEY ALL PLAYED AGAINST WHITNEY.

As God is my Witness

AND I FEEL LIKE WHITNEY FIGURED IT OUT HERSELF, AND IT IS WHY SHE PASSED BRANDY THAT NOTE....Nobody will ever understand exactly what I am speaking of here AND IT IS BECAUSE YOU ARE NOT ME. I HAVE BEEN RIGHT THERE WITH THEM AND WITNESSED THESE PEOPLE AROUND WHITNEY AND SO I KNOW WHAT I KNOW. This world has no idea the job they did on Whitney's life and how they lurked around her and taunted her and my brother's life altogether. I am sure if my brother Bobby reads this book, he will use his mind and think hard on what I am saying and bear witness secretly, but yes, this is what he saw too. If he doesn't admit it it's OK, because it will only mean that he wishes to let it go, but I now have the big picture right before me because even I have awoken today as to what transpired before me when Whitney was alive. The tape that Jonathon presented of Pat Houston speaking so ill about Whitney showed the world just how Pat felt and who she really is. If we all went back and looked at all that Pat has said and done then compared to what she has done now and since Whitney was murdered, I believe we all would see it as Jonathon Houston, our families and I see it today. This is a very sad case that could only be investigated BY THE FEDS, hands down...

A lot of people have always asked me, why Gary does not ever do anything about his wife, Pat doing all that she does to his so-called sister, Whitney. My answer is that he feels the same way about Whitney as Pat does, and that is the sole reason, (and in reality, I am being nice by saying this) she does what she does and is able to get away with it. All of the Houston's are down with it, including Mama Cissy. She is the matriarch of it all. And I am literally crying with tears in my eyes as I am writing this right now, because I know that I am right, and I am so disappointed in Gary and how he did Whitney.

As God is my Witness

I love my brother God knows I do, but it saddens me because I have to tell the truth of what is real with them all. I never knew the truth about him not being related to Whitney until later though. They had me fooled as well, and then to look back and see him doing what he was doing, and acting the way he was acting, it all literally makes me just cry, because I now know the whole deal of them all and how they were conspiring against Whitney for her estate all this time, and that is so cold. ALL OF MY QUESTIONS ARE NOW ANSWERED TO ALL I SAW AND COULDN'T UNDERSTAND.

And there is a lot that I am not saying here. But they all have God to answer to. What people don't fully understand is how serious it was with Whitney and Gary being at odds with each other. This is why I believe that he was the one who struck Whitney in that hotel room along with a couple other people. I believe they blocked Whitney in that room and did not let her out as she did try to get away from them who jumped her in that hotel room. I believe it was Gary, Nick Gordon and Ray J that was in that room when Whitney took her last breath!

I have said that they are all against Whitney and you can tell by watching all their behavior BEFORE & after, and right after Whitney's death. They sold all of her things right after her funeral. INCLUDING HER CATALOG! I believe they were making deals before her funeral even started. At least Ray J was making deals right away and in people's face while her body was awaiting the authorities to come pick her body up from that hotel. Ray J has no excuses for his actions. He (Ray J) was found in that hotel room on that phone with a person talking about the six million dollars they were going to get from this Whitney Houston foundation he was creating in Whitney's name.

As God is my Witness

He was offering them six million! I wonder what he thought he was going to gain himself. The Houston's must of stopped him, because so many people were probably ready to boycott it right away. It would have also given them all up. I think the world would have gotten that whole picture of their plot and that book would have been open for everyone to see it in full color. I believe that Ray J was one of the handlers for Whitney AS WELL AS Pat and Gary. I believe they all hooked up to expedite the mission. He was trying to make this world think that he was cool with Whitney, but all along, he was nothing more than a handler, is how I see him and feel about the whole idea of him.

This is why I would tell any entertainer to please be careful who you accept around you and people you befriend today because people will come and pose as your friend, and be nothing more than an enemy that are only there to set you up. I always think about my mother's words, which were, you will never find anyone who will love you in this business. And no matter how nice you are to people when they come before you, it doesn't matter because they have one mission and one focus, and that is to get rid of you. You have got to watch people and take on no new friends if you are in this business. Not just anyone that'll walk up to you acting friendly. Now, if you meet people otherwise just be careful, they cannot be brought is all you have to do. Screen people well and be sure that you know who is who for real around you. Also, watch even those you've known a lifetime too. They can easily be brought for a small or great price to do you in baby. I don't care how much you think they like or love you; a lot of people are easy to be brought today because everyone loves that money. Whitney was surrounded by people in her own so-called family that she could not trust.

As God is my Witness

Whitney is not really Gary's sister. They have different mothers and fathers, which means, Pat and Gary Houston's daughter is carrying no blood of Whitney's either. Well, all you have to do is look at them and their daughter. This is easy to see anyways because none of them have anything of Whitney's. That is the main reason why love is not there with Gary and it's why he doesn't do anything to stop his wife Pat from doing all that she does with Whitney.

If Mama Cissy was not her real mother, Gary most definitely wouldn't be her brother by blood because Cissy is not her mother and Poppa John is not Gary's father, so there we have it. This is just a sad case and a very serious crime that has occurred with Whitney Houston's life, my niece's life, and also my nephew's life. They used Whitney for her voice and the money she could make for that family, is all. OK, let's go on...I do not want to give this too much of my energy because it is too depressing right now.

REHAB

Ma Brown and Cissy Houston, both had gotten together to put both Bobby and Whitney away in rehab. Mama Cissy did it so much worse than how Mommy did it with Bobby. Mommy was a bit gentle and did it to where Bobby just went in willingly because she spoke with Bobby and cried with everyone about it. I honestly believe that Whitney would have gone in that same way had Mama Cissy been just a bit gentler with her and not so demanding and hard with her. Bobby wanted the help anyway, so it may have made the difference there because he was ready at the end of the day. He was the one who was more willing because Bobby did not like drugs like that, and it wasn't hard for him to give them up, and he was always the one out of the both of them trying to give it up.

As God is my Witness

Yes, he was at one time very seriously trying to get Whitney to just come on and stop and go in. He even tried to quit several times before they decided to step in. He tried so hard to get Whitney to quit doing drugs, but Whitney kept saying that she was just not ready yet and did not want to stop. This is what people didn't know about Bobby and Whitney when they were doing drugs. Bobby was at least trying hard to stay away from drugs, I have to give it to him. Whitney would sometimes throw that up in his face telling him she wasn't ready and just making him feel bad during this time. I felt sorry for Bobby because I knew how hard it was for him, and he was continuing doing his best to stop and had actually stopped at one time and was doing really good.

The day that Whitney went into rehab was the day that Mama Cissy pulled up in a limo. Bobby was not home; I think he may have been on his way into the rehab center. Whitney and I were home, with Tina and Gary happen to be there that day for some strange reason. And now that I look back, he may have been communicating with Mama Cissy before she got there. He was probably there letting her know who was there and what was going on, because it wasn't really normal for Gary to be there, and it was pretty strange this day that he showed up. I have said that Whitney was never really that comfortable with him around, and she surely was not ever comfortable with his wife Pat ever coming around. So, she surely was not there this day.

Mama Cissy showed up out of nowhere bum- rushing Whitney by surprise. Whitney was not pleased with the way Mama Cissy came to her, so she was very rebellious this day. Mama Cissy pulled up, came into the house with this strange smirk and frown on her face and looking at Whitney, letting everyone know she meant business.

As God is my Witness

She wanted folks out of the way so she could talk with Whitney. She started with Gary, and told him to leave, then she told Tina to leave now! Tina grabs her stuff and leaves. After they both leave, it is just me and Whitney standing there with Mama Cissy. I was ready to walk out just to give them their space to talk. However, Mama Cissy says to me, "No, Lele you stay, you don't have to go anywhere!" So, I did not move, I just stayed. During this time Whitney is trying to get away from her. As Whitney is walking in the Kitchen she is cursing at Mama Cissy! She said, "GET THE EFF OUTOF MY HOME B&%$#! GET THE EFF OUT OF MY HOUSE NOW B! Mama Cissy is not moved at all by Whitney's screaming at her. She is just smirking her face up at Whitney and giving her strange looks without saying a word, and half smiling and grinning at her.

I kept looking at Mama Cissy, because I could not believe the faces she was making at Whitney. Whitney was extremely uncomfortable at this time, and she began running upstairs, and she kept yelling at Mama Cissy to stay clear away from her and get out of her home. I thought it was kind of odd and weird the way Mama Cissy was acting with Whitney while Whitney was screaming out of control at the top of her lungs. It was very unusual for a mother and daughter to me. It was most definitely something wrong with this picture, and I could not put my finger on it at that moment. Something that I had never witnessed between a mother and daughter. I saw a lot in my life, but this was very, very, very different. I am waiting for her to say anything such as, "I love you Whitney, and I am only doing this for your own good." She did not say anything like that to Whitney. Mama Cissy just kept staring at her with a smirk on her face without saying one word, and she kept following her around the house.

As God is my Witness

At this point, I am at a loss for words wondering how this is going to end. By this time, I am looking from Mama Cissy to Whitney, because I am in between the both of them and I am totally confused. Whitney is now making her way up the steps to run upstairs (unbeknownst to us at this time, to jump out of the window to get away from Mama Cissy and follow Tina)! Tina was leaving in a car or had the car running waiting on Whitney. Mama Cissy finally said, "No, don't you go up those steps come back here!" Suddenly, Whitney pointed her finger towards Mama Cissy and said, "IF YOU DON'T GET THE EFF OUT OF MY HOUSE B! GET THE F AWAY FROM MEEEEEEEEE B....!" I had never seen Whitney this upset ever! I had never seen Whitney curse and call her mother the B word either! When Whitney said that, I said, "Oh no Whitney!"

My first instinct was to protect Mama Cissy, because she is our elder and mother, of course. I could not just stand there and let Whitney talk to her like that. I said, "Whitney, come on sis, don't disrespect your mom like that!" And I said that because I do not care how we feel about our parents or any elders and what they do, we are not to disrespect them at all and at any time, regardless of what they say, how loud they yell, or whatever they decide to do. We are not to ever raise our voices or talk back to our parents, period.

If looks could kill, Mama Cissy and I would have been gone the moment that Whitney looked at the both of us after I said, no Whitney, this is your mother don't cuss at her! She looked at me as if to say, "That is not my mother!" That is exactly how Whitney looked at me! I felt so bad right then for Mama Cissy, because I never disrespected my mom like that and could not take Whitney doing it to hers right in front of me. Little did I know at this time, Mama Cissy is not really her mother at all.

As God is my Witness

Today, after analyzing Whitney's entire life, and all that I have learned thus far, today I can understand how Whitney was feeling after I found out everything she had gone through and what she had to endure with Mama Cissy. It was just things that I did not know right then and there while all this was going down. I knew that Mama Cissy and the Pastor had raped Whitney, but now I know, she is not her real mother! I knew that a real mother who was as close as Mama Cissy was with the Church could never do this to her own daughter, I said to myself! No real mother would do any of the things that Mama Cissy has done to Whitney altogether.

Whitney was getting ready to have a serious breakdown at that moment of her life. You would have to have been there to see it to understand where I'm coming from. Whitney had been through a lot of things that you will probably never get to hear or know about now that she is gone. At that very moment, before I could get it all out of my mouth, and when I said, don't yell at your mother, she gave me this look that I will not ever forget nor ever be able to explain to anyone. Now that I look back, I know what that look was on Whitney's face. After all that has transpired, I know now just what that look was all about, so help me God! It was a look from her as if to say, that is not my mother!

All of this happened before I knew anything about this woman Teresa Graves, who people are saying today, looks exactly like Whitney. I had never seen Whitney this upset with Mama Cissy. I was in total shock and could not say one word to Whitney. I could tell by her actions that this was the time when she was not going to listen to anyone because she was so upset. Whitney continues up those stairs without saying anything else to Mama Cissy, and she jumps straight out her window!

As God is my Witness

She would not allow Mama Cissy to come near her. She goes up the steps and into a room upstairs and jumps out of the window to follow our sister Tina, and wherever the two of them went from there is history. It was not long after that they found Whitney and Tina together in a hotel, and from there she went into rehab.

Long story short, she and Bobby were both now in Rehab. Now, once they went in, they both (in separate places) had to pick just one (1) family member that they chose to come and see them. The facility made them do this and asked both Bobby and Whitney to pick just one family member that they wanted to come up to see them. They both decided to choose me.

I now had the job of going up to see both of them whenever they needed me for anything, and no one else in either family on either side could come because they both picked me out of everyone in both of their families.

I had to visit and talk to both of them all the time or when they requested me, which was just about every day, I had to speak to their therapist, and on top of it, I had to be that person that went between the both of them when it came time to talk for them. I had a job to do, and I did it well with both of them. I had to talk to their nurses for them, relay messages to the family for them, and give reports and everything. This was a very emotional time for us all, but I had to do it for them because I love them both dearly. I cried many times leaving Bobby and Whitney because I wanted the best for them. Meanwhile, I also had full legal court ordered custody of my niece, Bobbi Kristina. They made Whitney sign papers on giving Krissy up to someone she trusted for full custody before she went in there, which was "court ordered" and she chose me.

As God is my Witness

That job was not bad at all because Krissy was used to being with me all the time anyway, and I enjoyed keeping her and making sure she was OK. It was just the way that this whole thing went down, which was crazy! I could not believe how they did Whitney when they came in and (what we call) bum-rush her! They threw her up against the wall, emotionally.

She is a grown woman who is very intelligent and has a mouth to speak, talk, and a mind to make decisions for herself. I am sure that had they done it in another fashion or respectful way, Whitney would have gone in along with Bobby, willingly like him, and there would never have been all the noise coming from her. But they treated her as if she was this crazy deranged woman who was uncivilized, incoherent, and incompetent, and I didn't like it myself.

I am still living with Bobby and Whitney during this time. And after Whitney completed her program, I believe Mama Cissy thought that rehab was not enough for Whitney, and so, she wanted and requested that Whitney go in another place for some more time. Even though Whitney felt that she was done and did not need it. It eventually turned out that she was right, because once she got clean, she remained that way. All this noise about her doing drugs and being found in that bathtub in the Beverly Hilton hotel was a big lie.

Whitney was clean and had been clean and they know it. Her room was staged by Pat and Gary Houston who made it look like she was still on drugs, if anyone thought that. Whitney was clean and I am a witness and so is the coroner who took her autopsy. Just look at her pictures the night before at the Kelly Price party! Whitney looked so good could not tell she wasn't doing drugs anymore? I can and none of them can fool me.

As God is my Witness

Plus, she was pregnant I had already revealed it because I couldn't wait to tell everyone. They did not want her to have that baby either! They didn't want that because it was my brother's baby! That is two children they killed of Whitney's! I am asking everyone to please go and look at her in the videos, the night before she was found in that hotel, where she sang with Kelly Price. She was clean and sober, and they tried to make it look like she was on drugs after her body was found. She looked really good, and Whitney had not done any drugs in a while and there was a reason why she hadn't done any drugs. She was pregnant again carrying my niece or nephew when she was killed.

Back to rehab ...OK, so, Mama Cissy had Pat Houston out of all people, help her with a "court order" where a judge signed off and forced Whitney into rehab immediately. It was so cold how it took place and how they did Whitney. I had left the house and was out that day, and Whitney called me frantically asking me to hurry up and get back to the house! I had no idea what was going on and I kept asking Whitney to tell me what was wrong! She would not tell me, she just kept saying, "SIS GET HERE RIGHT NOW AND PLEASE HURRY!" I rushed there, jumped out of my car, and ran into the house to see what it was that Whitney was rushing me for.

When I walked in, Pat Houston was standing off near the back wall with her hands in front of her as if she was some kind of soldier in the army just standing there looking really nervous to me, and trying to look as if she was innocent. Whitney's attorneys were also there, and they were standing there trying to get her to sign off on the court-ordered paperwork to put the custody of Bobbi Kristina in my name. When I entered the door Whitney was huffing and puffing pacing her floors! She said, "Here sis, sign this!"

As God is my Witness

This is going to allow you custody over Bobbi Kristina, while I am away at rehab! I looked around and saw that her attorneys and Pat were just standing there silently and not saying a word and just watching me sign everywhere Whitney had me to sign off at.

In my opinion, they all looked guilty as to how they did all of that to Whitney. This was another episode of Whitney being so upset and to the point where it looked to me as if she was going to have a breakdown. I believe in Whitney's mind, Pat thought that by rushing Whitney like that, she would have no choice but to let Pat take custody of Bobbi Kristina right then and there, but Whitney wasn't having it. She said, hell Naw! Pat is not going to have custody of my daughter like that. "She said, "My sister Leolah is the only one I trust to have custody over my daughter!" So, I signed the papers everywhere she wanted me to sign, which was in quite a few places. After Whitney and I went through all of this that day, Whitney said to me, "Did you see that witch Pat, she was standing there hoping I would throw her custody of Krissy BUT NEVER WILL I!"

I already knew that Whitney would never do that. Whitney was so upset this day. I knew that Whitney knew what she was doing, by having me sign in all those places, so, I just followed her lead and just signed. Afterward, Whitney told me then, that she was so tired of Mama Cissy putting Pat in her business! Whitney hated that more than anything! Whitney did not ever approve of Pat ever coming anywhere near her house or her family, so she was VERY upset that Pat was standing there with her attorneys (whom I do not trust) this day. She did not appreciate her being there and being around her, or even calling her phone.

As God is my Witness

She has cussed Pat out on so many occasions, and it had never been anything nice. (ASK MY BROTHER BOBBY HOW WHITNEY FELT ABOUT PAT HOUSTON, HE WILL TELL YOU)! She looked at Pat as this puppet for Mama Cissy, and she said that Pat always had other ideas about her as well where Whitney just could not put her fingers on it half the time. It seemed to Whitney that they were always doing something sneaky and against her all the time.

I know for a fact that Pat and Gary were both watching every move that Whitney and Bobby made. How does anyone follow newlyweds to a whole other state, and newlyweds who don't mess with you? I knew something was wrong with that picture!

It was already clear that this was the reason that Gary and Pat both moved to Atlanta Georgia, and following Whitney and Bobby everywhere they went, because they came there right after they got married, and it was obvious then. Red flags went up then, but I just could not place my finger on it. Our whole family thought this was doing too much, and we wanted to know why they had kept their eyes on Whitney so much AND NOW WE KNOW WHY. You do not bother and follow a grown woman and her newlywed husband to another city and keep watching them unless it is a bigger picture than what we can all see. It all came out in the end because Pat and Gary moved like two people who just did not care what they did to Whitney or how they were seen. They were bold with it.

OK, now Whitney is out of rehab. I am thinking, it is time for her to take back the guardianship from me, but 'she would not ever do it.' Long story short, after Whitney did her time in that rehab, I asked her on many occasions if she was ready to take back the custody of Bobbi Kristina, but she was not ever ready for some reason.

As God is my Witness

Therefore, to this very day, my signature is still on all that paperwork and court orders as Bobbi Kristina's "legal guardian." As I think about it today, "Whitney did that on purpose by not taking back in case anything should happen to her, I am sure she did. Now that she is gone, I can now see why she did things the way she did them. During the time they went into rehab, they were honestly at a point of changing their lives.

The divorce was something Whitney regretted ever doing and she said that. I think that there were certain people in her ear and forcing it on her at that time. They were trying to get rid of Bobby because they had plans to do to her what they eventually did to her. The both of them just needed to sit down and talk about where they had been and where they wanted to go from there with their lives and then stay married to each other. Everything was moving fast after the rehab, and people were in the way to destroy them, and they were successful in doing that.

The only problem here was, when Whitney found out it was a mistake that she made, she rushed to fix it and she finally did, because after she literally begged Bobby to remarry her, he finally said, yes, and they were getting back together, but they had already had a lead way on Whitney, I believe, and so it was too late, they killed her while she was in that hotel. I still to this day cannot believe she is gone, and my niece was killed and on top of that my nephew as well! These people are demons that have to answer to God, if they only knew. This is why you cannot allow anyone m your business or circle, I do not care who they are, you have to always keep people away from you and your family, period. People are not supposed to be in your business and that up close in your life like that where other people have control over you, and you have no control.

As God is my Witness

I think that is what got them so mad with her that she was getting back with Bobby, and they panicked. They both just needed people around them that they could seriously trust. They carried a lot of weight on them, and this is what I believe people took advantage of with them. I was surely one of the people they could both trust. My brother Bobby will always until the day that I leave this world, I will always be trustworthy and have his back. I can only speak for myself and my immediate family. Bobby and Whitney together had just been through so much and just needed people to genuinely love them and have their backs, and they needed to recognize who was who and who they can trust.

They were surrounded by people who were against them, and it wasn't from Bobby's side of the family, but Whitney's side. I do not know anyone from her side that was seriously happy for the both of them except for her Aunt Bey, her cousin Shelly, cousin Aleah and Dionne Warwick, and the Drinkards. Those are the only ones that I know of, and it all showed up in the end and after she was gone.

It had to be people who understood that they really loved each other and understood the real struggles in their lives that they lived and were experiencing as being the entertainers they were. You would have to have known what they have been through and were still going through at this time. If anyone has ever been around them like I was, then you would understand where I am coming from. There were too many people trying to run Whitney's personal and private life for one. You cannot do that to a person who is an adult and married. God will come after you Himself when people get like that. They had no business to be all up in Whitney's business like that and focusing on what she did and what she wanted to do with her life, it was her business and her life alone.

As God is my Witness

But like I said, she was always that money maker for her family and they would not let go of the grip on her. They had a grip that was too aggressive with Whitney in my opinion. I have said it loud that Whitney Houston was the slave trophy to her so-called Houston family members who all depended on her to make money and bring it home so that they could all live lavish lifestyles, hands down. See, people do not think you see them as they were out there. They don't think about the consequences they will come to face when they are out here doing others wrong. There is always someone whom God will place there as a witness.

I will tell you something about God and how He handles people like Mama Cissy, Pat, Gary and the rest of them. What goes around will soon come back around again, and when it does you can bet your very last dollar, it will be so much harder for the person 'doing wrong.' This is why people need to stop and think about what it is they're doing when they harm other people. God has always been in the business of chastising people and teaching them a lesson. He is now here striking at people even quicker now because time is at hand and the day of doing wrong has been over, and this is what I am here to tell people whether people care to listen or not.

It is even so sad the way Gary and Pat are even treating Gary and Monique's children. You must answer for even that whether they will believe it or not. Their children have been treated wrongly by their own father Gary Houston and their stepmother Pat. I have always loved my brother Gary just as if he was Bobby or Tommy. I never once thought that he had it in him to do the things he has done to his very own children. I am so disappointed in him for how he has treated his children. I cannot like a man that is that weak for a woman that he would allow her to tell him how he should deal with his children.

As God is my Witness

God knows that I hate to talk about things like this, but when it happens around you, you have to say something about it. The terrible thing about Pat and Gary doing this is that they do not care who knows what they do to Gary's children, and it becomes even sadder, and there is a need to talk about it. I just do not like people who do not treat their children properly. And I am not talking about petty stuff here. I am talking about some serious things that I witnessed myself that were so ugly to do to any human being.

For one, they were trying to keep Jonathon from seeing Krissy while she was in hospice. He paid his last monies ($500) that he had saved up to come to Atlanta to see his cousin and could not see her the whole time he sat up in hospice because they would not allow him. I had no idea of this until it was all over. I think that they were afraid that Krissy was going to wake up and talk and tell him something. These people were like demons walking around my niece's hospice room trying to regulate things. Also, when Jonathon tried to speak to the officers in authority in the beginning when Krissy was found, to tell the officers just what he thought might be good information for Krissy's case.

Gary, Pat and Donna Houston all lashed out at Jonathon and told him to shut up and keep his mouth closed! They said, "Whose side are you on!" They were angry that he was trying to help the authorities! This told me that yes, they had something to do with it. I could not believe my ears when Jonathon relayed this to us! I said, "Are you serious Jonathon? They did not want you to talk to the authorities and give them information that may have helped Krissy's case?" This told me that these people were not only glad and happy that my niece was where she was, but they may have had something to do with it.

As God is my Witness

What so called family or loved one will do this kind of thing? He said, "Donna, Pat, and Gary called him on the phone and yelled at him saying, "Whose side are you on, shut up and keep your mouth closed?" I said, "Dear God, WOW!" So, you mean to tell me that they were not on Krissy's side?

Did they have something to do with this, I thought? There is no other excuse that I can think of that fits this kind of behavior. Of course, Jonathon wanted the authorities to know what Krissy said the day before she was found in her bathtub! Of course, he thought it would be good for them to know exactly what was going on with her and what state of mind she was in and what she said to him that day. But these people and/or culprits did not want the authorities to know what went on with her because they had something to do with it, I believe. And had he continued speaking to them he would mess them up and reveal something that would lead to them, the Houston's, is what I get out of that.

Those in authority needed to hear this! Are you kidding me? These people are extremely evil to say such words while my niece was laying there dying. I could not wait to tell the world this news because it's wrong to do. This made me feel like none of them cared at all that even Whitney was gone either.

Then for little Gary, Whitney's brother, Michael's son to say, "That's what Krissy gets!" He said that when Jonathon told him that Krissy was in the hospital dying because she was found in her bathtub. These are all the Houston's whom Whitney Houston took very good care of, reader.

As God is my Witness

Can you imagine what was going on in Krissy's mind as she was getting beat down in her living room by Nick Gordon, knowing that Pat Houston, Nick Gordon, Donna Houston and Gary Houston had something to do with her demise? I am sure that Krissy got it, and it all came to her as she was stuck in that house at that moment. I hate to think of it because I am so upset that I couldn't be right there with her and her mother. None of this would have ever happened on a Brown's watch! Not in a million years! According to Jonathon, little Gary was angry at Krissy because he thought that she should give them money right away after her mother was found dead! I have never seen people so hungry for money after being so spoiled and having it all.

I am sure that wherever these people are today, God is dealing with them in His own special way. I do not know, nor do I understand what these people have been eating in their lives. However, in my opinion, they have such a beast and animalistic spirit and soul to me. I had never witnessed a family being so wickedly mean and having so much animosity towards an innocent person that has done nothing to them. My niece was not even given counseling for her grieving for her mother's death. They had no regard for her mourning her mother's death at all and did nothing to help her towards that. Bobbi Kristina needed love, not people surrounding her talking about how much money she should give them. How can you say that about someone you are supposed to love? Well, there is no love at all if anyone is wise enough to understand these kinds of people. They did it because all of them were a part of the demise of Whitney and Bobbi Kristina, is how I feel about this. I mean, you cannot make this kind of stuff up.

I would not dare put something on anyone that did not belong to them. All of Whitney's family had it made when Whitney was alive without ever having to worry about any monies.

As God is my Witness

Whitney loved that young boy little Gary, as if he was her own son. She gave him the world when she was alive, so I cannot understand the greed and the attitude of this family over her money. Why is everyone so stuck on her money the way they are? I am asking but of course, I already know the answers because I investigated everything in this case. While Krissy was in hospice, they treated her and Jonathon Houston so badly about caring about his own cousin. Of course, Krissy would have wanted Jonathon to see her. If these people were not demonic people, I do not know what demonic means. What hurt me so bad was that Jonathon spent his last $500 to catch a flight to get into Atlanta from Los Angeles. It was the last of the money that he had saved up for his schooling. A school that he gets "no help" paying for.

When he gets all the way here to Atlanta, they do not allow him in to see his own cousin Krissy who is laying up in hospice "where they put her!" I was in hospice and saw Jonathon when I walked in. I assumed he had seen Krissy because he was sitting there with the rest of the family. I did not know that they were not allowing him in, and he had not been in. When I walked in, my thoughts were that everyone in there had already been in and seen Krissy. See, Jonathon is a very quiet and humble young man. The kind that doesn't bother anyone, and he's a very respectable young man who is well-mannered at all times. Therefore, he would not make noise and commotion about it. Had I known they did this to him I would have made sure he saw his cousin. I just had no idea until a much later date. It goes on and on about the things they have done to Jonathon. I had never understood why Gary and Monique separated in the first place. I later found out that Monique left him because she was tired of the bad treatment and all the unfairness going on in their lives.

As God is my Witness

Monique is that Michelle Obama type of woman "for real!" She is a woman of class and integrity, and she walks with her head held high at all times, while being so head-strong! And she has never allowed this world to take her down into the pits with them. She is a woman who demands respect, and she gives it as well. She has always been one of those women who loves God and is careful with who she chooses to allow in her space. I like that about her because she has a focus that she will not let anyone take her away from. Monique has always been my type of person. Whitney loved Monique too, she really did.

Unfortunately, I do not see anything like that about Pat. Anytime people steal another's person's name just to be seen and crave attention from people in the world there has to be an imbalance somewhere in them. She is comfortable with Gary and all the games and secrecy they walk around with. So, that tells you right there the mindset of this individual without having to do too much thinking of why. Monique and Gary seemed to be a good strong couple when I first met them being together. Monique was that type of woman who more than likely did everything she could to encourage Gary to get clean and stay that way. She was on a mission to help him get clean when she was with him.

I believe that Gary is soon to get a rude awakening from Pat and so is Donna and so is Pat herself. Anytime you live your life the way these people have it is only one way out when you do not repent with the Master. The God of this universe and time is always on time. None of them have any idea what they are going to experience for the evil they have done, but then again, they may already know. Monique and Gary have three children together to ensure their well-being.

As God is my Witness

When Monique was trying to get Gary long term help, Mama Cissy and some other family members turned on her and did not stand by her side when she needed him to go into certain programs. Where was that support for a woman with three children at? Monique has been through a lot with Gary, and I know I was not there to see all of it, but from what I know, heard and seen altogether, it is so unjust and unfair for any human being to have to suffer and go through what she did.

There is a lot that this world just does not know about these Houston's. Just think of how they all did Whitney by saying they needed her in a program. My thing is they all wanted her there, only so that they could control her with getting that money, because they needed her to continue making that money for the family as she always has been. Yet, it never seemed to me that Mama Cissy was too concerned with Gary going into a program. Could it be because he is not bringing any money into their home like Whitney was? Perhaps this is why she did not bother to ask him to go into a program when she came up from New Jersey to force Whitney into one. Her sons were on drugs

longer than Whitney, so why was there no concern for them, I wonder? If you are going to care for one child, should not the next child be loved enough to get him help as well? Gary surely needed it even more so at the very same time they came for Whitney. I wonder to this day why Gary was skipped over and not given the same attention. It was not long after that Whitney bore witness that she now knew who Jesus was! I had never been so shocked in my life! Whitney and I used to study the Bible together.

As God is my Witness

<u>WHITNEY BEARS WITNESS OF ALLAH GOD AND JESUS!</u>

I love the Bible and you cannot be a Muslim and not read and study that Bible. You have to know that Bible front to back when you are a student of Minister Farrakhan's. The Honorable Minister Louis Farrakhan will tell you that. She and I both loved to study the Bible together. Whitney was interested in Islam after we had studied so much together. I never remembered ever opening the Quran with her sitting in front of me. Yet, I would quote scripture from the Quran and repeat what it said many times to her.

It was always the Bible with me and her because I remember Farrakhan saying, "You cannot tell a man if he is wrong about what he believes in unless you read his book, meaning holy book that he believes in." And I have always studied the Bible just as much as I study my Quran. I remember visiting a Church one Sunday, and this woman tapped my shoulder and said, "It's good to see your Bible beat up!" She said that because she knew that I was Muslim, I guess from the garment and head-piece that I was wearing, and yet, I was in their Christian Church that Sunday, standing up clapping and bearing Witness to what the Pastor was saying this day.

I was also asked to speak by their Pastor, so I spoke in their Church as well, and spoke to the whole congregation, to let them know how much Minister Farrakhan teaches us to visit other Churches and worship with other people anywhere we are invited. I talked with them about how there is only one God, and we all have our own way of worshipping Him, and that was OK. They all thanked me for my speech and appreciated me being there and even offered me to come back to their Church anytime I was ready.

As God is my Witness

I did that often because love to go around to different places of worship no matter what religion people are, I love any house of God's. But I just wanted to say that because I felt you needed to hear that, I never opened my Quran in front of Whitney, and she stood before me, AND AS ALLAH IS MY WITNESS! SHE STOOD RIGHT IN FRONT OF ME AND SAID, OH MY GOD LELE! ELIJAH MUHAMMAD IS THE JESUS!!! OH MY GOD HE IS THE JESUS!!! I said, "Yes, Whitney He is indeed!" She said, OH MY GOD, I HAVE TO TALK TO MINISTER FARRAKHAN! She could not sit down after that, she was pacing the floors in her living room. It was late at night and too late to call Minister Farrakhan right at that time.

She bore witness that Allah was God, and that Jesus was The Most Honorable Elijah Muhammad ON HER OWN THIS DAY! She understood who The Honorable Minister Farrakhan was too. We studied that Bible this night together because I wanted her to see just where Jesus was at in her Bible. Yet, I had never said this to her this night as we studied together, and she got all of that with the help of almighty God- Allah. He gave it to her that evening! Allah had to give it to her for her to say like that. I don't know at what point she got it but she got it that night for sure and as God is my witness! I WAS SOOOO HAPPY TO HEAR HER SAY THIS!

There are too many Christians who are walking around, and they miss it in this country as they read that Bible. I wanted her to seriously focus in and understand what she was actually reading because a lot of people won't even admit it, or tell you, but they really can't understand their book (Bible). I didn't either at one time in my life when I was studying as a Baptist. I would get stuck all the time not knowing what this or that meant.

As God is my Witness

It was not until I studied Islam and read my Quran and then went back into the Bible, that I finally understood the Bible. The Quran and the Bible are basically saying the same thing, but unless a Christian reads that Quran, they may never understand what their reading in their Bible.

Whitney Houston said it best. I don't care how long a person goes without ever looking in that Quran, I do not believe they will ever understand what they are actually reading in their Bible until they do. I once seen an article where they talked about how I, Bobby Brown's sister was trying to convert Whitney to Islam. First of all, let me say this and please hear me. It is totally against the religion of Islam to try to convert or talk someone into being a Muslim. First of all, ALL BLACK PEOPLE IN THIS COUNTRY ARE ALREADY MUSLIMS. WE DON'T KNOW IT OR MAY NOT EVER COME TO BELIEVE IT, BUT OUR FOR-PARENTS WERE ALL MUSLIM'S WHEN WE FIRST GOT OVER HERE IN THIS COUNTRY. YES, INDEED THIS IS THE TRUTH OF US COMING OVER HERE IN THE BEGINNING SAYS MINISTER FARRAKHAN AND I DO NOT EVER DOUBT ONE WORD COMING FROM HIS MOUTH, EVER. SO, I CANNOT MAKE ANYONE ANYTHING THEY ALREADY ARE. YES,

INDEED, EVERY SINGLE BLACK MAN AND WOMAN IN THIS COUNTRY CAME FROM A PARENT THAT WAS MUSLIM BEFORE WE WERE CHRISTIANS IN THIS COUNTRY. OUR SLAVE MASTERS BEAT AND KILLED US INTO EVERYTHING WE HAVE KNOWN SINCE BEING OVER HERE.

As God is my Witness

WHETHER WE LIKE IT OR NOT THAT IS WHAT HAPPENED TO US. THEY TORTURED OUR PEOPLE UNTIL WE WALKED AROUND 'CLOSING OUR HANDS' TO PRAY LIKE THEM. WE AS MUSLIMS, WE HAVE ALWAYS OPENED OUR HANDS (TO RECEIVE OUR BLESSINGS) TO PRAY. OPEN HANDS ARE LIKE OPENING YOUR ARMS TO HUG AND LOVE ON SOMEONE, RIGHT? WELL, IT IS THE SAME WITH PRAYER. BEFORE YOU PRAY, YOU POSITION YOURSELF WITH OPEN ARMS, AND YOU MUST KEEP YOUR HANDS OPEN TO RECEIVE WHATEVER IT IS YOU ARE ASKING GOD FOR, AND IT MAKES PLENTY OF SENSE, DOESN'T IT?

THAT IS WHY WE PRAY WITH OPEN HANDS. AND THEY BEAT OUR PARENTS UNTIL WE SAID WE WERE CHRISTIANS JUST LIKE THEM. YES INDEED. NONE OF US WERE CHRISTIANS BEFORE WE GOT OVER HERE, LET THE TRUTH BE TOLD. BUT GOD IS ONE AND THE TRUTH HAS SET US FREE AND NOW WE CAN GO BACK TO OUR FATHER WITH OPEN ARMS AS HE HAS OPENARMS TO RECEIVE US.

I only wrote in caps here so that you see these words well. Please know that I am not yelling. Back to forcing someone to become a Muslim. No, we do not try to force our religion on anyone. Second, Whitney used to call me to the table to hear what I had to say about Islam. She was just as interested in it as I was interested in teaching her. She was the one who initiated it after watching me and learning what she did about what I was telling her. Overall, she saw something in me that made her know that it had to be a good and better way of life that I was practicing compared to what she knew about me. She was very curious and wanted to learn more.

And she did, and so, she also came to understand it the more we studied; and this night she got it all in and God showed her something to snatch her attention and she was now aware! Whitney got it in that very moment of us studying, and she was so happy and so full at the same time. We both had tears in our eyes as she kept saying, Elijah Muhammad is THE JESUS LELE! And she was 100% certain, I could tell by the way she said it to me. Whitney Houston was awoken on that day. I wish I had of written that date down, but we were just so excited I wasn't even thinking about a date. I thank almighty God-Allah for allowing me to see my sister stand before me and bear witness like that. Nothing could have made my day better that day. I said praise be to Allah the real and true God of this universe and time. Whitney Houston was so happy this evening. I knew she would have to GET IT someday soon though.

She felt like a lot of other entertainers were starting to not only study Islam, but they were also following the religion of Islam, and they love it, and so she was very curious to get to know what it was that was so good about it. She would ask me, "Why is everybody following Islam nowadays?" I said, it's because people are waking up Whitney to the truth is all, and they know that something is wrong with the way things have always been here being in this land. On top of it, it is the real religion of ours AND God's.

I said, Whitney, Islam only means peace beloved." It is a peaceful and such a beautiful religion, I told her. We talked about how even Michael Jackson and a whole lot of other entertainers were also studying Islam today. I said, Whitney, a lot of people do not usually get it until after everything else has failed them in life, were told. She asked me, why I loved it so much.

As God is my Witness

I said, for me, I always felt something was wrong with the Bible, and I always believed that it had been tampered with for some reason. I said, Whitney, this is the proper religion of God, trust me, you will see. I said, this is the reason why it is said in the Bible that THE TRUTH WILL SET YOU FREE! The prophets knew we were going to be lied to, coming over here, and so, they knew that our slave masters were going to take every single thing away from us while enslaving us back then.

I said, they took our God, our religion, our culture and even our names away from us. And this is why in the Bible it is said that GOD WILL GIVE US OUR NAMES BACK! They named us and gave us their names. I said, and you have to remember that all of this took place over 400 years ago, so today when people hear Islam it seems so foreign to them, and that is because it has been so long ago that none of us could not relate to the truth coming to us like this, unless we have studied our history to know. And so, they expect God's children to recognize the truth when it comes and I do indeed. I bear witness that the time is NOW and Islam is the true religion of God's hands down.

We all have no excuses because the truth is now here in the world with us. Some are listening while others are not but it is the true religion of God's, and all the scientist and scholars know it, and that is why they will never sit down with Farrakhan at a table and try to challenge Him or say that He is lying because THEY CAN'T! They KNOW THAT HE IS TEACHING US THE TRUTH in this land. Islam has not been a secret to any of the scholars and scientist here in this land. Minister Farrakhan broke it down and taught us the time and it all makes so much sense to anyone with just even a little bit of sense and intelligence.

As God is my Witness

Our parents suffered so much back then that they prayed and asked God for deliverance, and now it is HERE! God sent us our brother Farrakhan, just as it is written in our holy Bible. I don't know why people can't believe that after all that is already written in our Bibles.

God sent us a Man, His Son and our brother who looks exactly like our Father. A divinely spirited Man who He made in His image and after His likeness of Himself, as He made us as well. It is already written that His own people would not accept Him. The Bible talks about how He won't even be respected in His own home, but yet, people from all over this earth will crown Him as THE MESSIAH! That is because they are educated and wise to the facts. That is just how Farrakhan is recognized by THE WISE MEN and it should tell us something. We are a people who have to wake up now. It's all over and we still want to stay in our graves. We just have to wake up now and understand where we are at.

Well, I do RECOGNIZE Him and I do understand who He is and His mission, and I am a tiny little vessel in this earth who is wise enough to see something that makes a WHOLE LOT OF SENSE at the end of the day. And so, I am only here as a little warner to people for the beautiful things that are about to take place in the coming of God Allah. He has come to get His people, like it or not and ready or not.

Now we have a way back home to our real Father God. And last, because of all the affliction and oppression that we had been under being over here in this strange foreign land, all that we have gone through and endured for so many years, we have lost our way and do not know what it's like to really serve our God anymore.

As God is my Witness

And so, YES OF COURSE it makes all the sense in this world to me, to have a Man born of a woman to teach us how to come back to God and serve Him. I cannot understand why some people can't see this! People really have a problem with following A MAN OF GOD'S! HOW CRAZY AND RIDICULOUS ARE WE TO THINK WE DON'T NEE ANYONE! The white man has made us into savages in this earth and you mean to tell me that you can't understand that we NEED LEADERSHIP IN 2024? And it isn't just ANY leadership. This is a REAL MAN OF GOD'S I CANNOT UNDERSTAND WHY PEOPLE CAN'T SEE THAT LIKE I DO! WOW! Who would be upset with that and think we don't need to follow such a Man of God's? DID NOT JESUS SAY, PICK UP YOU CROSS AND "FOLLOW" HIM? If you can't do that, whoever you are. I feel so sorry for you. And I say that with all due respect.

It makes A LOT of sense because we have been under Satan's rule for over 400 years! WE HAVE TO BE TAUGHT ALL OVER AGAIN BECAUSE SATAN HAS MADE LITTLE DEVILS OUT OF US ALL, IS WHY. Of course, we need someone to teach us how to come back to God. And so, when we learn how this all came about, we can appreciate it and be obedient soldiers for God without fretting our faces up acting like we don't need it. Boy, we are some hard-headed and rebellious people I tell you.

BACK TO WHAT I WAS SAYING ALTOGETHER. IN ORDER FOR GOD TO DO THAT, WE NEEDED A STRONG LEADER (Farrakhan) TO STAND UP AGAINST THE DEVILS THAT ENSLAVED US. WELL, OF COURSE WE ARE DEALING WITH THEIR CHILDREN TODAY BUT IT IS ALL THE SAME BECAUSE THEY HAVE NOT CHANGED IN THE LEAST...AS WE CAN SEE.

As God is my Witness

THE MOST HONORABLE ELIJAH MUHAMMAD DID IT
FIRST AND THEN HE PREPARED FARRAKHAN AND SENT
FARRAKHAN TO CONTINUE THE WORK RIGHT HERE IN
THIS COUNTRY. AND FARRAKHAN HAS DONE A
MIRACULOUS JOB AND DONE IT SO WELL THAT I AM SURE
THAT GOD WHOSE PROPER NAME IS INDEED ALLAH, IS SO
VERY PLEASED WITH HIM, MAKE NO MISTAKE ABOUT IT,
EVER. YES, BRING US BACK TO GOD THE PROPER WAY
FARRAKHAN! AND THAT IS WHAT I BELIEVE IN WHILE
SOME OTHERS MAY NOT THINK WE NEED ANOTHER MAN
TO SHOW US THE WAY. YOU ARE WRONG AND SO WRONG
I CAN'T EVEN BELIEVE THE IGNORANCE OF US AS A
PEOPLE NOT BELIEVING WHAT IS REAL, EXACT AND
RIGHT ON TIME.

I have always thought it was very ignorant and arrogant to
think that we can remain the way we are and as we have been taught
by our slave masters. No, we have to learn all over again how to come
back to God and serve Him, of course! Before it is all over, this whole
entire world will come to Islam because God has come for His people.
Only thing is, if you don't want Him, He will not force you. He is here
for the people that want Him, regardless of your skin color or what
you have done in this world, if you want God, of course He wants you,
period.

BUT WE MUST BE WILLING TO ALSO REPENT FROM
OUR EVIL. We have to remember that we cannot continue hurting
other people AND CHANGE the way we think and do things in this
world. That's all we have to do it is very simple. We also have to
"want" to be better and then just STRIVE to do better.

As God is my Witness

Again, I was telling Whitney that Islam means peace and it was always what Jesus said, whenever He left from amongst people before and after he spoke to them. He always said, "As-Salaam-Alaikum!" This is how you greet in meeting someone, and it is how you say good-bye when leaving someone. It means, I wish God's peace on you! There is only one God of course, and we just all have our own way of devoting our love to Him. Therefore, we call Him by the name we love best. It doesn't matter what religion you are there is only one God.

God is called by many names as it is written in our books. I have always tried to tell people, my children call me Mommy, my father gave me the nickname, Buddy-Buddy, and people I grew up with call me Lele including my mother. However, I am one person. The same is true with God, whom we call by many names, He is one but is called by many names. I am one of those people who can go to any Church, any Mosque, or any synagogue in this entire world to worship God and study with anyone without being nervous or afraid at all. When you're a convicted person and you believe wholeheartedly, you do not worry about "where" you go to worship your Father... I can go to any house of God today and be so comfortable because I am 100% positively sure that Allah is THE GOD.

I am convicted in my belief, so I am not bothered by anyone else's religion, and it is a pleasure to worship with others. I can study with anyone in this world including an atheist because I respect anyone's religion and choices in this life.

Furthermore, I am not afraid to walk in the house of God anywhere on this planet, because I am convicted in my belief When you are convicted in your belief, and you understand who God is, and you understand His mission, you know that there is absolutely nothing in this universe to fear. When you have the proper understanding of God, there is nothing to fear when you walk inside of any Church, Synagogue, and any Mosque or anywhere in the world and sit down.

Therefore, Whitney and I, having different opinions, ended up coming together as sisters, studying together more often, and agreeing with one another and seeing eye to eye with one another after all. When that finally happened between us two, I was so happy! Right before the divorce, Whitney called me on the phone one late evening asking me to come over to keep her company. She did this a lot, always wanting to study the Bible together with me. Sometimes we would argue about it, but it was always in the best manner.

We would discuss things regarding what is being said in both books. There were times when we had peaceful studies without arguing. This night she and I were studying together, and talking about things that were in the Bible. I was explaining to her who The Honorable Minister Louis Farrakhan is, how she can find Him in the Bible, and who The Most Honorable Elijah Muhammad is, and how she can find Him in the Bible as well as Master Fard Muhammad. As Allah-God is my witness, after I said something about them to her, and then pointing it out in the Bible and explaining it to her, she became overly excited! Yet, she got quiet for some reason. She finally got it and understood this night.

As God is my Witness

She stood there and I could tell her mind was thinking about what I had just said. She rushed to the guest bathroom, stayed for a moment, and then came out speaking in tongues! She came rushing out of that bathroom speaking very loud in tongues, and so loud and so passionately that I honestly thought she was crying! In fact, I never understood when people spoke in tongues like this, because I just did not ever understand what they were actually saying. But this day, when Whitney did it, I was looking directly into her eyes. I was shocked at how passionate her spirit was in delivering this speech in tongues to me. She had tears rolling down her face and she just kept shouting that The Most Honorable Elijah Muhammad was the Jesus! I mean, I had never seen someone so passionately doing this! As God-Allah is my witness, Whitney Houston was standing right in front of my face bursting out loudly ...and IN TEARS!

She says, OH MY GOD LEOLAH! ELIJAH MUHAMMAD IS THE JESUS OF THE BIBLE! HE IS THE REAL JESUS AND HE IS ALIVE!! LEOLAH, THIS IS WHAT YOUR SUPPOSED TO BE DOING!!! OH MY GOD, OH MY GOD DEAR JESUS, I GOT IT! HE IS THE JESUS, LEOLAH!

I had never seen Whitney being so serious about something! She meant every word she was saying to me at this time she began crying while still shouting! Then I began crying and we just cried together! I said, "Yes, of course, Whitney! That is what I have "been" doing. I have been telling everyone that He is the Jesus who everyone has been waiting and looking for, and yes, HE IS ALIVE AND WELL TODAY!" I said, "It is exactly what I have always been trying to tell you, Whitney!"

As God is my Witness

It was a surreal moment in time. I had wished that someone else could have been there to witness this with us! Were both so full this evening. This was a very emotional moment for me and Whitney. At first, I could not believe my ears and eyes! I could not believe that Whitney Houston was standing before me saying the Most Honorable Elijah Muhammad is the Jesus this whole world has been looking for. Whitney was saying all of this and looking me straight in my eyes. We were both standing there crying and hugging each other as she bore witness that The Most Honorable Elijah Muhammad was the Jesus of this time, and the Jesus this whole world had been looking for.

Then she knew who The Honorable Minister Louis Farrakhan was. Whitney was so fired up she was shaking and crying and having a moment. This was so surreal. I kept saying, Allah-U-Akbar over and over again, which means "God is the Greatest!" I kept saying it because I was not sure if she would ever get it while we had been studying together because I was happy! Once Whitney got that, her whole face was completely different, and she was a new person to me at that moment. I believe this helped her to stay clean as well, little did people know about her. Whitney was a different person I am sure to a lot of people, and it was because she was now getting ready and preparing herself for God.

I think overall, she was also running away from the Houston family that she no longer wanted to be a part of, because of the reason she knew they were only around her for. Whitney Houston felt unloved with the Houston's. And I say this again, with all due respect. And I do not mean to sound harsh, but the only way to tell her true story is to just simply tell it. There is no way to sugar coat this it is what it is at the end of the day.

As God is my Witness

Anyone who knows me, they know that I always speak truth regardless to whom or what. I pray to God that I have not made anyone feel upset or angry at me because this is not about me. This is about a woman who was suffering with her identity, which no one seemed to ever want her to come in contact with.

Whitney Houston couldn't even be herself and it was literally killing her to play this role that everyone was so used to seeing. She was over that, and it is a crying shame that they killed her all because of her money and her estate that they snatched away from her daughter by murdering her as well. I am sorry but this is the truth of it all. Had she lived, she would have been a Muslim no doubt about it!

I am just so grateful to God that she got it before she left this world. Her light was turned on right before she was killed, and she had come into this new knowledge of God, and it happened before they took her life. I pray to God that He is pleased with her. It may have been why she wanted her husband back too, because she wanted a new life for herself with Bobby, and she was now finally ready. I really don't believe that she used drugs anymore after that night of our last Bible study together.

That was when I believe Whitney began keeping herself together and clean off drugs. I am so grateful to Allah that she bore witness that The Most Honorable Elijah Muhammad is the Jesus that this whole world has been looking for. She said, "Wow, it's right there in the Bible for people to see!" We both just fell into each other's arms...and both of us were just in so many tears! We cried like we had never ever cried before, together! We must have held each other for about 1 to 2 whole minutes after that, and she continued to say it repeatedly.

As God is my Witness

I had always had a feeling that Whitney would one day finally get it because she loved God so much, and I always knew this about her. I really and truly miss my heart-to-heart talks with her. We cried together on a few other occasions that I cannot go into right now, but not like this one. We had always told stories of the good, bad, and ugly of our lives, but this evening was so much different for us. She felt God and she was awoken because Allah-God gave it to her as he wanted her to know Him. All that stuff about me forcing her was not true because no one can just force anyone to come into Islam. You have to want it yourself if your eyes are open to accept your own and your God, period.

Whitney suffered and endured some horrific traumas during her life, but she never gave up on believing in her God. She knew her Bible front to back. I am just so glad and grateful to God that she bared witness before her life was taken and she went to our Father. Regardless of what we ever experienced in this life, we are taught in our Bibles and Holy Qurans to always love and respect our people, and we are to do it even more than they love and respect us, regardless of what we go through with them.

Yes, it was hard talking to her in the beginning of our discussing God and Jesus. I never imagined Whitney ever doing that and saying that to me, and I did not think she would ever get it, because she called herself a die-hard Christian without understanding that we were both believers in Jesus and I was only there to awake her brain to reality. We used to argue because she was always confused as to what I was really trying to say to her. She just didn't get it at the time.

CHAPTER 12
WHITNEY'S FUNERAL

This night was a night that God brought us both together, and I honestly kept saying in my mind, I don't want to argue with her tonight because she is going to be loud and tell me that Jesus is her Lord and blah, blah, blah. LOL! I was humbled all the time, and t was nothing like that. After I pointed it out like I never did before, she finally got it and she was shouting for joy because she

Really now understood. And when that happens you can't deny it because it is there right in your face to bear witness. I thanked Allah-God for a long time since her death, and I still thank Him to this day that Whitney and I had that experience. Not many people know that Whitney had a closed casket at her funeral. Her body viewing was the place where you could see her, but her funeral was a closed casket funeral because they did not want anyone to see that Whitney was beaten to death after so many people saw her beat up face at her body viewing. But it's OK, I am here to set the record straight and tell the truth. With all that has been said, and for what I am about to say. We are not God, and more than anything, we are not perfect people, and we all have our own flaws, mistakes and demons.

None of us stand without sin, and so at this time, I humbly ask you reader to simply try as hard as you can to understand just why I have felt it necessary to tell this story for the world to hear. I am not revealing this information to discredit or talk down on anyone, and especially Mama Cissy, but instead, I am speaking to give you an inside look a Whitney Houston's real and true life as it was because it is the truth first that counts for something. Second, because we need to change and do better as a people. What she had to deal with coming up as a young girl, and who she was as a person and how she endured the pain and agony of being a Houston child was far more painful than anyone can imagine. I can't even explain it all right here, let the truth be told. It is so much that has happened and so much they have done to her. This book is nothing compared to what Whitney really went through. It is so important to know the real Whitney Houston and how it was for her living with who she was.

There are going to be some of you who are not going to believe this, while so many more will surely believe it beyond a shadow of a doubt. In any event, again, I do not speak out of anger or emotions but instead for the sake of God and purposes of getting this truth out to this world so that Whitney Houston may have justice once and for all.

This world needs to know that Whitney Houston was a person who stood facing a lot of demons that surrounded her life. She was born into a world where she was not given a chance to choose her own life and what she wanted out of her own life. She was brought into a family that made decisions for her at a very young age, not knowing for some time who she really was and where she really came from. It startled me when I found out the truth about her life. I asked myself, why did not the people she loved and knew as her family not love her enough, and just enough to simply stand and help her out of a situation that was forever haunting her and making her uncomfortable. Why didn't she not have anyone around her that loved her enough to just make the proper sacrifices to make her life a lot better than what was forced upon her, knowing who she was as a person.

As God is my Witness

I never understood why Whitney called me her "Angel" because it came out of nowhere one day around Thanksgiving time. There were many people in our presence when she said it and kept repeating it to me, and even they asked her why she kept calling me her angel? Whitney never answered them, nor did she ever answer me, as I tried asking her many times why, was she calling me her angel. She would stand there staring me directly in my eyes without blinking, and while looking at me with such a serious look on her face, as if she knew something that I or no one else knew.

Today I understand it as God giving her a sign of something, or perhaps she may have had a dream that He sent her of me, fighting for her or something, I don't know but I'm here. I am here fighting for her and my niece and my nephew today, to bring them some justice, and if nobody else steps up to help me in this, it's totally OK with me because the God that I believe in has His many soldiers with me, and He has His own way of bringing justice to every one of us and I trust Him with everything in me! And more importantly, it is He, God, who is most definitely leading me to do what it is I am doing today.

This world has no idea what Whitney Houston really suffered as a human being and how she so boldly dealt with it all her life. The media has had their chance and wasted a whole lot of ink whitewashing her name, telling lies about who Whitney Houston was and so on. They have taken a lot of time to do a lot of damage to such a beautiful angel that gave herself to this world. They have chosen to ignore the fact that not only I have said that Whitney did not have any drugs in her system, but the coroner who did her autopsy also stated that she did not have drugs in her system.

As God is my Witness

He said that it was only a "minut amount" of drugs that she had, and it is not hard for us to see that she was indeed clean if we would pay attention to her, as she was partying and singing with Kelly Price the evening before her death. You can see it right there that she was clean!

Whitney was a Queen who literally gave up her life to make others happy in this world. She knew how to make others feel good listening to her voice. What I mean by giving up her life is this. She was never happy being used as a singer and one who brought in money for her family.

No, she was not, and it is why she did not wish nor desire to even sing those songs that they wanted her to sing anymore. It was not because she did not like singing anymore, because she did love singing! She just loved God so much more, and so much that she wanted to sing for Him for the rest of her life she had left in her. I mean, she was in her 50's when they killed her. Her idea was to sing gospel and grow old doing it.

And if you do not believe that Whitney Houston was murdered, I feel so sorry for you for missing it. I would not say such a thing if it were not true. Whitney loved gospel songs and those who knew her knew that she loved singing about God and Jesus, period. That was what Whitney desired from her heart. BeBe and CeCe Winans can tell the story better because they both were up close with Whitney as well, and they knew her truth when it came to what she wanted to do with her voice for God. She struggled with not wanting this life of singing the way she was anymore. Don't get me wrong, Whitney loved to sing as we all know she did.

As God is my Witness

It was not the singing that she was tired of, it was the songs that she wanted to sing for God because of what her spirit was telling her to do. She gave love through her voice, and it was such a powerful thing. Whitney Houston was a beautiful person that had a strong spirit, and a person who hardly anyone ever got to know completely.

Many will say they knew her but not very many can say that they really did, unless they could also tell you who she really was, if they are sincere. Whitney Houston was a woman who loved God so much that you heard it coming out of her voice whenever she sang. She carried a lot of love in her heart but could not ever be the woman who God created her to be because of all the trauma she endured in her life, if you understand me. I don't know if many people will say that they know the depths of how much she really loved God and Jesus. Some do know, but not when it comes to the extent or the depths of her soul as she yearned for people to really know.

Why am I saying all of this, you may ask? I am saying this because Whitney's family (the Houston's) did not want her to sing anything her heart desired. They are really people whom I believe never got to know the real Whitney. I believe this because they were too fascinated with the money she made, and too caught up in forcing her to be whatever Clive Davis wanted her to be, I would humbly say. I cannot write that I believe they loved her, because I would be lying ifl said that. They have given me every reason possible to believe otherwise, and as much as I would love to say that I cannot. If no one else understands what I am saying, I am sure that God does. And I say this with all due respect to anyone who may feel offended, but it is my truth of how I truly feel and believe.

As God is my Witness

I am sure that Whitney has told someone several times that she wanted to sing for God. I would bet my life that she was ignored when she did. Why do I say that? Because she would only mention it to those who were important enough in her career to have heard that. In any event, I want Mama Cissy to know that I am in no way trying to speak evil of her, nor was that statement intended or directed solely at her. I am just a woman who loves my sister Whitney, and I feel obligated to tell the truth of her story, as I believe she would want me to. Second, I am a woman who has a passion for helping my people out here to become better people, if I can at all do so. I am also a person who knows the reason I am here in this world.

I am doing what God desires for me to do and nothing more. In any event, we have to know that, if we never look at a problem and try to solve it, it will never be solved and will continue to be overlooked to repeat itself in our history of this life we live. In other words, it will continue to go on and lives will continue to be hurt and become devastated, and this will continue to go on as long as we live if not given the attention it calls for. It just cannot keep happening without us ever desiring to talk about it, and without us being able to heal from it and more importantly, we must do something about it now, so that this does not repeat itself in any family ever again in this life or the next, where we will leave a whole generation of our children behind.

We cannot run away from things that need to be faced, dealt with and resolved in our communities. And this is something that plagues a lot of our lives in this country, yet it is always swept up under a rug in many families. Some people choose not to deal with it at all, and I do not believe in that.

As God is my Witness

Again, none of us are perfect in this world, but we still must do our part in trying to make a better world for ourselves and our children coming behind us. We should always be eager to break the chains that we carry around our necks, while others keep their foot there with it.

There is a lot of sadness and abuse that happens within our homes and communities. If we do not summon our strength to stand up and speak truth, and deal with it to make changes in this world of ours, God will hold us all accountable for our actions regardless to who we think we are. It is too many of us out here that are going against what God wants and what people who are human beings want. It is terrible when people are in positions to help themselves but are held hostage and not able to do for themselves. These are people who have God-given rights to live their lives just like everyone else who is left alone to live theirs.

The music industry is a perfect example of what I am speaking of It will not allow people to be people they really came to this world to be, and it is not fair at the end of the day. People would feel a lot better if they were left alone to thrive and live out their lives here in this universe as our spirits guide us to. Too many people are out here trying to play God having power over human being's lives, while smiling and pretending to have their backs. They do this while being evil, selfish and carrying a lot of greed in their hearts. No man or woman has the right to take a life away from a person just because you want something they have, something that they have worked so hard for.

As God is my Witness

I happen to love speaking out to help my people because in helping them, I am helping myself and my generation of people who will also come into this world with the same ideas of entertainers and singers and actors. I also have grand children who are in this world, and I would not ever want them to go through what Whitney and many celebrities have gone through because someone thinks or believes they are better than them and this gives them the authority to take control over their lives. I would snap and go completely off and ask God to forgive me, if I thought someone was trying to do that to my child or grandchild.

If I am in my grave, I will find a way to come back and deal with that person who had the balls and nerves to do such to my children. Today, we as black people in this country, we must heal and get far away from the most outrageous, insane and evil ideas that are doing nothing more than traumatizing and devastating our lives, just because a person has a lust for doing evil.

I been through a lot in my life, and I found God and the peace that I need to help others in this world and give back as God would want me to while I live in this world. It is the least that I can do considering how many times God has been there to save me and see me through all of my trauma in my life. It would be a crying shame before God, if I sat down and allowed things to go on, on my watch and I keep my lips tight without saying something, or doing something to help those who need to hear these words of encouragement, so that they can pick up their strength and boldly move on in this world, with the faith of the God that they believe in. I would be less of a woman of God, if I stood by and saw evil done and I kept my mouth shut for fear of someone or something that has absolutely no power over the God that I believe in.

As God is my Witness

With all due respect, this is a sick world with a lot of sick people in it that have never really lived a real life. I am talking about myself to because I have been cheated myself and have not really lived in this world as God intended for us all to live. Whitney Houston was a person that so many people used for her money. She was used because it was an easy thing for someone to do to her. And the way she was used was in a way where people knew they could get away with it, so it made them bold, and proud of what they were doing. And it was so easy for them that they didn't even care who saw them doing what they did to her.

It is a sad and ugly thing that was done to her. The very sad part of it all is that it was people whom she cared for dearly that did her so wrong. It was people who for a long time had a chance to repent with God for the evils they had been doing to her and others, and for so long.

A lot of people do a lot of things in this world because they think or believe they can get away with it because they always have. And of course, they do especially if they have been getting away with it for so long. It can get so good that they invite others to share in their evils, promising them their share or their prize in helping with their evil. And all they do is call another and ask. It is up to others, the decision they will make in bringing harm to another individual. And so, blood is now on the hands of all of those who have chosen evil to do to God's people, who have come into this world to live out their lives, but found it cut short because of wicked people they have somewhat and somehow trusted with their lives. Some sleep well at night while others have a hard time in their life from that day on. It depends on whatever Gods sees fit for them will He allow.

As God is my Witness

Some even end up sick with disease and illnesses they can't seem to shake, and heartache and trouble that they go to bed crying about, that just won't go away. There are all kinds of things that happen to people after they have done such a horrific thing to such beautiful souls in the world, and for no good and/or logical reason whatsoever do they continue to do this. Meanwhile and all along, the evil doers may have all the power and money and fame in this world, but they forgot one thing. Something that they should have thought of before and/or while they were deciding with someone else's life.

They never gave it thought that they too must one day leave here, and the thing is, they don't have a clue as to how it will be on the other side. They may think or believe it's one way, but they cannot ever be sure, and who's says that God owes a person anything when they have done such grave things to another human being's life, by taking it. No one has ever come back to tell them how it is or how it will be for them when they go. These are the chances people foolishly take when they take the life of another human being. They don't know what they will suffer when they leave here. It will depend on God what He will do with your soul after He allows you to go away from here, and finally meet your fate.

People who will be so bold to do such evil things, have no clue as to how it will be when it is their time to go, and they do not know if they can even handle what has been planned for them after what they did to someone else. They may have to try to endure something they do not have even the slightest chance of enduring. This is why we should never ever entertain a single thought in our head to do such wicked things to people. Especially when you don't even know the Man who has power over your soul. I don't know what people believe or how they think.

As God is my Witness

But for people to do such evil things, someone had to tell them something for them to believe that they can do things, and nothing will happen to their soul. The one thing I want people to think about and remember is this.

We are all only here for just a little while. And when we go, we are gone for forever. Some say that some will come back, while other souls will not. If I were you, I would think 10 times before trying to do harm and take another soul, because you do not know what is on that other side where you will indeed have to go. That is all I will say for now. Whitney Houston was a person who suffered lot of things while she lived. I thought that she needed serious therapy for the things that she went through and had to live with. We all have different ways of coming out of our trauma or getting the therapy that we need to carry on in this wicked world.

I do not believe Whitney ever spoke to a therapist regarding her history with her family members. Yet, I will say that it was a thing that was so very necessary for her. Whitney has been through a lot with people who have set examples for her life from a young age. They had deceived her and used her so much until it was literally bothering her soul. She was crying out for help but was only seeking the help of God. She did not like this world and the life that was chosen for her once she learned who she was.

I also do not believe that she has ever gotten an apology from anyone either. She had very serious problems and issues that were haunting her life, and she was doing her best to remain sane with what she had to live with, yet she was tired of living if you understand where I am coming from and she was not suicidal at all, so please do not ever think for a half of a second that she was.

As God is my Witness

She just wanted her life to be better and the only way it could was if certain people stayed clear away from her. She wanted nothing more than Bobby Brown, her husband and her daughter Bobbi Kristina Brown. She made a statement one day and said she could live on a little island for the rest of her life selling lemonade, as long as she and Bobby were together and had their children with them, and I believed her. I believe that she was preparing to do something great with her life, and they had her phone tapped and heard her talking about it, is why they made that move on her so fast.

WHITNEY'S WAS RAPED AT 12 YEARS OLD!

This next thing I will talk about is something that happened to her, and it devastated her soul in such a way that she carried this with her everywhere she went in this world. On top of it all, there were a lot of other things that were haunting her. OK, let's go so I can get this part over with because I can't stand to even think about this part.

And before I go on to say this, please know and understand that this came out of Whitney's mouth. This is not hearsay it came straight from the horse's mouth. She talked about how the Houston family Church Pastor; Mr. Carter raped her along with her mother. This is what Whitney Houston had to carry with her all the days of her adult and childhood life. This is something that bothered her soul and made her cry on certain occasions. I believe this was why she could not ever get rid of her drug problem as well. If not, it had a heck of a lot to do with it as to why she took so long to become clean away from drugs, and why she did drugs for so many years.

As God is my Witness

Yes, this is a sad story, and I believe she would want this world to hear this after all that she had to suffer leaving this world. I am not the only one who knows about this happening to Whitney. She did not only share this with me. There are a few people that know this story about Pastor Carter. This was a man from their Church back in New Jersey, who was with her mother,

Mama Cissy, at some point in her life. Whitney was about 12-year-old when all of this happened to her. After Whitney did so much for her Houston family, she is murdered in a hotel where her so-called brother Gary and his wife were both present, and then her body is carried off for her funeral, which is held in this man's Church. I cannot think of anything else right now that would be more disrespectful to a human being. To have her going home services in such a place is hitting way below the belt.

It is a betrayal that is most definitely unheard of. The same Church they had her funeral in, belonged to that same pastor who raped her. I am going to tell the story and be done with it. I hope and pray that from this day on, parents will think five times before they act and make the best decisions out here in this world when it comes to their children. On the other hand, I pray that we all get the help that we need to overcome such things and help to prevent these things from ever happening again to anyone.

Whitney said, Mama Cissy, was cheating on Papa John one day with this man, Pastor Carter, and he was in their home this day lying in bed with Mama Cissy when Poppa John was not at home. I believe Poppa John was at work and of course, did not know this man was in his home and bed.

As God is my Witness

Whitney said, she went to enter her mom's room for some reason, and also like any other day she felt like opening her mother's bedroom door. Except this time when she opened her mom's door, she realized Mama Cissy had company and was lying in bed with this man, Pastor Carter, and this was the man who would rape Whitney.

After Whitney opened the door, she shut it fast! She tried to back up after closing the door. Mama Cissy yelled to her, along with the pastor, they both told her, nah, nah, nah, you come on back in here Nippy! The Pastor was also saying, Nab Nab, Nab, yeah, come on back in here girl! They both made her come back in there, and take her clothes off, and get up in that bed with the both of them. The rest is history and for you to imagine for yourself, but Whitney said, they both raped her. Whitney had her virginity taken from her that day. I do not wish to repeat it all because it is too much for me right now. It is a painful thing to hear, and it already took me a while to get this whole story out to the world. This is a very painful story to have to tell, and yes, it is the absolute truth, Whitney did tell us this.

And Whitney telling us this story let me know that she had been seriously traumatized and heart-broken at a very young age. She had been crying out for a long time, and always had Mama Cissy right there in front of her forcing her to be strong and just take it. This is why I know that anytime Whitney was in the media smiling and talking about her mother in front of any camera, it was because she was trained to do that. She was miserable and that is why Gary said to Mama Cissy when she invited him and Pat over and asked them what happened to Whitney, it is why Gary said, "You knew she didn't want to be here anymore." They knew that Whitney was tired after so many years being abused by them and burdened... I think Whitney was fed up!

As God is my Witness

My belief is that Mama Cissy threatened her and made her say nice things concerning her whenever she would interview. Yes, and while I am here speaking on this, Whitney was literally trained by Mama Cissy from a young girl. I don't even believe that she was treated fairly being Poppa John's daughter by another woman either. Whitney, I believe was treated so unfairly being in the Houston family all her life.

Even with her singing, I strongly believe it was all strategically planned by Mama Cissy, who very cleverly forced her to sing from the beginning, and she tried to make the world believe that it was Whitney who started the idea of wanting to sing. If you go back and look at that movie about Whitney's life, you will see that it comes on and starts with Mama Cissy standing right in front of her training her to sing.

As soon as I saw that, I told everyone who was sitting and watching it with me, "Look at this I knew it!" I strongly believe it was a situation where Mama Cissy basically placed her in the choir as a young girl and was throwing hints around Whitney to get her to say that she wanted to sing. That is why Whitney says that in her interview with Oprah. Mama Cissy, I believe made sure that Whitney was always "mindful" to say that in the event it should come up that she was not her biological mother. I so believe this and will never believe any other story when it comes to how Whitney started singing.

I also think Mama Cissy brought her around Aretha and all the other singers during that time and wanted Whitney to desire it for herself. This was part of molding her into this person and lifestyle where she wanted that fame so badly. I am telling you this is what God has given me to say.

As God is my Witness

I saw through even the movie they put out entailing their lives together and how Whitney came up. It is all a part of their Hollywood schemes. I hope you can understand where I am coming from right now. I cannot imagine putting a young baby through all of that. I am saying to myself, "Of course Mama Cissy placed her directly in there as if Whitney was a piece of her property.

As far as she knew back then, Mama Cissy was her real mother that was doing this for her. I am sure after her rape; she knew that Mama Cissy was not her real mother. And I say this with all due respect to Mama Cissy. I believe that is why she sang so well. It made me so very full of sorrow for her, as I watched how strong Whitney was as a woman. She was always dealing with who she was, versus who she wanted to be and who she could have been. She just could not be herself at all around her Houston family, and I believe some of them knew this but cared not.

In my opinion, Mamma Cissy always wanted her to act in a certain way when the cameras were on her. She had to talk a certain way to not let the world know anything about what their family was really like. Whitney had suffered so much in her life and had been through far more than people could ever imagine she went through. I felt like she deserved far more than what people who were close to her were offering her. She was not honored properly when she left here, nor was she respected while she was alive, in my opinion.

I have never felt so bad for Whitney once I learned her funeral was going to be there. This has given me the idea and forced me to believe that Mamma Cissy is not her real mother. I cannot see a real mother doing this to their real child. What I am saying is, perhaps that was why it was so easy for Mama Cissy to do that to her.

As God is my Witness

Knowing what I know, it is so easy for me to believe that Teresa Graves is Whitney's real mother. There is no way that a mother would do this to their own child. Now, Mama Cissy is known for being in the Church and doing a lot of things with her Church. However, a lot of people have talked about the wrong she has done in this Church. I hate to say this, but I have spoken to some members of her Church that just don't like it when you mention her name. I believe it comes from the problems she's had with some of the members, as elders in that Church.

I don't know what happened or who it happened to or with, but I do know that something or a lot of things has happened where they do not have respect for her in that Church. They don't even like it when you say her name around them. Now, again, I am not speaking ill of her, I am just speaking of what I learned. Something terrible happened in that Church with her and some other people and they are very bitter.

There is no doubt in my mind that Whitney Houston was brought home by Poppa John when she was a baby, for Mama Cissy to raise as her child. I was told by a Houston that Mama Cissy gave Whitney to Clive Davis for the sole purposes of making money, and I believe it after knowing what she did to Whitney along with that pastor.

Now I see and understand why things went the way they did with her in that family. Everything does make even more sense to me now and now I can see why everything that has happened and transpired as it has with this funeral. I am saying to myself, wow, this is why no one really cares about Whitney. And I now believe that it is why no one desires to even fight for Whitney.

As God is my Witness

We are living in a time when everything is being revealed in this world. I am putting this out here, so that it may help other families do better with their children, whether biological or adopted, we must do right by children, period.

We have been saying that what goes up must come down, and whatever you put out here in this universe, the universe is obligated to return to its sender. We hear this all the time, and we pay no mind until it hits home. We all must deal with the truth being revealed today because we are living in that time now. I believe God allowed this truth to come out for us to find out about Teresa Graves because it is just that time.

No matter which way you put this, Whitney did not deserve what happened to her. And then, for people to intentionally lie about how she left here, knowing she did not leave that way is another thing. There is just way too much evil going on in this case and too many lies being told when all we have to simply do is tell the truth and get it over with to please God.

People have done some of the most wicked and dirty things to her, and they are walking around as if nothing ever happened. I think they wanted people to think she took her own life. These people to me seem to not have a soul anymore. I am so grateful to God that I do not have a heart like that. I have prayed that my sister, my niece, and my nephew are all resting in their graves with God's peace.

As God is my Witness

WHITNEY AND BROTHER MICHAEL

Now, there is something else here that no one will probably believe, but I believe it. It was said from close family members and sources that Whitney and her brother Michael Houston, were both sleeping with each other when they were young children and conceived a baby girl together. This was a big thing in the Houston family from what I have been told. Other Houston family members said that everyone knew this was going on when it was happening because it was happening way too often, and Poppa John used to come home from work and look forward to separating them all the time because they would always be in the same room with each other.

They said this went on and on and they could never be separated. Everything now makes sense to me as to why everyone was treating Whitney the way they were and acting the way they were with her. Now, I see why Donna Houston is acting the way she does with anything to do with Whitney today and now that Whitney is gone. I believe she knows this as well, and I also believe that it is why she does not have a real genuine love for Whitney, and she is a part of all the conspiracy going on today.

See, in my mind, and the way I feel, they all don't care for Whitney, and they have some sort of vendetta for her because of their own personal hang-ups about her that have been with them for a long time now. Donna has two children by Michael, and I can imagine how she must feel knowing all of this. From what I have been told, Donna has been around a long time, and she went to school with Whitney. Everything has been so clear to me now, and it has opened my eyes to where I understand everyone's actions, all the way up to even Mama Cissy.

As God is my Witness

WAS WHITNEY THREATENED BY MAMA CISYY TO NOT TELL ON HER? Now, I thought about this and I said, I wonder if Whitney ever told her father, Poppa John what happened to her when she was molested by Mama Cissy and that Pastor. I don't know why but this came to my mind. And I am sure, if I thought about this, someone else has too. What I believe happened was this. Mama Cissy was bold enough to do it to Whitney believing she can get away with it for one reason.

I thought that she may have done it because perhaps she was aware that Whitney and Michael were both in their room "humpin around." I can believe that because a little girl and a little boy thinking their doing something but really ain't doing anything. On the other hand, Poppa John doesn't really know that though, and in fact, none of them know, but they are assuming that Whitney and Michael are both having real sex at 12. Yet, reality was that they were just always caught humpin around.

It was not until that pastor raped her; did she experience real sex. After that, her and Michael's meetings got real! Whitney was only 12, when the pastor raped her, keep in mind. Yet, it has been said that she and Michael had a baby at 15-16. I figured this out myself. I believe Mama Cissy placed fear in her heart to not tell Poppa John, and if she did, she would tell Poppa John that she caught her either trying to do something with the pastor, or she was found but naked with Michael; which would piss Poppa John off really bad, if he was to think that of Whitney. Because the way that I heard how this was going down, it made Poppa John extremely upset at Whitney and Michael.

As God is my Witness

Now, this baby could have been Michael's or maybe I am wrong, and maybe this baby was the pastor's and I got it all wrong! Who knows the truth after all? There is one thing I do believe, and that is that Whitney never told Poppa John she got raped by them because she was afraid of Mama Cissy and what she could do to her, I believe. Now, this is just my story and what I think may have happened as to "why" Whitney never told her father.

It makes sense to me and I can see and believe Mama Cissy going there and doing something like that. Whitney did say he took her virginity so maybe that pastor was her first. I thought Mama Cissy told Whitney, "Listen, if you tell your daddy, I am going to tell your father that you're lying and that it was "you" and blah, blah, blah. Whitney that I caught in the bed or you who was trying to sleep with the pastor! Why would Mama Cissy say that to Whitney you ask?

Because a reliable source who grew up with them told me that Poppa John used to be very upset whenever he came home from work because he always caught Michael and Whitney in the room with each other. Mama Cissy may have threatened Whitney and said, "If you say anything, your father won't believe you because he already knows you're a hot thing messing with your own brother.

In other words, Mama Cissy knew that she could tell Poppa John that no, Whitney was caught trying to come onto the pastor, if you get what I am trying to say here. I can see that happening with Mama Cissy for some reason. Therefore, Whitney doesn't say anything to her father for that reason, and/or fear alone of Mama Cissy and what she may do to her if Whitney did tell. Now,

As God is my Witness

MICHAEL HOUSTON RAPE MY NIECE!

I did not find out until I went to another state and this man mentioned to me that my niece was raped by her own uncle Michael Houston! I had to hear this years later, and while being in another state when I visited someone. When I got home, I asked certain family members had they ever heard this and they said, yes, he did! I could not believe what I was hearing! I said, this is unbelievable, and why didn't I hear about this? Nobody has given me an explanation but I bet it was probably because they knew I was going to go off!

The man telling me this story, showed me the documents from the courts where it was said that Bobbi Kristina was raped by her uncle Michael Houston. He also told me that he infected my niece chlamydia! I AM LIVID!! I am her aunt, and I aint never had any kind of infection or disease in my whole life! Now I have to listen to this news of him doing this to my niece!

A baby girl that probably was a virgin when he did rape her!!! THA FAMILY IS TOO DAGGON DEVIOUS AND IT MAKES NO SENSE AT ALL! HE HAS DAUGHTERS HIS SELF!! This was too hard for me to handle because I AM WONDERING WHY NO ONE PRESSED CHARGES ON HIM? What the heck is wrong with this man, and then what is wrong with my family? I am not understanding this!!! And why didn't they throw his but in jail? Why did he not get charged for raping my niece!? My niece was very young and too young to even think about suffering a rape and on top of it he gives her chlamydia, and from her own sick uncle raping her!!?? OH NO I CAN'T EVEN TALK ABOUT THIS THIS IS CRAZY! Does anyone realize how traumatic this was for her? OMG! It is very traumatic for ME to even hear it... I'm telling you!

As God is my Witness

They knew better to tell me because had I known I would have done something. He would have been in jail for doing such a terrible thing like that to my baby! Men have no idea about what they take from a girl or woman when they do that. That's why in Islam they cut your head off if you mess with a woman, and I don't blame them. I do not feel sorry for people who would rape anyone. I am saying, how did this happen to her and when did this happen, and how old was she at this time, I am wondering?

Why didn't someone tell me about this happening to my niece? See, this is what I'm talking about when it comes to Whitney's so-called family members. I can't imagine what was going on in her mind as this grown man was doing this to her this is insane! This man tried his best to show me these court documents, but I told him I did not want to see them.

I didn't want to believe it. I wanted to make sure I spoke with someone at home first before I really looked at the documents. They said it happened in Atlanta I believe. I still haven't studied these docs because I am so hurt! My niece been through so much in her short-lived life. I wish someone had of come to me to tell me so that I could have been a support for her and done something about it. I had no idea this happened, and I actually blocked it out of my mind believe it or not.

I had forgotten about this. I always said that Michael Houston loved Whitney and I would have never thought he would do this. If you had asked me, if he would ever do anything to harm Whitney, I will always tell you no, he would be the first to hurt someone that he thought was trying to hurt Whitney in my opinion.

As God is my Witness

Well, I hate to talk about this but now I see the mind of these Houston's and it's very disturbing to me. I cannot bear to talk about it anymore, this is breaking my heart too much. If Donna Houston, Michael Houston's wife, ever wrote a book and told the absolute truth, I wonder what that book would be like. In all honesty, I used to feel so sorry for Donna Houston, because she seemed to have endured a lot of stuff with Michael. One of the things that I always admired about Donna was, she appeared to me as a strong woman and a very good mother when I first met her. In fact, I always thought she was an excellent mother who was raising her children properly. Her and Michael have a son and a beautiful daughter Blaire. How would he feel if a man did that to his daughter?

They have so many issues, but in reality, they are not alone. This happens in a lot of homes across this country. They have probably done everything under the sun to Whitney. I would bet that he did the same to Whitney when she was younger. After I saw Whitney go through things with Donna and her mother Mama Cissy concerning her hard-earned money, I lost respect for Donna. I see right through her today, and I believe she is another person playing the role and acting like she loves Whitney, but really never did. She is probably still harboring feelings that Whitney slept with Michael, her own brother, who is the father of both of their children.

Call it what you may, but this is what I get out of all of this that I have witnessed and seen transpire with these people thus far. Donna was working in Whitney's foundation for a long time, and everything was going smoothly, the foundation was open and looking good to me when Whitney was alive as far as I could see. Today, I wonder what that foundation looks like.

As God is my Witness

I would expect Donna to be more sympathetic to what Whitney had to deal with while living under that roof with Mama Cissy, and not hold any animosity towards her. And to involve yourself with someone else's finances and try to control that because you feel some type of way, is a whole other thing to me. If I am ever asked the question, I will speak the truth and say that I believe that all of them used Whitney and were robbing her and spending her money. I so strongly believe this with all my heart.

What I get out of all of this is that Mama Cissy had no real feelings for Whitney as a real mother would, and so, this is why she allows all of them to use Whitney as well. I felt like they were not treating Whitney right from the door, and in my eyes, they all had no right over her money like that. I used to think, "WOW" what is giving them all this authority over Whitney's money like that?

The worst part of it all to me was that Whitney seemed to not be able to fight them back for some reason. I don't know what it was they had over her. The only thing I can think of is Whitney's contract that Mama Cissy signed for her with Clive. I seriously believe that she signed Whitney's life away and Whitney was too embarrassed to reveal it to this world, honestly.

I have honestly always thought it was Mama Cissy and the deal she made with Clive that kept Whitney held down and tied. I always thought perhaps Whitney felt obligated to that contract or afraid for some reason. I always respected Donna and took my hat off to her because she seemed to be a woman of strength. I had no idea all of them had something against Whitney, until I saw it for myself when she left here.

As God is my Witness

Like I said, I always thought Donna was a good mother. Those thoughts left me when I learned what little Gary said about Krissy. It now appears and seems to me that Donna was training this child up to hold something against Whitney and her daughter all this time. I could tell how little Gary acted towards Krissy and then how they all said what they said to Jonathon about talking to the authorities to help Krissy's case. They did not want that because they were actually happy that my niece was where she was! There was no other excuse for their being so angry.

All this stuff is hitting me like a ton of bricks today! I wonder if Whitney knew this, and I now see why none of these people participated in her wedding. Of course, they are going to act like they like Whitney, in her face and of course around other people, and act as if they are happy for her while she is alive. But I believe that all of them were happier and their happiest when both, she and her daughter died. Yes, I wholeheartedly believe that not one of them cared two cents for them.

As far as I am concerned, Whitney was surrounded with all these people that just cared absolutely nothing for her. I am so saddened that I can't say this any other way. It is just the truth to me today, after learning how Michael and Donna's son, little Gary just coldly disrespected Bobbi Kristina, by saying what he said as she lay in that hospital very near to death, it forced me to dislike his actions and who he is as a person, but of course I love him as my nephew or little brother. It's sad when you think about it. Where have we taken our next generation of people? His parents should not be OK with him projecting this kind of ignorance onto this universe. As much as I love little Gary, my heart is so broken, knowing he said that. I could have never imagined him doing such a thing to Krissy.

As God is my Witness

His whole character to me is now off and so different, and I feel like they are all strangers to me now, and people whom I do not know. That was very ugly, and I now see him as a very selfish individual. I could not find any other words for him. When you can act that way and lash out at someone who has not done anything to you, and a person who just does not owe you anything, I must question how he was taught and raised now. That was a very ugly way to show up for your so-called cousin who needed our prayers and love at such a time. It added on to all my thoughts in my head about everyone. I have now concluded in my belief and opinions about them, that all of them are only interested in Whitney's estate money and whatever they can get their hands on of value that belonged to her.

Please know that I bear no malice towards anyone, and I am saying this without any anger in my heart. It is just my opinion at the end of the day. God knows that I cannot hate anyone, but I will always be quick to tell the truth, and especially when it is necessary to say. I am a right-is-right and wrong is wrong, person every single day of the week. I believe in fairness, respecting others, and understanding others regardless of who or what at the end of the day. I just do not like it when people cannot be considerate of others, and they seem to become monsters as soon as a person is deceased. It bothers my soul how people can be so inconsiderate towards the wrong people.

DOES WHITNEY & BROTHER MICHAEL REALLY HAVE A CHILD?

It was said that when Whitney and her brother Michael had a baby together many years ago, Mama Cissy forced Whitney to give this child up for an adoption. I have heard that Mama Cissy supposedly and allegedly gave this baby up, because Whitney was too young, and

As God is my Witness

on top of it all, it was her brother, Michael who fathered this baby. This could very well be a rumor put out here without any facts attached to it. But as the days go by, I am starting to believe it more and more because of what Whitney wrote in her will and from what I have learnt and heard regarding this whole ordeal. In Whitney's will she stated that, if she had any children out here in this world, she wanted that child to have a part in her estate.

Of course, any mother would want that for their child, and it is only right that her child gets it. If this person whom I believe to be her child, is her child, then, yes indeed, she should get anything coming to her that belonged to her mother.

It may also be true that this child or woman is still out there, and Whitney has now left her in this world. If I am wrong in thinking this, then I am wrong, but I don't believe that I am wrong. It is a young lady by the name of Rena Houston, who is well over 30 or probably even over 40 years old now. I am not certain of her age, but I do believe she is Whitney's child. I met this young woman, after she contacted me through Facebook, I believe, if my memory serves me right. She introduced herself and told me that she believed she was Whitney's daughter, and that she was told that she was the daughter of Michael and Whitney Houston.

I could not believe my ears. She said that she wanted nothing more than to just simply reunite with her real mother. She told me some things that she remembered as a child and said that she remembered Whitney getting beat a lot by Mama Cissy when she was a baby girl in Whitney's arms. With tears in my eyes, I continued listening to her over the phone as she explained this to me. I could not believe what I was hearing.

As God is my Witness

Of course, I did not have any proof of what she was saying, but my heart still melted as I listened to her. She talked about how she witnessed Whitney being abused and hit and/or beat a lot, while she was sitting in her lap while sitting next to her in pampers when she was a baby. She remembers Mama Cissy and others treating Whitney so badly she says. I never got the chance to know for certain if all of what she was saying was the absolute truth, but I had no reason at all to "not" believe her. In fact, I thought she was telling me the truth as she was telling me everything about her. Time was passing and a lot was going on with Krissy at the hospice during this time. I had a whole lot going on in my own life at this time and it became so hectic.

I was trying to save Krissy while Pat and Cissy Houston were fighting Bobby in a court to take Krissy's estate away from her own father, my brother, Bobby. It was so traumatizing and painful to have to witness how cruel they were to even attempt such a thing after someone's parent dies. They both tried so hard to take a child's estate money from their own parents; and so, they go and retain an attorney, who would actually fight that child's parent for their own estate money, that their mother wanted for her child. This is unbelievable but so true.

I don't even like talking about this, because it is so wrong and so ugly of anyone to do to someone else with their own child, and it just breaks my heart to even think about it. They knew that it was never Whitney's desire to do any such thing and they also knew that Whitney would be furious over what they had done. The things they put Bobby through in this state, they will have to answer to God for that. And to think, all that Bobby Brown did for the state of Georgia, all the years he's been here in Atlanta.

As God is my Witness

He's put people in office and stood by them when they needed to use his mansion for elections, he has never said no to anyone when they needed him, and for people to not be there for him when his wife, daughter and son were all murdered is so ridiculously cold and so mean of people. People surely have no problem with kicking a good man when he is down! But God sees everything and they will have to answer one way or the other.

Bobby did a lot of good in the state of Georgia. His good heart put so many people through all kinds of schools, colleges, he's paid so many people's mortgage, he bought people houses and luxury cars, and you name it Bobby Brown surely helped anyone who asked. Bobby has done a lot of wonderful and important things for people, and far more than anyone has ever thought to mention, he has done for them. And this is the thanks he gets from the state of Georgia. A place where he has given a lot of money to help a lot of people, and especially those in authority.

This is a cold world and the people in it are doing so much wickedness, and they even have children of their own, and I guess, don't think about what will happen when they leave them one day. What comes around surely goes back around in this universe, we can all bet that.

You would think that those who consider themselves wise would measure right and wrong properly and just simply do right for once and for the sake of integrity and respect. I think it's a money thing, if you ask me. I have been literally forced by people, since the death of Whitney, to believe that people were just paid off to do what they did to Whitney, her daughter and my nephew.

As God is my Witness

The nerve of people seriously startles me, and to the point of me having to go into deep serious prayer with my God and asking that His justice be served on those who deserved it for doing wrong while knowing what they were doing. And let me tell you something you may not know. Allah is a God who answers prayers to His children, you better know it.

They all knew that Whitney wanted Bobby over her estate; and me over Bobbi Kristina's estate. She wanted this for Bobby, whether they were married or not. The only reason I stood down and did not fight to be over Krissy's estate as Whitney wanted it to be, was only because I did not want to be in the media appearing as if I were fighting Krissy's father, which is my brother, for his own daughter's estate. When I learned that Cissy and Pat both had lawyered up, I flew to Bobby and told him to not allow them to make any decisions for his daughter's well- being. I even told him that we should both fight them together, but he refused and asked me to stand down, and so, I did out of respect for my brother.

I did not know that they wanted authority over her estate just so they would have the say to tell them to close her eyes! Where in this world do they do that at? They do that right here in Atlanta Georgia, I am a witness. They allowed these people to go against my brother and kill his daughter. Krissy had nothing else wrong with her, she had fought hard to live and she had already won! She was home free until they came in and took her life so unjustly. She had come out of that coma long ago from being in that first hospital and was doing wonderful and was curing fast!

As God is my Witness

There was nothing wrong with her that she needed to die and not come home with us. She had fought so hard to get where she was, and we were expecting her to come home with us. Yet, Pat and Cissy Houston fought for this hospice center to kill my niece! For what reason did they do this for, and who allowed them to kill her, and then starve her to death in that process? Dr. Jolie Harris III has said, "It was a Mercenary killing and I so strongly believe this now!"

Bobby tried so hard, but these demons fought him tooth and nail just kill his daughter, and they made sure they starved her in that process, how wickedly cruel! And they did this in his face. I never seen a man cry so hard when Dr. Jolie called me to tell me that he stood right there when Pat Houston stood in that hospice center and voted for Bobbi Kristina to be left there to die. He said, there was a bunch of people in that room and that Pat Houston was the only one who voted for my niece to die. Should I say it again, did you hear me? It was just one against about 4 other people and they took Pat Houston's evil and demonic request against everyone else, and over Bobbi Kristina's own father.

A person who has no blood relation to her whatsoever had the authority to kill my niece. When I tell you that she or they have no idea what they did, trust me, they don't. And for those in that hospice center to allow her to have a vote all by herself, they along with Pat Houston have my niece's blood all over their hands as well.

Dr. Jolie said to me, your brother Bobby was crying so hard and begging them not to do this to his daughter, and they did it anyways. Yes, indeed this is what happened to my niece, who wasn't even in danger of dying anymore. There was nothing wrong with her that she had to die, as God is my witness!

As God is my Witness

They just allowed her to lay there without food and they were starving her to death. And I believe they did that because she wouldn't die! However, I also think eventually they did something to just out right kill her. As far as Whitney and Michael's alleged child, I have to keep it real, if I want to stay in the favor of God. I feel like I am good at discerning whether a child belongs to a parent or not. Back in the day, anytime I watched "The Maury Povich Show", the one thing that I was always good at doing was telling everyone who the daddy was, and I would always be right. I was of course wrong a few times, but for the most part, I am good at deciding who that daddy is. I just always had an eye for things like that.

It is why I believe that Rena Houston is indeed Michael and Whitney's child they both brought into this world. Do I have any proof? No, I do not, but I have a right to believe what I will. If Rena is really Whitney's daughter, then of course she is entitled and deserves all that she can get from Whitney's estate. It would not be fair for her to be left out of her mother's will and estate that would not be right.

And I must admit, it does make you wonder as to why Whitney wrote that part in her "will" and stated something to the effect of, "If there are any children of hers out here in this world, they are entitled to something in her will." I remember reading this while examining her will. For those who won't believe it, ask yourself, why would Whitney write something like that in her will, if she didn't think she had another child out here? I am not God and no one has to answer to me, but I bear witness to this world that Allah is a God that does not play all these games these people have played with Whitney Houston's estate, and I am here to tell and warn anyone that has done wrong with that will, you have no idea the things you will have to answer to Almighty God

As God is my Witness

Allah for. He is a God that you will one day bow down, reckon with and bear witness of in just a few more days mark my words. I also believe that her will was tampered with. The reason I say this is because I remember Whitney telling me that she left my Brother Bobby's name in her will. She always wanted Bobby to be over her will, regardless of whether they were together or not. She said that if anything were to happen to her and she and Bobby were not married anymore, she would still want him to be over her will. Those who have her will must know exactly what I am talking about. Yet, I am more than sure that they would never want this, and they more than likely did something to blot that part out of her will. But I am also sure that my brother doesn't care, not even a little bit. Bobby has never allowed money to be an issue for him, he'd rather do without it.

It is a sad thing when you write a will, and nobody that you think will respect you doesn't, and they turn around and disrespect you. Anyone leaving a will should be respected enough for others to simply adhere to it. However, we are talking about Whitney Houston who is worth a whole lot in this world, and a person who had a different kind of family, who had control over her whole life. Money and greed are overpowering the minds of those who care not for Whitney Houston.

Whitney's funeral revealed so much to me while I was sitting there. SHE HAD A CLOSED CASKET BECAUSE SHE HAD TOO MANY SCARS ON HER BODY AND THEY DID NOT WANT PEOPLE TO SEE THEM. SHE HAD LUMPS, CONTUSIONS, BUMBS AND BRUISES ON HER HEAD, HER FACE WAS SWOLLEN AND YOU WOULD HAVE KNOWN SHE WAS PUNCHED IN IT HAD HER CASKET BEEN OPEN. THEY DID NOT WANT THE PUBLIC TO SEE THAT. SHE EVEN HAD BRUISES ON THE TOP OF HER HEAD.

As God is my Witness

BRUISES UP AND DOWN HER LEGS, HER CHEST, HER ARMS, AND EVEN HER NAILS WERE CHIPPED, 'HER LIP WAS BUSTED SO MUCH THAT HAD SHE LIVED, SHE WOULD HAVE SURGERY ON HER LIPS.' SHE HAD DEFENSE WOUNDS WHICH TOLD ANYONE, SHE FOUGHT HARD FOR HER LIFE. WHITNEY HOUSTON WAS BEATEN TO DEATH, HANDS DOWN.

I had never cried so hard at someone's funeral knowing that Whitney had a punched jaw that blew her face up. Her cousin Shelly, Aunt Bey's daughter told me, because she went to the body viewing. I flew into town to go to her body viewing, but never made it because I just did not want to see my sister like that. Whitney's cousin, Shelly called me just as I was getting ready to go out my hotel door and over to the body viewing. She called to tell me that she was there for the body viewing and Whitney had a huge blown-up jaw! I did not go to look at her. I should have, but I couldn't see her like that. It would have been too painful for me to see her that way.

Furthermore, right at that body viewing, someone had taken her picture and leaked it to the media and for that reason, I was glad I didn't go near that casket that day. Everyone said it was Pat and Gary along with Raffles that took that picture, and that they got a million or more dollars for that picture. I believe it too.

I cried profusely at her funeral because I knew that Whitney did not put herself in that bathtub for one. Second, her body was laying inside of a Church where her rapist was the Pastor at (Pastor Carter). I knew how much that hurt Whitney all her life; and knew that her body should not have ever been in this place. I kept thinking in my head, why do they keep doing things to Whitney as if they hate her?

As God is my Witness

She has not ever done anything to any of them to deserve this, so why, dear God! I am literally crying out loud for Whitney at this point. Everything that she did not like, did not want, or did not do, they did the opposite. And I believe they do it purposely as a slap in the face to Whitney, especially Pat and Gary. I can just feel that it was very much intentional towards her. As far as I'm concerned, they are totally against Whitney, and they are very serious about openly disrespecting her without any remorse. They did this while she was alive as well, and they are still doing it in her death, and it is so evil and wrong in anyone's eyes. At this point, I feel that not one of them cares for her at all.

At the funeral, I sat behind Mama Cissy wondering if she was OK, and if Bobby Kristina was OK because she was sitting right next to Krissy looking weird to me for some strange reason. It appears weird the way they were just sitting there and not even recognizing each other. You may not understand this, but God had me fixed on how everyone was acting. The spirit in that Church was so dull and dark and void. It was like Whitney was not in that casket. I did not believe she was even in there to be more honest, and neither did my sons believe she was in that casket.

There was no body movement at all coming from Mama Cissy as she sat in that funeral staring down the whole time. I did not see her head turn either way the whole time. I did not see her at any time looking at Bobbi Kristina, nor to her left or right. It was as if she was not sitting next to her at all and just in a trans or something. She just kept her head straight without the slightest movement, and it was just different and weird to me. I have been to a lot of funerals, and I have never once in my life, saw anyone act the way she was acting on this day.

Especially because she is supposedly Whitney's mother, and I am sure she was feeling at least something. I stared for a minute, then I said to myself, why would she put Whitney in this Church like this, this is such an unbelievable thing to do.

My God, this man, and her mother seriously traumatized Whitney when she was just 12 and put her through a lot when she was just a young girl, according to what Whitney has told us. He murdered her, by murdering her spirit as a child, because she had never been the same after that. I know and understand because I have been through something similar. And Minister Farrakhan stated one day, "Whenever you rape a person, you have murdered them, period!"

I feel so sorry for Mama Cissy as well, because she 1s a woman who, more than likely, had to also gone through a lot of things in her life as well to get to a place like that and be OK with something like that, I am sure. But my God, why would the both of you do this to Whitney, and you know no child ever deserve anything like this, I am saying to myself And if Mama Cissy has nothing to do with Whitney being in that funeral home, and Pat did that on her own, I would think that Mama Cissy would come behind Pat and make sure that she has set up everything correctly for Whitney and as Mama Cissy would want the best for her daughter's funeral. She would have had to OK everything done by Pat if she let her do everything, which I am sure she did.

Also, another thing that I don't understand. If my child is found in a hotel, I am going to investigate thoroughly and find out what happened. Also, I am going to look at her body because I want to see my child. Did she not have to identify Whitney's body, as her mother?

As God is my Witness

And then, if she had the chance to see Whitney's body, which I am almost certain she did, or was at least asked by the coroner to see it, "why did she not want answers as to why her face alone was all beat up?"

There are a lot of questions I had in the beginning, and of course, I have them all answered now, but it never sat well with me the way everyone has acted since Whitney's death. Whitney's face alone was swollen to where, anyone looking at her knew that she was punched in the face and beaten up badly. Why did Mama Cissy not want answers after seeing her daughter that way?

I would have gone directly in front of a camera and had a press conference after seeing Whitney like that. Someone would have to tell me who punched my daughter's face out like that. I do not want to say anything bad about Mama Cissy, and God knows I have tried to be as nice as I can and go easy trying to be respectful at the same time, but I must tell the truth and get this off my mind, because it is bothering my soul. There is no way to sugarcoat this, not even a little bit. Because at the end of the day, it is not I nor my brother Bobby that has ever been ugly or harsh towards anyone. We have always respected any of Whitney's family. But time is out now for standing by and allowing this kind of thing to take place on my watch.

I have a duty by God to speak the truth, and so shall I do it very respectfully and humbly as I possibly can. We are the ones who continue to stand and bear everything thrown in front of us. We are the ones who are and have always been suffering the evil deeds of others in this family. There are people who have no right whatsoever to do the things that they have done and are continuing to do with my family members.

As God is my Witness

These people are no relation to us or to Whitney, and they are walking around here holding her estate as if they are worthy to be in such a position. Someone is getting paid off and the "FEDS" need to step in and do something about this case. I have never experienced anything this traumatizing and more devastating in my life. It has even taken a toll on my children in my home. We are so shocked today to learn that there is absolutely no blood running through any Houston's veins that match Whitney's blood except Whitney's father, Poppa John.

It is just so sad how Whitney was left without anyone caring enough to help bring her some kind of justice and that is the reason why. Something was always so very wrong with this picture. I am saying this with all due respect to anyone who ever loved Whitney. I am not saying that all Houston's hated Whitney, because I do believe that her brother Michael loved her genuinely and over everyone else.

It was even a sad thing when her godmother Aretha failed to show up for her at her funeral. Whitney's beautiful cousin Dionne Warwick had to break the news to everyone on that podium that Aretha wasn't showing up that day for Whitney. It was just so sad to know that they really expected her, and I did too, but she was a no show that day. I cried so hard for Whitney because I could not believe what was going on. Her casket was closed, plus there were just not enough real people speaking on her behalf that got up on the stage. I wanted to go up there and just talk to everyone about what Whitney would have wanted everyone to hear at her funeral. The only people that I saw genuinely were, Dionne Warwick and BeBe & CeCe Winan's, Aunt Bey and her children including Shelly.

As God is my Witness

This was a very sad event that day. Pat Garland goes up and speaks, and she says nothing meaningful about Whitney in my opinion. But she gives Clive Davis far more respect and attention, and the way she did it was so obvious that she was trying to please Clive Davis. People laughed at her after the funeral was over, but I found nothing funny. I said, this is a sad day. I felt like Whitney's funeral was so weak, and it was so disrespectful to me, and it was very dry and dull.

I found it to be very bootlicking when I saw Pat get up on that stage and do that. I said, to myself, this is an angel, an Icon and a very important soul we are talking about, and this is how you all do Whitney? It was Whitney Houston's funeral, and for the sake of God, why did you all have it here? Why would Pat Houston get up there and focus on Clive and not Whitney at Whitney's funeral? It made no sense to me or anyone else at all.

I mean, it is OK to say something nice about someone or anyone, there's nothing wrong with that, but it was the way she did it, and how she did it, you would have had to be there to see it. Everyone knows, when you have a funeral, you are to focus on the person laying in that casket. Pat said a lot of things to Clive Davis to make him feel good, and as if it was his funeral, is what I felt and got out of it. Many people agreed with me and were saying the same thing.

It seemed to me that she intentionally disregarded Whitney to praise Clive, and she did it proudly. In my mind, I kept saying, she is being sarcastic towards Whitney. The whole time I sat there I thought about that bathtub water that someone put Whitney in. I do not for one second believe that she drowned in any bathtub, of course not!

As God is my Witness

Those bathtubs at the Beverly Hilton Hotel are small, and too small in my opinion for a little baby to drown in. I believe Whitney was killed before she was placed in that water. That water was too hot for her to be sitting in all that time anyways. I don't know anyone who would take such a hot bath like that and be able to sit in it. I am 100% certain that her body was placed in that bathtub after she was murdered. Besides, Whitney did not ever get in that hotel bath water. I said this many times and don't know if people are really listening, or even understand the seriousness in what I have said, but it is a true statement.

THE DEMONS CAME FOR BOBBY!

Also, as I was sitting at this funeral, I noticed right away that they were going to be starting trouble with us or my brother. They did not want to leave well enough alone and let it be peaceful for Whitney. I am not saying that Mama Cissy did anything because she did not move at all. I believe this was all Pat Houston's doing. However, being that Mama Cissy does not like Bobby, it is a possibility she told them before we even got there to treat Bobby this way, who knows?

The thing was that someone wanted so badly to put my brother Bobby out of this funeral. Before they even started, I could feel the spirit in the air, because God was with me, and He was downloading information to me. He was letting me know the minds of the animals that were in there orchestrating the evils and preparing to release demons right into that funeral. The person that sent this man over to my brother Bobby to ask him to move his seat was nothing more than a hater of Bobby Brown and Whitney Houston, I am sure. Now, this is at my brother's wife's funeral, and they did this to my brother for the purpose of trying to make him feel uncomfortable, I am not stupid.

As God is my Witness

People have a lot of nerve and should leave people alone, because you never know what folks got on their mind, or what they are capable of doing at such a time like this because of a mindset. It was a dangerous time to be playing with someone's emotions at a funeral. And then, I dislike people who throw rocks at someone and then they hide their hands as if they have not done anything. We knew and felt in our gut who sent that man over there to Bobby, and we talked about it afterwards.

Certain evil people have always been so jealous of Bobby and Whitney's relationship because their marriage has never been a happy one. And Bobby and Whitney had a happy one and they loved each other, so you see, hatred was in the house this day. But God sees everything, and He does not like ugly that is for sure. When you bother someone for no reason, and except that you are just sickly jealous of a person; God has a special huge surprise for people like that today. He will make them wish they had left folks alone. See, God is a warrior who takes good care of His children that are warriors too. He's not a punk and He does not allow His children to be one.

Many people love to do things and hope that they will never be exposed. They had no idea that I was watching their every move, taking notes, and doing my investigations for Whitney and my niece still at this time. It is for this reason; I must write this today with the absolute truth about people and who they truly are. There will be no bruising my family members and we tum the other cheek and let you get away with it. No, Bobby has not done anything to anyone for them to send some man over there to agitate my brother's spirit as he and his children are mourning his wife and their stepmother at her funeral. That was so disrespectful of them to do that at such a time. Bobby sat there so quietly and peacefully that day without saying one word.

As God is my Witness

People were saying that it was Pat Houston that had done that, and yes, I do agree. We do not know who sent this man over to bother us, but what I do know is, they had no regard for not only another human being's "life" but also little children that were sitting there with my brother that saw that behavior coming from these animals. See, when you can taint children's hearts like that, I have lost respect for you. I want to tell you this so that this world is not fooled by the rumors and lies that have been going around regarding that incident with Bobby Brown at Whitney's funeral.

Bobby did nothing wrong and he said nothing to anyone at any time at all. There were absolutely no words coming out of his mouth. I believed that they wanted smoke from Bobby that day; and it was a fine day to get it and become very surprised at the outcome, and who was there waiting to protect my family. They wanted to put him out of the funeral, I am sure. But Bobby was a better man about it; being as respectful as he possibly could that day. Let me tell you how it went down. I was sitting right there to witness it all.

This man had all the room in the world to just bend down and whisper right into Bobby's ear from the aisle that was clear for him because Bobby was the first person seated sitting right there next to the aisle. There was not anyone in this troublemaker's way, if he came down that aisle where Bobby was sitting on the end of that bench. In other words, Bobby was the first person sitting there had he came down that aisle and whispered in his ear. Yet, guess what this trouble making man did?

Instead of walking down a clear aisle where no one is in his way. And when I say no one, I mean absolutely no one was in this man's way, the aisle was clear without just one person in his way.

As God is my Witness

Bobby is sitting right there at the end. This troublemaker comes from way on the other side, near the wall, where there are so many people standing against this wall, he had no room to pass them in the first place!

I am hoping you're picturing a Church, with an aisle in the middle, and people on the left and people on the right. The Church is full, but picture it as if you were to walk in the front door of this Church. OK, the aisle directly in front of you is the middle and it is "clear," because everyone is sitting down except for the people all the way over against the walls of the Church way over away from the middle aisle and over on the walls at the left and right of this Church.

There are people to the left sitting, and people to the right of you sitting. OK, now, if you were to just simply walk straight down this aisle, you will see Bobby sitting to your right, but closer to the front. Bobby is the first person in his seat on the bench, so, if you just walked straight down, all you had to do is whisper in his ear, because he is the closes to you and the first one sitting right there on the end!

You don't have to excuse yourself, bother anyone else, or push your way through anyone, all you have to do is walk straight down the aisle and there he is, you can whisper in his ear what you will, without bothering anyone. But no, that was too much like right and easy. And it is obvious you know exactly where Bobby is, because you came directly to him! Therefore, somebody had already spotted us walking in the Church and taking our seats. OK, from the top of the Church, this man walks all the way over to his right at the crowded walls, where there is a huge line of people who are standing up with nowhere to sit down, and people who could hardly breathe, because it's so crowded!

As God is my Witness

He walks all in between them, excusing himself, and making them all uncomfortable. Now, it is so obvious, he's doing all of this just to show everyone in the Church, where he was going, which was over to Bobby. He knew all eyes would be on him and people would see him make his way to Bobby. He's going through all of this and excusing himself through all these people coming down that wall. He now gets to our bench, and my and Tommy's sons are sitting right there at the end, so they are first to get up as this man comes through bumping everyone's knees and harshly excusing himself now.

Then I got up, then my brother Tommy got up, and last is Bobby and his children and then finally he reaches Bobby. He bends down and acts like he is there to politely whisper in Bobby's ear. And anyone in their right mind can see this demon for who he was. Without Bobby saying one word, he gets up and he asks all of us to get up and move as well.

We respectfully to our brother, we get up and we move back one bench, altogether. This man has already walked on the way he should have come in the first place. He goes right on out on Bobby's side like it wasn't nothing. I said to myself, how ignorant can someone like him be? After we all got up to move the first time, this man came down the aisle once again and he does the very same thing and coming the very same way! He walks by all of us in that very same way by bumping our knees again! Again, you can clearly see that he wants others to see him do this to Bobby.

By him doing all of that, of course, forced all eyes on him at this funeral so that they can see him calling himself coming for my brother. This demon knew exactly what he was doing by trying my brother.

As God is my Witness

And with all due respect, I dislike people who will start trouble like this, and they expect you to allow them to continue disrespecting you and think you will just take it. Wrong family, wrong time. I then whispered in Tommy's ear and said, "Tommy, I'm telling you right now, I am not moving again, it's clear to us what he is trying to do.

I called Bobby because now he got up to leave! Bobby doesn't answer me, he continues walking over to Whitney's casket with his son little Bobby. I immediately say, tell Bobby to come back down, he doesn't have to leave. Tommy says, nab, he's coming back, chill, he's coming back. I didn't buy it and I knew this man had frustrated my brother and forced him out of his seat. I said, Nab Tommy, he better not come whispering in our ear because I'm not moving! Tommy said, "Chill hang on... don't get upset."

Bobby had moved twice for them, and then he got tired and just politely and very humble, he got up, walked up to Whitney's casket, kissed her, and walked straight to the door and just walked out holding his son, Bobby Brown Jr.'s hand. It went exactly like that without any words being passed at all.

I sat there and witnessed the whole thing from beginning to end. Bobby never said two words to anyone. Whoever started the rumor about Bobby Brown having words with someone at this funeral, it was a straight up lie. Furthermore, nobody put my brother out of that funeral. You would have heard the Brown's going off completely if that happened. Besides, if they had laid a finger on my brother, it would have been a war up in there. And it would have been on them because they did everything, they could agitate us and force us out of our seats.

As God is my Witness

What I will not tolerate is that kind of disrespect at a loved one's funeral. I had people on the inside and the outside who were ready for whatever they were on. That was the one thing I was not going to sit back and allow to happen. Sometimes you must simply go to war to establish peace. People start things being unaware of how it may end and it's not a good thing to do all the time, especially when you don't know a man. And regardless of who anyone thinks they are. There is only one God in my book, and every man has skin that tears. People should be careful to never get to a point where they don't think they have to give respect to another human being, especially a humble one who deserves it, and is giving it to you.

Every man deserves respect, I don't care who you are. When you disrespect another man, you may have violated a serious law. Some people have no idea the depths of another man's law. All I know is, had anything happened, we would have been in our right to defend ourselves. Another thing, you cannot carry on and just continue to do things to people and expect them to just sit down and stand down on every single disrespectful thing you decide to do to them. No, we are living in another time today. "We are not some chumps you can just walk up on and do your dirt and think you will get away with it. Bobby's a man, and I am a woman just like anyone else." I give respect, and I demand the same.

Here is a man (Bobby) who has not done anything at all to any of them, and they act like demons coming for him as if he did something to someone. Whoever sent that man over there, they had no respect for Whitney, because if they did, they would not ever disrespect the man she loved more than any other person in this world when she was alive.

As God is my Witness

That was straight up jealousy, if you ask me. As God is my witness, we were sitting there minding our business, being quiet and all. Yet, it was not enough to just let Whitney rest and we have peace at her funeral. They had to come for Bobby because their evil ways could not be still. What they didn't realize was, they did this to not only him, but his children as well, and that's a No, No.

Also, they told another lie about my brother and his daughter. As God is my witness, Bobby, and Krissy never had any words whatsoever at this funeral, as the media lied about that too. Never once did anything like that happen. Krissy sat there the whole time crying about her mother, and she did not move, not even a little bit.

CHAPTER 13
WHAT HAPPENED OVERALL ... AND WHO REALLY KILLED BOBBI KRISTINA BROWN?

OK, here we go. Reader, I want you to first know that "no one broke into Whitney's hotel room, nor did Whitney Houston get murdered by some drug dealer, as many people have tried to say, as well as those who believe this facade. Those lies were made up by certain people who want the public to believe this." Please always keep this in mind whenever you think about Whitney Houston. Her death happened in that hotel while she was around her own so-called family members and associates. Whitney Houston was an Icon, and a famous woman who did not have a lot of people around her, as we all know.

You also need to know that she was in this hotel for two weeks prior to the Clive Davis event. Which told me that someone probably had her come there early so that they could have a head start on getting to her and seeing to it that she did not leave there alive, if you understand me. Why she was there for two whole weeks before the Clive Davis event, and who asked her to be there earlier, is a mystery to me knowing how Whitney hates to be in LA without Bobby.

One of the things I'd like for you to keep in mind 1s that Whitney Houston was a very smart and wise woman, who handled her own business, and she was a woman who never needed a manager. Whitney Houston managed her own career for so many years, all by herself and after her father Poppa John managed her, and she did not hire anyone to manage her at any time after that, as Pat Houston said she was her manager. I am here to tell you that was a bold face lie coming out of Pat Houston's mouth. You have no idea how true and serious this truly is. I say this like that because, for Pat Houston, to continue walking around saying, she is or she was, Whitney Houston's manager, and literally posing as such, is very serious with me for several reasons. First because I know, and I am 100% certain she is not and never was.

Second, it is serious because, I believe wholeheartedly that someone murdered Whitney for her estate money and for her legacy. For Pat to lie and we know it's a lie, it forces us to believe that she has played a great part in Whitney's demise. It is why I have always stood up and told the world that Pat Houston was and still is today "lying" about being Whitney's manager. No, she is not, and she has never been Whitney's manager, and anyone who knows Whitney for real, they know that what I am saying is the absolute truth.

I did not say that to just lash out at Pat, because I believe that she has something to do with Whitney's murder. I didn't say that out of my emotions of being angry with Pat either. Yes, I was and still am angry about all of this. Yet, today, God has given me peace with knowing what I know. And I have said that because it is a true statement, period.A person listening may say, "Well, why does it matter and what kind of weight does it hold and why is it that important to keep saying, Leolah? It is important to understand what actually happened to Whitney Houston. If you were found beaten in a hotel, and then someone you know, but have never liked, they suddenly stand up to tell the world, they managed you, and they grab your estate from your child, go to court to fight your child after doing everything under the sun to hunt your child down, and they set your child up to be murdered, and when that doesn't work, they kill that child slowly in a hospice center by starving that child to death, and to top it all off, they win in a court of law against your child's biological father to have rights over your child's life, so that they can make decisions on her life and have her killed! Would you like that? Let me say this again, in case you didn't get it.

They have your daughter murdered in a hospital when they know your daughter does not have to die. I am sure that anyone hearing this would be upset. As God is my witness, I have not exaggerated one word of this. All your important things are being sold, including your "Catalog" which was sold almost immediately after your death. I cannot make all this stuff up, and no matter how hard it is to believe, it is the absolute truth, as God is my witness.

What is even worse, all, not some, but all of your family, whom you grew up with, and who are supposed to be there and fight for you, none of them are not anywhere around to do so. Those close to you are doing absolutely nothing good for you. In fact, they are acting as if they hate you and are so happy that you and your daughter are both now gone. Yes, this is what I believe, this is what I see, and this is the only thing that I fully understand wholeheartedly.

To top it all off, Pat Houston made that statement in the media about being Whitney's manager, just so she could gain the attention of Whitney's fans as she's ripping Whitney off because, Pat had been on a mission to take everything she possibly could from Whitney, including Whitney's fans. If you knew the relationship of these two people, you would not only believe what I am saying, but you would know and then you would see this whole picture for yourself, and just as the rest of us see it. See, it's hard to believe one thing, if you already have your mind set to believe something else.

As God is my Witness

But just as sure as you are reading these words, I want you to know, that is not true at all about her being Whitney's manager. Furthermore, I cannot allow her to get away with lying about Whitney, because Whitney herself would be devastated and have a pissing fit, to know that Pat was doing everything she is doing today in her name. Trust me when I tell you that Whitney Houston was indeed murdered in that hotel room on February 11, 2012. She was also beaten to death in that hotel room, and whoever murdered her, did it to obtain her estate and to take her legacy away from her. That is another reason Pat stood up to tell that lie. To top it all off, they even went as far as to kill her daughter, so that her daughter, which is my niece, would not inherit her own mother's estate.

This is why Leolah is stressing this all the time, because it is the absolute truth, as God is my witness. Whitney Houston dying in a bathtub at the Beverly Hilton Hotel, from a drug overdose and drowning, is ridiculously foolish to believe. First, when I finally came to my senses and realized how hard it was for an adult to drown in that hotel bathtub, I was traumatized to know they would even say such a thing and get away with it. It is almost impossible to drown in those baby bathtubs. Also, I know plenty of people who have gotten high over the years and have taken baths in much bigger bathtubs and even gone into swimming pools and never drowned themselves.

Whitney Houston was no foolish woman even when she was using drugs. She was not using drugs while she was at this hotel, let the truth be told. According to the coroner, he determined the fact that, she had a very small amount in her system, and not even enough to kill a baby. If you ask me, the way he described it, it could have easily been residue from the past.

As God is my Witness

What I believe it was, was that someone tried to poison her, and it was why it was a small amount in her system. I really believe someone drugged her and ran and hid from her afterwards. They did not want to face Whitney once they realized they hadn't killed her. The behavior and actions of other people running around this hotel acting suspicious, it placed me in a position to believe they were trying their best to murder my sister and her daughter at this hotel.

My family and I knew things about Whitney and how she operated and did things that she never ever in all her years deviated from. One of those things was that she never ever went without "security" and especially when she was out of town in LA.

Whitney's security had to always be at her hotel room door at any given time. In this case and because she was in LA, we believe, and we know that there was a second security guy who was not recognized as being there at that hotel when all of this happened to Whitney. Who he was, is another unanswered question.

The one question I have for her security man, Ray is, where were you when Whitney was being beaten to death, and why were you not there with her at all times as you were being paid to be? I'd like to seriously know his excuse for not being with Whitney.

Everyone else has lied about Whitney. I seriously would like to sit down and talk with Ray with the hopes of the truth told to me. Because one lie leads to too many lies, and then before you know it, they have been telling them for so long, that the world starts believing only the lies because it's the only thing the media will keep in your face.

As God is my Witness

But we are going to keep that energy outdoors for now and get on with this truth that this whole world has been waiting for. OK, let's go! Like I said, I know things about Whitney and how she did things that she would never deviate from. Another thing that is so impossible with Whitney is that she will not ever sit down in a "hotel bathtub." Evidently, the culprits did not know this, and they tried to sell us this lie from the beginning, but you cannot fool those of us who knew Whitney. We all believe that this idea originated from Pat Houston's mind.

I said this to many of my family and friends. Every single one of us said the very same thing once we figured out why she lied about being her manager in the first place. We all said, "OMG! No, she did not go there and lie, knowing that Whitney couldn't stand her and would not ever do that!" It was also said in the media so that when she was seen out here handling Whitney's business in public, she would gain the respect of Whitney's fans and they would (in her mind) become her own fans afterwards.

A lot of people have said that Pat Houston was always so jealous and envious of Whitney just like Gary was. I will also say that I do agree far beyond a shadow of a doubt. I happen to know a whole lot more than what the public knows about Pat and Whitney, and it is old news for all of our families, but new to the people in this world. Therefore, I won't blame people who didn't know and went on to believe her lies. While I am here and to be even more honest, I have started to believe that the night before Whitney was found, she became aware that Pat and Gary both were in Los Angeles. I believe that she did not even know they were there in LA and became aware of them being there when she was at the Kelly Price party.

As God is my Witness

I say that because, I have studied the pictures that are online, that were taken of Whitney the night before her death, at the Kelly Price event party. Looking at these pictures, it seems to me as if Pat Houston was following Whitney around. Whitney seems agitated and angry about something. Go and look at these photos to see for yourself. It seems to me as if Pat's presence amongst Whitney was irritating her, and it is why Whitney seems to look frustrated in the pictures.

It was no surprise to me or us who knew their relationship. I still believe it to this day that Pat and Gary followed Whitney without her knowledge that evening until they popped up at that Kelly Price event. The one thing that was missing was Whitney's security.

Why is he "not" right there every time they snap those pictures? I have not yet seen a picture of Ray, Whitney's security, who is supposed to be following Whitney and be right there with her. If there is one, I have not seen it yet. But even if it is one, he should be in every single one is what I'm saying. Where is he?

For some reason, I believe that Whitney felt alone while she was in LA at this time. I know that my brother Bobby was out of the country on a tour. Krissy was with her, but it is a fact that Whitney was looking for someone to join her in LA at this time. I heard that she asked my sister Tina to come to LA to be with her during this time, and she also asked her niece Aleah to come.

This told me that she didn't have anyone there with her and Krissy and had to feel alone. Pat Houston sat on Oprah and said, Whitney was there doing an infomercial for her, which none of us believe for not even a half of a second.

As God is my Witness

To say that Whitney was doing an infomercial for Pat Houston, is just like saying, Whitney was going to take Krissy's hand and jump off the empire state building somewhere. It would not ever in the history of this life happen, period.

When we all saw her on Oprah, telling Oprah that, we all knew in our minds that Pat Houston was sitting there lying to Oprah about Whitney. Everyone that did see it said, "Why did she lie like that, she knows that we know that her and Whitney never held a conversation for more than a minute, and if they did Mama Cissy forced her to talk to Pat or even about Pat whenever Pat would just try to talk to Whitney." As a matter of fact, my brother, Bobby, had been married to Whitney for about 15 years, and I can't remember not even just one single time where Whitney spoke to Pat, like just saying, hi, and had a full conversation with her.

I am very seriously saying this. I am also sure that my brother Bobby knows exactly what I am talking about. Bobby himself was even shocked that Pat and Mama Cissy, both took him to court and fought him with his daughter's estate. During this time, Bobby cried on my sister Tina's shoulder saying, "Why is Pat doing this-she knows Whitney hated her!"

But see, it into really Mama Cissy whom I believe brought Pat into that family as a handler for her to keep watch on Whitney. And so, we believe that it is always her pushing Pat up there with Whitney, and/or forcing Whitney to have dealings with Pat. It doesn't matter what Pat says or does, Mama Cissy is going to back it up, simply because, like I said, she is a handler for her, and Pat is only doing all of Mama Cissy's work for her, if you get what I am trying to say here. I am only being honest in saying this.

As God is my Witness

If Whitney was alive, Pat would be nowhere near her estate, trust me. Anything Pat says of Whitney is going to be a story made up by Pat and we all know that. I also heard Pat tell Oprah, she was on a whole other floor than Whitney which sounded suspect to me as well. She was on another floor, but was there when Whitney's body came up dead, is very suspect to me. This was another thing that told me in my head that Whitney did not know that Pat or Gary was even in that hotel in the beginning.

I strongly believe that Whitney" death was planned and plotted out by Pat and Gary Houston, and they got a room at that hotel that week, or that day or whatever day they both checked in that hotel. I believe they both only came to that hotel to get rid of Whitney and Krissy.

Pat and Gary Houston both, knew that they had to scheme and plot their way into Whitney's space to even get that close-up on Whitney to do what they did to her. Trust me, I have been out on the road with Bobby and Whitney, I also lived with her and Bobby for a long time, and I know what I am talking about. With that said, you should know that I have studied how Whitney does things. I learned them because I was employed by her, and I've seen how she and Bobby both rolls. I know what they will and won't do. I am also their sister for crying out loud. Therefore, of course I know far more than a whole lot of other people in this world know.

I know what my brother Bobby and Whitney both will say yes and no to. I know when they are serious about something or not so serious. I know if they liked someone or if they really didn't at all. I know when they would lie in someone's face, when they are joking, being real or just being themselves.

As God is my Witness

When it comes to my sister, Whitney, I knew her like the back of my hand, and nobody knew her better than Bobby, of course. One thing for certain, whoever placed that lie out there about that bathtub surely didn't know Whitney at all, because she would never get in a hotel bathtub. So, that told us that whoever said that they didn't know Whitney at all, which was Pat Houston. Unless she just forgot altogether that we were listening to these lies. I personally do not know what led her to think that we were going to sit quietly and not say anything after they did what they did to my sister and niece.

WHAT HAPPENED AT THAT HOTEL WITH WHITNEY!?

OK, here we go, let's really get into it now. The very first thing that happened at the Beverly Hilton Hotel was, Whitney's niece Aleah got a call from someone who was there at the Beverly Hilton Hotel and saw something going on with the people who were with Whitney and thought she should report it. This person called Aleah and told her to get her Aunt Whitney out of that hotel because something very weird or fishy was happening or going on against Whitney and the people she had around her, which was Pat and Gary Houston, Ray J, Nick Gordon and whoever else was there in this hotel around Whitney and my niece. This person saw some sinister things going down and was trying to reach out to someone to tell them.

It was scary enough for her to contact Aleah and tell her to get her Aunty Whitney away from there because they knew that Whitney was in danger. Aleah said to me, Aunty LeLe, I called Aunty Whitney right then and there to make sure she was OK, and she sounded fine. In fact, she said that Whitney was in a good mood and told Aleah that she was having a good time, and even asked Aleah if she wanted to come to LA? Aleah told her that she couldn't because she had other very important obligations with her son. Now, I believe Aleah when she said, Whitney was happy. I can tell you myself that Whitney was happy at this time for several reasons.

For one, Whitney and Bobby had just had dinner in Los Angeles, and took Krissy with them to tell her that the two of them were now getting back together for another marriage. Whitney was happy that Bobby had finally said "yes!" This was a lot to be happy about for Whitney because she had been begging Bobby to remarry her and he finally said yes, after so many No's.

I and my siblings are witnesses to this, and we are very sure that this happened just like that. On top of this, she had just found out from the doctors that she was pregnant! Yes! Whitney Houston was pregnant by my brother, Bobby Brown. After Whitney's death, Krissy told us that Mommy had just got her doctor's report back saying the "pregnancy test" came back positive. Some people may not desire to hear this truth, but Whitney was for sure pregnant by Bobby, and we found out late because she found out late. Yet, this was great news for us all.

Now, again, Whitney had just literally begged my brother to re-marry her because she was so sorry that she had asked for that divorce, and she so desperately wanted her family back together. We knew this, but it was not for everybody else's ears back then. And so, not a lot of people knew this news yet. I am not sure if Bobby knew about the baby yet, because, the thing was I believe, Whitney was going to reveal it to him once he had gotten back to the States if she did not tell him beforehand.

As God is my Witness

And let me just remind you that Bobby was "overseas" at this time of her death. He was on his new tour that so suddenly came up right before all of this just so strangely happened to Whitney and Krissy at this hotel. Bobby had not toured for so long, but now his brother is no longer his manager and setting his dates, but who is because he is suddenly all over the place and everywhere away from his wife and child at this time? And even more strangely, my brother Tommy, who had been Bobby's manager, and "the best" manager for him, and responsible for his success, is no longer his manager anymore. Something is very wrong with this picture.

He is so far away, that he can't get to Whitney to be with her as she laid in that hotel dead for all those hours. It seems to me as if someone planned this thing and orchestrated it to go down just as it had. Meanwhile, Pat and Gary Houston are both in this hotel, running from room to room taking things out and placing things in it, to make it look a certain way for the authorities.

I don't care who you are, if this does not sound weird to you, well then, I don't know what is weird and strange anymore. It sounds like this was all a set up and happened right when Bobby was out of the country. It made me think that perhaps Whitney's phone was tapped, and they knew all this that was about to transpire with Bobby and Whitney coming back together and they got rid of her before he or she could get back. Those were my exact thoughts.

In fact, it seemed to me that around this time, he is always doing a show, or is just out of town whenever Whitney or his children need him. I thought this was just too inconvenient, and strangely coincidental. Even when Krissy was laying up in the hospital it was weird.

As God is my Witness

It was like, oh, Bobby, your daughter is in hospice, and I know this is hard, but I booked you a show out of the state. I am not certain who sets his tour dates, but this was all done while Krissy went into the hospital and hospice as well and started with Whitney being out of the country. I felt so bad for Krissy, because she always needed her father right there with her, and after all these years of not touring, he is now so suddenly touring in and out of the country going everywhere when she needs him the most. OK, back to Whitney. Now, Whitney is at "The Beverly Hilton Hotel" for the Clive Davis event that she had gotten invited to. She checks in at this hotel 2 weeks prior to this event.

I and my brother Bobby both know for a fact that Whitney does not like LA like that for one if Bobby is not there. Therefore, somebody had to have told her something to keep her in this hotel for that long before this event took place. She likes to be in & out of Los Angeles because she does not like LA. But I will say that Bobby was now there in LA, and so now she was there more because she wanted to get her husband back and she did.

While I am here talking about this, let me tell you something to keep in mind. When her body was found they said, Whitney's LA license was sitting on a table and pulled out of her purse. When I heard that part, I knew someone had to have placed that there. Think about it, why would an LA license be sitting outside her wallet out of everything else in her wallet? I know why and I will explain what I believe. First, again keep in mind that Whitney doesn't even like LA. For her to have an LA license is very strange. Second, she lived in Atlanta, so why would she have an LA license now, she lived in Atlanta?

As God is my Witness

I believe someone "planted" that ID and placed it there because they wanted the authorities to write it up as LA being her home, which I believe is untrue. Why would I say that you may ask? Because the plot is to get her estate monies and perhaps, they thought it be best to say that she lived in LA because they have different or better laws in LA, when it comes to a person's "estate" after they have died, if you are following me. I am almost sure that somebody else besides Whitney placed that license there, simply because they wanted it to be visible to the authorities. They want those in authority to believe that Whitney Houston now lived in LA.

And I am here to tell you that Whitney did not live in LA, she resided in LA for that time, but Atlanta was her new home. Why would she live in LA and her daughter lived in Atlanta? Does it make sense, at all? I did not think so. Ok, so that's like the 10th red flag. Don't forget that my nephew witnessed Pat and Gary both in the hallways running back and forth staging that hotel room before the authorities had gotten there. So, that could be our answer right there. They could have gotten that from somewhere and placed that license there. I am certain that they ran through Whitney's wallet, make no mistake about that part. More than anything, who and where did they get that license from, because I would bet all the tea in China that Whitney did not get an LA license?

Whitney had a Georgia license so how did that LA license pop up? It seems to me that someone knew someone at that DMV, and they have secretly and under cover discreetly gave that to Pat and Gary Houston. I honestly believe this, and I have a right to believe whatever I will.

As God is my Witness

Now, again, it had to be a good reason that Whitney would go there that early to that hotel. Otherwise, she would not have been there 2 weeks prior. I believe someone gave her some story and tricked her and had her come there two weeks prior, so that they could get an early start on taunting her and doing what they wanted to do to her, having enough time to make sure she was gone before this event took place.

STACY FRANCIS LIED

Now, I know that you see pictures out there the night before of Whitney having a good time singing with Kelly Price. But, also here, she is seen looking up-tight and disgruntled, not so happy when Pat Houston is (seemingly to me) following her around this party.

I see this in the pictures that someone kept taking of her and Pat for some strange reason, this night. I saw those pictures and I knew immediately that my sister was not in any way happy. In fact, she looked very uneasy and uncomfortable to me. Of course, this was the night before her death. I kept saying, whomever the person was taking these pictures, they sure seem to keep getting Whitney next to Pat for some reason...

Now we knew what happened the night before because we got word about what happened at that Kelly Price party with Whitney and this person who literally "lied" about Whitney, and on top of it, she also violated Whitney's body at that Kelly Price party. If you haven't heard about it, let me tell you and explain it to you as it came to my ears, from the source and witness's mouth. This is a person who saw everything go down from the beginning to the very end that night.

As God is my Witness

We have a reliable and credible eyewitness and a trustworthy person, who saw everything go down between Whitney and this Stacy Francis girl, who lied about her and Whitney's ordeal. Stacy Francis lied by saying that Whitney and her were arguing about Ray J, this night.

This woman Stacy Francis even went further with this lie and appeared on the Dr. Drew show and told this BIG LIE TO THIS WHOLE WORLD ABOUT WHITNEY HOUSTON wanting to fight her because of Ray J, the day before Whitney's body was found in that hotel. When I first heard this, I knew that it was a lie because I know Whitney and I also know that she did not like Ray J like that. I just could not figure out why this girl was saying this in her interview. I wanted to get to the bottom of this lie, and my blessing came, because God brought it straight to my door.

I am so grateful to God that He watched over Whitney like this. I said to myself, "God is not playing with anyone today!" If you are caught out here lying in this very hour, you will be exposed because we are living in that time now. We must be careful that we do right and speak the truth because God is watching and He surely has His angels out here at work baby. I knew that God was with me, but I did not know that God was going to bring a witness before me that quick to confirm with me that it was in fact a lie.

I know a lot of you reading this may not know who Stacy Francis is, because I did not know her either before this, but you can go look it up on the Dr. Drew show back in 2012, right after Whitney Houston was found dead. You will see Dr. Drew interviewing this girl Stacy who appeared on his show right after my interview with him, and after Whitney was found in 2012.

As God is my Witness

But OK, let's get to who told me it was all a bogus lie! My girl, whom I have so much love and respect for. A sister, who is well educated, wise and very intelligent, and has a lot of class, morals, and integrity and carries herself extremely well out here in this world. The one and only, "Omarosa Manigault Newman!" The queen who blessed the Donald Trump apprentice TV show, some time back, with her beautiful and so gorgeous presence. She is a former political aide to former US president, Mr. Donald Trump, and has no reason to tell a lie about this woman Stacy.

Omarosa and I spoke in Los Angeles face to face while we were in a green room getting our makeup done and preparing for our interviews this day. I was in LA to appear on the Doctor Drew show, and she was appearing on another show with Nancy Grace I believe.

She said, "Leolah, I was there, and I saw the whole entire thing from beginning to end, between Stacy Francis and your sister Whitney." My mouth literally flew open! She said, "That girl, Stacy Francis, she told a BIG HUGE LIE, and you can tell her that I told you, because that wasn't right what she did to your sister Whitney! She said, Leolah, I was right there, and I saw the whole thing!"

She said, it went exactly like this, Leolah. Whitney was standing there minding her own business; when Stacy Francis walked directly up to her and grabbed Whitney's BREAST and SQUEEZED them! Omarosa then said, Whitney went completely off on her and she could not believe that Stacy walked up to her and did that and disrespected and violated her body like that. She said, Whitney immediately snapped, and totally went off on Stacy Francis! That is what all the commotion was about with Whitney and Stacy Francis after all.

As God is my Witness

Stacy Francis got on Dr. Drew's show, and straight up lied about Whitney, and today she is another person being revealed as a liar! Omarosa said that Whitney said, "How dare you do that to me, don't you ever come anywhere near me and touch my body like that again! I do not play that mess!" I am sure that Stacy physically hurt Whitney by doing that to her because that's like squeezing a man in his private area. And why would a woman walk up to another woman and do such a perverted thing and violate her body like that? You have no idea what Whitney has been through in her life, so why would she try her like that? All this talk about Whitney arguing with her about Ray J, was just a HOAX and a bold-faced LIE AND IT WAS MADE UP!

It was a story that either Stacy or whoever asked her to do that (because I believe someone asked her to do that), and for whatever reasons she or they concocted the lie up for after she did it, it made me to believe that she too was a part of the Whitney Houston take down. Of course, I believe Omarosa's words because of her character and person she is and has always been out here as a straight-up sister, and I trust her word. Omarosa said that nothing like that happened regarding Stacy and Whitney arguing about Ray J. She said that Ray J had absolutely nothing at all to do with it. I could not believe my ears as she was telling me this creepy stuff! I could do nothing but shake my head. I said to myself, "That is such a perverted sick thing to do to someone's body!"

Now, I am thinking to myself, what else have they lied about and done to my sister since she had been there in that hotel because someone saw something and was afraid enough that they called all the way back to New Jersey from Los Angeles, suggesting that Aleah call her Aunty Whitney and check on her.

As God is my Witness

I literally saw stars and was so upset behind this lie! I said, there's no telling what they were doing to Whitney all night and that is also probably part of why my sister was so upset in those photos the media placed out there with Pat walking behind her with Whitney looking so upset and angry at something.

In my opinion and the way that I see everything after investigating this case, it seems to me like they were taunting and bothering Whitney, and probably all night long they did this. When I saw her with Pat, I knew that something just wasn't right with that picture. After Whitney's body came up, and I saw those pictures of Whitney and Pat going around,

I said right there immediately that Pat had to have her media friend take those pictures because she wanted to be seen with Whitney that night before. That is exactly what came into my head upon seeing those pictures. With all due respect, I see both Pat and Gary Houston as clout chasers. See, it was all part of the plan to get Pat out there with her, so that when Pat did her interviews, she could say, see, me and Whitney were together the night before. I think that is the only reason why Pat was there with Whitney following her at that party. We all knew Whitney and she would not be with Pat, so something was very wrong with that picture.

But I want to say this. With all due respect, I am convinced that those pictures were nothing more than a set up to make it look like Pat was cool with Whitney. Everyone whom I know and who knows Whitney said the same thing. First, you can look at Whitney's face in those pictures and see for yourself that Whitney was not happy with Pat following her around.

As God is my Witness

Whitney had that look of disgust and anger on her face, to all of us who know her. If you go back and look at Whitney's face, she is very upset every time Pat is near her. Whitney does not mess with this woman, I am telling you, reader. So, why is she with her now right before Whitney's death? I can answer that for you. Pat planned that and had someone there taking those pictures I would bet all the money I had.

On top of it, Whitney doesn't even look good with Pat being around her. See, you reader, you have no idea or clue as to Whitney and Pat's relationship, but we as Whitney's family members do, and so, we all know that it is "very weird and odd" for Whitney to have Pat that close to her at this party.

My brother Bobby knows exactly what I am saying. Knowing my sister's relationship with her and knowing how Whitney rolls out there in those streets is another game baby. Whitney did not want this woman anywhere around her at all. Therefore, we were sure that something was very wrong and going on. Whitney had not ever trusted her, never wanted her around her, and did not approve of her ever coming anywhere near her or her family at any time. Meaning, Bobby, Whitney and Bobbi Kristina and us as her family, period. Whitney would argue with her Mama Cissy about Pat a lot when I lived with her and my brother Bobby.

Furthermore, she always told us that she would never grace a space with her in it ever again, because see, Pat has done some things to Whitney that are very serious and things Whitney could not forget. This is where I began wondering if Pat and Gary, both had followed Whitney all the way there to that party "without Whitney knowing" it, until she got there to that event.

As God is my Witness

I would BET they did. Especially when I heard Pat tell Oprah that she was there in that hotel "on a whole other floor" and not on the same floor as Whitney. See, all of this may sound OK to you, because you don't know the real deal. And Pat knows this, and it is why she continues to lie. Anyone who travels with Whitney is normally on the same floor as her. Especially now because Bobby was not there with her, he was overseas.

Whitney would want people closer to her because she just never trusts hotels and the things that go on in them. There are a lot of things that are going on with this Whitney Houston case that just don't sound right at all to me. That bathtub lie was that first red flag for me and then it was like dominos.

Also, Pat and Gary are known for following Whitney everywhere she would go, and without her knowledge on many occasions. They would do this with no problem of looking weird to themselves. I guess they were so desperate for whatever they had plotted out for Whitney. I am a real eyewitness to them both following Whitney around "without" her knowledge. I even saw them following me when I first got custody of my niece, Bobbi Kristina.

I should have known then that they were up to something. I feel so sorry for Whitney now, just knowing their secret agenda today and why everything was going the way they were. Whitney Houston's life was a sad one. It made no sense for these people to get away with doing her like they did.

Today, after looking back, I know why they did that. They were doing all that following us around to create a paper trail for a much later date, like today. And what I mean by that is this.

As God is my Witness

They wanted to set up something for those in authority, like a judge, so that they could say they did things in the past and I guess for a long time, is what they will probably lie and tell them. They wanted to say that they were with my niece Krissy, and doing things such as taking her to her doctors, etc.

But I never witnessed them taking my niece anywhere, I DID. I am the only one who did all of that because it was a court order that ONLY I COULD TAKE CARE OF KRISSY, AND I WAS WHITNEY'S CHOICE, PERIOD. I had full custody from the courts, and not even Bobby and Whitney could take her to school, pick her up or basically do anything with her until they got clean, which they did right away. Whitney was not stupid, and she must have known or felt something sinister about all of them.

Now I see why she acted the way she did with all of them, and why she loved my family so much. I just wish she could have been more vocal about the actual things they were doing and who they were. My guess is, after being born into such a life with such people, you at some point cannot believe they would go the lengths they went to do all of what they had in their hearts to do to her. You have got to be an evil person and not have respect for another man's life to do what these people have done. If they think they can deal with HELL and what is prepared for them, oh well. They have no idea what their hearts have set up for them.

Pat never did things with my niece Krissy until Whitney was dead and gone. I can now see Pat and Gary in full clear vision now and I am now aware of their scheming and plotting on Whitney.

As God is my Witness

When I saw them follow me to Krissy's doctors' office, when I had custody of her, I thought it was very creepy, I used to get so upset with them acting so weird, and I just ignored them. They are so sneaky, I said. My God what do they have in their minds, I would wonder? Now that Whitney's gone, and they have done all they did, I can see clearly now what they were doing all along. Today, knowing what I know about them both, Pat and Gary are nothing more than criminals to me. I can now see, now that Whitney's gone, what they were doing all that time that we were overlooking them, and not realizing that they were plotting all along.

They wanted that trail for the courts because they were coming after Whitney's estate money for Mama Cissy. I can tell now that, they only wanted it for the money, because they sold Whitney's catalog so quick, and like right after she died. So, you see, it was all done for that money, hands down baby, make no mistake about it! And they plotted this thing out for a long time.

Which means they were just waiting for the right chance in time to take her out. They are some fake and phony people who were always, and for a very long time, after Whitney for her estate and money. WOW is all I can say. As I am sitting here, I started remembering how it was even when Whitney was doing drugs at her house. I believe Gary sometimes came over to give Whitney drugs.

He would come around looking so suspicious all the time. When he came over, he would act very strange. It was like he was there just as a watch dog just to see what was going on. See, there thing was to be a feeder. It's almost like him and Pat both knew, and once Bobby was out of the way, they had Nick there enabling my niece with drugs after Whitney died.

As God is my Witness

They made sure they got to my niece to make sure that she was going to like drugs, and she was going to get hooked on them because they figured she needed a pacifier to sooth her pain of losing her mother. Gary did this same thing with Whitney when she was alive. Pat used those same tactics on Krissy by way of Nick when Whitney died. They first followed Whitney and Bobby all the way to Atlanta from New Jersey. And they did this right after Bobby and Whitney got married. So, you see, they had a habit of following Whitney all the time without her consent, as she also told me in the beginning.

I lived with Whitney, so I know the deal. The fact that somebody told Whitney to take a bath sounded "really" strange to me. Whitney never took baths in a hotel so I knew that would never happen, and we knew Pat was lying again. Whitney would not ever sit down in a hotel bathtub at any time, nor would she allow Mary to tell her to take a bath. On top of it, Whitney never talked to Mary like that, so I and everyone else who knew Whitney knew right away that it was a lie and that Pat had to have her relative Mary say that. It did not sound right nor make sense when Pat Houston told Oprah that Mary told Whitney to take a bath. I do not believe it ever happened and no one else does either, because it didn't. I know Pat made all of that up. Whitney doesn't even hold conversations with this woman Mary, or Pat.

Now, check this out. Pat was also telling Oprah that Whitney's "makeup artist" came to that hotel to see Whitney to do Whitney's makeup, right. And Pat stopped her in that hotel lobby. Now, this is not something that Pat was supposed to do, and she knows it. Nobody bothers Whitney's makeup artist or hairdresser at all or at any time whatsoever.

As God is my Witness

For Pat to say that she stopped that woman in that lobby it let me know she was holding her up trying to stall her because she knew that Whitney was being beaten to death on the 4rth floor of that hotel right at that moment. I believe Pat Houston was the look-out person, and she was making sure nobody came to disturb them while they were killing Whitney, I believe. Pat knows that Whitney never allows Pat in her business like that. So, or her to stop that woman in that lobby was a red flag for me which let us know that something was very wrong.

Pat says, she told the makeup artist to sit right there in that lobby, and she told Mary to go all the way upstairs to ask Whitney if she was ready for the makeup artist, when she already knows that woman came to that hotel for Whitney and Whitney already knows that she was coming, so she can go right upstairs without being bothered by Pat! First, Pat was not supposed to be in Whitney's business by stopping that woman. That is a No go, and everyone knows that! We all know that this is a no, no! OMG!

This is 2024, why couldn't Pat just call her brother Ray, Whitney's security on the phone? He is supposed to be at Whitney's door anyways! But you see, Pat forgot again that we know how Whitney operates her business. No one has ever stopped Whitney's people from going to her whenever she called them. Pat knew what she was doing by holding that woman right there.

If this world only knew Whitney Houston and how she operated, you would know right off base that Pat was doing something sinister, and she was indeed guilty of something. It is why she stopped that makeup artist in that lobby.

As God is my Witness

A few minutes later she said that she went upstairs herself and was walking the hall on Whitney's floor and saw that makeup artist in the hallway standing in front of Whitney's door screaming! She skipped the part where Mary was supposed to let that woman know if she could come upstairs or not.

I understand it as Pat lying, while others have no clue. Oprah says, OK, so you said the "hairdresser" was at the door screaming at first. As her and Oprah is sitting there conversing, Pat first said it was the makeup artist that was at the door, and Oprah asks her to run it by her again. Oprah says, "OK, so, run this by me again, so, you said the hairdresser was at the door screaming right?" Pat goes on to say, "Yes, so, the "hairdresser" ...and Blah... Blah... Blah. I was listening, so I caught it quick because I already knew she was lying. I said, OH NO, HOLD IT RIGHT THERE! PAT FIRST SAID, THE MAKEUP ARTIST WAS AT THAT HOTEL ROOM DOOR SCREAMING, AND NOT THE HAIRDRESSER! NOW, SHE CHANGED IT TO THE HAIRDRESSER?

So, you see, she was tripping up in her words. I immediately said, see, look at that right there, Pat was nervous and guilty of something, and it was why she was tripping up in her words. Another thing, she is hardly looking at Oprah as she is talking, it is literally killing her to look in Oprah's face. She knows that she must or needs to, and so, she was struggling, or else people would say something about how suspicious she looks and sounds right now. I saw a whole lot of guilt with her talking to Oprah.

I said, which one was it, Pat, the hairdresser or the makeup artist? Now, this is when it is supposed to be fresh in your mind, because it just now happened. So, why the mix-up?

As God is my Witness

Where is the confusion coming from, Pat? Reader, please go back and listen carefully and you will see what I am talking about here, reader. It's on YouTube, the video of Oprah and Pat right after Whitney's body was found in that hotel. Pat first said it was the makeup artist that was at that door (of the room Whitney's body laid in on the floor), screaming because she found Whitney on the floor dead. Then she said it was the hairdresser.

My belief is that she was so guilty and nervous that she just did not realize what she was saying at all, and she was making stuff up as she went along because she was forgetting what she was supposed to say. She was literally losing it if you ask me. It did not sound right to us for a few reasons. Let me explain something to this world and please listen well, because this is very important to know and detrimentally important to this case as everything else is too.

First and foremost, Whitney's makeup artist and/or hairdresser or anyone who Whitney has ever hired for her personally, will always go straight to Whitney's room without having anyone stop her in a lobby. I am sure that Whitney's makeup artist knows what I am talking about if she is reading this book. Even she or he knows what I am saying.

I would bet anyone any amount of money that it never happened to that makeup artist to get stopped going to Whitney's room or anywhere, in all the years of working with Whitney. But on the day that she gets stopped, Whitney is in a room dead. Come on now, this is not good and we all know it. The reason being is because first, Pat does not "ever" get into any of Whitney's business, by speaking to anyone who comes anywhere to see Whitney.

As God is my Witness

She would have cussed Pat out, had the circumstances been different and happening in another time and the day was a regular normal day for Whitney. Whitney has that relationship with her people, and they know what to do when they come to that hotel to see Whitney.

They do not have to even entertain Pat at all because she has nothing to do with Whitney and her business. Plus, she is never around Whitney like that. Ask my brother Bobby, he will tell you. And it sounds like that hairdresser ignored Pat and went on that floor anyways, from the looks of how she explained her being on that floor all sudden after she had just left her in the lobby.

If my memory serves me correctly, I don't think Pat explained properly how the hairdresser ended up on Whitney's floor, after all. In other words, she did not tell the full story of what happened after she told the hairdresser to wait in the lobby. I think she skipped all the way up to being on the floor walking and then she just heard screams.

So, you see, there are a lot of things missing, and a lot of suspiciousness going on and I know exactly why it all seems bogus. First, Pat has not ever had anything to do with anyone connected to Whitney like that. No, that hairdresser did not have to stop in that lobby and wait for Mary to go all the way up in an elevator to ask Whitney anything. Whitney would probably, and more likely, not even open her hotel room door for Mary. Pat thought it was safe to tell these lies and perhaps she was going to get away with them. Nobody went to Whitney's door at all to check anything trust me when I tell you. Let me tell you what happened, because I know, and I am 100% certain that this was the deal!

As God is my Witness

I believe that Pat specifically went to that lobby to intentionally stop Whitney's makeup artist in that lobby to 'stall her out', so that she would not get in that elevator and go up to that 4rth floor and hear Whitney's screams, as they were beating Whitney to death! She knew that, if that makeup artist went on that floor, there whole game would have been busted wide open.

Pat knew that Whitney was being dealt with in that hotel room at that time, and that is why she met that makeup artist in that lobby. After she told her to sit there, she herself went up on that floor to see what they had done or how far they had gotten in killing Whitney. If Pat is reading this, she knows that I am telling the truth. I can't prove it, but it is the truth in my head. This is my opinion, my belief, and I feel this in my gut. Now, let me open your third eye. Remember when she told Oprah that she "had not spoken to Whitney ALL DAY and was even avoiding her calls? OK, well let's start right there and let's make some sense of this. OK, so Pat told Oprah that she didn't talk to Whitney nor answer her calls "all day, right?

Even though I knew why she was hiding from Whitney, she never told anyone "Why" she didn't answer Whitney's calls all day. Now, here is a person who just said, Whitney was there for her to do an infomercial for her new candle line. Plus, Whitney is only there for the Clive event as well.

Now, if Pat was there with Whitney and everything was well and good with her working for Whitney, then why didn't she just answer the phone when she saw Whitney calling? What held Pat back from answering that phone at such a critical time. All the events going on and that is supposedly "why" they are there right? Just picture this and ask yourself, does it sound right?

As God is my Witness

It's crunch time at this time! You got Clive's event today, you're supposedly there to help Whitney and I'm sure Whitney needs things because the show or rather event is about to start the Clive event! Whitney's supposedly doing this infomercial for Pat this day, but Pat hasn't answered Whitney's phone calls, "ALLDAY, says Pat? Yet, Pat says she's not picking up her phone? And she wasn't shy to tell on herself either. I guess she told the truth there because she didn't know what may come next with the authorities. So, she told the truth in case someone checks her phone.

Yeah, right, she knows what Whitney wants is why she's not answering that phone. I wonder what they did with Whitney's phone, and did the authorities ask for it? Why did they not investigate this case knowing Whitney was beaten like she was? All this blood on all their hands is something God will ask them when they face Him, I hope they know. Third Eye Stuff!

How would she dare stop Whitney's makeup artist in the lobby and tell Mary to go all the way up in an elevator to ask Whitney if she was ready, if she hadn't spoken to Whitney all day? Now, you see, that doesn't make much sense, does it? You haven't spoken to Whitney all day, but you put yourself in her personal private business by stopping her hairdresser in that lobby and telling Mary to go ask if Whitney wants her hairdresser upstairs. When I tell you that Pat most definitely has something to do with the demise of Whitney Houston, please believe it and count her in and stick a pin in it because one day it will all surface and come to the light. Everybody knows that Whitney is very personal with her people and when you see them coming you are to have nothing to say.

As God is my Witness

That woman knows what to do because she already spoke to Whitney and Whitney is expecting her to come straight to her room and did not tell her to check in with anyone. How much does anyone want to BET that none of Whitney's people ever had to check in with anyone. What I'm saying is this. Again, she stalled that makeup artist up in the lobby so that she would not know what they were doing to Whitney altogether. God is a witness for me!

Now, she told Oprah her room is not even on the same floor as Whitney right, so what is Pat even doing on Whitney's floor and how did she just happen to walk by on Whitney's floor and hear the screams coincidently? Then she tells Oprah that she walked slowly and told a stranger who opened her door to call the police! Third eye Stuff Again ... (think about it) You haven't spoken to Whitney all day, you ducked all her calls, and knew nothing about nothing going on with her that day, BUT YOU WILL STOP HER MAKEUP ARTIST AND HAVE HER SITTING IN THAT LOBBY STOPPING HER FROM GOING TO WHITNEY'S ROOM?

There is no way on this planet that you can explain that to anyone and get away with it. Pat knew that Gary was upstairs beating Whitney to death, and with so much anger and force, he did not allow Whitney to leave out of that room because his intention was to end Whitney's life right then and there. He also had help from another individual, I just cannot put my finger on that other person, but I believe Gary Houston did this and is that main culprit, I am sure.

I strongly believe that he had help to do it and that help was Nick Gordon and/or Ray J, and that is my belief. Now, it could possibly be someone else, but Gary Houston was the actual person that did the most work in killing Whitney.

As God is my Witness

I do not believe that Gary killed Whitney on his own and by himself. I do believe it was more than one man. I believe they surrounded her in that room and did not let her out and she did try to get out, trust me. For Whitney's security guy Ray to tell me that room looked like a tornado hit it, it told me that Whitney was in there fighting for her life! Her body even told anyone that she literally fought for her life. Wounds, marks, bruises and scars all up and down her body. Her face was even swollen so why did those in authority overlook that and suppress the information and not give it to the public? Whitney Houston was murdered, and they all know it.

With all the technology in this world, who has to get in an elevator to go up to the 4rth floor to ask one simple question when you could just easily pick up your cell phone and call someone? I am sure Whitney's makeup artist knows exactly what I am saying, and if she is asked, she may not want to get involved, but I would bet all the tea in China she would say, yes that was odd and unusual to happen with Pat stopping her in that lobby because Pat herself was a part of Whitney's demise, and she knew what was going on and taking place on that 4th floor of the Beverly Hilton Hotel that day and at that moment.

Furthermore, anyone else would bear witness and say, "that is what Whitney's security is for, if you have a question, just call her security and ask him, he is supposed to be right there with her at her door anyway, so where was Ray at during this time? It is 2024 and people have phones, but she asked Mary to go up in the elevator. Pat Houston was covering for her husband, and she looks pretty much crazy at this time coming with that one.

As God is my Witness

But see, no one had to ask anyone anything so she figured she could say whatever without being questioned at all woman in that lobby like that. Whitney couldn't know, she was being beaten to death at that time, I'm sure. That is critical to me and in my mind. And where was Whitney's security at, and why was he M.I.A.? The whole story just did not sit well with me at all.

Then I didn't like the feeling I got when I heard what went on with my sister and Stacy Francis the night before. The lie about Whitney arguing with her over Ray J. So, this whole thing has given me a lot to think about. After hearing that about her and Whitney, it made the hair on my neck stand up, because it told me that whole story. It told me that they were 'taunting Whitney", and probably that whole night.

I had already known that was not something that Whitney would do. It seemed to me as if Whitney was seriously being targeted that night at that Kelly Price party. I wasn't even there so I can imagine what others saw themselves, and I pray to God that someone would step up and say something. How do you walk up to another woman and just touch her breast like that!? Stacy Francis seriously violated Whitney's body by doing that and she literally embarrassed her at the same time, and then added on to that AND LIED to destroy my sister's character with the public.

She knows nothing happened with Whitney being upset with her about Ray J, and then she turned it around and tried to make Whitney seem like that bad person. God only knows what else and who else had done something to my sister this night. And then, I am thinking about Whitney's security Ray, and where he was in all of this.

As God is my Witness

Whitney has never deviated from always having security with her and right by her side, so, where was he at, as Stacy Francis is violating Whitney's body at this time? See, I keep thinking about all of this as I look at these pictures of Pat following her around at this party at the same time. What were they doing to my sister, I am asking myself at this time. When a person acts like this, it tells you they have no respect for themselves or anyone else I do not appreciate her making up that story and trying to make my sister look like some sick puppy in love with Ray, because trust me, Whitney was not ever interested in Ray J.

I strongly believe that somebody told Stacy Francis to do that to Whitney. I could be wrong, but I don't think that Stacy Francis did that on her own. I saw a video of her, and I tried so hard to study her a little bit so that I could understand who she really was inside and as a person and human being. I think, if she was not around certain people, then yeah, she could easily be a better person. I believe that others influence and entice her to do things that she really isn't feeling sometimes. She seems to be a nice sister, just hanging with bad company is all.

I have asked God for guidance, and I trust that He has guided me with this; so, I believe that as my spirit tells me. It is so sad the things that people would do and the depths they would go to concoct such a lie. I feel like they could try to tear Whitney Houston's name and character, and on top of it all, it was a part of the conspiracy they had going on to make Whitney appear as if she was a mess right before her death. I am telling you; this is all I can get out of it. Besides, Whitney has already told me she has never had anything like that to do with Ray J in the first place, and of course I believe my sister, she had no reason to lie to me.

As God is my Witness

As she explained to me, she had no relationship at all with this person Ray J. All people have to do is simply give it a thought, she was married to Bobby Brown, and VERY SERIOUSLY LOVED HIM, and she never did that whenever he spoke with girls, so that plot did not work with us who really know Whitney and her character. That is dead out the window and gone. But now that I know that did not happen; it forced me to think that Whitney was being taunted that evening. The look on my sister's face in those pictures told me what was going on with her at that party.

I believe it was the beginning of them coming for her without her even knowing what time it was with all these people doing weird and crazy things to her that night. Because I'm sure a lot of other things happened that night that we know nothing of, because they were coming for her all the other days leading up to that day. Only God knows what else happened that night.

And again, as I have said, I do not believe that Whitney even knew that Pat and Gary both were there with her until she saw them at that party. They will follow Whitney whenever they feel like it without her even knowing it. They did it with me when I had custody of Krissy, so I am a witness to their actions. Now let's talk about what may have been happening to my niece earlier that day.

Bobbi Kristina gets found in the bathtub the day before Whitney is found, and I will tell you exactly how I believe this all went down that day from what information I gathered. Keep in mind, someone is doing things to both Whitney and Krissy while they are in Los Angeles at this hotel the day of and the day before. Keep in mind, "all of this is going down with Whitney Houston having 24 hr. security", does this sound all right to you?

As God is my Witness

It surely sounds like a setup to me. It tells me that people know far more than what they are saying. I certainly can't stand down and act as if this doesn't seem fishy. You can't make up, this is real. We are talking about an Icon, Whitney Houston. Phones are ringing and nobody is answering Whitney's calls. Ray J said he even regretted the missed calls. Pat on Oprah saying, "she did not answer Whitney's calls" all that day, and when I watched "Whitney interrupted Clive Davis's meeting" with Brandy Ray J's sister while she sat with Clive and Monica. I believe wholeheartedly, the note that Whitney passed Brandy was for her brother Ray J. I believe they were running around that hotel doing stuff to Whitney all week and probably the whole two weeks she was there.

Don't forget! Ray J said he regretted the missed calls, so could that mean that Whitney was dialing his phone too, and he was sending her to his voicemail because he was guilty of what he did with her as well? It seems evident to me and a whole lot of other people they were doing things against Whitney for these whole two weeks in that hotel. They all seem to know something, but there isn't anybody talking because they all know that Gary is the one who struck the blows with Whitney, I believe.

I also "very strongly" believe that Ray J may have "tried" to slip something in Whitney's food or drink and "it made her hot," and that is why she was "WET" looking for Ray J, and ended up stepping in front of his sister Brandy who was meeting with Clive Davis that day. Whitney seemed to do everything she could to let them know she was on to them and they knew it. You MUST go and look at this video on YouTube for yourself. There is a video out on "YouTube" with this on it. It is Whitney interrupting Clive Davis, Monica & Brandy during, I believe, a live interview they were doing together.

As God is my Witness

I believe that Whitney felt like they were doing something to her, and she wanted the world to know that she was not going down without a fight, or at least giving us clues as to what was really going on in that hotel that day. She was "wet" when she came before them. We have not paid attention to see this picture for what I believe it is.

Whatever Whitney had in her system, I believe it forced her into that water that day, and I believe that is why she walked up to Brandy, his sister, handing her that note for Ray J. I really do wholeheartedly believe that that note was for Ray J.

PLEASE DON'T FORGET THIS!

Now this is Whitney Houston who did not have drugs in her system (says the coroner) and who did not wish to get high anymore because she was carrying my "brother, Bobby Brown's baby" plus she had "been" clean and wanted to remain that way.

I believe Ray J taunted her and wanted her to get high or offered her drugs and she turned them down, and they all, being sneaky, had him sneak something in her drink and/or food that made her hot and wanting to jump in that water that day! I can see Ray J teaming up with Gary and Pat for this event because this is what they all do.

They love feeding people drugs. With her turning them all down now, they found a way to get something bad into her system by slipping something into her food or drink that dissolved fast without her knowing. But Whitney is smart, and she knew what they did. They knew Whitney was clean and did not desire to do drugs anymore.

As God is my Witness

I believe they did this and then they all disappeared away from Whitney, and it is why she kept her daughter close to her that day. They all made sure to stay out of her sight around that hotel. none of them showed up until her body was found in that room. I would BET Pat had not even spoken to Whitney since Whitney saw her at Kelly Price's event.

Krissy had eaten something as well, and it made her feel woozy after eating, and then she just woke up in her hotel bathtub!" Now, this was the day before Whitney was found. It makes sense to me, I don't know about you, but it all makes sense to me. It seems like they were all trying hard to get both the both of them in those bathtubs that day at the Beverly Hilton Hotel. But it was hard for them to do.

I believe they were all running around that hotel trying to duck and hide from Whitney and was probably kept saying to themselves, we cannot let her see us, she knows what we are trying to do, because Krissy came out of that water, and when she did, she ran to Whitney's room crying. Now, we all know how any mother is going to react to her child being targeted like that. Of course, Whitney is going to call everyone's phone, but none of them were answering their phones. I thank God that Ray J and Pat said it out loud in the media that they had missed calls from Whitney.

And the fact that they did not answer her calls helped me to crack this case. See, I am no fool. There has to be a good reason why no one wants to talk to Whitney when she calls, and what better reasons would a person have to NOT answer their phone? Of course, I believe in my heart that this was the deal. I also believe Whitney either took it upon herself or perhaps someone she was talking to, they told her to come down to Krissy's room to talk to them.

As God is my Witness

This is where I think Ray comes in at. The only person I believe Whitney trusted at this time would be her security, Ray. Because I don't think she would have walked down that hall and in there alone knowing that she was that upset and she knows how her brother Gary and her get when they argue, she knew it would be bad, so she had Ray go with her, and She (leaving her own room), left Krissy in her (Whitney's) bed.

She threw on her robe being naked and all, and she proceeded to go down that hall into Krissy's room or the adjoining room, to talk to someone; and she never came out alive. I believe when she got into that room they were in there, she and Gary got to arguing and Gary began hitting her very hard! And so hard that the blows he was throwing at her were so devastatingly surprising to her, and this caused her heart to bleed in that moment from the pain she began feeling. What I mean by that is, Whitney was so shocked that he would hit her so hard as if he wanted her dead, and she knew this.

I honestly believe this. And after they got started, she tried to leave outside that room to get away, and they would not allow her to leave. They surrounded her in that room and beat her until she closed her eyes. Whitney was shocked at how they all just stood there around her and would not let her go out that room. I also believe that Ray her security could have been right there with her, and she was probably looking to him to help her, but he knew if he did, they may do something to him because it was now going down in that room that they were not going to allow her to live through that. Yes, it is a possibility that Ray just stood down and let it all just go down right there in front of him.

As God is my Witness

Of course, he could have helped as well as Jonathon believes he has something to do with it. But I personally can't see Ray doing that to Whitney, so I do not know about that one, but again, I could be wrong. Then again, something tells me, no, that is not true, he just let it go down because he knew their plans long ago as well. They could have threatened Ray to stand back. See, everyone was out for Whitney's estate and money, make no mistake about that. Gary took this opportunity and ran with it, because he was thinking in his head, all the years of their plotting, scheming, and planning, and watching Whitney's life for all those years could now be all over, if he (Gary) would just expedite this mission and get this over with and end it for Whitney right now. Meanwhile, Pat is stalling her makeup artist in the lobby, and she is lurking in those hallways waiting to hear the words that Whitney is now gone.

And so, when she heard the screams, she knew that Gary's job was now over. And that is why Pat was so calm, cool and collective when Oprah asked what she did upon hearing the screams? Pat said, oh, no, I just walked slowly and asked a stranger or someone that opened their door to call 911. Wow! Yeah, Pat knew what was going on! She knew her husband had just killed Whitney. Pat at that time probably took a deep breath and said in her mind, YES THANK YOU SHE'S GONE! Because trust me when I tell you, they could not wait for the day to get rid of Whitney.

I am telling you it is a hate there that I cannot describe that Pat has for Whitney. Reader, you, have no idea or clue as to the level their feuding was on. There was no relationship there and this is why I say that Pat is lying about this.

As God is my Witness

People have no idea, and a few people may think that Pat is innocent of this, but as God is my witness, he is going to prove me right and show this world that, "YES, EVERYTHING LEOLAH HAS SAID IS REAL AND TRUE, AND THEY ALL HAVE A PART IN WHITNEY HOUSTON'S DEMISE." God is going to show any and every person that is seriously interested in knowing this truth, that I was correct. Wait for it because it's coming. Yeah, I believe Gary was thinking about that money and Whitney's estate and how he and Pat could forevermore enjoy Whitney's money that she worked so hard to obtain all her life.

That is "why" it was so easy for Pat to go into that hospice center and tell them she wanted them to kill my niece and let her die by starvation. Wow, how evil can a human being be? She and Mama Cissy did that because first Whitney is not Mama Cissy's child, and second, they have no use for Bobbi Kristina being here being over her mother's estate because they could not have what they wanted.

It's all about GREED AND WHITNEY'S MONEY at the end of the day. There is nothing else to this story but that. Yes, they did that because Krissy was fighting so hard to stay alive and she was successful. My niece wanted to live and come home with us. Gary ended it so painfully for Whitney because she went out with a hell of a fight. She did not make it easy for him. He won with her, but God had never taken His eyes off NONE OF THEM. All of them had been doing things around that hotel against Whitney and Krissy and then they ran away where Whitney could not see them. Ray J was probably in and out. Gary and Nick were doing the same.

As God is my Witness

Whitney had gotten it at the last minute realizing they were all out to get her, and that is why she walked up to them handing that note to Brandy. I am telling you, all of them are guilty one way or the other. I connected the dots with Ray J because of Whitney walking up on Brandy and Krissy's ordeal with Ray J soon as Whitney was pronounced deceased. It was obvious when Ray J came to that room and forced that pill on my niece. It told me they were all down with that. He was seriously trying to get rid of her because like I said, the plan was to take them at the same time.

That was plan A. Krissy first and then Whitney last. They wanted to be able to say that because Whitney found her daughter in that bathtub, she committed suicide right behind her. See, I added it up and got that from when the coroner said he got that phone call to be prepared to pick up a body at that hotel, remember? But there was no body because my niece came up out of that water. Then after Whitney dies, Ray J is right there suddenly to try to see to it that Krissy took that pill, and they were going to reverse and say the same thing.

I can't make this up, this was so easy to conclude because of all their actions in that hotel. I thank God for all that I have learned in my investigations. I thank God for Ray and Pat making statements about those missed calls and all. They helped me too. My niece, Krissy felt this same (hot) way when Ray J gave her a pill, and this is how I got that idea of "the water" and being hot and them wanting to be in water! It was all because of Ray J! Whitney was looking for him because of that water ordeal.

As God is my Witness

Krissy said, she too was also "hot and needed water" after taking a pill that Ray J gave her to take that day her mother was found. Ray J is a part of this murder, make no mistake about it. Anyone in their rightful mind would easily say the same. Whitney had to jump in that water to cool herself off from whatever it was that someone had given her unknowingly, and I believe that someone to be Ray J, of course.

If my memory serves me right, it was the second time Whitney had jumped in a pool of water that same day. I believe Monica asked her, "why are you wet again?" And just so you don't get confused. When Krissy was found in her bathtub, she was in her room and had ordered food in her room. Now, we don't know who was in her adjoining room with her at this time, or where Nick or anyone else was, but I would bet it was Nick who probably laced her food or drink. What we have to keep in mind, is that Pat Houston had Nick Gordon do EVERYTHING that was happening to Krissy and Whitney because se, Pat had to have someone else do it only because Whitney would not allow her around her like that. She could not get close or up on Whitney to do anything.

We don't know if someone else brought her food to that room or she had just eaten some other food and got really woozy and sleepy immediately after. But she did not remember after eating because she passed out. It was not until Ray J seen her that day, that Whitney's body was found that Krissy was asked to take this unknown pill that he kept forcing her to take that threw her into a seizure and she was rushed to the hospital by ambulance the same day. Now I see why he said, I was lying about him being there at that hotel. He didn't want anyone to know he was there and had done that to my niece.

As God is my Witness

But what else has Ray J done? See, that is all that I know of him doing but he was probably doing other Ish, I'm sure. God knows what he did to Whitney because she was furious at him, I could tell as she handed Brandy that note. She could not find him and like he said she called him, but he didn't answer his phone of course because he said he had missed calls.

Ray J just seemed to be doing some things at this hotel and was seen there acting weird. We are absolutely 100% certain that Ray J gave my niece, Krissy a pill that threw her into a seizure and rushed to a LA hospital by ambulance that day. I would not ever put something on someone that was not true, that is not me. This happened after Whitney was pronounced dead at that hotel. Krissy was rushed to a nearby LA hospital, simply because she was having a "seizure" from what Ray J had given her, I never lied about him.

My gut feeling tells me that Whitney went looking for him and thought it was OK to pass his sister that note to give to her brother because Whitney was "that" upset with him stemming from whatever it was he had given her. I know my sister and there would be no other reason for her to hand Brandy anything. Trust me Whitney had nothing else to say to Brandy Ray J's sister. Whitney told us all that she never liked Brandy. I hate to say it, but see, I have to be honest in order to get you to understand what really happened and took place here.

I can see the behavior of everyone and by their statements, it tells me what was going on in that hotel. Every person I know agrees with this scenario that I came up with after doing all of my work for this case. Everything adds up and makes more sense than anything else. And until somebody brings me something different, this is what I ride with.

As God is my Witness

OK, so, Krissy is in Mommy's room and Whitney 1s gone. Remember now, Krissy wakes up in her mother's bed in room 434. This is very important to remember in this case because they keep saying that Whitney Houston died in her room, which was 434. But Krissy tells us that she was in that room and Mommy was gone when she awoke that day.

Whitney was in someone else's room that day, and if not Krissy's room, then I think someone lured her into another room, but "whose" room could that be? Ray would have a room next to Whitney, of course. But I think its Nick Gordon's room. And that may be why he stated on that tape, "I HELPED PAT WITH WHITNEY DEATH! I'm not going down for Krissy! I believe Whitney got up to go down that hall and she went into Nick's or Krissy's room or Nick's adjoining room, or another room because that is where everyone would be hanging out at.

That is where someone lured her into. You can't go into anyone else's room because they wouldn't allow people to hang out in their room. The people who I know that were most definitely on Whitney's floor would be 1. Krissy & Nick (with adjoining rooms) 2. Whitney's security Ray. And that is probably it. Ray J was a visitor whom I believe was hanging around Nick Gordon, Gary, Pat and Brandi Burnside, and was with them all in Nick's room.

I got a feeling in my gut that he and Pat both were running from Whitney the whole day and then everyone just appeared after her body came up. And see, this is why Ray J said he wasn't there after I said he was. His publicist had already given her statement and said he was there. She placed him there by giving that statement, don't forget that.

As God is my Witness

Then she came back to say, no, it was Ray Whitney's security that found her body. And see, I believe Ray J's publicist was doing what she was used to doing by reporting what she knew. Then someone told her to go back and say, no Ray J wasn't there. She probably didn't even know what they were doing and thought she was doing something good by reporting that for Ray J.

Krissy said the rugs were soaked in her room, and really wet under Whitney's body when she was found, as the authorities had said. So, if the rugs were wet it would have to be Krissy's room that she was in. Unless there was a lot of water in other rooms which I doubt. Krissy had already told us her rugs were wet. In the bathroom where Whitney's body was found was a pitcher, a bottle of alcohol and some kind of towel, it was all sitting in that tub. I believe this is because Pat and Gary were running back and forth cleaning up Whitney's blood and stuff in that room. That's why they went running to clean up that room, because they did not want the authorities thinking someone killed her, so they staged that room right in front of my nephew Jerod.

I had a vision that they stole all of Whitney's expensive items and they placed cheap stuff in that room. Now, when the authorities got there to see everything, they had no idea, probably that Pat and Gary had just left cleaning up and rearranging that room.

When they got there, they saw all these scars and bruises on Whitney along with a swollen jaw, a busted lip, and they saw that she needed surgery, because it was busted up so bad. She had bruises everywhere on her body, and contusions all in her head and just scars everywhere on her body. Yes, Whitney Houston was clearly jumped and beaten and her body was messed up pretty badly.

As God is my Witness

And did you know a police officer sued the police department after they came out to get Whitney's body? Yes, Sgt. Brian Weir of the Beverly Hills Police Department said he caught Sgt. Terry Nutall, peaking at Whitney's nude body under the sheet the day she died in that bathtub and the Sgt. was caught lifting the sheet and saying things about how good she still looked at her age. He did all of this as her body lay there for hours. Whitney's body was once again violated! All this stuff is a shame before God. Her body had to lay there for many hours before they would even lift a finger to come and get her.

And the thing about this is, Bobby asked my elder brother Tommy to stay there with her because he was overseas and couldn't be there for Whitney and Bobby knew no one was going to look after her properly. He just didn't want Whitney to be alone with people that did not care for her body because he knew how her so-called family were with Whitney.

This is a crying shame. Whitney had a robe on as well, please remember that and don't forget it. She was waiting for her makeup artist to come, and they wanted to get her before that because once the makeup artist came it would have been over and she would have made it to Clive's event, and they did not want that. They probably knew and plotted to snatch her out of her room before that makeup artist came. It's all evident how all this went down, I'm telling you...

Yes indeed, this told me that someone lured her out that room or she ran down there to that room with the mind to just cuss folks out quick, and then return to her own room, but she never made it back to her room. I can't get over the fact that her jaw was so big either. Anyone looking at her knew that she was punched in it a bunch of times.

As God is my Witness

They knew that she was surely fighting someone and fighting hard. Her fingernails were all chipped up and had defense wounds. Yes! This is how Whitney's body was, but they don't want people to know. This is very sad they did not go any further with Whitney's case. God has some repaying to do to some folks, believe me. I don't know who allowed this to slip through their paperwork; but Whitney surely had a bunch of signs of foul play. I am talking about major bruises on her body. All those people around her there is no telling who jumped her.

I also heard from a reliable source that Whitney caught Mary stealing something of hers in that hotel. Whitney told Mary, Pat's relative, "When we get back to Atlanta, you cannot come anywhere near or around me ever again!" They said that Whitney caught Mary stealing something from her and she then cussed her out. I said, WOW! Does that run in their family because Whitney told us stories of Pat stealing from her too, and several times.

Life is real and you would be surprised at the things these people have done already. We all knew about Whitney's wedding ring that Pat and Gary stole off her finger. I am going to get that ring away from them. My brother paid for that ring, and they do not get to keep it. In Whitney's voice, "H*ll Naw!

My sister Tina met the guy, who is supposedly Tyler Perry's relative. Tina said that he told her that Pat and Gary Houston took Whitney's ring to a jeweler when Whitney was alive, and tried to sell Whitney's wedding ring to him, but he turned it down because he noticed the ring to be Whitney's that Bobby brought her. There are people out there in the world who know what Pat and Gary have done to Whitney. Yes, this is a true story that you can't make up. Whitney had realized they had stolen it around one thanksgiving.

As God is my Witness

However, they returned it because it popped back up in the house. Now, Gary is the one who brought it back into Bobby and Whitney's home. It was so obvious because of the way he did it. Whitney knew that it was him that took it. I have told Bobby to get his ring and our mother's piano. I must go after my mother's piano that Bobby brought her as a gift. It's a beautiful white piano that someone said Donna or Pat has in their home. My mother is gone, and she wanted me to get her piano and so I shall go after it and retrieve what belongs to my mother.

My thing is, how about asking for money if you need it that badly. I can imagine what they took of Whitney's, but you can't take anything with you when you leave here so they must turn it loose one day. Why keep stealing from someone? And then, it's probably true that Pat brings along her family members to that hotel on Whitney's dime. Remember she always has Mama Cissy in her back pocket.

None of them work for Whitney so why are they there at that hotel? You may think this sounds far-fetched because you have believed that lie that she has told people about being Whitney's manager, and I have told everyone that she "is not" her manager and I would not ever tell a lie on someone. I can only speak this truth to shame these people that are walking around lying to the public and ripping Whitney's estate completely off Pat Houston does nothing for Whitney today and everything she does is fraudulent because the state of Georgia is allowing it for Pat and Mama Cissy without knowing who they really are. I hate to say it, but these people really did nothing for Whitney except bring her a lot of heartaches. Now that Whitney's gone this woman who literally killed my niece is over Whitney's estate. My God what has this world became?

As God is my Witness

Whitney did not ever even trust this woman as far as she could see her, and this woman took her daughter out of here so sadly. And for her to starve my niece to death, it must have been some kind of wicked ritual they are a part of to starve my niece to death. And for this hospice center to allow it is crazy and unheard of I am sure that my niece saw a lot of weird things happening at that hotel while she was there with her mother. Whitney was trying to keep Krissy close to her because she knew that they were coming at her so hard and I am sure it was becoming harder for her to handle.

I viewed a video online of a woman at the Beverly Hilton snooping around with her children. She put it online for the world to see. They brought their cameras and went to the floor where Whitney's rooms were. The woman stated that the number of 434 had been missing; and that it was not on that door anymore. A lot of us believe they took the numbers from that room door and switched room numbers on that floor. On top of that, the media had been telling everyone that the Beverly Hilton Hotel had been remodeling that room. But my question is why?

When have they ever done that sort of thing when a celebrity dies in a hotel room or home for that matter? They usually keep that room or home just like it was and allow others to rent it out. After they jack up the price. What was so different about Whitney's ordeal at that hotel, I wonder.

With all due respect, Mama Cissy is not Whitney's mother, and I am so glad that I know this now because there was a lot of things that I could not understand where I was so confused about their relationship and now that I know that they are not related it all makes so much sense to me now.

As God is my Witness

Pat got the OK from Mama Cissy to do as she pleased with Whitney, and she ran with it like a chicken with its head cut off. One reason why I knew that she wasn't just in that hallway on Whitney's floor without knowing what happened to Whitney. She sat on Oprah saying she was just coming out of another room or something like that, and then she heard screams. Yeah, OK, well whose room was she coming out of on Whitney's floor and why?

I don't think I heard that discussion on Oprah. You had already said, you had told Mary to go up and ask Whitney if she was ready for her makeup artist, which I know didn't sound right because that is what Whitney's security is for. See, it is hard to fool me; a person that knows my sister, her business, how things go. I know a fake story when I hear it. I believe Pat heard Whitney's screams and everything else because it was Gary in that room beating Whitney to death. I keep thinking about her statements on Oprah when she said that she was on a different floor; and yet, wasn't on her own room floor when Whitney's body came up dead. She just happened to be so-called walking on Whitney's floor and heard screams? Yeah, right OK.

Think about this well and go back and listen to her statements. She heard screams and kept walking "slow" because I believe she knew what was going on in that room. But what was Pat doing on her floor? Her being on another floor should tell anyone the real deal. And the only people that could have been trying to harm Whitney would be Pat, Gary, Nick and Ray J, because they would be the ones in those rooms. Whitney's security Ray knows something because he was there also, and I am not going for that that he doesn't know what happened to my sister. I just will not believe it in a million years.

As God is my Witness

Whitney went into that room to approach them about her daughter being found in that bathtub and a bad fight that broke out, is what I believe happened. Someone lured Whitney out of her bed with Krissy, while Krissy was asleep. It is not hard to tell at this point the real reasons they were all around on Whitney's floor at that particular time, but one of them did it and they all know for sure who did. I also believe that it's a possibility that Pat could have held her brother Ray in his own room too, while her husband killed Whitney, unless Ray did it himself and lured Whitney out of her room altogether. Who knows, but what is real is that one of them did it! NO DRUG DEALER CAME INTO THAT HOTEL AND DID ANYTHING as some may think.

I want to say something else while I am on this subject. Jonathon Houston pointed out to me that Ray had on a chain on his neck that was likened to a music symbol. He said, "Aunty Lele, look on Rays neck when you go back out there in the lobby, look on his neck and observe that chain around it. You will see what I'm talking about." He said, he believed that Ray got that chain around his neck as a gift for killing Aunty Whitney. I said, well, what would that mean; because I couldn't understand what he was really trying to say. And Jonathon just said, it stands for him killing Aunty Whitney.

I believe Gary did it and Jonathan believes Gary, Pat and Ray all have something to do with it. We all feel the same thing. They all have something to do with it. I look to God for answers, and I believe that is what He gave me. I hold Gary Houston and all of them responsible for the death of Whitney and Krissy I believe that is why Nick said, quote: "I am not going down with Krissy's death if she dies, I saved Pat with Whitney!"

As God is my Witness

See, Nick knew he was doing everything pat told him to do. And he helped either Gary or Ray at Pat's request and that's why he said, I saved her with Whitney. She asked him to assist her husband. I believe that is another reason why Nick is gone today as well.

He is not here anymore to snitch on Gary and Pat and bust them out. I already know that Nick Gordon could not take Whitney alone and Gary or Ray or both had to help. It could have been Ray J and Nick too. It's just hard for me to tell who "Actually" did it but in all honesty, I believe it was Gary Houston that took Whitney out and Pat surely killed Krissy. These two people need to be investigated properly BY THE FEDS and dealt with by the authorities ASAP. They know exactly what happened to Whitney. Gary would gladly do it in a heartbeat because he has always been jealous of Whitney, according to some Houston's. One thing for certain, Whitney walked in that room probably and more than likely to see them to talk to them about her daughter.

She needed to know what was going on and how did her daughter end up in that bathtub like that. She wanted to know who placed her daughter in that bathtub. I believe a fight broke out and Gary killed Whitney. He could have been high off some sort of drug that just made him go crazy and he began hitting Whitney so hard and uncontrollable and he did not stop. This is what I believe. They were waiting to face her because they knew her life would now end, and she wouldn't get out of that room. I believe they knew that Krissy was asleep in Whitney's room and could not hear her mother's screams. I believe that everyone played their own part in her demise.

As God is my Witness

Whether they taunted her, tried slipping something in her food, or straight out murdered her, I believe they were all involved. Whatever it is that they did, I do believe it was more than just one or two people. I say this because they were all over the place in this hotel. Look at Stacy Francis's thing the night before. I mean, it is hard to tell who was down with what part of the demise. Now, I know Whitney and how her security is run. We cannot figure out why Ray was not there to protect Whitney. There is no excuse in this entire universe that he could ever give me, as to why he was not there to save Whitney from all this trauma.

And regardless of what anyone thinks or believes; again, they were cold bloodedly murdered for Whitney's estate and it's not right that these people are not answering for what happened to her. That was a very inhumane and cold way to take someone's life, and for the reasons she was killed. It is a sad day on this earth that she did not receive the justice she so well deserves.

Whitney never did anything to anyone to deserve what they did to her. My niece was an innocent child that had every right to not give out her mother's money to anyone that is only looking at her for her money. When Ray, Whitney's security, told me that the room looked like a tornado hit it, he had to forget that quick that I knew just how Whitney's security team has always operated. I imagined that room to be a horrific mess, and at what point did he finally get to her aid to see this room, and why was he NOT there, if he is innocent? See, all the questions should have been answered by an authority on that same day they found her like they did because trust me anyone looking at her KNEW and was SURE that Whitney Houston was indeed beaten to death, hands down.

As God is my Witness

I do not know what kind of investigations were done on the Whitney Houston case, but I do know it was extremely easy to solve and still hasn't been solved yet. With that said, I am sure no investigations took place at all. None of this stuff I am saying has ever been brought up because no one cares to help Whitney. No one in the Houston family is doing anything because they have her estate and Whitney was not really related to them, so I guess they just do not care. Her body had to appear really messed up to even them when they came up to her, so what happened? Why did they "not" investigate this case as they should have? How could they do this to Whitney?

I feel and I believe it is because it was planned so long ago. I so strongly feel and believe that these people had this planned from so long ago, and it is "why" Gary changed his name to Houston from Garland in the first place. Yes, I believe this is the absolute truth as to why he changed his name altogether. Just to think about her injuries makes me sick. She had a busted lip that was busted so bad that she would have needed surgery had she lived. Whitney had the wounds of a person who hated her. Her life was executed so passionately and so violently. The blows she was trying to endure as they were hitting her was so excruciating to her, I am sure it is what made her heart give out, and this is how she took her last breath. She was so shocked that Gary was beating her so passionately that it literally took her breath away. Come on now, something is not right with this, and we all know it.I will not accept the media to keep throwing this out there as if Whitney was on drugs and no one did nothing to her, because it is VERY clear that she was so violently killed. More than anything, I also do not believe a proper investigation was done on either her, nor Bobbi Kristina's body and the same with Bobby Jr., and it is very sad because the evidence was right there in front of them.

As God is my Witness

There are no excuses for this negligence, and someone needs to stand up and tell the truth so that my family can have the peace that we are looking for with this case. I am urging anyone, and anywhere in this world, who may have information of any kind, to just simply come forward and just tell the truth for the sake of God. If you are out there and you know something, I am here to tell you that God will not allow you to rest until you get that off your chest, out of your hair and into this universe of people all over this world who desires justice for my family members. Think about this as if it were you or someone you loved and cared about. Would you not want someone to stand up and tell the truth for you? Would you be OK with going out of this world like that? It is not fair, and everyone in their rightful minds knows that this is not.

With all that I know, it is very hard for me or anyone else to see Ray J as an innocent person. All the things he did to bring harm to my niece the day he forced that pill on her, it told me who he was and why he was there at that hotel. These are things that you just do not do unless you have a sinister agenda. I can see the trail and how Pat and Gary orchestrated all of this. It is so easy to see and believe.

I hate to say this, but Whitney told us from her own mouth that she did not like Brandy Ray J's sister. This is why I know, and I am sure, that Whitney would not have any other reason to walk up to her to hand her anything unless she had something not-so-nice to say.

Like I said, I believe that note was about Ray J, and it is why Brandy has not allowed anyone to see that note or even just say what Whitney wrote in the note. Think about it yourself, if you are intelligent. Don't you think that Brandy would love to tell this world what Whitney's last words were?

As God is my Witness

If it was something nice in that note, Brandy would have read it to the world because it would have been Whitney's last words or last thing probably written on a piece of paper. But she couldn't because it was nothing good to say in that note. Some people think that because Whitney did a movie with Brandy, they were cool, or they communicated with one another. I am here to tell you the truth regarding what I know about Whitney and her relationship as far as Brandy Norwood goes. Whitney told us from her own mouth that she did not like Brandy at all.

It stems from something that happened a long time ago, but Whitney just never forgave her for it, I guess. But trust me, she did not at all like to even hear you mention Brandy's name. Now, that's the absolute truth. Some of our family know about this as well as I do. And just because they did a movie together meant nothing to Whitney. Whitney has always been able to smile at people she did not like. Whitney would not have anything nice to say to Brandy or her brother Ray J.

As I have talked about before; when it comes to Ray J, we all know what Whitney was dealing with him for according to what she revealed to me. I don't care to repeat it anymore. I also know that my sister was strong, and she could do whatever it was she needed to do to keep the peace when she wanted to. I knew who she liked and who she didn't like. I knew who she faked it with and who she kept it real with. I also know that whatever was in that note was not in any way good, period. Brandy may have thought she and Whitney were cool, but I am here to tell you that they were not.

As God is my Witness

Furthermore, all of these people that were around her in this hotel at the time of her death, and when I say all, I mean "all" of them whom I mentioned earlier, and were in that hotel that day, they are guilty of one thing or another when it comes to Whitney Houston. People will appear as if they were cool with my sister, but keep in mind, it was nothing more than an acting job for them and Whitney.

My sister and my niece Krissy did not have anyone there to have their backs that day. It's strange how all of these people whom she did not mess with were right there at that hotel the day she came up dead! It is not strange in the sense of being surprised, but strange in the sense of weird as they say now; and weird like guilty weird. Something is very wrong with this picture, I'm telling you.

I also believe that at that point, Whitney finally got it, and she knew that games were being played with her, but I also believe that she just did not understand the depths of the games they were playing with her life, and how serious it was, or maybe she did, but just could not get out of that hotel in time, because of people doing things to keep her there to make sure she never left it alive. I am not sure, but one thing is for sure, she is not here alive today to tell us. Now, back to the story again.

Let us skip up to Krissy finding her mother dead. Krissy gets up and comes down that hall and she sees Pat, Gary, my nephew Jerod, and my brother Tommy amongst a few other people. She finds out her mother's gone and begins crying hysterically! My nephew Jerod tries to calm her down and looks to Pat and Gary to help him because they were right there! But he says to us, quote: Pat and Gary are both rushing in & out of that room where Whitney's body lay, and they are quickly taking things out of it and putting other things into it!

As God is my Witness

I could not believe my ears as my nephew was telling me this! Now, we all know that you cannot touch an area that the authorities have not seen yet, when a body comes up dead! It's called tampering with evidence.

Can you imagine being in a hotel, and let's say a white girl comes up dead; and it's a bunch of black people around this hotel room when the police arrive. This white girl is very clearly beaten to death with visible bruises upon her face and whole entire body! And to top it off, there are nothing but black folks walking in & out and all around her room and in that area, period. What do you think is going to happen to those who are there? Anyone can answer correctly to that and easily get the answer correct. Well, nothing happened to anyone.

I don't even know if anyone was even questioned at all, and this is one of the saddest parts of it all. My nephew Jerod Carter-Brown said that Pat and Gary both stepped over him & Krissy trying to hurry up before authorities got there to snatch whatever they could out of that room. He said they could clearly see that he needed help with Krissy, because she was all over the place, but they just looked and kept on going without offering a hand to help him with her. He said they did not move to help him, instead they were stealing Whitney's items and staging that room.

You are not supposed to go in there to touch anything at any time, especially not before the authorities have got there. And they are very aware of this just as any other person in this country knows. This was crazy to me, and I thought it was rather bold of them to do this right while someone is looking at them. But you see, this is how they have always been with Whitney all her life and/or since they've known her. They just simply don't who sees them. It's called confidence!

As God is my Witness

My thing is, who has made them so confident, is the question? Whitney had complained several times about them stealing things from her. It has never been a secret that the two of them were known for stealing things from Whitney. It had always been that main reason why she never wanted them around her.

OK, now here is where Ray J comes into the picture. Now, do you remember when he told the media that I was lying about him being at the Beverly Hilton Hotel? He said from his own mouth that I was lying about him being inside the hotel with Whitney and Krissy the day Whitney's body came up dead.

Ray J is making himself look guilty for lashing out in the media at me with lies. An innocent person is not going to act the way he acted towards me. I don't think anyone had a clue that we had been talking to Krissy, my brother Tommy, and my nephew Jerod, to name a few, at the time of Whitney's death. And it's not anyone else's fault but them, for what they think in their own mind. I guess, because he didn't see me there personally, in his mind, he thought he could lie about me to the world by saying he wasn't there. It shows you just how far people will go to lie about things. And that's a foolish thing to do in a case like this.

I am wondering, what is his reason for him lying? See, now Ray J, has me thinking. I said, "Why would he lie about that unless he was guilty of something and had something to hide!" What is he trying to hide, I'm wondering? I can't think of a good or valid reason why he would want to lie about that. If you are not guilty of anything, then you should have nothing to be afraid of.

As God is my Witness

You would not lie and say that you were not in a place that people know very well you were. I just always thought he made a mistake he was going to live to regret one day. And I am sure it was other people there at that hotel and on that same floor that day, but don't have anything to do with Whitney's demise, and they won't lie and say they were not there. What reason did Ray J lie for? What does he have to hide?

Like what's the lie for and why can't you just be honest and just simply say, yes, I was there, but I didn't do anything. It is because he was there doing things and that is his reason for trying to hide it. But I never said that he killed Whitney then. Honest people don't lie and panic. If you don't remember him saying this about me, please just go back and look at it, it's out there in the media a lot of people seen it. He made a bold statement in the media and told a lie about me, period.

He thought that I wasn't talking to my sister. At this time, I don't think anyone knew or even had an idea or clue that I was looking for a 3-bedroom condo for Whitney during this time, and because she had asked me to. She wanted to find her a spot where she, Bobby, and Krissy could just go and be away from everyone else at. They spun this idea in the media about me and I just remained humble not saying a word because I knew I'd have my day. When you speak the truth, you do not worry about anything. You don't have to lie and worry, and that is who I am. I am going to always speak the truth so that I can always sleep well at night and have my peace. Ray J was at the Beverly Hilton Hotel the day my brother and nephew waited for the authorities to come and get Whitney's body.

Besides him telling Krissy to take that pill he does another thing. Krissy did go to this hospital by ambulance because of Ray J, at this time of Whitney's death. Now this is all happening while Whitney's dead body lies right there waiting for the authorities to come and retrieve her body. So, Krissy is rushed to the hospital now because Ray J gave her this pill. My brother Tommy is staying at the Hotel with Whitney because Bobby had already asked him, to please not move and watch her body until the authorities get there.

WOW RAYJ!

Bobby is smart, he probably didn't want Whitney alone with anyone; there's no telling what would happen then. My nephew also tells me, when they were in this hotel waiting for authorities to come and pick up Whitney's body, Ray J is in this room on the phone with a beer in his hand and talking to someone about a "Whitney Houston Foundation!" They said that he was promising some guy $6 Million dollars for this new suddenly Whitney Houston Foundation he was either going to create or a foundation he had already set up. None of us know the details as to if or when this did take place as of today's date. While on the phone, Ray J says, "yeah man, I'm telling you, I got you, man, and its six million dollars in it for you man!

I said OH NO HE WILL NOT! He won't get a dime from any foundation in my sister's name, oh no he will not! I said, the nerve of people to even think the way they do. Now, I am not sure if this was before or after he literally forced my niece to take that pill. But, this same day, my niece was rushed off to the hospital in an ambulance. Whitney is lying there dead, and all he can think about is some foundation money, and a foundation in Whitney's name.

As God is my Witness

I said, is he out of his mind!? It makes me wonder, what else they have planned, because you see, this is all we know to have happened. I can imagine what else was in the cooker cooking up as Whitney lay there dead in that hotel.

I was so angry with this boy for saying all this! I'm thinking like, who does that!? I asked my nephew, where was your Uncle Tommy, and why wasn't he put out of that room, you all should have thrown him out of there! Before I could get another word out of my mouth, my nephew said, yes Aunty, Uncle Tommy threw him out quickly when he heard that; and told him to take that talk somewhere else! I said, "Good, I'm glad he did, and he's lucky I wasn't there because I would have snatched that phone straight out of his hands after hearing that." And with him giving Krissy that pill like that. ... I would be in jail today, had I been there, that's all I can say. I do not play that and anyone that knows me, knows that I do not play that.

Now that Whitney's dead in this hotel, all the sudden everyone is here now. First, she couldn't get none of them on her phone. Pat, Gary, and everyone else are now at that hotel doing all kinds of things. I'm saying to myself, at first my sister was trying to call all of you and none of you would answer her calls, but now look at all of you, you're all here now to see what you can take from her! I mean, they couldn't even wait until Whitney's body was just a little cold.

I could not believe the things I was hearing about everyone at this hotel on this day. Whitney was killed in cold blood, and I really thought that Pat and Gary would get arrested for it. I heard they were being investigated for it, so what happened, I'm thinking.

As God is my Witness

I hear about all the bruises that are on Whitney's body and I hear how the police officer sued the Beverly Hills Police Department or an officer he caught doing something terrible to Whitney as her body laid there. I commend that officer for standing up for Whitney and appreciated that to the utmost. I couldn't believe it. I was shocked that he sued and won! But I read a statement somewhere where it says, he resigned out of that police station. But I wanted to thank him for standing up for Whitney, I was grateful for that.

WHAT THE CORONER STATED!

The coroner said that Whitney only had a "MINUT" amount of drugs in her system and not even enough to get a baby high, and certainly not enough to kill them. Therefore, we know that drugs were not in any way whatsoever a factor or the real cause of her death. Now, let us look at this for one moment, because Whitney's whole body including (but not limited to) her legs, chest, back, throat, fingernails, and head showed signs of a serious fight along with signs of defense wounds.

enough for me. I did not believe a word Pat said while she was sitting there with Oprah. I feel like, she said to herself, she would rather see Whitney this way because I strongly believe that Pat was jealous of Whitney and my niece Bobbi Kristina. I will always believe that Pat knew what took place in that room.

She knew that Whitney nor Bobbi Kristina would not leave that hotel alive. I also believe that Pat and Gary both are extremely happy that Whitney and her daughter are now both not here to tell their story as it has really happened.

As God is my Witness

You MUST go and look at this video on YouTube for yourself. There is a video out on "YouTube" with this on it. It is "Whitney interrupting Clive Davis and Monica & Brandy" during a live they were doing together.

I believe that Whitney felt like they were doing something to her, and she wanted this world to know, and she also interrupted them so that they knew that she knew. She was not going down without a fight, or at least giving us clues as to what was going on in that hotel that day. She was "wet" when she came before them. We have not paid attention to see this picture for what I believe it is. Whatever Whitney had in her system; I believe it forced her into that water that day. I believe that is why she walked up to Brandy handing her that note.

Now this is Whitney Houston who did not have drugs in her system (says the coroner) and who did not wish to get high anymore because she was carrying my "brother, Bobby Brown's baby" plus she had "been" clean and wanted to remain that way. I believe someone taunted her and wanted her to get high or offered her drugs and she turned them down, and they, being sneaky, snuck something in her drink and/or food that made her hot and wanting to jump in that water that day. With her turning them down, they found a way to get them into her system by slipping something into her food or drink that dissolved fast without her knowing. This is why it is important to not drink anything around anyone, and never allow someone to hand you a drink. I would tell anyone not to even go eat at a restaurant where someone you do not trust invites you to. I am very careful about anything I drink or eat. I never allow anyone to poison me.

As God is my Witness

hII believe someone did this and then disappeared away from Whitney and it is why she kept her daughter close to her that day. And yes, you heard correctly. "My sister Whitney Houston was pregnant by my brother Bobby when she was killed." Krissy told us that she too had just awakened in that hotel bathtub full of water in her room the day before. She said she ate something and then she felt woozy after eating, and just woke up in her hotel bathtub! Now, this was the day before Whitney was found, in case you did not know. It makes sense to me,

I do not know about you, but it all makes sense to me. My belief is that they were trying hard to get both in those bathtubs that day at the Beverly Hilton Hotel. But it was hard for them to do. I believe they were trying to kill Krissy first and then Whitney so they could say that Whitney committed suicide after finding her daughter. But Krissy came up out of that water that day. I believe they were all running around that hotel trying to duck and hide from Whitney and kept saying to themselves, "We cannot let her see us, she knows what we are trying to do because Krissy came out of that water! And that is why I believe they would not answer Whitney's calls and it is why my sister is dead to this day! I believe Whitney took it upon herself or perhaps someone told her to come down to Krissy's room to talk to them; and she (leaving her own room) threw on her robe, left Krissy in her (Whitney's) bed, and proceeded to go into Krissy's room to talk to someone; and never came out! I believe this is what happened to Whitney Houston, February 11th 2012.

My niece, Krissy felt this same (hot) way when Ray J gave her a pill, and this is how I got that idea of "the water" and being hot! Krissy said, she too was also "hot and needed water" after taking a pill that Ray J gave her to take that day her mother was found.

372

As God is my Witness

I believe Whitney had to jump in that water to cool herself off from whatever it was someone had slipped in her drink or food. If my memory serves me right, it was the second time Whitney had jumped in a pool of water that same day. I believe Monica asked her, "was she wet again!" When Krissy was found in her bathtub, she was in her room alone and had ordered food for her room. Now, we do not know who was in her adjoining room with her at this time.

However, we are certain that Nick Gordon had a room next to and adjoined with Krissy's. We also believe it was the hang-out room for everyone because we knew how Whitney and Krissy roll when they are out of town and in a hotel.

My gut feeling tells me that Whitney went looking for him and thought it was OK to pass his sister that note to give to her brother because Whitney was "that" upset with him stemming from whatever it was he had given her. I really believe this because I know my sister and there would be no other reason for her to hand Brandy anything. Ray J said himself in the media that "he regretted her missed calls."

Therefore, it simply told us that he too was not answering Whitney's phone calls... as well as Pat Houston who sat on Oprah saying the same thing. She said she avoided her calls that day. I can see the behavior of everyone and by their statements, it tells me what was going on. Whitney paid too much money and is too big of an icon to not be protected. And after Whitney died; why did her entourage "NOT" see to it that Whitney's daughter has security after they found her mother like that; "If that was the case?" These are the questions that need to be answered and put forward to her so-called team that lost both on their watch!

As God is my Witness

All our family members know that whenever Whitney goes out of town; she has two security men right there at her disposal who stand at her door doing 12-hour shifts each. When she is home, she usually only has one; and that person is Ray; Pat's brother. But it depends on the events; sometimes, she will have two at home; and it used to be that way. My question is, how did someone get past Ray and the other security man that was supposedly there with her as hired security?

Ray needs to explain to the world what happened on that day because I and everyone else know how it goes with Whitney's security. Anytime Whitney goes out of town and away from her home, she has two security guys at her disposal. Who that other man is or was in Los Angeles, we do not know, but of course, I have an idea. Yet, this is still a mystery right now because the person I had in mind is now dead for some strange reason.

Now, I always liked Ray, Whitney's security guy, and I never had anything against him. I just want him to explain to me today where he was and why he was not at my sister's door. After all, she was paying him to be her security and protect her while she was there in LA I was too caught up in the moment to clearly think about asking him where he was until I put it all together, and by that time, he disappeared, and we lost contact with one another. I still believe that even if I did have his number, he would not speak to me regarding this though.

I am sure that Ray had a room there at the hotel along with his sister Pat and Cousin Mary, whom they brought along for the trip. These women could very well be lying and just saying anything per Pat's orders. I just do not trust anything Pat says.

As God is my Witness

I do not believe that Mary was even Whitney's assistant either. I don't even believe that Whitney brought Pat there with her either. If she did, then I believe that Pat herself brought Mary along for the extra help for her personal reasons of helping her with Whitney's death.

I don't know if it holds any truth, but I was also told by a family member that Mary (Pat's cousin or Aunt) stole something from Whitney while she was at that hotel and they had an argument and Whitney told her, when we get home, I do not want you to come anywhere near me! See, this is why I believe what I believe as to what happened that day. Everybody has got their mouths closed and I believe their mouths are closed to protect the one or few people who struck those blows with Whitney that day....

And with all due respect, I have to say this because it is important to this whole case. With all these people around Whitney and her daughter and being a so-called family, why didn't you all put security with Bobbi Kristina after losing Whitney? It was clear as to what really happened. It appears to me that Gary killed Whitney, and everyone is trying to suppress it and keep quiet about it.

WHAT MONIQUE HOUSTON TOLD ME

I got a call from Monique Houston. She told me she had a dream the night before Whitney's body came up on the news. Meaning when she awoke from this dream, she turned her TV on and heard them announce that Whitney Houston was now dead. She said to me, "Lele, before I tell you this dream, I want you to know that I never had a dream about Gary, and I was married to him for years and still never saw him in my dreams.

As God is my Witness

She wanted me to know how serious this was and how God had even given it to her that Gary did this And anyone who knows Monique Houston, I bet you they will bear witness and say that she is one of the most devout Christians they know. None of us are perfect, but Monique strives hard to live a good clean life and she has always been that way since I have known her. Plus, she is very spiritual, and she is close to God. She said that "she had a dream that Gary called her and asked her to pick him up. It was at night, and she got in her car and went straight to him. After he opened her door to get in to sit down, he took something out of his pocket to throw out the window and it was a GUN! She said he did it in a way where he was trying to be sneaky and did not want her to see this gun.

But in this dream or vision if you will, God was basically speaking to her to let her know that he had just murdered someone with that gun. She said that Gary was looking nervous, and she knew deep inside that he had just killed someone!

Now, she wakes up and it's all over the news that Whitney Houston is now dead! Monique and I both feel like we know that Gary killed Whitney. We both believe that is the absolute truth, and that God was sending her that message so that we will not be fooled out here in this world. Whitney had always called me her angel because she knew that I would be the only one to stand up for her.

Meanwhile, God had already set it up for me and Monique to be good sister friends from the time we met, so that we would remain in contact and help Whitney and this world to solve Whitney's murder. I believe this is the reason, and as much as I love my brother Gary Houston, I must speak the truth so that God is pleased with me.

As God is my Witness

With all due respect to anyone reading this, I feel like I am 100% sure of what I have said altogether. I can feel it in my gut that I am right, just as Monique feels it as well. I feel it in my heart, and I believe it wholeheartedly that Pat and Gary Houston, both are responsible for the death of Whitney Houston and Bobbi Kristina Brown.

All of them involved in one way or another and are guilty of something must face Him. The outcome with Him will be whatever God deems fit for all of them, and the same goes for anyone else. It was a terribly wicked thing to do to another human being. That is serious when you plot to take a life away from someone. They walk around as if they did nothing without repenting; and when we don't repent, we will place them in such a dark place that I know and I am sure neither of them is ready for, equipped for or can even handle. God loves humble human beings, and people who have beautiful hearts. When I tell you that the crimes that they have chosen to commit have been committed at such a horrible time in the history of our lives, you have no idea what this means as I am saying it.

We are living in a time where either we have to do right and stop acting as if we just do not have to do anything right and believe in Him. God has fire set aside for the hard stiff neck people who do not desire to come to Him. Those whose hearts are stone. I feel so sorry for some people because they have no idea what is coming. The day is approaching where not many will be able to bear it. God is He who gives the best chastisement, and He is a JUST GOD and one who is fair. Whatever our hands have done in this earth, so shall it be done to us, so shall we receive it right back in return. I have to say this because some people just do not know God or how this universe works. There is nothing out here more powerful than God.

As God is my Witness

Not man nor woman anywhere in this world. If we did not know that, then just trust me, we all are about to learn that, and how it goes down real soon. I have to say that because, some people been around evil so much, they don't know any different; or they do not believe any different, and they think they are safe out here in this universe, and so, when you mention righteousness to anyone that doesn't know God, or people who don't like righteousness, they sometimes become agitated, ignorant and arrogant, and they are not even afraid of God. But a time is coming when they will understand. It's at our door NOW.

There are levels of chastisement, so, either way it goes, we have to know that there is nothing that goes by God where He sleeps and does not see. We all have two angels reporting our good and bad to the Father. If we do wrong, it is coming back to us without delay in this season. When we do good to others, it is the same for it. God will whip the evil out of a person's soul, until those who are evil will finally get it right. The God that I believe in does everything for me and all of His children that He loves. Those who hate Him, trust me when I tell you, He knows who they are. Those who don't know Him will get to know Him, if they sincerely want to.

I just patiently sit back and humble myself because I know Him and how He works, and I am pleased with whatever He is pleased with. I want what He wants, and I like what He likes, and the hate is the same. I hate what He hates, while striving to be the best servant I can be for Him. Again, I'm not perfect nor do I claim to be better than anyone. I live and I try to be peaceful allowing others to live by respecting all people, having unwavering FAITH in my God.

As God is my Witness

If Pat or any of them was so good for my niece after Whitney's death, why didn't they see to it that my niece had security and was safe after her mother died? Meanwhile, they worked night and day to see to it that she was far away from us, her REAL FAMILY, because they were doing so many malicious things to her. They all had secret agenda's all along. See, this is enough to tell anyone who Pat and the rest of them really is.

Anyone would agree that after her mother died, if they were so remorseful and loved Whitney so much, they would have watched over her daughter and kept her safe. But they did not because the whole ordeal was to kill both. They played that game of "divide & conquer" with her father, my brother Bobby. They even had Donna Houston involved where they could change my niece's number when they decided they wanted it changed, so that she would not have contact with those who loved her.

When I tell you they played this game and were in it to win it, and it was so much so that Donna's own child was now on board to be happy about Krissy being in that hospital. This whole family was serious about obtaining Whitney's estate. I feel it in my gut, Mama Cissy came around whenever the attorneys were needed, to sign off on their fraud. This is how I see it; it is how it was done, and it is still today still in motion making sure they keep this thing going.

The federal authorities would have to step in now, to investigate this case and allow Whitney Houston the justice she so well deserves. When and if those of higher authority investigate this murder case, I guarantee anyone reading this, that they will find what I am talking about is so very much true.

As God is my Witness

Pat and Gary Houston are two people that are the very last people that Whitney Houston would even want near her estate along with Mama Cissy Houston. They have done a grievous thing with human lives, and it is a shame before God.

KRISSYS FUNERAL

As much as I wanted to, when Bobbi Kristina was in the hospital, after all these people plotted on her by using many tactics for their treachery against her, I just could not make decisions for my niece. My brother Bobby would not allow me to, and I can't blame him, in all honesty. God knows that I would have done the very same thing as a mother.

The only difference between us is, I would have taken my child out of that hospital and/or hospice center, and no judge nor person in this world, and especially an evil one, would NOT have stopped me. And any persons who thought they could get in my way, well, it would have been such a sad day for them is all I will say. They would have regretted the day they "tried" to challenge me with my own child.

Even though Whitney left it to where I was her legal guardian, I still stood down, and I respected my brother's wishes, which is her father, because at the end of the day, that was his child, and he gave her life. As I have told you, these people did some terrible things to Whitney and my niece, and on top of it all, they even went for my nephew, little Bobby. The one thing that they did not stop to think about was who these children belonged to. They conspired and played with the wrong family without understanding or knowing what they still do not know today.

As God is my Witness

There are many people in this world who do a lot of wrong and a whole lot of evil "to others" in this world. They do it without either believing in God or perhaps they just do not know or understand the consequences of one's actions today in this day and time. I am a person who happens to be a real believer in God. I am a person who understands who He is and what time it is in this world today. This is a very dangerous hour in the history of life. God is HERE and He has come to change things as we know it.

I say that to say, He is He whom I depend on at the end of the day. Some people who do not believe will not understand what I am saying while others who do will. In any event, justice will be given to my family members

whether one believes it or not or whether they understand it or not. All of those who have played one part or another, whether in the demise of my family members, or whether it was financially. All of them who did something sinister, wrong and/or evil, they may or may not know by now, that there are repercussions for what they did to the Brown family.

When I say that God is here and present, I mean that, and He will indeed let it be known to all of them exactly what they did. I serve an Almighty Powerful God, and if He hasn't yet, He will, and trust me when I say this; He will indeed make Himself known to all of those who took part in their demise. The God that I serve is not a milk toast God, where you can do what you want, and you won't be checked for it. Oh No, that's not who He is. You cannot pay Him off and compromise with Him. There is no such thing in that area with Him.

As God is my Witness

The thing about this is, and you can mark my words, this whole world will see exactly what God will do for you when you mess with His people and do wrong to His children. That's all I'm going to say. See, a person may not obtain justice by the system of the laws of this land, and that's OK. Yet, you will always obtain the justice you so well deserve whenever you are a believer in the God of this universe and time, make no mistake about it. Wherever the wrong doers are in this world, they should immediately get down on their knees and ask God His forgiveness, I can't stress it enough. And they should very sincerely repent for their evil and wrongdoing. Depending on how sincere their prayer, will He accept it.

All of them know what they did to my family members, and they have a price to pay just as my family members paid a price for doing absolutely nothing to them to deserve what they got. I am sure that if someone went and killed three of their family members, back-to- back just like they did mine, they would be pained and full of agony and would not like that. It's a picture that nobody wants to imagine, I'm sure. The murder of my family members is a clear indication that someone killed all of them to obtain my family member's estate, and that's the bottom line.

The one thing that I can't stand is a person who is not willing to get out here and legally hustle, work for themselves, make their own money, and in this case create their own legacy instead of plotting on another man's life to take what does not belong to them. And third, do it without forcing and climbing their way upon someone else's back to steal what belongs to them.

As God is my Witness

To this day, it is easy to see that the remorse is not there with anyone yet, because they continue to kill and murder others, even after they murdered Whitney. They went for her daughter and then someone killed my brother's first-born Son, Bobby Jr. It didn't stop there either, so many others were killed. Many people lost their lives all because of someone else's greed for money, and that's a sad case. What they don't know is that God has assured me what their outcome will be after all their wickedness, and I am pleased and at ease to know what it is I know today.

What I hate the most is that they would have the audacity and nerve to take someone's life that God gave them. They would plot, deceive and connive their way into a person's life and sneak them and kill them so viciously, brutally and so demonically. And people who did not deserve it at all. In fact, from what I know, many people lost their lives behind all this madness that has gone on and it makes no sense at all.

I am so glad that I am a person who does not worship money like that. And yes, of course, I love money, we all do! The difference with me is that I am not a person who is afraid to get out here and get her own without conspiring to take another person's life, regardless of how long it takes me to come up, I am patient. There are people whom I believe were enticed into doing this evil. I certainly would not ever allow anyone to whisper in my ear about helping them to take someone else's life, for their own money they worked so hard for.

A lot of people want money so easily and they don't want to do anything to work hard to get it unless there is a whole lot of blood on their hands.

As God is my Witness

With all due respect, I believe that Pat and Gary Houston along with Mama Cissy Houston, have always wanted what was in Whitney and Bobby's name. They have followed my brother and his wife around placing themselves in their business that has nothing to do with them now that Whitney is grown. And they did this for many years, which tells me, they had plenty of time to retract their decisions on invading their life like that. I am a witness to this, and I am sure of this because of the years that Pat and Gary both followed my brother and sister around after their marriage.

Like I said, after looking back I can clearly see their agenda and motive now. It's like God downloaded all the information right in my head and I clearly saw it all right there before me. It was so evident that they are trying to take out Whitney and their children, so that their legacy does not go to them. That is what I smell, what I feel, and what I see and understand here. What they forget about was that God has another plan, and a plan that they cannot avert nor stop once it is decreed. When I say them, I really am not sure as to how many people it is that are really involved here altogether.

What I do know is that there are people walking around right now having a good time spending Whitney's hard- earned money, while having sold many, if not all, of her personal things that belonged to her after the death of her and my niece.

They took her baby girl because they did not want my niece to live and be over her own mother's estate. That is the sole reason why Pat and Mama Cissy Houston killed my niece, as God is my witness. That is why they fought my brother in a court room for his own daughter's estate. I cannot make this up nor say this another way, it is what it is.

As God is my Witness

God knows I would not ever attempt to tell such a lie if it were not true. As for my brother's son, little Bobby Brown Jr., it is the same for his father's estate as well. It is why they took him out too. This is a very sick, sad and wicked world that we live in. Yes, I have said it and I have tried so hard to say it another way, but I cannot today. I don't believe in biting my tongue so I can't do that. I am not calling people names nor am I cursing at anyone, I am just plainly speaking the truth here. And I am also an imperfection person and a human being who is striving hard to focus on God and what He would want me to say and do.

Therefore, I will not curse or call names to anyone. At the same time, nobody knows how nonchalant these people were acting while doing this and after doing this. It was as if they did not care even a little bit and as if they had every right to do this evil to my family members, I will not lie about it. When the truth is necessary to be told you must simply stand without hesitation and just tell it. You have no idea how hard I tried to not curse as I was writing this. I was so angry in the beginning, because I was so hurt and so full of pain. But I had to sit down and ask God to forgive me and take my time writing this book. Because I never want to say anything that God does not want me to say.

Despite the evil done, I still must be my better self Also, I hope that by me doing this, I am an example of what this next generation of people will be, if they should ever experience anything likened to what my family has. Anyone who knows me, they know that I am built to be a soldier for the God that I believe in, and I have absolutely no problems whatsoever, doing whatever I am called to do.

As God is my Witness

The thing that hurts me the most is, I could have saved Krissy from all these people, but she was not my child, and so I could not do what I wanted to do for her because of my brother, Bobby. I believe I could have saved her from those people who came into that hospice center posing as certain officials and at the same time where nothing more than devils in disguise. I tried my best to get my brother Bobby to allow me to help him with all of this, but he would not allow me. He may not have meant any harm and was just so pained and confused, because of what he was suffering and going through. I understood him feeling that way, and I knew he had a lot on his mind and was doing his best to cope and deal with everything before him, especially without Whitney being there.

Another thing, not many people realize the stress and agony he was suffering altogether, but I did, and I still do today. We had just lost our mother and father, our other sister Bethy before them, and then Whitney and now Krissy and little Bobby, so can you imagine what Bobby Brown had to carry and endure altogether? On top of it all, I don't even like to imagine what he must have suffered at home with his new wife and family at the same time he is dealing with all of this. All I can say is, when God allows us to go through so much at one time, and even when we don't think we can handle it, we can.

We must understand that God gives His most beloved and adored people the hardest trials because He wants us to be strong, wise up and become one with Him. And it is our tough medicine that He also desires for us to have, along with the wisdom we need to know, so that we can see the difference and we are not fooled anymore.

As God is my Witness

There is a time in all our lives where we will have to make tough decisions, and without being fearful of absolutely anything but God. It is always for the better regardless of what kind of situation we are in. The "Faith" in God will always be right there as a challenge for us. I feel so sorry for people who don't even believe in God, because it then means that they have not experienced or gone through enough in this life to bow down and simply bear witness. We have no idea what He will do for you when you have that Faith in Him. I am a witness and I love God, and I am not ashamed to speak His name at any time. He shows up every single time without delay for His children, make no mistake about it. I am a living witness that Allah-God is the true and rightful God of this universe and time, and Muhammad is His Messenger and we as Muslim's love Jesus the Christ, make no mistake about it.

He does indeed work for His believers, know that. It is a deep situation with us and God that many are not ready for right now. And that's OK, because the time now will prepare us all even if we think we are not ready. We all hear the saying, "the harder your trials, the greater your blessings will be." This is so true, but on so many other levels are these blessings to come, if we only knew. Reality is, we are already blessed, and the mercy of God blesses us even more.

In this day and time, anyone who is desiring God and wanting to be with him, He is here for you, and we should be focused on getting ready and prepared because, the more we say, we believe in God, the more He is going to try us, and it is a beautiful thing. It is beautiful because God shows you, He is real. The one thing that we get confused about is the fact that everything He does for us is for our very own benefit. Some of us He chooses out of this world for His own purpose.

As God is my Witness

The moral of the story and/or the bottom line of what I am trying to say is, He tries us simply because He truly loves us. He tries us because He is trying to prepare us to really be like Him! And this is His world, and He has come to claim it.

I think a lot of people forget that part of this world belonging to Him. We have gotten so used to Satan, who has taken over, that we won't even believe in God anymore. Everything happens for reason and God allows what He will for His purposes which we should always try to understand if we don't. That is what makes it so sad to me. We won't even believe in Him and try God and keep in communication with Him so that He can continue to show and prove to us that He's real.

This world is unbalanced and unjust. A lot of good people suffer in this world just for being who they are. A lot of people have no knowledge of why we are here and what we are really supposed to be doing in this world and "why" we were given life in the first place. And then to get here and be here and do such evil as take another human beings' life is a very wicked thing to do if we only knew. Regardless to what anyone teaches you and regardless to what you believe out what you have been taught, everything must be dealt with by the almighty God of this universe and time. Everything will be dealt with if people would just be patient and obey God rather than anyone else. There is no reason to worry about anything because everything must take place as it is written.

Life is like practice for us to become one with the father. We will one day live in a world where there is no more killing, and it is just peace. We must know that and continue to stand strong as this world spins. Everything we go through is like a test in our trials.

As God is my Witness

Trials will either make one better or make a person worse depending on how they take it or deal with it. It really depends on one's belief system and their mental state at the end of the day. This is why it is important to never curse God in our trials. God is always there with open arms even when you are hurting. My son wrote a song or poem called, "Beautiful Pain." And I believe he was even younger than a teenager when he did, but that song always reminds me of a messenger of God's because my son explained in this poem or song how pain that hurts so bad is so beautiful at the end of the day. And not many can understand it or even relate to it if they are not really in that tone.

If your trial or experiences seem to be too hard for you to bear, I believe it is all your imagination. The saying, "God will not give you any more than you can bear is so very true. Many of us say this, but we don't really believe it, but God will never allow you to go through something and you not be able to bear it. Whatever He allows you to go through, you just keep your faith, stand strong and face whatever comes your way while trusting him and know that He will bring you through it. I don't care what we go through in this life, we should always give thanks to our father for allowing that trial before us, because it came to make you so much stronger, and we need it.

And then we must also try hard to simply understand that a lot of things happens by the decisions that we make for ourselves and have nothing to do with God, but He is always there to catch us because He is our Father, and He has never let any of us down if you really think about it. Now "that" we can count on and stick a pin in it. All I am trying to say now is that God is such a merciful God, and we really don't know how much He has had mercy on us.

As God is my Witness

If we did, we would probably fall out and cry knowing the love He has always had for us all along. A lot of things that we do in this world that we don't even think is bad, is bad in the eyes of God. We are people who don't even know right from wrong anymore. God has a whole different system and mind set and His own way of doing things.

While we are some savage people out here doing all kinds of evil thinking we know it all. We don't even know how precious we are to God and how much He values our life. And for others to take it upon themselves to kill a human being for some money is something that God does not like at all, nor does He take lightly. We don't even know who we are. We are a blessed people that He has come to save because He understands that we live in a wicked world. And for that He has placed His hands on us with so much forgiveness. But we cannot get it twisted not even for one second and think we can come to Him and remain in our sin. No, that is not the proper idea about God and us. There are also not enough preachers out here who are telling us this in the Church's and we are out here carrying on as if we are safe and we know.

Yes, it is true, we can come to God any way we are, but we cannot remain that way. We must strive to be better and change for the sake of God. There is a great blessing at the end if we would be strong and focus on doing right after we come. We have taken good for bad and bad for good, and bad seems to be fair seeming to us today. This is one of the reasons why the Bible says, "The mind of this world is foolishness with God!" It really is and we do not fully understand that. We just don't get it because of how we have been raised here in this country, and what we have been taught.

As God is my Witness

A lot of people reading this know exactly where I come from in saying this, and so many others don't. And even if we don't understand it's OK. Whatever we don't understand, then, all we would have to do is just very simply ask the Father, and He will never cease from answering you, I am a witness.

God has always favored my brother, Bobby and the rest of my family members, and I know this. Bobby has taken a whole lot in his life, and he has been able to stand amid it all, having ten toes down and standing tall! That's a strong man, who can continue to move on, while remaining humble and just striving to remain focusing on what he will. You cannot let this world get the best of you, you must remember who you are and who God is and what He can do for you, if we really believe in Him. God is a Man who will be your best friend, if we would only simply have that faith in Him that He asks of us. I promise you with everything in me that it is not a hard thing to do if we would only study and better understand this, we call life.

GOD WILL FIGHT VERY DEMON WHO STANDS BEFORE YOU AND YOU WILL WIN! YOU WILL WIN! ALL YOU HAVE TO DO IS FACE GOD AND "KNOW" THAT HE IS WITH YOU HAVING EVEN THE FAITH OF A MUSTARD SEED! "HE WILL FIGHT ALL OF YOUR BATTLES AND EVERY WAR THAT INVITES YOU!" HE WILL MAKE YOUR ENEMIES HIS AND DESTROY THEM AND PROTECT YOU RIGHT IN FRONT OF THEM, IF YOU WOULD JUST HAVE FAITH AND BELIEVE. GOD IS THE BIGGEST AND BADDEST GANGSTER I HAVE EVER KNOWN! AND HIS POWER IS NOT HIDDEN EITHER, A LOT OF US JUST SIMPLY HAVE NOT TRIED HIM. AND SO WE HAVE NO CLUE THAT HE MEANS EVERY WORD HE SAYS.

As God is my Witness

Now, back to my niece... I did not know anything until it was all over with Krissy, that Pat had done what she did to her by telling them to kill her. On top of it all, "THEY STARVED MY NIECE TO DEATH IN HOSPICE, AND THAT IS HOW SHE LEFT THIS WORLD!" I came to the hospice center one day to see Krissy and a nurse stopped me in the hallway. She walked up to me very nicely and said, "You seem to be the only sane person in your family, can I please talk to you?"

I was shocked because I didn't know why she was saying this. I quickly said, yes, sure, of course! She took me in a door/room and closed it behind us, and said, "Please do not tell anyone that I said this to you, please, because I don't want to lose my job; but they have removed your niece's bag from the side of her body and are not feeding her anything, and I been here for about two weeks and have not seen them give her even a drink of water!" She then said, "And I have children at home, and I can't stand to see this any longer, and I had to tell you this because I don't think you know this!" I could not believe my ears, but then again, I knew that they were there to see to it that my niece had not left that hospice center. I knew in my heart that they wanted her dead.

I am not just saying this, these people made it so evident by their actions and behavior, who they were and why they were there. You would have had to be there to see it for yourself. It seemed to me they were getting angrier and angrier that we were going up there to see her and they just wanted her dead so that they did not have to look at us anymore. This is exactly what I felt in my gut and in my heart. And if you were, you would not say it as nice and respectful as I am trying so hard to say it that is how ugly certain spirits were in this hospice center.

As God is my Witness

You would think that people would have respect for a family who is about to lose a precious child. No, and no, again, it was unbelievable! I am going to talk about this one person much more on a later date, because it is necessary that the world knows because we need to understand who we have out here in our society. I was so angry and at that point of her telling me my niece was starving to death. I forgot everything and was ready to do whatever I had to do to get my niece out of there! Bobby had just called my phone, prior to me arriving there, and he was the reason I was there at that time in the first place. He asked me to get there to hospice early to sit with Krissy until he got there, and said he was on his way to her and was coming in from out of town this day. He had been out of town doing another show.

Bobby had always called me and my sister Tina, often to be there when he was out of town on the road. For the most part, my brother Tommy was always there by Krissy's side trying to protect her as much as he possibly could. Meanwhile, Pat and Mama Cissy were doing everything in their power to fight my brother in court for his own daughter's estate. Pat did not want Bobby using up Krissy's and Whitney's money to pay for Krissy's hospital bills!

We are talking about his daughter's estate that HE IS OVER! THESE PEOPLE FOUGHT HIM IN A COURT OF LAW AND WON! WHERE DO THEY DO THIS AT? THIS IS WHY WE NEED THE FEDS TO STEP IN AND LOOK AT THIS CASE. Yes, she did indeed make noise about how he was wasting money, as she put it. In other words, they did not want Krissy to make it so that they could take over her money is all it boiled down to at the end of the day. Because there is no way that anyone would have anything to say about someone else's money that should be used for that!

As God is my Witness

That is what her mother and father worked for all their life! They did it to take care of what belonged to them. The nerve of these people vexed my spirit so badly, I could not see straight. I cannot make this up. We are talking about Whitney Houston's daughter who was in hospice because of her, let me remind you. Now, she wants to make a fuss about my niece's bills which have nothing to do with her.

I said to Bobby, are you serious, OMG dear God who do these people think they are? Bobby was even using his own money to take care of his daughter, and has always taken good care of his family, period. This world has no idea what my brother Bobby has done of good, nor do they know what he has suffered from the ignorant people in this world who don't know his heart. I will not lie and act like an angel. I was ready for war at this point. I had people trying to calm me down telling me to stay cool and remain humble because they were watching everything too.

Bobby was asking us to be there, I am sure, because he knew that Pat Houston had been given rights over his daughter's estate by a judge in Atlanta who granted it to her and Mama Cissy; or rather granted it 50% to Mama Cissy, and then Mama Cissy allowed Pat to step in her place when she allowed her to. Whichever way it went down, it went down and was done.

This was something that nobody understood because it is something that just does not happen to anyone as far as we understood or have ever known to happen, in this country. I, nor anyone I know, have ever heard of any judge granting anyone over any estate that did not belong to anyone other than their parents.

As God is my Witness

Whitney's "WILL" clearly stated that none of her family could be over her estate, and that was a No, No and if they did not come to conclusion or resolve who was to be over it, there were stipulations for them. The reality is, Whitney wanted me over it for Krissy according to Krissy's aunt who called me to tell me.

I stood down at the request of my brother to allow Bobby over his own daughter's estate. I did not want to be in the media fighting my brother over his daughter's estate. How would that have made me look? Therefore, I took my brother's words and believed that he was going to see to it that Krissy made it out of there safely is what I did. Unfortunately, she did not make it and they took it upon themselves and literally killed her in such an unmerciful way.

You have no idea what I suffered just watching how they did my brother and my niece while she was down. I wanted to fight because of what they were doing to her and my brother. I did not believe that my brother fully understood what was going on in there. Meanwhile, Bobby kept me out of the meetings they had concerning my niece. I asked to sit in there with him, but he just would not let me. He only wanted me there whenever he wanted me there and that was it. At the same time, I am trying my best to keep my cool so that I don't upset anyone and then be placed on the "Do Not Allow in List", if you understand me at all.

This was a nightmare because I had to sit back and watch these spirits to sit around my niece and lurk at her bedside while we visited her. I felt like they could not wait to be alone with my niece. I wanted my brother to just take her out of there and bring her home with us. I literally depended on doing this in the end. Doctors had already said that she would be fine and could go home with us to improve.

As God is my Witness

Yet, we felt in our hearts like none of the Houston's wanted that because it would have meant they would have to use Whitney's money to take care of her. Pat Houston said at one point (to Bobby), "Your wasting money on her (Krissy)!" Bobby became furious when she said this. He called us to tell us that she said this, and he was so angry that she had the nerve and audacity to get in his daughter's business and say such a thing.

I do not believe that those in authority and those from that courthouse fully knew the status of my niece, and how hard she had already fought to live. For them to sign off and just grant Mama Cissy 50% along with her father, over a child's estate, and a person who carries no blood whatsoever in her body of my niece, is a mystery to us all. We do not believe any judge from that courthouse who signed off on this paperwork ever came to hospice to visit my niece either. If any of them had children and had come and visited Krissy, I'd like to think the tables would have been turned for Mama Cissy and Pat. They had no right whatsoever to say or do anything they did, because for one, Bobby is her biological father. Second, Krissy is not related to any of them nor is any of them carrying any blood that places them as family to my niece.

This one day that I get there to hospice, and I bump into this nurse as I am entering the hospice center. She tells me this and is talking to me, as another nurse comes into the room where we were talking. She also says, yes, we needed to help my niece because of what they were doing to her in that hospice center. Now, this is around the same time this inhuman and sneaky woman was caught impersonating a nurse in this hospice center.

As God is my Witness

Yes, she was also in this hospice center at this same time, and yet, we knew nothing about it. "YES, YOU HEARD ME CORRECTLY AND IT IS PUBLIC KNOWLEDGE, PLEASE GO LOOK IT UP!" This fake nurse named Taiwo Bolatito Sobamowo did this.

This woman was caught in this hospice center after sneaking her way in there, so they say. She was in there doing whatever it was she came in there to do to my niece. We believe and are 100% certain that this woman was sent in there by Pat Houston. I also believe in my heart that this hospice center is not innocent either. There is no way that a black woman can sneak her way into a hospice center that is in a white rich area. That sounds like a set up to me and as far as I am concerned, it is a bunch of bolognas. We researched this woman, and we found that she is from North Carolina, which is the same state where Pat Houston is also from. Every person who heard this said, "Yes, it has to be Pat Houston who hired this woman." This even hit the news and then it just disappeared and did not last long for any of us.

We heard about her in the news and then it was not mentioned enough anymore. What does that sound like to you? She was arrested as a fraud and was a fugitive from another state, but what happened to her altogether? What did she do to my niece, first? Did she do any jail time for having done something while she was in there with my niece? Why did they starve my niece to death in this place and no one was brought to justice for such harsh treatment of a child and a patient while in their custody? In my opinion, these are questions that need to be answered by the Feds.

As God is my Witness

Back to the nurse....We are now done talking in the room, and I am making my way to my niece's room to see her and to look at her side, as she was laying on her bed. I literally saw "stars!" I could not imagine the things they were doing to end my niece's life! I had to literally stand there and look at her not having any food and no nutrition going through her body intravenously as she lay in this hospice center. My whole head began hurting! I have now approached her door, and now opened it to go into Krissy's room. One of the nurses followed me in and was standing there behind me.

When I opened the door, I noticed a doctor to my right of me who was writing something on her board. He had his back turned and didn't say anything to us. She and I are both standing there staring at Krissy after walking in. I am waiting to go over to her to lift her sheet up and see her side.

Krissy looks at me, and I speak to her and tell her I am here. As upset as I was, I knew that I had to remain humble for my niece's sake. They had been doing everything in their power to get us to act up so that they could have us leave. When I tell you that we were so peaceful and they could not stand it, please believe me. I and my sister, we both said on several occasions, "They don't want us here so let us stay humble!"

In fact, on me and Tina's first- or second day visiting Krissy, this nurse or hospice official comes out into the lobby and says, "Only Krissy's Aunt can be there with her at that time. We all said, "Yeah, Pat had this woman come out there and say that to us to -get us upset, because we just saw Pat walk back there with that woman. so that she could perhaps call the police on us and have us removed.

As God is my Witness

" I told my sister Tina not to fall for it", but we were not going anywhere, and we didn't. We paid no mind at all. I told Tina to just remain humble and just stand down at that moment and we would explain to this woman that we are the only Aunts to Krissy that is present in that hospice center. We both, very politely, made it very clear that we were in fact Krissy's blood Aunts and the only Aunts she had present in this entire place. That woman left us alone after that. Tina was about to snap and go off, and when she goes off, trust me she takes down anything and anyone in her path. I will not mention what I will do when I feel I need to.

I said, Tina, don't do it because we will only give her what she wants. This was a tactic that I was already expecting them to play out and use against us so that they could try to just be rid of us coming in there. This was an idea they used so that we would snap and then they would have tried to get us removed for good, and it would have given them the freedom to do what they wanted to Krissy, but it did not work. I just felt like I had to add that because I want this world to know everything that transpired with them, and everything they did to us in this hospice center. It was all uncalled for and so sneaky of them, I kept saying. I mean, no remorse, no sadness, nobody even looked like they were hurting behind my niece being in there but us. OK, back to Krissy and going into her room.

As I walk in her room, Krissy is laying there, and as usual and anytime you walk into her room, you can always BET that she had her eyes open. It seemed to me like Krissy was afraid of closing her eyes. Any time I walked into her room, and regardless of what time it was, she was either looking at television or just staring up in the air thinking to herself.

As God is my Witness

I always felt it in my gut, and always said that she was so afraid to shut her eyes and go to sleep, because she knew there were people there seeking to try their best to end her life. I thought to myself, if she did close her eyes and sleep, she wanted to get right back up, because I am so sure that she feared those lurking around her bed.

I never once opened her door at any time and witnessed her being asleep, and I visited her a lot! I am telling you; Krissy was afraid to sleep around them. She told her father, Bobby, that she did not want "any Houston" near her bedside. She only wanted the Brown's, Bobby tells us. So, I walk in and see Krissy laying there, and she's looking up into the air, and looking at the television as we are standing there looking at her. I walk over to her and say, hi baby, and I slowly and very carefully pull up her sheet, and there it is! Just as this nurse had just told me! OMG! I am now looking at it! I saw where they had removed her bag, and she was not receiving any food or any nutrition going into her body! I was a witness with this nurse and saw this myself. She had not been eating ANYTHING just as that nurse had just told me.

There was a doctor, who was standing there writing something on the board to the right of Krissy's bed on the wall, and right by the door. So, I now walk in and see this, and just as I was getting ready to ask the doctor a question, as to "why" my niece didn't have her bag on her side, the door flings open! Surprisingly it's my brother Bobby! I said to myself, this is unbelievable and right on time! I guess Bobby was even closer than I thought he was, in getting to hospice from the airport.

As God is my Witness

Bobby walks in cheerfully shouting looking at Krissy, "Hey baby girl it's Daddy, I'm here!" Of course, Krissy was happy to see him! I look at Bobby and say, "Bobby, is she even eating anything?" He says, yes of course she is, why you say that?" I said, "Well, where is her bag that was on her side, because I just looked, and I don't see her bag on her side anymore." I said, "She doesn't even have that bag on her side anymore, and that is where her food was going into."

Then, I asked the doctor, and Bobby asked the doctor as well, what is she having for dinner? Bobby says, "Yeah, what is my daughter having for dinner doc?" The doctor then says, "Oh, I'm just the doctor sitting in for her main doctor, you'll have to ask her main doctor that. He said that or something like, "You'll have to take that up with him." Bobby and I both asked, "Where is this doctor at Sir?" I personally thought that was very weird that he was there and said he knew nothing of her getting food but was writing things on her board as if he was the attending doctor for her. Now, I am asking myself, "How is he doing all of that, but didn't know what my niece was eating or had eaten?" I guess it is a possibility that he did not know, but for some reason, I felt in my gut that it was so different.

At this time, Bobby and I both asks at the same time, "Where is her doctor at right now, (so that we can ask him)?" The thing was, I thought in my mind, they all knew what she was having which was nothing! I felt like he just wanted to direct us to whomever it was that knew more about my niece, and that person who would tell us whatever they had already planned to explain to us had we asked. The doctor, while still writing something on the board, and not even making eye contact with either of us, he says, "Oh he's in the room outside this door and across the way."

As God is my Witness

Bobby flings the door open to Krissy's room to quickly go and see this doctor and of course, I am right behind him, because I feel it's necessary for me to go in as well and hear what this doctor is saying. Bobby immediately stops me right in my tracks and says, "No, Lele, you just stay back, I got this!" I said, "Come on Bobby, I need to go with you, please let me go, I'd like to hear what the doctor is saying too." He then says again, "No, I got this, just chill, and just stay back." As much as it hurt me to not go into that room with him to ask this doctor what was really going on, I was trying to make sure that I did not piss my brother off at the same time, and then make him uncomfortable, and we argued amongst ourselves. Therefore, I politely just stood back.

It seemed like not even 10 minutes went by, and here comes Pat Houston, walking in the door, and rushing into that doctor's office with Bobby and this doctor. Now, I am saying to myself, how come she is in there and I can't go in there? This is crazy and clearly a bunch of bull crap, I say! I'm thinking in my mind, Pat Houston should be nowhere near my niece right now what the heck is going on? First, Krissy didn't want her or any other Houston anywhere near her bedside.

Krissy seriously made this clear and relayed this to her father when she was in the hospital. She did not want them near her, and Bobby said he was going to keep them away, but for some strange reason he didn't, and they continued to be right there, and I could never understand it. Then, Pat obtains authority over my niece's estate, because of Cissy Houston, who placed her there. With all due respect again, she is not Whitney's real or biological mother. I can now see this whole picture that has been before us all, all this time.

402

As God is my Witness

I see now that all of this has been about money even with Whitney. Bobby and this doctor are in this so-called meeting in this doctor's office, talking about feeding his daughter food that any human being needs when they are in any hospital. Meanwhile that bag was still gone, and it remained gone, and did not ever come back to my niece. There were no changes in my niece getting food into her body anymore. Right after that I believe wholeheartedly that they planned on just taking her completely out.

It was not long after that we got the call that Krissy had expired! I said, come on now this is a bunch of bull-Ish! My niece was fine, and she was not on her death bed, they did this to her, I yelled! It was like God told me that they just killed her because we recognized that they were starving her to death. God is a just God and there are people in trouble, and with all due respect, I must warn them. There were people who did not care because I am sure all they could think about was dollar signs, but again, God is and the God that I serve is angry at what they did.

I strongly believe that it was just that they were at the point where in their mind, they knew the jig was up, and they knew we had realized that she was not getting any food, and so, some got together in their meeting and decided to just take her quickly after that to calm us down from them starving her to death. Oh yes, I could feel it in my bones that this is what they did. So, I believe they just took her out quickly after that. I felt it in my spirit and that they knew that we were going to make noise about my niece not being fed any food nor receiving any water and nutrition in that hospice center, and so they literally forced her death on her. There could be no other explanation for me as to why my niece just expired so suddenly.

As God is my Witness

It was not long at all after I complained about her food, and I will say, it was almost right after that when they pronounced her dead! This was one of the saddest days I had ever experienced in my lifetime. No one can ever tell me that they did not take her life like that and all because we were now aware that they were starving her. Krissy looked fine other than that and had been going strong. She had already come out of her trauma. I would never ever for not even half of a second believe anyone if they did try to say that is not what happened. As far as I am concerned, I know, and I am 100% certain that is why she was now gone so suddenly.

I and everyone else felt like they planned her death right after because they did not want to deal with us saying that she had no bag or food going into her anymore. What human being would do this to an innocent young girl who was full of life and a patient that was hospitalized in hospice? And she was indeed a strong child who was literally fighting against everything they were doing to her. Bobbi Kristina fought "hard" to stay alive and they know it. They could not understand how she was so strong and was still living after all she had been through.

I do not believe anything that comes out of anyone's mouth, from the Houston's all the way up to those doctors and I have to say that courthouse too. I knew what was going on and I wanted to snap at that point. It was so strange and weird how Pat Houston just walked in that door that day. I told everyone, "Yeah, Pat was close by and always ready, and it is the reason she picked that hospice center in the first place. My son said, Mommy, you said that in the beginning, before Krissy came there, Pat was going to make sure that Krissy came straight to that hospice center. I said, yep because I knew it.

As God is my Witness

I said, she intentionally placed my niece there because she wanted to be able to get to that hospice center the quickest way she could, and it was why she picked that hospice center. I knew that she wanted it as a convenience for her to be able to get there quickly when she needed to. As I said before, Pat and Gary followed Bobby and Whitney to Atlanta in the first place, so she knew that this hospice center was right there in that neighborhood. Oh yes, I had everything down to a T and I called it all out before it even took place because the Almighty God was downloading it all in my head.

Pat Houston also made those arrangements right there at that hospice center because she wanted to be able to be on top of things and see to it that my niece died sooner than much later. I can't even explain this like it needs to be said. Reader, you can't even fathom how these people orchestrated this thing, and how easily they did all of what they did for themselves and how disrespectful these people were to my family. It was something that my family will not ever forget as long as we live. But God knows and He is on it... trust me when I tell you. God knows that every word I am saying is the absolute truth.

Bobby kept telling me to stay calm and that he had it, and Krissy was going to be OK not to worry, but as the days were going by, the culprits were becoming more and more evident right before my eyes. They were becoming bolder and bolder and did not even care that they appeared the way they did to us. Even if you did not know them, and you were there, you would have known just by their actions and how they were running around that hospice center and doing what they did, acting the way they were, that they were there to see to it that my niece was no longer alive.

As God is my Witness

I told everyone that they looked and acted like people who won the lottery, no joke! That is what came to my mind as I saw them come and go into that hospital and hospice center. WOW! I said it to my sister Tina. I said, Tina they act like they hit the lottery, don't they? Of course, Tina said yes, they do! These are people who have children themselves and would do this to someone else's child. I hope their children are reading this today.

The thing about a case like this and with today being a time of truth; it is better for a person to come straight up and tell the truth to get God off your back. You can do this while remaining anonymous if you like to. You don't have to give up your name or anything else right now, but just come forward for the sake of God and the Jesus Christ, whom we all say we believe in. And let me tell you this, and this is very important to know. Whoever is out there and has information on this case. Please know and understand that this is your trial with God as well. And just like I am asking those who have something to do with it, to just simply repent with God. It is better for any of us that we take heed and know that God is going to hold us all accountable for what we know. Because if you do know then it was indeed meant for you to know, and now you must pass your trial with God by telling it to help bring justice to innocent people.

See, we must do unto others as we wish done to us, and we must repent for wrongdoing. Otherwise, their blood is sitting on your hands and God will see about you, I am telling you. This is how life goes, believe me. Either you deal with it now or it lays heavy on your heart for so many years or until you retire, and no one knows when that is. You will remember me saying this, trust me. When you remain silent, it is telling God that you fear people instead of Him, and that is not a good thing to do, if you only knew.

As God is my Witness

If you hold it in and say nothing, it will go all the way with you for as long as God allows you to live, and it will be on your mind to do the right thing, and as the days, weeks or years go by you will become more and more uncomfortable if you are still here. It won't be until you get this off your chest will you have peace, I am telling you. Why not get it out of your hair now, so that you will live a comfortable life after reading this book; because a lot of us know that this is the truth. If you know something, remember, their blood is on your hands now. I hate talking about this because I still to this day cannot believe all the evil things they did to my family, and especially my niece. Krissy knew what they were doing while she was in hospice. She was helpless and could not even help herself. God is not going to let these people rest I am telling you. No, He does not work like that. They did too much evil. And to target innocent people is a heavy ticket.

You have no idea, so many sick things were happening to my niece, and it was all beyond my control and out of my sight. It was absolutely nothing I could do, because of my brother. I honestly thought that we were going to bring my niece home, as the doctors told us we would. We should have never allowed them to get away with doing my niece like this. We must always be prepared and ready to save our children from the evil people on this earth, and we must do it by any means necessary. I was ready but I could not do anything without my brother, of course. Krissy did not have to go to the hospice. She was not supposed to go to the hospice. She was supposed to come home to us.

It was not very long at all after learning that my niece was being starved to death, that they took her life. Yes, I believe they ended her life in some sort of evil way after we all left that hospice center this one evening. And the way they did it was so sneaky.

As God is my Witness

They disrespected my brother and my entire family on a level where God is so displeased with them, trust me. Let me tell you how far they went even more while Krissy was in there. While Krissy laid in hospice, my brother, Bobby had it set up where he wanted "no one" to enter Krissy's room "alone." He made that clear and nicely asked everyone to respect his wishes, and do not go in to see her without another person present with you. This way it is always two people at a time going in, which makes it a witness for the other, if you will. Although, in my opinion, I thought in my mind and to myself, it did not matter if two Houston's went in together, because we believed anyway that they were all there to see my niece dead and gone, and so, we believed they did not care nor did any of them want her to come out alive.

None of us (Brown's) ever entered this room without a second person, from what I know; except, Pat Houston, and a woman named Bedelia Hardgrove, (who told us that she was sent into hospice center by and/or from the state of Georgia). I do not know of anyone else going in that room alone after my brother made it clear that he did not want anyone in his daughter's room like that. People are so lucky I had no authority over this situation. She said that she was there as a go-between for Bobby and Pat. The reason for this is something that we will never understand as long as we live.

This was something that I, nor anyone else in my family, ever knew, ever experienced, or ever believed in, especially after this trauma. I, very nicely, so humble and extremely kind, asked her on one occasion, "Who was she there for, and was it Pat or Bobby? My only reason for asking her this was because of the way she was disrespecting us and talking to us. When she answered, that even felt so harsh to me.

As God is my Witness

She said, "Neither!" But the look she gave me while she said it, it gave her away, and I could not understand it for a second. She was a beautiful sister that had beautiful features, but her spirit did not match her looks. I thought to myself, this woman is sitting her using that ole tactic the handlers use. I said to myself, OK, I see what she is trying to do here. She wants me to believe that she was there for neither of them, but she is here for Krissy's money. And the more she talked the more I believed this in my head. I was seriously thinking like this, and it was because of how she was making me feel. It seemed to me as if someone sent that woman in there as far as I was concerned. I'm not 100% certain, but the feeling I got from her was not in any way good.

And God knows I did not feel good at all, the way she was talking to US. She was just too harsh for no apparent reason, and I never experienced anyone of her caliber act or treat a human being the way she was treating us. Not one person did anything to her for her to act the way she was. At that point, and in my eyes and in my mind, my thoughts were, this is a crazy and evil woman. I felt like she was giving herself away because she appeared to be overreacting to me. I kept saying in my mind, was this sent in here by someone who is an enemy of ours.

I had never been so shocked at a person's behavior. I almost thought we were being punked for a minute, like that show punked where they fool you. When I see that she was serious, I'm thinking in my head, why would they send such a person acting this way? It was unbelievable and I really can't explain it. I mean, she was so angry at us and was acting as if we killed "a bunch" of her family members, I am so serious. What was so weird was that we never met this woman a day in our lives.

As God is my Witness

I kept saying, something is wrong with this picture, this is not normal for people to act this way for no apparent or logical reason to us. Then she said, "Oh, you must be Leolah?" The first thing that came to my mind was that Pat or someone else had to have said something negative about me for this woman to be talking to me in this manner. I don't know her, I never met her, I never harmed anyone she knows, so why is she acting like she doesn't like me and what did I do. I'm saying to myself, this woman better lay low, because she is in here doing a huge violation right now and don't know who she's playing with. She just came up in there disliking me as soon as she met me, and she knew who I was before I introduced myself, so I was not a stranger to her yet she is was one to me.

I said, OK, so they set us up and something is going on here. What is going to happen in this hospice center where my niece needs everyone to be polite and quiet in her room because she doesn't need to hear this kind of talk coming from this woman's behavior, I'm thinking to myself I was literally frightened for my niece because this was a woman who we did not know, and she could be in there with Krissy by herself and do anything, I'm thinking, Krissy could be really be unsafe if we're not here and certainly she is uncomfortable right now I am sure because Krissy can hear her tone loudly.

I was thinking to myself and hoping that this woman wasn't going to treat Krissy a certain way when we leave? I honestly was saying this to myself at this time, like literally! I began praying to Allah-God immediately for peace in the room. Then I kindly say, yes, I am Leolah.

As God is my Witness

In all honesty, in my most honest and respectful opinion, I immediately did not trust this person. I did not want to think this way, but this woman gave me no other choice but to not trust her. I actually feared for my brother Bobby's life and my niece's life because she seemed to be sent in there by someone who was not right in my mind, and she appeared to me as an enemy of ours. Something told me in my mind that she just wasn't right. I was honestly saying this in my mind because I had never witnessed someone of her caliber to act so harsh towards a family who was now in hospice mourning the idea of probably losing our beloved niece. This made absolutely no sense to any of us who crossed paths with this woman.

We could not figure this woman out nor understand why she was acting the way she was acting to save our life. She said that she was from the state of Georgia, but acted as if she was an enemy to us but more Krissy because she is the one in hospice and this woman was in my niece's "room" acting this way right by her bedside, as God is my witness! I will never understand that as long as I live. Me and my sister-n-law Carloyn said, wow, what did we do to deserve that, is something else going on? There was absolutely no need for her to act that way with us, and we could not understand why she was projecting this attitude towards us at this time.

We had just entered Krissy's room to see her and have prayer, and there she was sitting there by herself with Krissy and out of nowhere interrupting our visit with my niece asking questions and seeming like she was literally trying hard to make us uncomfortable. I said, wow this is unbelievable, who is this woman? I was honestly so afraid of what might happen to my niece under this person's watch if we were not there with her.

As God is my Witness

I immediately went into prayer, and then here she comes disturbing my prayer! I said to myself, dear God remove this woman please before I do something I may regret, please! I do not ever desire to see this person again. As I kept looking at her, as she kept talking, she was no longer a pretty woman to me anymore. Her looks totally disappeared because of her spirit. I said wow, she's no longer cute to me! She became so ugly to me all the sudden.

Chapter 14
DR. JOLIE HARRIS III, PROMISES TO SAVE KRISSY

Bobby called me while Krissy was in hospice and asked me to please meet this doctor who was flying in from Los Angeles to help Krissy. His name was Dr. Jolie Harris III, and he came all the way from Los Angeles on his own dime to work on her and bring Krissy's brain back to normal. She was not in a coma nor was she a vegetable or anything like that. She was just a bit messed up where she could be normal again. It was not life threatening or anything like that. This man was so serious about helping Krissy, and he looked at her and treated her as if she was his own daughter. Dr. Jolie Harris III came in very seriously, trying to help Krissy. He said he had patients who were worse off, and he saved them, and that Krissy's issue was a piece of cake for him. He promised us we would have a normal Krissy again.

Do you know how this made us all feel? We were happy and could not wait to see him give us our Krissy back like she normally was. Meanwhile, Pat and Cissy Houston did absolutely everything in their power to make sure Krissy that Krissy did not get the help that would have made her life normal again. Now that I am looking back, I see how Mama Cissy played this whole game in the media too. She did an interview right after the doctors told us Krissy was coming home and she would be OK. When they asked Mama Cissy, how was Krissy, she gave them a look and said something pertaining to she was not doing so good.

As God is my Witness

I was literally watching her as she was being asked, it must have been God making sure that I saw it because He opened my eyes right there to show me who Mama Cissy was after all. I could not believe it. I said to myself, why is she doing that and saying that when these doctors just told us, Krissy was coming home? OMG! I guess they knew what we did not know, and they had another plan.

It clearly played out in their favor, and it was only because I feel my brother did not fight it like I would have. I am not saying this to talk down on my brother, because I love him. I just don't have another excuse as to why my niece is not home with us. Bobbi Kristina is supposed to be here with us right now. There was no logical reason or explanation for her death. They tried to later say she had pneumonia while she was in the hospital, but I do not believe she did and certainly will not ever believe she had it at all. I had a nurse look at her paperwork and this nurse told me that Bobbi Kristina was "never' given any meds that were for pneumonia, which means she never had it. I am telling you; these people force me to believe that it was a huge conspiracy going on. For a nurse to tell me that and then I had to swallow that!

My very serious question is and has always been, "How in this world does a judge allow Pat and Mama Cissy to be able to say to a child's father, that his child should die! How they were able to decide my niece's life, and go against her own father and have the last say is NOT LAWFUL. This does not go down anywhere in this country and yet, it did happen in the state of Georgia. This was wrong on so many levels and THE FEDS NEED TO STEP IN AND VERY SERIOUSLY INVESTIGATE THIS CASE BECAUSE SO MANY CRIMES TOOK PLACE WITH MY FAMILY MEMBERS.

As God is my Witness

THIS WAS A VERY SAD DAY FOR US AS A FAMILY. PAT NOR CISSY HOUSTON HAD NO RIGHT WHATSOEVER TO KILL MY NIECE AND SAY THAT SHE SHOULD NOT GET HELP FROM A DOCTOR THAT HAD A 100% TURN-AROUND AND WOULD HAVE BROUGHT MY NIECE'S BRAIN BACK 100%! THIS DOCTOR PROMISED US HE'D DO THIS! THEY KNEW IT AND DID NOT WANT MY NIECE TO COME HOME TO BE OVER HER MOTHER'S ESTATE. THIS WAS MURDER IN THE FIRST DEGREE IF MURDER EVER TOOK PLACE IN THIS COUNTRY! THIS WAS SO BEYOND COLD BLOODED AND UGLY!

They literally did this to her because they did not want my niece to go home with her father. There are way too many people surrounding us because of that money Whitney had, I am sure. I think that my brother should have gone to a FEDERAL COURT TO GET SOME KIND OF EMERGENCY HELP.

I was wondering why my brother didn't have the help he should have. Bobby had new attorneys who seemed to be doing nothing like his old attorneys. I don't understand why people have people hanging around them that serve them no good, I could never understand it.

If I feel like someone is serving me no purpose, I am not going to have them around me wasting my time. I am a no-nonsense person who has zero tolerance for any bull crap. Bobby should have had that last word with his daughter's life. He did not want his daughter to be killed like that. And there was no logical reason for her to die, period.

If that was Pat's daughter or child period, and the doctor said that he or she can save her, all they have to do is X, Y, Z, and she will come back 100%, there is not a person in this world who could tell me, that she or anyone else would just outright kill their own child, and not give that doctor a chance! Krissy did not have anything else wrong with her.

She had fought like hell and beat her sickness in that hospital. They knew this but were angry that my niece survived what they had set up for her. We are talking about a good doctor who has receipts on what he did for his patients that had water in their brain. He brought them back like there was not ever any trauma done. This is a doctor who works miracles on his patients. This same doctor was the same doctor who stated that Krissy was not nearly worse than the patients he's dealt with and helped bring their brain back to normal. Krissy was in fact a better patient, which made it impossible for her to fail!

And what is worse they called this same Dr. to heal people in their family and he worked their miracles out! This is why we all know that what they did was so spiteful, and they knew this doctor was going to be good for Krissy and they did not want her to live out her life. They literally committed murder by killing my niece, hands down.

THIS WORLD SHOULD KNOW THAT SHE NEVER HAD THAT MUCH WATER IN HER LUNGS! NO! THIS IS WHY THE DOCTORS WERE SAYING THAT SHE WILL GO HOME AND BE FINE! BOBBI KRISTINA WAS NOT REALLY AS BAD OFF AS MANY PEOPLE THOUGHT SHE WAS! SHE WAS JUST SURROUNDED BY THESE PEOPLE WHO CALL THEMSELVES HUMAN.

As God is my Witness

First, when Nick did that to her and threw her into that bathtub, he must have drugged her up with something. But she did not die, nor did water hit her that badly after he threw her in that bathtub. HER CHANCES OF BEING BACK TO NORMAL WAS 100% AND DOCTOR JOLIE HARRIS III TOLD US IT WOULD HAVE BEEN SO EASY FOR HIM TO WORK ON HER AND HAVE HER STRAIGHT SIMPLY BECAUSE SHE WAS NOT IN SUCH A BAD STATE AFTERALL!

THE DOCTORS AT THIS HOSPICE CENTER WAS EVEN AMAZED AT DR. JOLIE, HE TOLD ME. HE SAID THEY WERE EVEN SHOCKED AT WHAT HE DID RIGHT IN FRONT OF THEM BECAUSE KRISSY RESPONDED WELL WHICH MEANT IT WAS WORKING. PAT SAID NO WAY TO LET HER DIE! I CANNOT MAKE THIS UP! CAN YOU IMAGINE WHAT MY BROTHER SUFFERED IN FRONT OF THESE PEOPLE? WHO THE HELL IS PAT HOUSTON? A HANDLER!!! HANDS DOWN SHE HAS TO BE!

I am sure you noticed my words are all in caps. I did that on purpose and made these words bigger so that you can see it in big letters and really get what it is I am saying. Our love for our niece was real and genuine, while those in authority did what they did to my brother and allowed these people to remain in her presence.

But who is this woman Pat Houston that stood in Mama Cissy place all the time, everyone is asking? My answer is that the only thing I can say out of my mouth is, "a handler for Whitney Houston by the permission of Cissy Houston, who raised Whitney." Furthermore, I hate no man nor woman in this world. That is not who I am. I am a person who just simply speaks the truth and nothing more.

As God is my Witness

She is certainly not a person related to us, therefore, no judge in this world should have appointed and placed her over my niece's life like that. If you ask me, I will tell you that I have literally been forced to believe that they all were down with taking my niece out of here.

THIS HAS TRAUMATIZED MY ENTIRE FAMILY! ON TOP OF IT, THIS HAS MAINLY LEFT MY ELDEST SON IN A TERRIBLE MENTAL STATE WHERE IT HAS SERIOUSLY MESSED HIM UP, MAINLY BECAUSE HE LOVED EVERYONE HE WAS SURROUNDED BY, AND SECOND, HE IS A FAMILY ORIENTED PERSON WHO IS VERY EMOTIONAL ABOUT HIS FAMILY WHEN THERE IS NOT UNITY AMONGST US AS ADULTS! AND FOR HIM TO WITNESS THIS IT BLEW HIS MIND! LIETRALLY! BECAUSE OF THEIR DEATHS AND AS GOD IS MY WITNESS, I AM SEARCHING FOR COUNCELING AND THERAPHY AS I WRITE.

OF COURSE I HAVE TO TELL IT. MY SON THAT I BROUGHT INTO THIS WORLD WILL NEVER BE THE SAME BECAUSE OF WHAT HE KNOWS HAPPENED TO HIS AUNTY WHITNEY AND HIS COUSINS WHO WERE MURDERED FOR SOME MONEY THAT PEOPLE LOVED MORE THAN THEY LOVED A HUMAN LIFE.

I AM CRYING AS I AM WRITING THIS RIGHT NOW BECAUSE THIS IS FAR MORE REAL THAN ANYONE CAN EVER IMAGINE. PEOPLE HAVE NO CLUE AS TO WHAT I'VE HAD TO SUFFER AND WHAT MY CHILDREN HAD TO SUFFER BECAUSE OF THE GREED OF OTHERS.

As God is my Witness

AND WHEN PEOPLE TAKE LIVES, IT DOES THINGS IN OTHER PEOPLE'S LIVES THAT THEY WILL NEVER KNOW ANYTHING ABOUT. I AM SERIOUSLY SO ANGRY AT THIS WICKED WORLD RIGHT NOW. I WILL NEVER UNDERSTAND WHY PEOPLE ARE SO CRUEL AND SO EVIL IN THIS WORLD. THE DEATH OF MY FAMILY MEMBERS HAVE LEFT US SCARRED FOR LIFE!

I cannot even fix my mouth to say anything other than that, and I say that with every humble bone I have left in me that they did not take out already. All these people have children at home. These doctors, the judge and Pat Houston herself. They all have children, and there is no way on this earth they would have done that and made that decision in front of Dr. Jolie had it been their child he was talking about.

I am a witness that this threw even Dr. Jolie Harris III into a depression!!!! He went into a depression where he was calling my phone crying all the time and telling me what he told Pat Houston to her face, and how she would have to pay for that with God if she did that to that baby (Bobbi Kristina)! Dr Jolie IS VERY UPSET AND ANGRY with Pat Houston. He said he told all of them, "If you do not allow me to do what I know I can do for this young girl who already won and fought so hard to stay alive, he said that God will not allow them rest and He will punish them! Of course they did not listen. He said, he told them, it is evil what you are doing, and God will not allow you to sleep well if you take this babies life!" They did it anyways and did not care who they were hurting! Pat Houston, of course, did not even care, not even a little bit and she stood by her decision.

As God is my Witness

BUT WHO GAVE HER THAT RIGHT TO EVEN MAKE A DECISION ON SOMEBODYS LIFE THAT HAS NOTHING TO DO WITH HER? THAT IS WHO'S HANDS HAS A WHOLE LOT OF BLOOD ON THEM AS WELL. I am telling you; it could have not been ME! That's all I am going to say.

This had to be all a set up though. Meanwhile, Dr Jolie said my brother was crying begging them not to kill his baby girl! Now where does this happen at? These people are murderers and cold blooded murdered at that. But this is the killer right here, listen to this! How does any doctor stand up and say, "Well, Pat has 50% and so does Krissy's father, according to what the judge ordered.

EYE OPENER!!!

IF TWO PEOPLE HAVE 50% AND ONLY ONE OF THEM IS BLOOD AND A PARENT AT THAT! HOW DO THEY SWAY OVER TO PAT'S SIDE... AWAY FROM THE FATHER'S SIDE? AND SAY THEY WILL GIVE HER WHAT SHE DECIDES FOR MY NIECE? WHERE DO THEY DO THIS AT? THIS IS SOMETHING THAT I AM BEGGING "THE FEDERAL AGENTS" TO PLEASE STEP IN AND LOOK AT! ... PLEASE! IF YOU ARE ANYONE OF AUTHORITY, PLEASE RE-OPEN THE DEATH OF WHITNEY HOUSTON AND BOBBI KRISTINA...AND BOBBY BROWN JR CASE AND I GAURANTEE YOU IT WILL BE NOTHING BUT LIES YOU WILL FIND!

AS GOD IS MY WITNESS!!! A TERRIBLE AND HORRIFIC CRIME HAS TAKEN PLACE WITH HUMAN LIVES AND MY FAMILY'S LIFE AT THAT. AND IT HAPPENED RIGHT IN THE STATE OF GEORGIA.

As God is my Witness

PAT HOUSTON IS NO RELATION TO MY NIECE AT ALL. HER NAME IS PAT WATSON GARLAND. SHE MARRIED GARY GARLAND WHO IS NOT EVEN BLOOD RELATED TO WHITNEY HOUSTON! THESE TWO PEOPLE ARE A FRAUD AND TOOK ON WHITNEY HOUSTON'S LAST NAME FOR THE PURPOSES OF OBTAINING HER ESTATE ALONG WITH CISSY HOUSTON WHO IS NOT WHITNEY'S REAL MOTHER!!! A VERY SERIOUS CRIME HAS TAKEN PLACE AND ALL OF THIS STARTED WHEN WHITNEY WAS A LITTLE BABY AND BROUGHT INTO CISSY HOUSTON'S HOME, HANDS DOWN. THEY ARE NOTHING MORE THAN MURDERER'S! I CANNOT MAKE THIS UP!

Chapter 15
<u>KRISSY'S FUNERAL</u>

Pat Houston should not have ever done that to my niece, knowing that we loved her, and my niece had every right to live! So, yes, again, I was so very angry when I was at my niece's funeral while sitting there saying my goodbyes to my beautiful niece. I could not get it out of my head what Pat Houston did to my niece and Whitney. I could have very well done a whole lot more. Instead, I very humbly got up out of my seat at this funeral, and I looked Pat straight in her eyes and said, "WHITNEY WILL HAUNT YOU FROM HER GRAVE FOR WHAT YOU DID TO HER AND HER DAUGHTER PAT!"

There was no way that I could have sat there in that funeral knowing everything that this woman did against Whitney Houston and her daughter, without saying something. As we sat at this funeral, I was hoping she did not come up on that podium. It was a horrible thing to see that these people did this, and they are not in prison yet. When I say that this woman Pat hates Whitney Houston this world has no idea on what level it is on.

And I was thinking about all of this at Krissy's funeral, and it is why I got up out of my seat and looked at Pat as she was walking up to that podium to speak and told her that Whitney would indeed haunt her from her grave, and I meant it. I felt like I had to deliver that message to her because of what she did to Whitney and her baby girl "and husband" for that matter. They have done a whole lot of things to my brother Bobby's family and so, yes, I was upset.

As God is my Witness

They took a lot from my brother and our family. Again, I have forgiven them, but they still need to be granted justice for what they did. Things that I do not like at all, I will speak about because how are people going to be accountable for what they do if we do not mention it to at least remind them of their deeds. See, they do things and hide their hands as if they did nothing, but I am not stupid at all and I can see a lot more than what they think I can.

There is no telling what my brother suffered by their hands since Whitney has been gone. At the time of Krissy's funeral, I felt like anyone who would do such wicked things as them, they deserved to hear what I had to say, regardless of where I have said it at. I said what I had to say, and I was leaving to go out of that funeral to speak with the media and give them a report on what was really going on.

Now, before I did walk out, I noticed some men walking towards me as if they were going to try to do something. Trust me, God had me so relaxed, and I looked at them and said, "Not one of you will come over here and put your hands on me!" I said, if you try to put your paws on me, you will not get it back! And I meant every single word that came out of my mouth at that moment.

Well, I had every right under the sun to protect myself had anyone tried to place their hands on me that day. I would have been within all my rights, to do what it is I am taught and trained to do as a human being and a Muslim woman.

Yet, a real Muslim woman is humbler, and she is not loud and making any trouble with anyone. Therefore, I am not too proud to admit that I was wrong, and I will apologize to anyone who felt ill in any kind of way because of what I did.

As God is my Witness

I am so sorry AND YES, I DO APOLOGIZE RIGHT HERE AND NOW FOR THAT. I had to flee to Allah-God and beg His forgiveness because that was not the proper thing to do, and I know better. That is not how we are taught to carry ourselves. I was totally wrong for standing up in that Church and doing that, regardless of how I felt. I was supposed to be respectful and humble myself and allow that funeral to take place. In fact, if I have ever made anyone feel ill or hurt anyone's feelings, I so seriously apologize to you! I was under a whole lot of pressure and not myself.

After I said what I had to say at that time, Tyler Perry stood up and he began running over towards me, and telling those security men, "They better not touch me, and that he has me!" At the same time, he was telling them, "Do not touch her, I got her!" Tyler Perry was on my team, trust and believe me when I tell you. It was not a situation where Tyler was upset with me and helped throw me out, as the social media has said. He and I walked out with his arm around me, and we were walking slow as we approached the hallway of this Church, and we spoke to each other and talked for a while in the hallway. Tyler Perry said some encouraging words to me, as I cried. After Tyler and my conversation, I walked outside to get some fresh air and decided to speak to the press regarding Pat. Not one person laid a hand on me and put me out of that funeral as the media again spun lies and said they did. No, I did not get put out of this funeral.

I walked out. I was just extremely upset at what I witnessed Pat Houston doing to my niece, and then at my niece's funeral she had all these white boys who nobody in our families knew as the "Pall Bearers!" I could not understand why Bobby allowed her to do that. We had all bet that Krissy knew not one of them. Krissy already has well over 50 young male cousins that could have been there to do that, and they knew that. It was just their evil intentions that held them back from doing the rightful thing by including our family to be there for Krissy at that last moment. People don't realize that they must suffer the very same things as they place out here in this universe.

I am sure by now many people know this. It was the wrong thing to do. Instead of them getting Krissy's cousins to hold her casket, she hires all these strangers to do this job! I kept saying in my head, "It's OK, because Pat Watson Garland has her day with Allah-God, make no mistake about it." See, God is very powerful. When you do spiteful things like that, He comes and chastises you. And it's done in a way where you will know that it is Him correcting you.

Pat was very disrespectful to my entire family by first killing my niece. She literally took my niece's life and did it in such a horrific and cold way. Krissy did not die from what Nick Gordon had done to her. And yes, it was true that Nick Gordon beat my niece bloody without any remorse, and drugged her up, and also drugged her up her own steps by her hair to that bathroom and then threw her in that bathtub to die. But my niece was so strong, and she came out of that because she wanted to live.

A lot of people do not believe Nick did anything. All you have got to do is go and get that police report it's all right there in black & white. Yes, Nick Gordon did this along with his girlfriend, Danielle, who was supposedly Krissy's friend, and supposedly Krissy's other friend, Max. Yes, they were all present and right there to see it all and did nothing to help Krissy. All three of these people were the cause of my niece being in that bathtub the day she was found. None of them helped Krissy while Nick was beating her.

As God is my Witness

They are all so very lucky none of my sons or nephews knew anything about this. He was so lucky that none of Krissy's BROWN family were there or just happened to pop up because Nick would have been gone and I hate to say it, but I don't know what would have happened if we walked in there and saw Danielle and Max just sitting there doing nothing. They would not have been able to explain anything and say they did not know, or they were afraid of Nick.

None of us would have believed it. This is why I love to speak out to the youth and talk to them about trusting people. They were not her friends at all. Nor did they help after Nick threw her in that bathtub. The authorities did not arrest anyone, nor did they even charge anyone with anything. This does not happen in the state of Georgia, ever! Well, I guess unless you have money. Krissy was found in that bathtub when that cable man got there.

When the police got there, they were supposed to make an arrest right then and there! They saw the blood on the walls where Nick was trying to clean it up and all. They knew that Nick Gordon had done this because of Danielle and Max's statements. It was no secret that Nick had committed this crime! So, why did they not arrest him? Had it been their child though, he would have been fried that very day. I am begging the FEDS to PLEASE step in PLEASE!

This is why I say, Krissy's blood is on a lot of people's hands, and God whose proper name is Allah, He is coming for every single one of the people who have something to do with the death of her life whomever they all may be. There is no hiding place for any one of them today. To this very day not one of them is being charged for either of their murders, but many people will pay for "not' doing their jobs too.

This is not at all a threat; this is just simply facts of what God is going to do to all of them who are guilty of holding their hands back from the so- called justice system. After all my niece went through, she survived the horrific tragedy and came out of that alive. Truth is, this is not a thing that is unheard of in this country. There are a lot of criminals walking around that need to be placed in jail and prison. Things like this go on all over this country every single day, and we all know it's true. Atlanta, Georgia is not the only place this happens at, and it is not the first time it happened, and it won't be the last.

KRISSY WAS NOT IN COMA WHEN SHE DIED...I mean, when she was "MURDERED!"

I want this world to know that Krissy was not in any coma anymore, and she had come out of that coma in the very first hospital she was rushed to when she was first found in that bathtub. She was in a total of about 3 hospitals and then hospice. She was first moved so that the Houston's would not be able to come see her. Something happened and they were right there again following Bobby to make sure they were on my niece's heels to deliver her up in death. Yes, this is what happened.

She was doing so very good, until they kept coming around her. Suddenly, her health goes bad, and she ends up in hospice after they start coming around. Yes, this is true, and it is so real. After that impersonating nurse, Taiwo Sobamowo, whom I believe was paid to go up into that hospital and do something against my niece, after she came and did whatever it was, she was there to do, that is what took my niece out of here. I will not ever buy the facade that she had nothing to do with my niece in that hospice center.

As God is my Witness

We all strongly believe that Pat who calls herself a Houston, she sent that woman in there, period. This book was way too much for me to write from the beginning and I was in too much pain to properly explain it all. It is hard because so much has happened and trying to piece it all here for you to understand was the hardest thing for me to ever do. It is far too much stuff to put here, and then, to explain it all where you see it as I see it, is not a walk in the park. The very hard thing to do is get it all in here. I almost thought I would never get to stop writing. I am already a passionate person when it comes to the truth. I just wanted people to seriously understand just what took place and happened here, so please forgive me for repeating things as well. Please try to understand because this was so much harder (than you will ever understand) to write.

A lot of very important and prominent people even know the truth. They all feel and believe that there is something very sinister about all that has happened here. I am hoping that people will stand up and do something to help Whitney Houston and my niece and nephew. I cannot allow them to go down in vain.

Dr. Jolie told us that Ray, Whitney's security looked at Pat (while Bobby was crying begging those doctors to not kill his daughter) and said, "Pat, you know if Whitney was here, she wouldn't listen to you, or no one else, instead, she would take Dr. Jolie in that room to her daughter and administer her those meds herself, and we all know this, Pat!" See, even Pat's brother Ray was trying to stop Pat from doing this to Krissy, he said. Pat just did not want Bobbi Kristina to live because she wanted that money I'm telling you, and she was probably saying in her head, yeah, but Whitney ain't here and I been given permission to kill her and so I am!

As God is my Witness

My thing is this, and this is very important, and I hope the feds pick this up and investigate it as they should. My thing is, why did those doctors go against Krissy's parent that stood right there fighting to not kill his daughter! We are talking about a man who has the money to save his daughter. My family are not some poor people that did not lack money or insurance.

Her father supported her and there was nothing standing in the way but Pat Houston who ILLEGALLY MADE A DECISION THAT KRISSY'S FATHER SHOULD HAVE BEEN RESPECTED TO MAKE! I say that all of these people have to be brought in and questioned and tell this world how they did that. They took a life illegally as far as I am concerned. Bobby is the only person who had ANY rights over his child's body and LIFE and should have been the very only person making decisions for her.

This is wrong in so many ways and they know it. We have no other choice but to believe that all of this was planned and my sister and niece, including my nephew, were all intentionally, deliberately and so cold bloodedly murdered. Who would believe anything else? There are no excuses for this. You cannot give somebody who has no relation to a person the right to kill their child. No, this cannot be left alone. They killed A BROWN! MY BLOOD! I cannot sit down and allow this. I am not their puppet.

I remember a time when we were at the hospice, I heard two people arguing loud! I heard Ray say, "You B!" You know the real word for it, I won't write it here. But I heard that and so, I asked my brother Tommy, "Who is that calling someone the B word Tommy?" My brother Tommy said, "Oh that was Ray, Pat's brother.

As God is my Witness

I could not believe my ears! Ray and Pat were in the back arguing about something, who knows. He very loudly called her the B word because he was pretty upset at his sister this day for some reason. With all due respect to my brother, and I mean this. I am not saying this against him, I am saying this because it must be said that this does not ever happen again in our family. But no judge, no police officer, or any other persons in authority would have ever been able to make that decision for me, I'm so sorry but I have to say this. A person that you know is only out to bring harm to your child goes and runs and hides behind all these people to have permission to kill our babies and they let her!? Pat Houston, of all people in this world, would have been the very last person that Whitney would have had in that room deciding her daughter's life.

And for the Houston's to place her up front as a spokesperson for them, easily told me that they have no love whatsoever for Whitney Houston, because THEY KNOW! They all know and are very aware of Whitney and Pat's relationship. They should not have been granted that satisfaction to do their evil on my family members. Some of the people in this world have a bad habit of doing some of the most terrible things to people because they think and believe they can get away with it. But I am here to tell you that I do not believe in a lot of things that other people believe in ....and God is so sufficient for me. Furthermore, the "GOD" that I believe in doesn't even condone this kind of behavior coming from anyone, He doesn't care who you are.

My belief is, there is a time for everything, and you must be willing to even die for what you believe in because, "if you do not stand on what you believe in and seriously mean it, you are destined to fall way down for anything." No man should have suffered in that way that my brother Bobby did.

As God is my Witness

At that very moment Bobby should have called on God and made Him sufficient for him. And this is to my brother Bobby. With all due respect brother, YOU HAVE GOT TO HAVE FAITH IN GOD BOBBY, HE REALLY WORKS! BUT YOU HAVE TO KNOW THAT GOD WILL BE THERE FOR YOU. YOU HAVE GOT TO TAKE A CHANCE AND KNOW THAT HE IS REALLY GOING TO BE THERE AND LET NO ONE STEAL THAT JOY OF KNOWING FROM YOU!

I PROMISE YOU HE WILL NOT LET YOU DOWN AND YOU CAN COUNT ON HIM. "IF YOU DO NOT EVER TRY GOD, HOW WILL YOU EVER KNOW" AND BE SURE THAT HE REALLY DOES WORK? ONCE YOU DO IT YOU WILL NOT EVER FEAR ANYTHING ELSE EVER AGAIN! PLEASE BE STRONGER IN GOD BOBBY AND KEEP YOUR FAITH WITHOUT DROPPING AN OUNCE OF IT! LET NOTHING BREAK THAT BOND WITH YOU AND YOUR FATHER. NOBODY DESERVES TO HOLD THAT CROWN BUT YOUR FATHER. HE WILL BE WITH YOU; YOU JUST HAVE TO TRY HIM AND NOT BE SCARED TO DO IT! GOD, WILL NOT LET YOU DOWN I'M TELLING YOU THIS IS REAL!!! WE CANNOT BE AFRAID HE IS ALREADY THERE WAITING ON YOU TO HAVE THAT FAITH! THAT'S IT!

And I don't care how big anyone may feel they are in themselves. It has nothing to do with how BIG MY GOD IS. I have been through enough under this Sun to know that God really works. I paid my dues out here, baby trust me. There is absolutely nothing under this Sun that could ever take my faith away in my God. And God KNOWS that I am not bragging AT ALL! I am not that person to brag & boast ignorantly.

As God is my Witness

No, that is not me, I am just straight up speaking facts, is all. God will equip any believer in Him with whatever you need to do whatever it is you need to do. We don't have because we don't ask (Bible)! Whitney had dreams, she had desires, she had goals in her life that she had never begun to start fulfilling for her dreams for her and her daughter. But she was on her way there as they took her life. She was a different person altogether in real life, and they knew it. Her strength was building up and her faith was getting stronger ....

They can't deny it if they want to. It is too much evidence pointing to Pat and Gary Houston when it comes to Whitney and Krissy's deaths. It is at the point now where we know that it was a big conspiracy and people got paid off That is not a secret anymore.

I heard Nick Gordon's say over the phone, while my nephew Jerod and he were talking. After Nick put Krissy in the hospital, he was very nervous, but also very angry at Pat Houston! His exact words were, "I saved Pat with Whitney, I am not going down for Krissy!" He kept talking about how he did not want to go down for Krissy's ordeal with him beating her almost to death in her living room. He became so scared as if Pat had told him to do that and now, he's about to go to jail because of it. That is exactly what we all felt as we were all listening to him in my living room, as he vented about the whole situation that had just taken place. And this was right after Krissy was rushed to the hospital after being found in her bathtub at her condo by the cable guy who came there to give my niece service that day. Pat Houston had put him up to it and he had finally got it done but was afraid now because he had come to his senses and knew he was in trouble. He started immediately blaming Pat Houston!

As God is my Witness

Pat and Gary had recruited Nick in to play brother for Krissy and for him to get close to Krissy. He was ready and waiting for Whitney to die, so that he could take over Krissy for Pat and get her on drugs. We all knew that Krissy was not like that when her mother and father were both together and married. No, and I don't care what anyone says, Bobby and Whitney sheltered Krissy and I never witness a time where Krissy saw them doing drugs. That is a bunch of bull. Look at Bobby's daughter Laprincia, does she not look like a decent child? Little Bobby was too, and they were both very intelligent children who were brought up properly. At least nondrug users.

When I flew to the body viewing in New York but did not go to see Whitney, it was because Whitney's cousin, Shelly called me to tell me how she looked. I was in New York in my hotel room trying to get ready at first when I was trying to go. My phone kept ringing constantly at this time, and it was Barbara Walter's people who continued to call me so many times. They kept calling my phone to ask me if I would allow Barbara Walters to interview me.

I respectfully declined and said not now but get with my attorney and we will see if it can be worked out but now was not a good time. I did nothing wrong, that is exactly how the game goes, I continued to say no only because I felt it was not time, as I was there mourning my sister's death. First, no one told me how they got my number. Second, they continued to call me to keep asking me the same question. I said to myself, who gave them my number for them to contact me. After a while, Barbara Walters herself called my phone and said, "Leolah, this is Barbara, I am "THE" Barbara Walters myself" I said, "OK," yes Ma'am, with all due respect, as I told your staff, I am not interested in speaking with you regarding my sister, Whitney Houston right now, this is my sister's funeral that I am in town for. If you wish to interview me, you may contact my attorney and from there, we will work it out later, but right now Barbara, I am here for my sister's body viewing and funeral, and again with all due respect, I will not be ready until after her funeral."

That was the rightful thing to do and so, I expected people to at least respect me as a human being and one who was seriously mourning for my sister. Right after I hung up my phone, it rang again and it was Shelly, Aunt Bey's daughter and Whitney's cousin. She was crying hysterically! She said, who did that to her Lele!? I said, Shelly what is the matter, who did what? She just kept crying unable to get her words out completely. Then she says, "I am here at the body viewing and her face is all swollen up Lele, why did they do this to her!

I said, "what, are you kidding me!? She said Whitney's face had a big noticeable swollen jaw! So, not only did they have a closed casket for Whitney Houston at her funeral, but they also "knew" that she was murdered by the bruises upon her face and body, and that was "why" they had a closed casket at her funeral. It told anyone looking at her at that body viewing exactly what happened to Whitney Houston.

Now, whether people want to say anything or not is another story, but I cannot and I will not allow my sister to go out like that. Whitney had way too many bruises on her body for anyone to disregard like that. That is so horribly disrespectful in my mind. This is why I don't understand why those in authority did not make any arrest the day they came up in that hotel and saw Whitney's body. It was a horrible sight to see Whitney that way, I am sure.

As God is my Witness

It was a terrible thing that happened to Whitney, and it is so sad that nobody else but me is willing to step up and tell the truth about her murder. I could do nothing else but shake my head and literally cry as I sat at her funeral. Whitney died a horrific death, and they know this. They beat both her and Krissy until they shut their eyes. Only difference there was, Nick Gordon did not kill my niece in beating her like that. Yet, he is still responsible for doing all the horrible things to her, but Pat Houston herself is that one who took Krissy's life.

Somebody put hands on Whitney in that hotel room and it is not hard to narrow down who did what. Like I said, it was Gary accompanied by at least one other person is what I believe, but I also believe that it was two more people altogether. I do not believe that Pat physically fought Whitney herself, and then killed her with her hands, but on the other hand, I do believe that it had to be between "Ray J, Nick Gordon, and Gary Houston" who was all in that hotel that day.

Many would say, "What! Did you say, Gary Houston, Leolah?" Yes, and yes again, because what this world did not know was the fact that Gary and Whitney did not get along at all. I have been told many times by other Houston's that Gary had been jealous of Whitney for a very long time and that he holds her responsible for his career and not being famous like her. They say that Gary blames Whitney for not having the success like she has had over the years. There are so many people out here in this world from all over the place that ask me time and time again, "Why does the Houston's allow Pat to do what she does to Whitney?" I believe the reason is because they all feel the same way at the end of the day. Otherwise, they would have been fighting for Whitney just like me. They all know that she was murdered, and no one could tell me differently.

As God is my Witness

They are just focused on her money and what they can get while she is no longer here. And with Pat Houston being her handler and feeding them whenever she feels like it, they feel obligated to her to do whatever it is she likes for them to do because Mama Cissy has placed her there. Now, who really is responsible for Pat being there other than Mama Cissy will probably always be a mystery.

Any man who does not stop his wife from doing all that she is doing today with that estate of Whitney's, has got to be down with it. So, where is the love for Whitney Houston in that family? There is none as far as I can see. I do not know anyone on that side and within that immediate so-called family that has ever genuinely loved Whiney Houston. This tells me that all of them are keeping quiet for only "that" reason, and that reason they feel will benefit them.

I have talked about her funeral and where it was. I repeat, her funeral was at the very same Church of the pastor or minister that raped her at 12 years old. This fact alone tells anyone the mind of the family, and these are the things they have done to Whitney, which tells me that there is no love, and they don't give a hoot who knows, likes it or wishes to talk about it. I don't believe they are ever bothered with anything.

I believe that Pat could not wait for Whitney to leave here so that she could pay her back after all the cussing out Whitney did to her. If you watch Pat Houston, you will find her to be a very sarcastic individual when it comes to Whitney Houston. They have stolen her name and now they are walking around with it and selling all her things and doing all kinds of sinister things in her name. Whitney used to cuss Pat out all the time. She never liked her calling the house for her.

As God is my Witness

Whitney would go off and threaten Pat and tell her that her sisters (Me, Tina & Carole) were going to jump on her if she didn't stop calling her house! Whenever a person says nothing at all when they are getting cursed out and called names all the time, you must assume they are always out there in what I call a get-back state of mind. I used to wonder why Pat never said anything back to Whitney. And what I mean by that is, I never seen Pat curse back at Whitney. Now, I can't say it didn't happen, I just didn't hear her that much, but it always sounded like Pat was humble and all this time I now know that she was patient because they had plans with Whitney. But Whitney yelled at them because of the bad and terrible things she found out about them that they did to her, like stealing her jewelry from her. There are a lot of things Whitney was upset with Pat and Gary about.

It is no surprise to me that they would do whatever they possibly can the very first chance they get. The thing about this is that it is even sadder that Whitney's family are all sitting back allowing it, as if they are also angry with Whitney. I feel that Pat and Gary are both enjoying all that they are doing to Whitney because it's like payback time to them. It is not enough to kill her and sell all her things and make all the money they can from her name.

They had to take her daughter, my niece, Bobbi Kristina because Whitney told her to not give them anything after she was gone. They felt like they had to kill my niece to get to that money. Reader, you just do not know or understand how much wrong has been done to Whitney Houston, and there is not enough paper for the real story, especially since she has been gone now. Destroying all the valuables that were sentimental to her and Bobby was sure part of the evidence to me.

I went to Bobby and Whitney's home and saw things in their garage that Pat and Gary had to have thrown away and no one else. I saw important sentimental things of Bobby and Whitney's that looked intentionally damaged with holes and things in it. Things you would not believe anyone would have the nerve to even touch. I am sure she never thought that I would talk about this in this book, but I had to because I went back to that house and saw how they trashed all her stuff and even I lost a lot of clothes in that house. A woman reached out to me on social media and told me, her husband was hired to clean that house up. OMG! I don't even want to say anything else, SMH. He even found a lot of stuff.

STOLEN INSURANCE MONEY

Whitney also said she found out that Pat took out insurance policy money in her (Whitney's) name for, I believe, $10,000. Right before Whitney was found she had revised her "WILL." In her will she stated that she was not responsible for any insurance money that someone else took out in her name. I said, OMG! This is what Whitney was talking about. Whitney told us that Pat Houston had taken out $1OK from her insurance money. I wonder what she used that money for? I have never seen anything like how these people have treated Whitney. They all treat Whitney as if she is a human trafficked child and they care nothing for her! I am so serious! I don't know what I would have done had it been me. One thing is for sure, I would never let them get away with it. When you steal money from me, you take it from my children's mouth and that's how I look at it and I am like a big Mean Mama Bear when I feel like you violated my children. I will move to HELL & HIGH-WATERS! And it doesn't matter how high that water is, it will be out of my way!

As God is my Witness

The world has it now and can see just what she has been doing and still is doing with Whitney, and her belongings ever since her funeral. I believe that Pat is still on a rampage and out to make Whitney look so bad. I honestly believe in my heart that Pat is still angry with Whitney because it shows in her actions. You don't know because you reader, don't know that relationship. But if you knew, you would be able to see it as I do.

I believe that she is determined to do whatever it is she can to make all the money she can from Whitney's name, and it is a crying shame before God that she even doing all that she is in doing with Whitney's things. See, if they knew God none of this would be going on.

OK, Now, listen to this one. The Los Angeles County Chief Coroner stated, when he saw Whitney Houston's body, she was in a room where the rugs were soaked and wet. Reader, please pay attention to this real good because something is just not right here. OK, now, Krissy told us her rugs were soaked in her room at this hotel when she awoke in that bathtub at that hotel, and then she ran down to Whitney's room but naked! OK, now, please keep this in mind.

The day that Whitney was found in the Beverly Hilton Hotel, Krissy had awoken in her mother's (Whitney) bed, and she got up to get dressed, and opened the door afterwards to go down the hall to find her mother and BOOM! That was when she found out Mommy (Whitney) was dead! Don't forget Whitney left her room and left Krissy there asleep to walk down that hotel hallway to go to another room (that someone evidently lured her to) while Krissy was asleep in her (Whitney's room).

As God is my Witness

So, you see, Whitney was "not" in her hotel room when they found her body because Krissy had already told us that she was in Mommy's room, and when she awoke, she got dressed because she didn't know where Whitney had gone to. Again, Krissy opens Whitney hotel room door and proceeds to go down that hallway...only to find her mother deceased. So, Krissy is now leaving room 434. Now, where this other room is where Whitney was found is sort of a mystery-but then again, I can guess! It was more than likely Krissy's room or the adjoining room to Krissy's which was Nick Gordon's room WHERE EVERYONE WOULD BE HANGING OUT AT... TRUSTME!

Something is telling me that Whitney got up to go down that hallway and into Krissy's room. And this is of course the room that Whitney was beaten to death in and found dead in. The thing is, I believe it was Krissy's room because it would be the only room where they could hang out in because Nick Gordon, I am sure, shared an adjoining room with Krissy. It could have been someone else's room and that is why Pat and Gary both were running in and out of trying to stage it before the authorities got there. Who knows but I think I got it right. ...

Remember, now, Krissy awoke in that bathtub the day before and ran to Whitney's room but naked because someone took her clothes out of her room. And remember, because that happened to Krissy, Whitney had kept her baby girl in her (Whitney's) room with her all night trying to reach people to ask them, "why was her daughter found like that, and who took her clothes out of her room?" None of them were answering her calls for all that day and so, it is now the next day and the day of Clive Davis event.

As God is my Witness

Evidently Whitney was still calling around, but they were still ducking her calls all day yesterday (or probably more, but we at least know they did not answer her calls these two days). Now, I have already "proved" that Whitney was not in her room 434 .... If that is the room, she checked in upon entering that hotel for the Clive Davis event as they have been reporting. OK, so Krissy awakes and goes down the hall only to find out her mom is dead!

She is hysterically crying all over the place! Krissy falls right there on the floor in that hotel hallway and meanwhile Pat and Gary both are running back & forth from room to room taking stuff and situating everything before the authorities get there! They are moving fast taking stuff out of Whitney's room and I am so sure they were stealing Whitney's things because my nephew was standing right there watching them do all of this.

Krissy is out of it, and she is crying so much right now. Pat and Gary, both see her in this condition, but they do nothing to console her right now, instead they step over her to keep going and get whatever it is they were trying to get out of that room.

CORONER ON THE PLANE

My nephew Jerod Brown Carter told us after Whitney's body was found, he got on the plane to come back to Atlanta and saw the Coroner Ed Winters on the plane, in his seat. How ironic is that they would sit next to each other. My nephew said he and Ed Winters were exchanging names as they sat next to each other on this plane. They were talking and making conversation on the plane as normal passengers because they were sitting right next to each other.

As God is my Witness

He told Mr. Winter's that he had just left the Beverly Hilton where his aunt Whitney had just been found murdered. And Ed Winters says, "Wow! Yes, I do remember seeing you that night in the hotel. I am on my way to Atlanta right now to do a presentation on Whitney and Michael Jackson." My nephew stated that Mr. Winters told him that he was Michael Jackson's coroner as well.

My nephew asked him if he thought it was foul play with Whitney's death. He said, look, take my card, I do not want to talk about it here but let's talk because the Brown's need to know that there was foul play with Whitney's body." My nephew took the card and said, OK, will do. However, by the time he called, he said that they said that they had so many people calling pretending to be the Brown family that they did not know who to trust and they didn't want to talk over the phone. I never got a chance to even call and speak with this man. Yet, it made me wonder who my nephew also told and gave the number to because that should not have happened unless you are speaking to a lot of people, and you told the wrong people, and they are now taking it upon themselves to act like they are a Brown. No one else should have had that information.

The coroner's office had become suspicious and I could not blame them. They just did not know who it really was they were speaking to on the phone. They said that we could go there in person, but at this time, I wasn't back in Atlanta yet, and I was moving around. This took place right after Whitney's funeral... I thought about that real hard later. They said they could not even be sure who was who anymore and they did not even want to take a chance talking over the phone.

As God is my Witness

I was shocked! I said, "What!! How could this be?" I never got my hands on his number and so, I never got a chance to speak with this coroner or anyone else at his office. My nephew confused me at this time though because he called Nick Gordon on the phone pretending, he was on his team supposedly to just get info out of him to see what he did to Krissy. We already knew the deal because it was evident that he had beaten Krissy down in her living room, so we already knew that Nick tried to kill her. But I don't think my nephew believed it or just didn't want to believe it. On top of it, the police report that we later read stated that Nick Gordon beat her down in her own living room with Danielle and Max both right there and none of them were doing absolutely anything to help my niece and just stop him.

I really thought my nephew was just acting this out to get Nick to talk and tell us what happened, but it did not work out that way I have to say. My nephew gets Nick on the phone, and he asks Nick, "Hey Yo! Nick, what happened man?" Nick hesitated for just half of a second and then he just burst out into so much fear! His voice was shaky and trembling! He first started out telling us what happened from the beginning, and then he just suddenly and out of the blue said, "OH, I'M NOT GOING DOWN FOR PAT, I ALREADY SAVED HER WITH WHITNEY, I'M NOT TAKING THE FALL FOR KRISSY!" This young man sounded so guilty anyone listening knew right then and there that he was guilty! We hadn't seen the police report yet at this time but we just knew he had to do it!

Nick went on insinuating about how Pat did that to Whitney, and somehow had him in it, but he was not going to go down for Pat with Krissy because he had already saved her with Whitney's ordeal!

As God is my Witness

Everyone that was sitting in my living room, their mouth flew open! We could not believe what we had just heard! I said, Jerod, please hurry and get me that copy so that I can get it to the authorities, please! My nephew left and did not show up for a few days to give me a copy. When he did return to me, he did not have that part on the tape. It had been erased off I said to myself, WOW! And at this time, he was all on social media asking people to pray for my niece and had us thinking and believing that he really cared about his cousin Krissy. Yet, I could not believe that because of what he did. As much as I love my nephew, this is the truth and I cannot sugar coat this and think that something else happened, because I know that it didn't. I've had to make copies plenty of times with tapes, so I already know the routine of how it goes. You cannot easily erase something unless you press the erase button so there was no excuse, real talk.

And the only reason I am talking about this is because I am about the truth and I don't care who you are I will tell it. This is a serious case and so this needed to be said. I have to hold those accountable and not let anyone get away with anything. My niece lost her life and she is not here today, and so, if no one else cares, I certainly do. Anytime you do something like this and think it should go unheard, Leolah is the wrong person to do it to. Everyone will learn that lesson about me if they don't know already because I am about the truth and shall always speak it regardless to whom or what.

No, nobody gets a pass with me anymore. Life is too short and I take it very seriously and always have. When I feel like I am at a point where I can't even trust my own family, I have to reveal it because I do not want this to happen again. I love them all, and it's OK, because God is sufficient for me. I did not see that one coming, just like many did not see this coming with me revealing it.

As God is my Witness

In any event, I will not allow people to do things on my watch and think I will not mention it. No love lost for my nephew, I just know that I cannot ever trust anyone with my or my children's life out here today. Krissy was like my child and if you can do that to an innocent baby girl and take the side of a stranger or another person, just to deliver truth, then I have to ask questions about who you really are altogether and what is your motive for doing that to us. That was a blow I could never allow anyone to get a pass on, it was so foul.

This just gave me another reason why I cannot trust anyone today. I didn't yesterday either, but he just brought my guard up even further now. And so, now, I would never be able to understand that. I had no choice but to believe that he was protecting Nick Gordon instead of his cousin Krissy.

I honestly believe he did that for fear of losing Nick as a so-called friend. I should have known because I kept calling him on the phone telling him to please hurry and bring that tape, so that I could get it to the authorities as soon as I possibly could, but he kept me on hold and the longer he did the more I felt uncomfortable. I also had already told one of the detectives that we had the tape, and that Nick's voice was on it saying this about Pat. So, for that reason, I was so upset that he did not bring that tape to me. It didn't really matter at the end of the day because I had at least 9 to 10 people in my living room that heard it that day.

I was just hurt for my niece that her own family could not be trusted and that broke my heart. Nothing or no one should ever be an issue when it comes to your family regardless of what. This detective wanted me to bring it into him, but now I couldn't because Jerod was so strangely holding back this tape.

As God is my Witness

It was another cold blow against my niece who was already laying helpless in a hospital awaiting justice, and he had the one piece of evidence that could have busted this case wide open. After going through all of this, I have become like Jesus, when he was in the pulpit and someone said to Him, your mother and brother are outside, and Jesus said, no, my mother and brother are those who are in here with me. I say that to say, I don't care who you are today, Leolah is a changed woman who gives no one a pass anymore. I am a loyal, trustworthy and very serious about life person, and so I expect anyone coming in my path to be that same way, period. If not, I am the wrong person to try to befriend.

If I detect any fake, phony, hating, unreal, plastic, lying, jealousy, envy backbiting or whatever. If I feel like you are not worthy to be around me in my circle you will not get anywhere near me, and you won't even know where I rest my head at because I am taking no chances with anyone today. I just cannot trust people anymore and I am done with taking chances. People have no idea what I had to suffer fighting for Whitney and my niece and nephew. It has been a lot of unnecessary pain and heartache from others. And so, the best way to win at that is to never have folks around you until you are absolutely 100% sure they are valid and worthy.

Today, I don't care who you are, if I see you moving weird out here, I will not trust you, period. That was so cold to do to Krissy after this boy did what he did to her. Krissy has a whole lot of other male cousins who really does have her back though. There is close to 100 young males altogether in this family who are around Krissy's age and/or a bit older, so it's a lot of young males in our family.

As God is my Witness

I of course forgave my nephew already, but forgetting what people do is something that we just cannot do because you cannot make more room for disappointment to welcome itself again if the opportunity arises. He told me that he did not know what happened to that part of the tape. That was all he said to me after coming to my home to bring it to me. And as he played it back, I can clearly hear how he erased it. It was almost as if he wanted me to know that he erased it and that is what I did not understand. I immediately said to myself, OK, I am dealing with another person I have just become introduced to. The actual reasons why is the only place I got stuck at because I could not come up with a reason why to save my life. I said, WOW! Unbelievable, you would do this to your own flesh and blood? OK, time for me to sign out.

Who would want that to happen to them? I hate it when I cannot trust a family member. We already have haters/enemies outside our family already, and now we have one on in the inside and that is dangerous. That was nothing to take lightly baby, and trust me I did not.

That was deep and it sent a serious message to me. Of course, I never looked at him the same way after that. We are living in a time of God revealing everyone to everyone. I cried so hard for Krissy that day, and at the same time, I felt so sorry for my nephew as well, because he has no idea how people look at him when you are disloyal like that to your own family. I was just happy that a lot of other people were at my home, and they witnessed and heard Nick's voice for themselves. I honestly believe in my heart that he wanted that relationship to remain attached to Nick because he had in his mind that Nick could or would somehow be a benefit for him with his career. That is what my spirit was telling me.

But what he didn't know was that that same spirit was also telling me that it would not happen for him because of his heart and because of what he did and who he did it for. I heard a voice tell me not to worry because what he had in mind was already gone. Today it appears as if that voice was correct because Nick is not alive anymore to even help himself let alone anyone else.

KRISSY'S FRIENDS

I thought about all the stuff that Krissy's friends were telling me about Pat Houston and Nick Gordon, and how Pat was trying so hard to manipulate Krissy's friends and trying to get Nick and them to do the same.

Krissy's friends told me that "Pat and Nick" were both really faking it with Krissy all that time and Pat and Nick both were really a team and that they were only "acting" and faking and pretending to be enemies only around Krissy so that she would think Nick was on her team. Yet, Nick was working for Pat all along.

They said that all the yelling at Pat Houston on social media was all fake with Nick and that Krissy did not know what they were doing together and to her. They said that Pat told Nick to do certain stuff, like make Krissy think that they were enemies, but they were close to each other. It was a game they played as they preyed upon my niece and got her to where they wanted her to take her life. They said that Pat had Nick giving Krissy drugs and forcing her to drink all the time. I thought it was so weird that Krissy was even doing that because she never touched stuff like that.

But see, they knew that, and they knew that once they killed Whitney, they had to place a boy in Krissy's life to keep her busy because otherwise she would have been around us and we would have taken over with Krissy and made sure she was alright. They thought this out good like devils and did everything they did.

Krissy hardly did anything when Whitney was alive. Krissy was sheltered and stayed close to her mother and father. The only thing she was known to do was go to school, come home and play with her friends and go to the malls to shop and that was it. They told me that one of Krissy's friends was found dead and she was a young girl! I could not believe it! Today, I am wondering how many people died after Whitney and Krissy left here. It is a lot of people.

I even heard Whitney had two security guards who worked for her and was with her at this Clive Davis event, but the man in question is also now deceased! He was a young man without any health issues from what I hear. It's a lot of strange deaths taking place. Whitney's cousin Micky is another person who was strangely deceased. She was the one person who took care of Mama Cissy and told me she hated Pat Houston with a passion for what she and Gary did to Whitney. The list goes on and on.

JOSHUA IS GANG RAPED!

After people popping up dead, Krissy's friend Joshua who happens to be a very young Caucasian male friend of Krissy's, he calls me, and says, "Auntie, Lele, I GOT GANG RAPED BY 5 GUYS and I know it was Pat Houston who sent those men to me, and I am in the hospital right now! I almost dropped the phone while this young boy told me this.

As God is my Witness

He and his mother both believe in their heart that it was Pat Houston who sent those guys his way. These guys busted his backside out! I could not believe my ears when he said he thinks its Pat Houston who sent these men at him! He stated to me how his mother was so afraid and that she was moving him away and out of the country, because they did not want those guys to come back. They said they believe that Pat was going to send men back to him and they were so afraid. He said, "I cannot talk about this part for too long Aunty Lele, because it will upset me to the point of serious depression!" OMG! I felt so bad for this young man. Who could do that to someone, In Islam you die for raping a man...or a woman!

How does anyone do this to a young man and go to sleep at night? He said that five big grown men came upon him snatched him into a vehicle, took him away, and violently raped him! They put him in the hospital! I would not wish this on my worst enemy, my dear Father God, I am thinking!

There are a lot of sick people in this world that will have to answer to God, is all I can say at this point. The one thing I won't do is place blame when I am unsure. But he said he strongly believed it was Pat Houston who sent those men his way. I am not certain who did that to him, but whoever did that is a sick and perverted person. To rape a young man and do that to his backside is ridiculously sad! I can't even think of that. I don't even want it in my brain!

Everything is happening to people is always pointing straight at Pat Houston though. I was told that Pat even did that to Micky Whitney's cousin who took care of Mama Cissy. I had no idea Micky was even dead. I hadn't spoken to her in about 2 to 3 years and was wondering why I hadn't heard from her.

As God is my Witness

Then I was speaking to someone, and they told me that Micky was dead and the person who told me said, "It was strange that Pat Houston ended up in New Jersey and all of a sudden Micky dies!" They said, Whitney's cousin Felisha also passed, but I didn't know that either or what the cause of her death was and haven't heard anything regarding her death or how she even left her, but I do know she was young. We all know that Nick Gordon is gone. I was surprised he couldn't figure that out for himself and ran after he did that to Krissy because I knew he wasn't going to be here long after watching him on the Dr. Phil show. He was now a weak link after that ordeal. I guess he didn't have the best acting skills after all.

All the things that I felt and thought about Nick Gordon were real though. I know for a fact that Nick Gordon was planted by Pat Houston right after Bobby and Whitney's divorce. Nick was sent in to go around Whitney and Krissy for the sole purpose of making sure Krissy did drugs and alcohol. That was the mission of Nick.

I also strongly believe that it is why he is not here today. I think that after they finished using him, they had no more use for him and just did away with him. But like I said, he began coming around Whitney and Krissy "after" Bobby and Whitney's divorce, and not any time before. I just knew that it was Pat who hired Nick because we had never met this young man or ever seen him in any of our lives. The media kept spinning things out there about how Nick lived with Whitney and Krissy and grew up in Whitney's home. All of this was nothing but bald-faced lies being told to make people think that Nick was legit, but all the while he was not, he is what we call a handler". Every person in our family said that they had never once met nor seen Nick in person. I believe the only people that knew him were Pat and Gary Houston.

As God is my Witness

None of Krissy's other cousins knew this young man except Jerod and we don't know when they met but we know they knew each other. On top of it, it makes me wonder today, what my nephew saw Nick doing to Krissy while he knew the two were together.

I am now wondering if Jerod knew that this boy was abusing Krissy at all. Krissy's friends told me some stories that let me know that Nick did not care anything for my niece. I just wish that young girls could break away from such boyfriends no matter how much you like someone, if they are not treating you right it is a sign from God to stay away from them. This goes for anyone.

You cannot be so caught up in relationships to where it is hard to walk away. Place God first in your life and allow Him to guide you, because the signs will come. God will show them up for you to see just who they are so that you can make the right decision with your life. You must make the right decisions so that you can stay safe out here. It is very important to watch people and pay attention to their actions and their demeanor. Even when it's people you love. Always be willing to accept the truth about people when they show you who they are. You don't have to hate them, but you must get away and stay away from them so that you are safe out here.

It is plenty of people in this world for you to quickly move on before you become attached and become hurt. Whenever you get that first sign, RUN! You will know because God is always there to tell us. People hang on because it's their bad decision. But God don't play He will show you quick! That is just like Pat doing what she did to my niece. I said to everyone, "Pat only had Krissy on that Reality show to tear her down before this world because "they wanted a judge to see Krissy as incompetent so they could pull that estate away from her.

As God is my Witness

THIS WAS THE MAIN REASON FOR THATREALITY SHOW. And just as sure as I said it, it came to pass and happened. They had gotten together and took my brother to court to gain access to Whitney's estate through Krissy. I KEPT TRYING TO GET TO KRISSY TO TELL HER THIS. I sent note after note on Facebook trying to get her to listen to me. I had no other way of contacting her. Then she finally got back to me and said, Aunty Lele, I missed you, let's get together and have lunch I missed you so much! It would be the last message she sent me through Facebook.

Nick was to keep her busy and away from the Brown's and keep her drugged up. That was his job overall. I believed everything I heard about Nick because it proved to be correct after hearing the lies in the media about how he lived with Whitney and Krissy. We all knew that was a lie that Pat had placed out there. Especially when Krissy just outright told us that she knew that Pat had her on that show 'just to tear her apart" Krissy said, "SHE KEEPS HOUNDING ME FOR MONEY, AND I'M NOT GIVING HER ANYTHING!"

Why did she do the show, you may ask? My belief is that Pat Houston told Nick to sweet talk her into it. And we know how young girls are when it comes to their boyfriends. I was young and gullible, and so I know. Anything your boyfriend asks you will do.

And Pat knew this and it is why she brought Nick Gordon into the picture from the beginning. It was because she knew that Whitney nor Krissy doesn't get too close to her or Gary and they needed someone else there for starters to be in the way to do whatever she needed done. And she picked a weak young man like Nick. I am telling you, and trust me, I know exactly what I am talking about. Pat got Nick to con her into doing everything Krissy did.

As God is my Witness

All you have to do is look at my niece before her parents got their divorce. See, Bobby and Whitney both were tight and they kept their daughter close when they were together. Nobody could get in their way and do anything to either of them by themselves because they were too close and they together kept an eye on Krissy. And that's why Nick was brought in "after" their divorce, if you understand me at all. That is the only way I can see my niece doing it. That that is most definitely why she did that show with my niece. Pat did not want to do that show without Krissy because it was all about letting the world see Krissy in the condition that SHE, Pat Houston got her in! If Pat is reading this book, she knows that everything I am saying is the absolute truth.

Pat did it and wanted her there so that the world could see Krissy the way she was after Pat had Nick give her drugs. Pat set that whole thing up so that Krissy could look bad, and at the same time, she could not wait to introduce herself to the world to be seen as well, because Whitney never did anything with her, and she hated Whitney for not ever inviting her into her life. You reader, just have no idea how everything I am saying is so true. Pat knows herself that if Whitney was here, she would not ever be able to put Whitney's daughter on a show nor would she be able to get on any camera and tell this world that she is Whitney's manager. That would not ever happen if Whitney was alive, and she knows this. Just think about it, and look back at Whitney's life and then look at everything Pat has done since her death. Whitney wouldn't do stuff like that.

Remember I said I had never seen Pat inside of Bobby and Whitney's home until we had to sign those papers for me to be Krissy's guardian. The only time she did get a chance to come around was because Mama Cissy forced Pat in there with Whitney and that was it!

As God is my Witness

Whitney could never stand her to come around her and her family. Nobody really understands this relationship between Pat and Whitney but us, and Whitney's family is not going to tell you what I am saying, because they are own with Pat and against Whitney too. But, one thing is for certain two for sure, they know that I am 100% correct in everything I'm saying.

They way this woman was able to kill my niece in cold blood and then starve her to death after they agreed to let her go home is unbelievably wicked. It was not like she was in a coma or something like that. She had been doing good and getting so much better. Yes, this is what Pat did and it can be proven if she feels like I should not have said anything about it. Everything is documented in that hospice center.

They gave her no food! No nutrition! No water! No nothing! Yes, I said it; and it is 100% true! We never thought Krissy was going into a hospice center. They had to have done something to hurt her to force her in there. We all thought that Krissy was going to another hospital in the beginning. Krissy came into that hospice center unexpectedly and out of the blue. What does that tell you? I am sure Pat did things at the request of Mama Cissy at times too and it could have been most of the time, who knows, I sure don't put nothing past anyone after this. Yes, Mama Cissy did not want Krissy to live as well, I am so sorry if you do not believe what I am saying. I know and I understand it is hard to believe but this is so true reader. I hate to say it myself. This is a truth that I did not want to face. None of them wanted Krissy here over that estate money. They wanted it for themselves.

As God is my Witness

ROBYN CRAWFORD & MONIQUE HOUSTON

Robin Crawford and I had a conversation at Bobbi Kristina's body viewing. Robin Crawford said to me, "Think about it Lele, when has Mama Cissy ever did anything pertaining to being a grandmother to Krissy? When she said it to me, I could tell that she was trying to wake me up to something and she wanted me to think! Robyn had me thinking and I could not do anything but bear witness to what she was saying. Monique Houston has even told me some things about how she treated her own grandchildren by Gary and Monique, so this had me thinking for real.

After witnessing how Mama Cissy has allowed Pat to do all she is doing to Whitney, I had to question her motherhood because I could not understand it. I have it now because I learned the truth of all that has transpired. It was forcing me to believe all the accusations against Mama Cissy altogether that were before me. The truth was right there, and I could not act as if I did not understand it and see it.

I had never cried so much for Whitney after learning the truth of her life and what she went through. I kept saying to myself, why couldn't they just love her for being who she was after all these years of just being around her? Were they all just jealous of her because she did not belong to them by blood, I asked myself?

This was a lot to swallow for someone like me that has witnessed a lot transpire between them. I am a witness that Dr. Jolie Harris could have brought my niece's brain back to normal. She was already doing wonderful! And reader trust me, my niece was not "that" bad off as you are probably imaging.

As God is my Witness

No, she had never had that much water in her lungs or brain after all, and Dr. Jolie proved it directly in front of their faces that he could easily work with Krissy.

Pat still voted, no and said nab, I say kill her! Who is this woman Pat Garland, who calls herself a Houston that has obtained my sister's estate along with her daughter's estate? This is what I'd like THE FEDS to investigate because all these deaths were plotted out as God is my witness.

The doctors told us that she would be fine before we left that hospital, and she was in no way close to death. If we must bring those records up, we certainly will. I am saying what I am saying because they are facts and not hearsay or lies. I have every right under the law and under this sun, to say what I am saying. My statements are 100% true to the letter. And in my eyes and in my mind, I see Pat Houston just as I see a devil. She is a very sick and inhumane person that must be stopped at once.

This world does not know how hard my niece fought so very hard to stay alive! After all Krissy had been through, and after all the fighting, she had already managed to stay alive! God is not pleased with the way this all happened trust me when I tell you. Pat has done a lot of evil things to this family.

When I think of them, and how good Whitney was to all of them, and then, what they did to her in return, it breaks my heart that the greed and nerve of them all is so selfish and mixed up with far too much pride makes my stomach sick. I am so sorry; I cannot think of anything nice to say about them. God knows that I wish I could say something nice, but I can't!

As God is my Witness

There is absolutely nothing I ever witness nice about them dealing with Whitney, not ever! I sure wish I could have spoken with the coroner who examined Whitney's body. He may have given me more information. I wanted to ask him why they blotted out so much of Whitney's paperwork. It is a lot of yellow everywhere hiding the words of the coroner. It may have happened after he died too is what I'm thinking. One thing for sure, he was really concerned with the condition he found Whitney's body in.

He seemed to want to tell the truth about what happened to Whitney. I do appreciate his honesty in reporting what he did in Whitney's case. Yet, I will never know if it was more for me to know. In any event, we know that she was beaten to death and so, no one will ever be able to tell us anything different because that is a fact without any guessing or hearsay. As of today, this coroner is now dead as well and no longer with us in the world to tell us anything. Of course, it is possible that he died from an illness that took his life, because I think he was up there in age. But on the other hand, it just sounds weird to me that he is no longer here in the world and died not long after he does these examinations on Whitney and Michael Jackson.

Whitney body coming up dead in that hotel made me think of her song, "Heartbreak Hotel." She was a wise woman and she even played in that movie Cinderella, and no one knew why she did, but I know now. I wonder if this was plotted out from so long ago and her songs were even prepared for her death. Whitney Houston tried to live a private life with just a small circle of people, but the thing was, she did not know or understand who she was surrounded by. She most definitely had some harsh handlers around her.

As God is my Witness

We have got to take our lives more seriously, especially entertainers today that continue to see a habit of things that so strangely take place around them and learn from the mistakes of others. Life will always have stumbling blocks, and anything can fall down that pipe for you but overall, it will be whatever we make it to be, and we do have control whether we want to believe it or not we have control. The important thing here is to make plans and guard those plans as if your life depends on them because it really does. And get what you want out of this life and keep in touch with God because you will need Him more than many believe. Wake up and face anything you have set up for yourself and make changes to what is needed without fear.

Beware of those who smile much and tell too many jokes to throw you off, while expecting you to laugh when nothing is funny at all. There is nothing or no one that is more important than you at this time so welcome the peace that comes in your path with open arms and never get it confused. Avoid confrontational people and unnecessary ill treatment coming from those who say they love you. And far more important, love yourself and be there for you when you need whatever you need without hurting the next man.

Those that come with baggage, tum them around at the door and let them know that there are no rooms available, and you're all sold out. It is a lot of good people in this world, but there is also a lot of untrustworthy people that will come around you, and you must be extra careful, especially if you are in the music industry. Everybody wants to be on top of the world but won't bust a grape for God who created it for you. How insane is that? I pray that people who read this book take their life very seriously and let this book be a as a benefit and a blessing to their life and take precaution.

As God is my Witness

Be very careful trusting people and watch them good and guide your life by any means necessary, and don't get attached to people and personalities who mean you no good. Keep in mind your only here for a little while and when you go it is for forever. I am hoping that people will turn to God and repent for what they did to my family members. Each person knows what they are guilty of, be it small or great.

People who are out here murdering people and doing wrong against another human being, they should get on their knees and ask God for forgiveness right now, if they only know what I know. I'm just a little warner for God is all I am. I would also like to say, if Ray J did nothing at all, then he should be that man and step up to his plate that he served himself by the decisions that he made for himself. Nobody made none of your decisions for you but you. You can't get upset with me for speaking the truth of what you did. You walked into the Beverly Hilton hotel, and whatever took place on that day it went down, you remember, I am sure. I am sure it is still with you.

If there is any loyalty in your blood at all, and if not for Whitney, well then let it be for the people who loved her but step up to the plate and just help bring justice to her if she was a close friend of yours is all I am saying right now. What if it were your daughter, your sister or your mother or niece. What would you want people to do if nobody was owning up to the truth?

I did not place anybody in that hotel, they walked in there on their own, so why be upset with me? I don't have anything to do with anyone going in there, so if anyone is upset, they can only be upset with themselves because that is who was there. Perhaps Pat and Gary did, but I did not.

As God is my Witness

I have not lied to anyone by saying anything I've said. Everything I have written in my memoir is the truth. I would never waste a moment of my time to dare talk about something that wasn't true. For anyone to ever say that I am a liar about them being in a place they were in fact at is nonsense. Why would you do that to yourself and what is it that you don't want anyone to know, if you are innocent of any and everything? If you didn't do anything there should be nothing to worry about. Whenever anyone throws rocks into a pile of dogs the very only dog that is going to bark is the dog that got hit. The other ones are just going to continue doing what it is they do because they have no reason to make noise. I dislike it when people are bullies and the target good people who have never done any harm to them.

I remember doing time in prison and when I went to prison, I never called back home to tell anyone I was in jail because I always believed in, if you do the crime you stand on business and do that time. That was just me and I could not ever bother anyone, especially my parents. I never felt it right to put my turmoil on anyone else and I always felt it was only fair for me to deal alone with what I created for myself, even if it meant I had to starve. I stayed in prison for almost 2 years without calling a soul. A phone was something I never used in a prison to call anyone, and someone reading this is a witness for me because they know I am telling the truth.

I did my time standing on my head as we used to say, in prison. And so, all I am saying is this. I am cut from another clothe. I never feared anything, even before I even fully understood the fact that there was not anything to fear at all. I am cut from a different clothe in this world. The whole time I was down not one of my family members knew where I was.

As God is my Witness

I came from a 2-parent household where I had parents who basically spoiled their children and would die and go to hell for their children whether they were right or wrong. Anyone that grew up in our neighborhood and knew our family knew that we had the best parents. We had already been famous even before Bobby went to Hollywood. Everybody knew the Brown family because of the names we all made for ourselves back then. There was nothing that our parents wouldn't do for us because they loved us so much.

My mother and father were "real providers" for their family and never said no to anything we ever asked them to do for us. In other words, I could have gotten the help, but I didn't want it coming from my parents who did not deserve what I had done, by the decision that I made for myself I was always the one who was most independent out of my siblings. I made God sufficient for me at such a young age. I used to go in my room and talk to him all the time, and I did it secretly just between me and Him, even at that young age. I have always lived by certain principles, and I always moved by whatever my spirit told me. It was the God in myself that I paid close attention to all the time.

At a young age, I could walk in a room and literally feel people and my intuition never failed me because I paid close attention. I set boundaries for myself that I was always serious about and did not wither. You may ask, how did I survive without help while in jail? Well, here is the truth of it all...I survived in jail because I protected this one girl who was getting jumped by three girls who were bullies when I entered prison. These girls were older than me, but I feared nothing or no one and so, I threatened them and told them if you mess with her, all 3 of you will have to deal with me. They outnumbered me and knew that I was younger than them, but more than anything they knew that I was very serious, and so they all backed up.

As God is my Witness

The moral of the story is, they never bothered this girl ever again the whole time I was there. This woman is still alive today and is my Facebook friend. She found me and when she did it was the first thing she said to me on Facebook. She said, Leolah, I had been trying to find you because you have no idea the impact you left on my life. I protected her because I hated bullies, and I would challenge them even if it meant I was going to get beat up! LOL! I was used to pain and wasn't afraid of it, and I was always ready and on go for whatever they felt they needed to do. Well, the young girls man knew that I did this favor for his girl and so, now he is bringing me up monies to take care of myself and he does everything for me after this point. He evens comes to get me when my time is up, after they released me.

I never liked it when people bothered others and did it just for the sole purpose or reason of knowing that "they CAN do it!" That is so ugly to me and so weak of people. Because you know you can get away with something, you do it because the opportunity is right there in front of you. Little did they know that in life, it is also an opportunity for you to think wisely on and your chance to do the right thing. It is a challenge for your heart, and it is that time that you show up as the human being you are in that very moment. It is also something that can determine your destiny at the same time. Because if you would jump at such an opportunity and prey on a weak and humble spirit, then it tells others who you really are.

More than anything, angels are watching everything we do and reporting it to God, says Minister Farrakhan. I did not learn that until so much later in my life, and after being introduced to Minister Farrakhan, who is indeed "A Real Man of God's "and God's Man with the Messages that we should all take heed to.

As God is my Witness

I don't like it and I can never stand down and allow someone to harm others in any way whether physical, spiritual or emotional, and on my watch. No, because it's wrong to treat people like that at the end of the day. What bothered me more was that this girl was a young girl like me, and she was so beautiful, but she just didn't think she could fight and defend herself, and I happened to dislike those kinds of actions coming out of people. I never liked people messing with other people because they were jealous that they were good looking or looked better than them. That just pierced my heart and my spirit so badly, and I felt I had to do something to help the person who was being targeted.

But back to my parents, no, I did not think it was fair for my mother or father to be burdened with my foolishness is why I did not bother to involve them. I was so used to suffering it was a piece of cake for me back then. I always had in my mind, if l did the crime, I should do the time without bothering anyone else with it. I hate no man or woman, but what I must do is let people know exactly what transpired at this hotel because crimes were committed, and the crimes were done to my family, and that is very personal to me.

It doesn't bother you if your heart is not involved with the person who is harmed. It doesn't bother you if you have an unremorseful heart that is in love with doing wrong to others. Whether or not you did anything, you owe this world an explanation. If you didn't do anything when it appears that you did, then tell the world what really happened is all you should do. Never mind me, but this world would feel so much better if people would step up and just tell us what happened if they are innocent.

As God is my Witness

What I am revealing has nothing to do with me, it is just the absolute truth of what they did, and so they cannot be upset with none other than themselves, because they are the ones who did whatever it was, they did, not me! All I am doing is speaking on the truth and what they did while they were there at this hotel and if it is any difference then let us know. This is not a situation where I did anything to anyone. It's not fair to Whitney or my niece that they lost their life like that in that hotel. They messed up big time by killing my niece after they killed my sister.

After knowing what Krissy told us, I began thinking and praying to God to show me what really happened to my niece in that hotel that day. Then God sent me a vision in my sleep is what I call it. I had a dream that "Krissy walked up to me as I was sitting at the top of the bleachers in a football field. She came over to me looking so tired. She came straight to me and just laid directly in my lap on top of a pillow that I had sitting in my lap. Without saying a word, she just laid down, and I then started rubbing her head telling her to rest, and she went to sleep.

When I awoke from that dream, I felt like I knew the interpretation and it was that God was trying to tell me, yes, Krissy did make it to her pillow after locking that deadbolt on that hotel door, and then she laid on her bed and knocked out. This told me how they removed her clothes. Yes, I believe it was not until after that, where she had her clothes taken off her body and placed in that bathtub at that hotel. After that, they took her clothes out of that room, and they did whatever they did with them. I said then that Pat probably kept those clothes for her daughter or someone else has them, but someone took my niece's clothes from her hotel room that day before placing her in that bathtub.

So, you see a lot of wicked things were going on in this hotel and it was going on with all these people surrounding Whitney Houston and my niece. I believe it was God who sent that vision to me to tell me that yes, Krissy did in fact lock that deadbolt on that door, and then she proceeded to lay down on her bed to go to sleep and she did in fact, get in her bed.

In my mind, this was the deal, and it was why I had this dream. Now, if it is true after she laid down and was out sleeping, they took her clothes off stripping her but naked and then they placed her body in that bathtub to kill her. I strongly believe that this is what happened because this is what makes sense and it adds up to what my niece has told us happened. Besides that, when I was going through this and fighting for my family, and investigating this case, I was very In-tune with God as well so please keep that in mind. I did a lot of praying and fasting because I know the power of prayer and fasting. I believe they then took her clothes off and threw her body in that bathtub and were trying to figure out what to do next.

BOBBI KRISTINA'S BODY WAS WARM TO THE CORE AT THAT MORGUE!

The thing that hurts me and breaks my heart even so much more is the fact that, my niece, Krissy's body was warm to the core after they took her body to the morgue. Her body had been in the refrigerator unit for approximately 24 hours after her autopsy, so she sat in there for about a day, and yes, her body was very much so warm says that coroner in his notes. On top of it all, she had SALIVA on her lips! THIS MEANS SHE WAS STILL ALIVE! WE NEED TO KNOW HOW DOES THIS HAPPEN AND ON WHO'S WATCH DID IT HAPPEN ON I WONDER?

As God is my Witness

When I tell you that my niece was tortured, you have no idea what she endured before she took her last breath. If the people in this world want to know why I was so upset and screaming in the beginning of all of this, it is simply because of all the things that I was learning about my niece in my investigation. This is not supposed to happen, and then, "why" is it happening for real, and who is responsible for this, for real?

Please don't forget that Nick Gordon was that person who Pat Houston brought into my sister, Whitney Houston's life. None of us had ever met that boy before Pat Houston brought him around Whitney and Krissy, and she did not do it until after Bobby and Whitney's divorce. They knew that Nick could not come around us and do what he was doing. They know they would not have gotten away with it if so. He was literally "PLANTED" or "PLACED" into Whitney and Krissy's life for the purposes of helping with their murders. The tabloids are spinning so many lies about him staying in Bobby and Whitney's home, and so- called growing up with Krissy. None of it happened and not one of us ever met this young man, Nick Gordon. I personally never saw him, not even once.

Pat and Gary Houston, both gave themselves away, by even spreading that lie through the media, and telling that lie to this world, knowing that we knew the real deal with this young man. No, he did not grow up with Krissy and Whitney in their home. How is this going to happen, and not even my brother Bobby, who is Krissy's father, and Whitney's husband, don't even know him and never met him before? I believe that is why Nick Gordon is not here today. He began to get weak and lose it and he would have opened the can of worms for them, is why I believe he is dead now. I am 100% sure how he came in and what his mission was.

As God is my Witness

It was all too easy for us to figure out. See, they figured, Bobby is not around anymore to protect his wife and daughter, so, he won't be there when this boy Nick does all that he was asked to do to Whitney and Krissy. That is how and why they brought Nick in. They needed someone around Whitney and Krissy because Whitney would not dare allow Pat and Gary Houston around her enough for them to get her, trust me when I tell you this is why they went and got Nick Gordon. It was easy to see through Nick Gordon. He was that weak link. After he did Dr. Phil, I knew it was over for him because he was all over the place.

The lies that he and they told brought me straight to all the evidence. They made it so easy for all of us to figure out. I just followed all trails, and it was easy to figure out what they did. I practically helped Bobby and Whitney raise Krissy and was living in their home and we never ever once laid eyes on a Nick Gordon. They placed him there and had a much harder time killing Krissy. My niece ended up surviving every trap they set for her. But they kept going until they got her. I'd like to know who asked Whitney to stay in that hotel for two weeks which lead up to the Clive Davis event because they did that to have lead way because they were focused in on two bodies they were trying to eliminate before this event. OK, let's sum this all up right here. First, Whitney is asked to stay in this hotel for 2 weeks, she's at Kelly Price event and it was Stacy Francis (who is a friend of Ray J) taunting Whitney with violating her body the way she did. Their doing all they can and who knows what else Whitney and Krissy were both going through in this hotel? Yet, Whitney's security (Ray) was nowhere around to help Whitney in all this, and meanwhile, we clearly see Pat Houston behind her at Kelly Price's party or event, and Whitney very much so looks disgruntled there.

As God is my Witness

Then we have the phone call to the coroner about picking up a body. The very next day it is Whitney's body instead of Krissy's, and then after Whitney's death they came for Krissy, her daughter, AGAIN. I am sure they did multiple things to end my niece's life. Then, they call in Brandi Burnside for help because it's a possibility that she can get up around Krissy and do whatever they ask her to all they had to do was promise her a spot on a TV show... AND THIS IS A PART OF RAY J AS WELL.

Here, we have a young girl, my niece (Bobbi Kristina BROWN) who's mourning her mother's death! They just found Whitney dead in this hotel and Ray J IS INDEED IN THIS HOTEL and he forces my niece to take that pill that quickly throws her into a seizure, and she's now rushed off BY AMBULANCE to an LA hospital! Yes, and this is THE SAME DAY HER MOTHER IS FOUND DEAD IN THIS HOTEL.

While she was there in that hospital, they had Brandi tell the nurse she needs to be committed to some "Psych Ward" and that doesn't work, so they just plan to get my niece back in Atlanta because my son told Krissy to RUN. Kelsey told Krissy they were setting her up and to get out of that hospital now! They catch up to her in Atlanta and do multiple things that did not work and one of them is, they plant that knife into that vehicle telling Krissy to drive it SO THAT HER SO-CALLED FRIEND "DANIELLE" WHO SHE CAUGHT SLEEPING WITH NICK GORDON won't kill herself.

As God is my Witness

They told Krissy a made-up story that her friend Danielle was sorry and that she didn't mean to get caught with Nick Gordon and she was so sad and was so sorry about what she did to her friend Krissy. Yeah, right, sure she was sorry. They did this still playing games with my niece just so my niece would feel bad for this girl, who was "never" her friend at all.

But Krissy gets in that car to drive it as Joshua has said because he was in fact A WITNESS WHO WAS THERE AND WITNESSED THIS WHOLE THING GOING DOWN RIGHT IN FRONT OF HIM. Joshua said that my niece Krissy, got in this car to drive it and they had "already" stuck the knife in her tire ...so that it would assure them that she would have an accident- AND SHE DID! AND THEY DID THIS SO THAT SHE WOULD EITHER DIE, OR THEY COULD JUST MAKE MY NIECE SEEM UNFIT TO BE OVER HER MOTHER'S ESTATE BECAUSE THEY WANTED IT! YES, THIS IS THE TRUTH AS GOD IS MY WITNESS! And my niece, she "still" doesn't die there, but the thing that was more important to Pat Houston, was that they had that incident as evidence, in case Pat Houston needed it for "the courts" to prove to a judge that she was unfit.

Meanwhile, EVERY SINGLE THING and/or EVENT was happening "because of Pat Houston's set up. She was orchestrating it all and bringing people around my niece to expedite this mission for her. Yes, indeed, they did all of this as God is my witness they did. OK, and now at this point, she still didn't die, and they tried trick after trick after trick, and Krissy was still not dying. Meanwhile Krissy said, Pat was constantly begging her to do this reality show, but Krissy is still saying NO! Pat has not let up on begging my niece for money and whatever else she was begging Krissy for.

As God is my Witness

Pat is also trying to get my niece on this so- called Reality Show TO SHAME MY NIECE AND MAKE HER LOOK BAD TO THIS WORLD. Krissy continues to tell her NO, until she finally does it for some strange reason. And we all said that Pat "must have" gotten Nick Gordon to change Krissy's mind and do the show because it would be the only way she would do that show. And Pat is doing all of this to Bobby and Whitney's daughter, "knowing" that they would not ever condone this such behavior coming from Pat Houston, to place their daughter on national TV, with the ideas that Pat had in her mind to do to their child.

According to what Joshua told us was that Pat Houston was TELLING NICK TO KEEP HER SEDATED AND HIGH AT ALL TIMES. This was done to try to make it look like my niece was some drunk or drug addict that belonged somewhere or anywhere of her choice. And let me tell you this reader, you can believe it or not, but this was exactly Pat Houston's intentions as she placed my niece on that show. Her "main" idea was to shame my niece and get her committed somewhere so that they could snatch that estate away from her.

If you can't see this picture reader, it would only be because perhaps, you just do not want to see it, or because you just don't believe it. Either way, it is the absolute truth, and I am telling you that this is exactly what it was. They committed "so many crimes" even before killing Whitney and my niece, and they need to be brought to justice for it. From what Joshua told me, about how Pat was orchestrating everything, and Krissy's other friends telling me the same, I strongly believe that Pat Houston was telling Nick to hurry up because they could not wait any longer for Krissy to be down and out and they wanted Krissy out of here!

As God is my Witness

Joshua talked to me about the note that fell from Max or Nick's pocket while they were trying to get Krissy into that car where they had stuck that knife. He said, it was a card folded up and it fell as they were "ACTING" as if they were struggling trying to get Danielle to not get in the car and drive it to commit suicide.

Joshua said that they were all acting because Pat had them doing it pretending as if Danielle was going to kill herself all because Krissy wouldn't talk to her anymore after finding her with her boyfriend Nick. This was the whole thing they were playing out for Krissy. He said, the card falls out of Max or Nicks pocket, or hand and he said he did not touch it until he left from around them and when he got away where he could look at it and observe it, it was a post card FROM PAT HOUSTON that just had her address and a "SMILY FACE" on it. No words, no instructions or anything, it was just a sign for whatever they talked about in person, he said.

The rest of Krissy's friends told me things just like this and they were all convinced that Pat Houston had Nick doing things to Krissy. They said, Nick did not care for Krissy not even a little bit. So, them being around Krissy all the time without seeing what was going on, of course I believed them because they all had the very same stories about Nick. And to find out that Pat and Nick were both on social media arguing in public but was pretending at the same time just made my hairs stand straight up on my back. I said, you mean to tell me that it was all a hoax. They all said, yes Auntie Lele it was, Pat and Nick were both just playing a game with Krissy's life by pretending to be upset with one another.

As God is my Witness

So, I get it, the first thing that came to my mind when they said that part was, Pat had Nick there spying on Krissy as well with her money, because Nick even had access to my niece's bank cards and was getting money out of her accounts.

Pat's job was to act like she didn't know this but was the main reason it was going on all along. I believe every word that came from Joshua's mouth whenever he talked about Pat and Nick. This is that same young man who was kidnapped and gang raped by 5 adult men who sent him to the emergency room from busting his backside out so bad. He said, "Aunty Lele, as I looked at this post card, I said to myself, it only has Pats address on it with a smiley face on it to send a message!" I then asked him to repeat the address to me that is on this post card, and when he did, I knew that he knew what he was talking about. I believe after that post card was delivered to that boy, Pat Houston forced Nick to do Krissy in and hurry up! That is the reason for his behavior after he did that to Krissy, He said, "I am not going down for Pat, I saved her with Whitney!" It all makes sense to me as to everything that transpired with my sister and niece, and no one can change my mind because I have it clearly right here before me. I have all this evidence that points to Pat and Gary Houston.

Not to mention that Jonathon Houston told me out of his own mouth that he "knew" that his own father and stepmother did this to his cousin Krissy! Now I see why Donna Houston, Pat and Gary Houston all told Jonathon to shut his mouth and asked him, "Whose side was he on!" It is because they did not see Whitney or my niece as family to them because, they ARE NOT any relation to them at all. Everything has added up to be exactly what it is, and no one can deny it because it is what it is at the end of the day.

As God is my Witness

After that Car accident, Nick Gordon beats my niece nearly to death and he places her in that bathtub with the hopes of her to be completely dead. She doesn't even die there and so everyone is now afraid that the truth will come out because Nick is on Dr Phil FAKE CRYING and acting weird and foolish trying to place blame on my brother Bobby (which did not work at all). I must talk about the Dr Phil interview as well because the way they did that was too obvious to me. I knew something was strange about the Dr. Phil & Nick Gordon interview. The only person invited was Nick Gordon on a Whitney Houston case? WOW! After one of the greatest Icons of all times were murdered and/or even just dead. Let's say she just died in a hotel. You only have one person in your studio to interview out of all of Whitney's people and it's Nick Gordon who beat her daughter down nearly to death leaving her in a bathtub the same way her mom went out.

No other family members were invited. I am sure no Houston's wanted to come and sit because they orchestrated everything and helped! But you couldn't invite not one of "The Brown's?" Oh yeah, that was off limits because that would have been too right to do. Yeah, I see this whole picture and how things were done, and it doesn't look good at all. Evidence was too clear for me and so easy a second grader can figure it all out. I thank everyone for how they acted and everything they did to help me solve this picture.

Anyone who was present at that hotel did that to themselves and exposed themselves to whatever we can clearly see. If you haven't done anything, I would ask you to come and sit down with me and tell me that looking me straight in my eyes. And now I believe that perhaps Ray J did put Stacy Francis up to do that to Whitney at that Kelly Price event by squeezing her breast.

As God is my Witness

I have a good feeling in my gut that Ray J either asked or told her to do that to my sister. It looks like more than a few folks were seriously down with the conspiracy of Whitney Houston and her daughter Bobbi Kristina.

People were just down with doing all kinds of things to my sister and my niece, and they did it as if they were just two people easy to play with. It was easy because the family of Whitney Houston made it so. And that is why you see "no one" from Whitney's family wanting to go after Pat and stop her from all the evil she is doing to Whitney and against her estate. She sold Whitney's CATALOG FOR CHRIST SAKE! SHE DID THIS NOT LONG AFTER WHITNEYS DEATH. WELL, SHE HAD BEEN PLANNED IT I BELIEVE. ALL OF THIS WAS PLANNED AND PLOTTED OUT BY PAT AND GARY HOUSTON, HANDS DOWN.

What are the odds of an Icon being found dead and all these people present; and none of them saying a word about it, THINK! And if you are not guilty of anything you go on about your business and have no worries regardless of what anyone says, right? Ray J saying he wasn't there, had already given himself away. We are 100% certain that Ray J WAS THERE! I am 100% convinced that Ray J has something to do with the demise of Whitney Houston and Bobbi Kristina Brown, and it is clear to me that he has something to hide because he wants people to believe that he wasn't there at the Beverly Hilton Hotel. If you did nothing malicious then why are you trying to hide the fact that you were there? This is 2024 and God is exposing everything under this Sun that is wrong, evil and wicked. Katt Williams said it best, he said, "It's Up for All and All lies will BE exposed in 2024, No Matter Who You Are!"

Chapter 16
LAST BUT SURELY NOT LEAST!!!
BOBBY BROWN JR.

My nephew Bobby Brown Jr. I saw my nephew, Bobby Jr., the day before he was pronounced dead, and he looked so good! Anyone looking at him, knew that he was clean, hands down. Little Bobby was clean and sober, and I will never believe that he just took something and killed himself. That is a lie and a cover up for what someone again did to another one of my beloved family members. My brother Bobby was in Atlanta with us the day before and we all met him at a restaurant. I happen to be sitting right next to my brother, Bobby as he was facetiming little Bobby in the restaurant where we met up at. He passed the phone to me and said, "Say hi to your Auntie Lele, Bobby!" Bobby Jr., smiled at me and said, hi, aunty and was smiling from ear to ear! I had never seen him look so good as we began talking to each other.

My nephew didn't even look like he was smoking weed anymore, he looked so good! I told him right there how good he looked to me. All of us who seen his face that day was amazed at how good he looked! I am so sure that my nephew was clean and sober. Now, as much as I don't want to, I have got to tell this story for you, reader, to understand my nephew, Bobby Jr's true story. Not long before that, Bobby Jr. called me on the phone and told me he was homeless in Los Angeles and very seriously needed a place to stay until he could do something, such as go home to his mother Kim Ward in Boston. Kim Ward is Bobby's "first love, and they had three children altogether.

As God is my Witness

Bobby and Kim have always been close and at least they have always communicated for the sake of their children because they had to raise their children together. I could not believe my ears when he called me and said, he was homeless, so hungry and hadn't eaten anything and had nowhere to go.

Now, when he called me, last I heard, I thought he was staying with his father, my brother, Bobby Brown in Los Angeles. But when he called me late this night, he said, Aunty, I am homeless and have nowhere to go out here in LA. I said, WHAT, ARE YOU SERIOUS, LITTLE BOBBY? WHERE IS YOUR FATHER, AND WHY ARENT YOU THERE AT HIS HOUSE WITH HIM?

He then said to me, "Aunty, yes, it's because of my father's wife Alicia, she said because I lost my job, I cannot stay with them and so, she put me out of my dad's house. I said, you got to be kidding me, unbelievable? Reader, you have no idea how much this devastated me, and made me feel at this very moment of him telling me this, and so, putting it in words is something hard for me to do right now, but I can't write too much on this I am hurting too much but I will try.

I tried so hard not to cry as he is talking to me because I just could not believe what he was telling me. I just burst out crying for my nephew! I said, Bobby, tell me what happened and why did she put you out of your father's house baby, please! He then told me how his so- called co-workers were always teasing him at his job whenever he came into work, and they did it all the time. He said, he tried to work and ignore them as they made fun of him and passed judgement by saying that he shouldn't be working there if he was Bobby Brown's son and so on. I mean, my nephew is not the kind of person you want to tease and do that to.

As God is my Witness

He's not the confrontational type who even talks to a lot of people because he's so shy and all. This last day at work, he went to work, and he argued with these people asking them to please leave him alone and let him work because that was all he was there for anyways.

One word led to another, and they fired him for whatever reasons behind such foolishness that "they themselves" should have resolved without firing him. Anyone who knows my nephew they know he is so far from being a troublemaker and would never bother anyone.

There is no way that they should have done that to him, because they should have known that these people were bothering him all the time and making fun of him being Bobby Brown's son and having to work where he was working. The nerve of these people messing with him got to me more than anything. He also told us that Alicia, his dad's wife, put him out of his father's house "only" because he had lost his job. Where is the love and support of a family when you need it? And people wonder why the youth is out here selling drugs and doing things they shouldn't. It's because of parents like her that care nothing for children. I can't even get into it like I need to because my spirit is just that vexed right now. But anyone reading this that has a heart, they know where I am coming from.

Well, OK, I had to think quickly to get him off the streets! LA is a dangerous place and no place for a young black man to be at alone and especially at night. I felt so helpless when my nephew told me this because I really didn't know who to contact in LA at this time. The people I knew were out the country on vacation and I did not want him going to just anybody's house.

As God is my Witness

At that time, it was better for me to trust a stranger to be honest because at least I know he'll be treated better. I immediately got him some help from one of my Facebook friends who took him in.

I started to reveal her name, but I felt it was better not to right now. It was a person I had never met, and I had to go with my gut feeling and decide on who I was going to trust my nephew with going into their home. It happens to be a very nice and kind woman who got in her car and picked him up and brought him home with her. She was so very happy to do it this for me. After she got little Bobby with her, she told me that my nephew was so nice, so respectful and so kind, and that she could not believe how beautifully spirited he was. She fell in-love with lil Bobby after allowing him to stay in her house for over a week. Everything I told her of him was true she said because she got a chance to experience it with him face to face. I did not exaggerate even a little bit with her. She told me, the one thing she appreciated about him was that he told her he had just stopped smoking. She is a vegan and a very clean person and of course, keeps her home clean. Therefore, she was hoping that she didn't have to ask him to not smoke weed around her and her grandchild and so on. She said, "Leolah, your nephew didn't even smoke weed anymore, and I was so proud of him and how he respected my home while he was here.

After she heard he was found deceased, she said, Leolah, I am a witness that your nephew didn't even smoke WEED anymore! He was looking good and was clean, and I said, "I know, because I saw him just one (1) day before his death and he looked marvelous and extremely good, so, I know someone killed him, period." She said, he was most definitely clean, and I had absolutely no problems at all with him, and I even allowed him to have his girlfriend there with him because he was so peaceful and respectful of my home, she said.

As God is my Witness

I knew this because I know my nephew, and no one can tell me anything negative about him. I could never thank this woman enough for what she did to help me at such a time. Now, she took little Bobby in not long before he was found dead. But I am going to leave that right there because I just can't do anything about it right now, and talking about it brings on other things for me. It hurts me too much to even think about it, let alone write the things I am feeling in my spirit. I have spoken out a lot on social media concerning my brother's wife, and it's something that I don't like doing (for the sake of God) anymore.

The one thing that baffled and surprised me was the fact that my son Kelsey told me, he looked it up and found out that Bobby's Jr.'s body was found in a condo in LA that was owned by Alicia, my brother Bobby's wife. I am saying to myself, "How does Alicia throw my nephew out of the house where his father pays the bills and lays his head at, and he ends up dead in a condo owned by the woman who put him out? It just doesn't make sense to me at all. On top of it all, my brother Bobby had 'just left Atlanta' to go back home to LA only to find his son dead.

My nephew was just homeless with nowhere to go and after staying with my friend in LA when I had not too long spoke to him about. He told me that he was staying somewhere with his friends after that. I am trying to find out how he got from there into Alicia's property which was also somewhere else besides his father's home where he and his wife both stay. I am thinking to myself, and why did he have to stay in this place and not there home? These are questions that I ask which I cannot understand or get answered.

As God is my Witness

Now, when I asked what happened to my nephew and how he was found, I was told, my brother Bobby was home with his wife Alicia, and he was somehow not feeling good and asks his wife Alicia for his medicine that his doctor(s) prescribed for him. Alicia then allegedly tells my brother Bobby, "Oh, you got to go and get your medicine from the (Alicia's) condo. My question in my head was, why is his medicine not in his own home where he stays, and who brought my brother's medicine to that condo and why? But my family member that is telling me this, says that Bobby goes to this condo to pick up his medicine so that he could take it, and when he arrives at this condo, he finds his first-born son, Bobby Brown Jr. dead.

There is a young white girl currently in this condo with my nephew at the time of his death. Bobby J is still lying in bed, and Bobby my brother walks over to him to shake him to get up! Little Bobby doesn't move, and his father finds out he is deceased. Now, there was a young Caucasian/ white girl there with my nephew, and she's been there with him the whole time but has claimed that she did not know he became unalive. This girl says, "I don't know what happened to him, I thought he was asleep all this time.

I do not trust this girl whoever she is. By the way, this girl is not a mystery to anyone from what I am hearing. I find out later that she is seen online with a camera showing off the "Fentanyl" as she was laughing, smiling, and playing with it on video right there with my nephew, and as if she was telling the world what she was about to do to him, with it! She was showing this off online where people can clearly see this at. I knew that whatever happened it had to be someone slipping his in his food or drink and it is the cause of his death because my nephew would not ever take such a drug, plus he was not using any drugs not even weed anymore.

As God is my Witness

He had even given up cigarettes from what I am hearing and had only smoked weed in the past. I personally cannot understand what anyone in my family is doing about the situation because they don't tell me everything. Therefore, I do not know what they are doing about it. Whenever I say something, nobody wants to hear me or tell me anything, and meanwhile the very thing that I am always trying to save my family from including "people," I always get ignored and then, BOOM! The worst has happened, and everyone is silent about it. Nobody wants to deal with anything it seems to me. For some strange reason, this girl is not in jail for it as I write.

She has been given a pass I guess and as far as I know, this girl is still out there just like Pat Houston and the rest of them, without having been questioned or even given Bobby Jr's parents or our family a proper explanation as to what really happened to my nephew. Now, they mentioned something about drugs, which is very disrespectful to me. I want them to know that this is not something I believe not even for a half of a second. It is ridiculously absurd and such a crazy, unreasonable, and extremely unacceptable narrative to continue to flash in the news and I don't like it at all.

There is no way that my nephew was even doing drugs and I am so tired of the media blasting drugs as the problem whenever they find someone dead-when they know and are sure he didn't do any drugs on his own. They have been using this as an excuse because of the "Bobby Brown & Whitney Houston" drug persona that they have been flooding the tabloids with for years, but it doesn't work with me and it never will. Of course, all of this sounds so suspicious to us. My nephew never told me or anyone that I know that Alicia let him stay in a place she owned.

As God is my Witness

When I last spoke with him, he was kicked out from their home and had nowhere to go and she wasn't even speaking to him from what he told me. I remember the sad look on his face as I looked into his eyes during the facetime call between him and his father. It made me want to cry just looking at him and imagining his pain he had to walk around with not having a place to sleep.

This young man has always paid his own way while he was living in LA, struggling to get his music out there for people to hear him. He barely asked anyone for anything, including his father. I don't think he depended on his father for much, he just needed a place to stay until he could get on his feet properly. And knowing little Bobby, it would have been short term because he is so independent. I sent him money anytime he asked me, and I was happy to help him whenever I could because he never asked me for anything. With all due respect, the reason why my nephew's story is here at the end of this book, is because I had made the decision to not write his whole story in this book because I did not want to say anything that sounded negative regarding my brother's wife Alicia.

But you can't talk about certain things unless you mention her. I don't like talking about people, period and I am so tired of things happening by the very same people and people are losing their lives and nothing is happening behind it. There is no justice giving anywhere we tum. This is crazy and insane already. I am not a troublemaker nor am I anyone who speaks lies out here to gain fans or money. No, that's the last thing that anyone should ever think about whenever they see my name anywhere. Some people may ask the question, well, why don't we sit down as family and resolve our issues? We can't because we can never get together with others coming between us as a family!

As God is my Witness

I have personally tried to on many occasions but to no avail do I ever get the respect of a sister who just seriously loves her family and is concerned with where we are going as a family. We have too many outsiders saying this and that and things that don't even matter to keep us separated and disunited as a family. I get tired and I am only human at the end of the day for crying out loud. Speaking of outsiders, my brother Bobby's so-called attorney who likes lyi8ng on people, he too is a person who comes between our family affairs when he should be respectful and simply mind his business.

HE LIED ON ME AND SAID I WAS LYING ABOUT MY BROTHER BOBBY BEING HIT BY THAT CAR. YES, ATTORNEY CHRIS BROWN, BOBBY BROWN'S ATTORNEY, TOLD A BOLD FACE LIE ABOUT ME SAYING THAT MY BROTHER BOBBY WAS HIT BY A CAR, AND IT IS NOT OVER. I WANT A PUBLIC APOLOGY FOR HIM LYING ON ME, BECAUSE BOBBY WAS INDEED HIT BY A CAR AND HIS ATTORNEY CHRIS BROWN MORE THAN LIKELY WAS ONE OF THE FIRST PEOPLE TO KNOW THAT BOBBY WAS HIT BY THAT CAR. SO, THEREFORE, OF COURSE HE KNEW AS HIS ATTORNEY. THEREFORE, WHEN HE LIED ON ME, HE WAS CERTAINLY ALREADY AWARE OF WHAT HE WAS DOING AND HE DID THAT INTENTIONALLY AND SO HE OWES ME AN APOLOGY BECAUSE CHARLAMAIGNE THE GOD OF THE BREAKFAST CLUB GAVE ME DONKEY OF THE DAY BECAUSE OF HIM AND SO, YES, I AM ALSO GOING TO NEED AN APOLOGY FROM HIM AS WELL. I AM COUNTING ON IT...

As God is my Witness

Back to my family issues. I have tried on several occasions to contact them and try to resolve our issue and bring peace amongst our family. I never held hard feelings for my brother's wife. I always respected her and looked forward to treating her like family when she first married my brother. They got married very quickly and did not invite any of us to their wedding which was very strange as well, but I still respected them. I held no hard feelings at all about that because everyone has their own rights to do what they will. I am just curious to know "why" they did not invite any of Bobby's family members.

Perhaps I would understand if I knew the real reasons why. Nobody is doing anything to deserve the harsh treatment all the time. It was never a situation where she knew anyone yet, and someone upset her or anything of that nature. I had never got to know Alicia when she first married my brother, and so, we'd like to know why she thought it was a good idea to "not" invite any family members. I am sure she had her family there with her and Bobby. Was he comfortable without any of us there? If that answer is yes, then that's a different thing altogether and the problem is not her. But what reason would Bobby have out the blue after and before that even with Whitney, we were all a family and doing so many things together.

I mean, I just can't imagine Bobby being comfortable without his family at this wedding. We were all invited to him and Whitney's wedding, and I was actually "IN" this wedding by the choice of Whitney herself, so we can't be that bad. In fact, Whitney kept this family together along with Mommy and Daddy both. When Bobby and Whitney were married, Whitney asked me and my younger sister Carole (Coop) to be her bride's maid. It's just really weird when you leave out family without an explanation is all I am respectfully saying.

As God is my Witness

Another thing, whenever someone spoke ill of Alicia back then, without having known her yet, when the family and friends were speaking so ill about her, I was the only one who told everyone to leave her alone and allow our brother to be with whomever he wanted to. I made it clear to everyone that it was none of our business who Bobby decides to be with. As long as he was happy, that is all that mattered to me at the end of the day. I said, he is a grown man and is living his life. It just hurt for me when things were directed at me as a single person where I had to say, hold on now, I am not your enemy.

Then to find out how his children were being treated and how she had been and still is separating Bobby from everyone was all unnecessary unless you see the bigger picture in "why" she was doing what she was doing altogether. Everything became exposed to where I understood the game after all.

It led me to understand what is really going on to cause all the confusion and/or bad behavior. And I don't care who you are, I am going to speak truth and let that be it, because at the end of the day, it's God that I am looking to please and no one else. My father always told us, if you don't STOP doing a thing that is needed to be stopped "it will eventually stop you!"

Back to Bobby Brown Jr. My nephew was a hard-working young man who just ran into a set back and lost his job. He is Bobby's first- born son for crying out loud! There is something very wrong with this picture, and somebody has to tell me something because something just isn't right with all that has gone on. There are a lot of strange things going on around my family members. I didn't want my nephew in Los Angeles from the beginning.

As God is my Witness

I told him he could come and stay with me, and he would be so happy and more peaceful if he did. Yet, I couldn't get him out of LA. In time. I feel so bad saying this because it hurts me to my heart that my nephew is not here with us anymore. I can't imagine what he was going through in his mind being out there in LA and going through that with people he didn't even know. I was going to leave little Bobby's story out of this book because it hurt me too much to write. My heart could not take telling his story in this book. I just couldn't do it after all I had to write for Krissy and Whitney; it was too much. It is going to take a lot of prayer to get through what my family is going through.

Lastly, they did a so-called autopsy on my nephew and then they held back the results which they seemed to be trying to make us believe they did not know. I did not believe it for a second. I said, now, there is no way that they did an autopsy on Lil Bobby, and don't know the results. In my mind, I thought it was because they did know what it was, and they found out that someone had poisoned him or did something terrible to him, and they just did not reveal it to us. Too many strange things were happening, and my brain is far too intelligent for me to think that it was something otherwise. No, I strongly believe my nephew was poisoned and killed point blank.

LAST WORDS

There is too much evil in our world against our human race of people. It's even sadder when it's our own people doing their own people and we don't fully get it and see it as a problem. That alone is insane. We need to know that whatever comes around shall go right back around to its sender. If Krissy, Whitney and Bobby Jr., were their family and came up dead in their families, every single one of them

487

would be upset and who knows how much. But you see, they don't have to wear the shoes we are forced to wear. They don't have to mourn family members in the same fashion we have to, so they don't feel what we are feeling.

They are not missing their dead family members that were murdered in a hotel room or beaten down in their own living room. I don't think they seriously realize what they have really been doing amid all this happening and going on. They seem to lose sight of the real world we live in. I would bet all the stacks of Bibles, they are so far lost in time and have no idea what time it is out here right now with God.

Whitney revised her will right before all this happened to her. Maybe she felt they were coming for her and tried to change it right away. I don't know but what I do believe is, they fraudulently compromised Whitney's WILL. Yes, indeed we all do. Yet, I nor my brother Bobby care not even a little bit, about money like that. I am totally concerned with how they killed them altogether and how they got away with it. That is where I come in at. You don't take someone's life and do it so arrogantly and as if you "can" do that and get away with it. Whitney did not owe anyone a single thing.

She worked hard for whatever God blessed her with, and for people and other so called human beings to take her and their lives so lightly and so brutally, they should get on their knees and ask the Almighty God of this universe and time for forgiveness ... because the time is here and NOW where God has come to deliver all of His true and righteous believers in Him. This is 2024 and God is exposing everything under this Sun that is wrong, evil and wicked. Again, Katt Williams said it best, "It's Up for All and All lies will BE Exposed in 2024, No Matter Who You Are!"

As God is my Witness

Lastly, did you know reader, that Pat and Gary Houston along with Mama Cissy Houston, they all sold Whitney Houston's CATALOG to a company named: PRIMARY WAVE? That alone to me is suspicious the way they did it. In my opinion, they did this just to have all of Whitney's HARD-EARNED money, so that they can live lavish lifestyles with her dead! Thing is, they knew that they had to do it over her dead body! Yes, that is why they took her out. That is the reason why Pat Houston ALSO killed my niece as well.

Pat and Gary Houston along with Cissy Houston has a VERY, VERY, VERY HEAVY PRICE TO PAY WITH GOD FOR THE MURDER OF WHITNEY HOUSTON BROWN AND BOBBI KRISTINA BROWN. WHOEVER IS RESPONSIBLE FOR MY NEPHEW HAS THAT SAME PRICE TO PAY, AS GOD IS MY WITNESS THE PRICE WILL BE PAID IN FULL...AGAIN, KATT WILLIAMS SAID IT BEST, "IT'S UP FOR ALL IN 2024! ALL LIES WILL BE EXPOSED IN 2024 NO MATTER WHO YOU ARE.

THE END ....

<u>MORE TO COME LATER!</u>

Chapter 17: <u>Whitney's Autopsy Report</u>

County of Los Angeles, Department of Coroner
Investigator's Narrative

Case Number: 2012-01022   Decedent: HOUSTON, WHITNEY ELISEBETH

Information Sources:

(1)   Beverly Hills Police Department-Report #12-0806   (310)285-2156
        Detective Hyon

Investigation:

On Saturday 02/11/2012 at 2104 hours, Sergeant Publicker from the Beverly Hills Police Department called the Los Angeles County Coroner's Office to report a natural versus accidental death of a 48 year-old black female that possibly drowned in a bathtub. On Saturday 02/11/2012 at 2120 hours, Lieutenant Brian Elias assigned this case to me. I arrived on-scene at 2220 hours and I cleared the scene on Sunday 02/12/2012 at 0135 hours. Prior to my arrival, the decedent was removed from the bathtub by her personal assistant and bodyguard, and then Paramedics placed the decedent onto the living room floor in order to render First-Aid. Also prior to my arrival, Paramedics moved the couch from out of the living room, and placed it on the patio in order to render First-Aid on the decedent. The decedent's purse was on that couch, and the decedent's California driver's license had been removed from the wallet, which was inside the purse, prior to my arrival. Also prior to my arrival, the majority of the decedent's prescription medication bottles had been removed from a brown bag that was on top of the table in the southeast corner of the living room, and then placed on top of that same table. After completing my investigation, I changed this from a natural versus accident to an accident. The decedent possibly overdosed on a narcotic substance, prescription medications, over the counter medications, and alcohol. Minor trauma was noted and there are no signs of foul play.

Location:

The incident occurred and the decedent died in the bathroom inside her room #434 at the Beverly Hilton Hotel located at 9876 Wilshire Boulevard, Beverly Hills CA, 90210.

Informant/Witness Statements:

I spoke with Detective Hyon at the scene, and he told me the following:

The decedent checked into the Beverly Hilton Hotel on Monday 02/06/2012. She was here for the Grammy award ceremony on Sunday 02/12/2012, and there was a pre-Grammy Party at the hotel on Saturday 02/11/2012. The decedent was last seen alive by her personal assistant on Saturday 02/11/2012 between 1445-1500 hours. The decedent complained of having a sore throat that had been lingering for the past few days. Before she left, she told the decedent to go take a bath, to start getting ready for tonight. The personal assistant then left to go pick up items at Neiman Marcus. The personal assistant left Neiman Marcus at 1525 hours, and per the door key, she entered the decedent's locked hotel room at 1536 hours. She went into the bathroom, and she found the decedent lying face down in the bathtub, unresponsive, with the top of her head facing west. The bathtub was filled with water, and there was water on the bathroom floor, however, the water was not running. She called out to the bodyguard, and they pulled the decedent out of the bathtub. The assistant then called downstairs telling them to call 911. They received the 911 call at 1543 hours, and Paramedics from the Beverly Hills Fire Department arrived on-scene. On Saturday 02/11/2012 at 1546 hours, Paramedics from Rescue 1 determined death. On Saturday 02/11/2012 at 2135 hours, the water temperature in the bathtub was 93.5 degrees. There are no signs of foul play.

Scene Description:

The Beverly Hilton Hotel is located at 9876 Wilshire Boulevard in Beverly Hills. Room #434 was located on the 4th floor in the southwest portion of the hotel. The living room was located in the west side of the room. Located in the northwest corner was a chair and then a computer tower with a Fedora on top of it. Located along the north wall, central portion was a dresser with a

Investigation:

On Saturday 02/11/2012 at 2104 hours, Sergeant Publicker from the Beverly Hills Police Department called the Los Angeles County Coroner's Office to report a natural versus accidental death of a 48 year-old black female that possibly drowned in a bathtub. On Saturday 02/11/2012 at 2120 hours, Lieutenant Brian Elias assigned this case to me. I arrived on-scene at 2220 hours and I cleared the scene on Sunday 02/12/2012 at 0135 hours. Prior to my arrival, the decedent was removed from the bathtub by her personal assistant and bodyguard, and then Paramedics placed the decedent onto the living room floor in order to render First-Aid. Also prior to my arrival, Paramedics moved the couch from out of the living room, and placed it on the patio in order to render First-Aid on the decedent. The decedent's purse was on that couch, and the decedent's California driver's license had been removed from the wallet, which was inside the purse, prior to my arrival. Also prior to my arrival, the majority of the decedent's prescription medication bottles had been removed from a brown bag that was on top of the table in the southeast corner of the living room, and then placed on top of that same table. After completing my investigation, I changed this from a natural versus accident to an accident. The decedent possibly overdosed on a narcotic substance, prescription medications, over the counter medications, and alcohol. Minor trauma was noted and there are no signs of foul play.

Location:

The incident occurred and the decedent died in the bathroom inside her room #434 at the Beverly Hilton Hotel located at 9876 Wilshire Boulevard, Beverly Hills CA, 90210.

Informant/Witness Statements:

I spoke with Detective Hyon at the scene, and he told me the following:

The decedent checked into the Beverly Hilton Hotel on Monday 02/06/2012. She was here for the Grammy award ceremony on Sunday 02/12/2012, and there was a pre-Grammy Party at the hotel on Saturday 02/11/2012. The decedent was last seen alive by her personal assistant on Saturday 02/11/2012 between 1445-1500 hours. The decedent complained of having a sore throat that had been lingering for the past few days. Before she left, she told the decedent to go take a bath, to start getting ready for tonight. The personal assistant then left to go pick up items at Neiman Marcus. The personal assistant left Neiman Marcus at 1525 hours, and per the door key, she entered the decedent's locked hotel room at 1536 hours. She went into the bathroom, and she found the decedent lying face down in the bathtub, unresponsive, with the top of her head facing west. The bathtub was filled with water, and there was water on the bathroom floor, however, the water was not running. She called out to the bodyguard, and they pulled the decedent out of the bathtub. The assistant then called downstairs telling them to call 911. They received the 911 call at 1543 hours, and Paramedics from the Beverly Hills Fire Department arrived on-scene. On Saturday 02/11/2012 at 1546 hours, Paramedics from Rescue 1 determined death. On Saturday 02/11/2012 at 2135 hours, the water temperature in the bathtub was 93.5 degrees. There are no signs of foul play.

The first glaring notice on page 1 of the <u>Investigation Narrative</u> is that when the coroner investigator arrived on the scene, she states that prior to her arrival at the scene Paramedics moved the couch from the living room and placed it on the patio to render First-Aid on the decedent. They said that Whitney's purse was on that couch, and so was her California driver's license.

As God is my Witness

WHEN DID SHE GET A CALIFORNIA DRIVERS LICENSE? I NEVER KNOWN WHITNEY TO HAVE ONE. Then they went on to say that it had been moved from the wallet which was inside her purse prior to his arrival. I WOULD BET THAT PAT AND GARY DID THAT BECAUSE THEY WERE DOING THINGS LIKE SITUATING EVERYTHING TO MAKE IT LOOK A CERTAIN WAY.

Also, prior to the investigator's arrival, the majority of her medication bottles were removed from a brown bag that was on top of the table in the southeast corner of the living room, and then placed on top of that same table. How do they know all of this? And who told them all of this happened? THEY ALSO SAI THERE WAS A WHITE SUBSTANCE IN A SPOON IN THE ROOM WHERE SHE WAS FOUND. YET, THE CORONER STATED THERE WAS NO DRUGS IN HER SYSTEM! PAT AND GARY HOUSTON AGAIN PLACED THAT STUFF THERE!

Question #1 Sergeant Publicker, from the Beverly Hills Police Department, he called the Los Angeles County Coroner's Office to report a natural versus accidental death of a 48-year-old black female that possible drowned in a bathtub. Then Lieutenant Brian Elias assigned this case to "who" is the question was this person Detective Hyon or Kristy McCrackin the coroner investigator?

THIS IS NOT COMPLETE AN IT APPEARS IT'S INTENTIONALLY DONE.   EITHER THAT OR THEY KNEW IT WOULD NOT BE INVESTIGATED. DID YOU KNOW ANOTHER OFFICER, "BRIAN WEIR" SUED THE BEYERLY HILLS POLICE DEPARTMENT "AND WON!" YES, HE BUSTED ANOTHER OFFICER MIS-TREATING WHITNEY'S BODY AFTER THEY ARRIVE. GOOGLE IT YOU'LL SEE.

Also, on the case report it states, "Identified by Kristin McCracken" and it is signed by her. On the Forensic Consultants Report/Criminalist Report by Detective Publicker Hyon there is no mention of him moving any medicine, or a purse so who moved what? Another issue is that they do not have no other information from the witnesses being the bodyguard or the assistant signed by them. So why is the detective acting as the sole witness and where is their information at least a name, there is nothing.

The second glaring notice on page 228 Informant/Witness Statements: The assistant left Neiman Marcus at 1525 hours (3:25pm) used her door key (15:36) hours and entered the decedent's room went into the bathroom found the descendent face down in the bathtub, unresponsive with her head facing west. THE REASON THEY HAD A KEY TO THIS ROOM BECAUSE IT WAS NOT WHITNEY'S ROOM AND SHEWAS SET UP I'M TELLING YOU! NONE OF THEM WOULD HAVE NEVER HAD A KEY TO HER ROOM-THIS DOESN'T HAPPEN! AND THAT WAS NOT WHITNEY'S ROOM! IT WAS KRISSY'S ROOM WHICH WAS CONNECTED TO NICK GORDON'S ROOM! TRUST ME I KNOW WHAT I AM TALKING ABOUT. I WOULD BET IT WAS NICK'S ROOM.

They stated the bathtub was filled with water, and there was water on the bathroom floor, however the water was not running. The assistant called out to the bodyguard, and they pulled the decedent out of the bathtub. WHITNEY HOUSTON DID NOT HAVE AN ASSISTANT...MARY WAS PAT'S AUNT OR COUSIN AND WHITNEY DID NO DEAL WITH THEM! SHEWAS SET UP BY ALL OF THEM ....

The assistant then called downstairs telling them to call 911. They received the call at 1543 hours (3:43pm), and the paramedics arrived on the scene at 1546 hours (3:46pm) and the paramedics from Rescue 1 determined her death. On the same day on 02/11/2011 at 2135 hours (9:45pm), the water temperature in the bathtub was 93.5 degrees. OK I do not know how dumb these people think other people are, but I digress.

First, who determined the "EXACT TIME" that the assistant left Neiman Marcus? THIS IS ALL PAT HOUSTONS DOINGS SHE IS SAYING ALL OF THIS TRUST ME! Was it from a receipt, store security footage, etc. Why did the assistant call downstairs to make an emergency call? Did they not have cell phones or a phone in the room? And third, from the time that she was pulled out the tub to the exact moment. The downstairs desk was notified to call 911 exactly 9 minutes passed by (3:35pm - 3:43pm). Fourth: If the case report synopsis on page 227 was written as if it was the coroner why does the detective/witness/informant statement contradict this major flaw. Nothing is right with this case.'

The huge discrepancy is the timeline that the is on both the synopsis and the investigators narrative is that one says the paramedics arrived at (15:46 = 3:46pm) and 15:55 = 3:55pm) with the latter showing possible relevance, and the first being questioned because if the authorities were called at (1543 = 3:43pm) how is it possible the authorities were on the scene and determined death at (1546 = 3:46pm) literally 3 minutes later. Also, if this is not correct, why was this incorrect report not ever corrected? This is just the tip of the iceberg of this report. Now let us get to the water temperature, did they get those undeniably wrong results.

How is it that the bathtub water temperature was 93.5 degrees "6 HOURS LATER?" That means that the water had to be hot enough to cause extreme burns on the body. Boiling water cools down below 65 degrees after just 30 minutes depending upon the environment. So how is that logically possible in reality? THIS IS A BIG LIE!! OK now another discrepancy how is it that the paramedics had to literally move furniture "OUT" the room to do CPR? Was CPR or revival methods done prior by the security guard or the assistant.

THIS DOESN'T SOUND RIGHT BECAUSE FROM WHAT I KNOWTHEY WAITED AWHILE FOR AUTHORITIES, AND PAT HOUSTON SAID HER BROTHER RAY GAVE CPR, NICK GORDON SAID HE GAVE CPR SO WHEN DID ALL THIS CPR TAKE PLACE?? Remember "Who were THEY and WHAT WERE THEIR NAMES?" and all this furniture had to be moved for little ole Whitney 5'8 141lbs and very thin.

And please keep in mind that Nick Gordon said on Dr. Phil, that he did CPR on Whitney Houston, and his mother coached him from Florida on the phone. Then Pat Houston said, she watched her brother Whitney's security, Ray, give Whitney Houston CPR and he was exhausted, and she basically told him to stop she was gone! Who is telling the truth here? Was CPR administered to Whitney Houston at all? And if so, by who? They all placed themselves right there with Whitney to do this if it was done....and They cannot even get a simple time right! Reader as you examine this report coming up, look at all the yellow marking that is hiding the words in this report! It is unbelievable how they blotted out all of this report! Is this even LEGAL and how can they get away with this.

As God is my Witness

This is proof that someone 1s hiding something here! Unbelievable!!! Another thing, I and anyone that knows Whitney knows that Whitney Houston would never get in a hotel bathtub. I have said this so much that I am sick of saying it. It would never happen AND WE ALL KNOW IT! Pat Houston lied right there. Pat also stated that Mary said that she told Whitney to take a bath. Reader, if you only knew how serious this was in me saying this. Whitney doesn't even talk to Mary OR PAT, and Mary is afraid of saying two words to Whitney trust me! If Mary would ever say something like that to Whitney, she already knows that Whitney would tell her to jump in a bathtub FIRST before she took her advice and got in one.

Evidence:

On Saturday 02/11/2012 hours, I collected a plethora of prescription medication bottles, prescribed to the decedent, multiple blister packs, and a loose tablet from off the top of a table in the southeast corner of the living room. I also collected a capsule from off one of the tables in the west central portion of the living room. I also collected an empty blister pack from off the floor in the southwest portion of the living room. I also collected a bottle of prescription medication, prescribed to the decedent from off a table In the northeast corner of the bedroom. I also collected loose tablets from off the same table in the northeast corner of the bedroom. I also collected a bottle of prescription medication, prescribed to the decedent, a bottle of a supplement, and a loose tablet from off a 3-drawer dresser in the southwest corner of the bedroom. I also collected a bottle of prescription medication, prescribed to the decedent, a

They can not even get a simple time right!

ALL OF WHAT PAT HOUSTON STATED WAS NOTHING MORE THAN LIES ON TOP OF LIES AND THEY KNOW WHAT HAPPENED TO WHITNEY HOUSTON BUT THEY ARE KEEPING IT TO THEMSELVES. I BELIEVE THEY ARE COVERING FOR GARY HOUSTON, NICK GORDON AND RAY J! YES! Like I said, I don't even believe Whitney knew that all of them were there at that hotel. Pat gave me that idea as soon as I heard her tell Oprah that she was on a whole other floor and not on the same floor with Whitney.

As God is my Witness

Me and a few other people said right away-"Yeah and I BET Whitney didn't even know you all were in that hotel with her. Pat Houston has told too many lies and I would BET if she did a "LIE DETECTOR" test it would blast with so many negative colors it would prove she was lying about every single thing she ever said. NOW I WOULD BET ON IT!! NOBODY BELIEVS ANYTHING PAT HOUSTON SAYS NOT OR A SECOND!

CASE REPORT

COUNTY OF LOS ANGELES									DEPARTMENT OF CORONER

APPARENT MODE: ACCIDENT

CASE NO: 2012-01022

SPECIAL CIRCUMSTANCES: Celebrity, Media Interest

CRYPT: SEC1

1

LAST, FIRST, MIDDLE: HOUSTON, WHITNEY ELISEBETH

AKA: HOUSTON, WHITNEY

ADDRESS: 360 HAMILTON AVENUE #100

CITY: WHITE PLAINS **STATE:** NY **ZIP:** 10601

SEX	RACE	APPEARS	DOB	AGE	HGT	WGT	EYES	HAIR	TEETH	FACIAL HAIR	TO VIEW	CONDITION
FEMALE	BLACK		8/9/1963	48	66 in	151 lbs	BROWN	BLACK	ALL NATURAL TEETH	NONE	Yes	FAIR

MARK TYPE	MARK LOCATION	MARK DESCRIPTION
SCAR	LEFT FOREARM	INNER, LOWER-OLD HEALED

ADDRESS: **CITY:** **STATE:** **ZIP:**

RELATIONSHIP: **PHONE:** **NOTIFIED BY:** **DATE:** 2/11/2012 **TIME:**

SSN: **DL ID:** D9834026 **STATE:** CA **PENDING BY:**

ID METHOD: CALIFORNIA DRIVER'S LICENSE

LA#	MAN #	CII #	FBI #	MILITARY #	POB	NEW JERSEY

IDENTIFIED BY NAME (PRINT): KRISTY MCCRACKEN

RELATIONSHIP: NONE **PHONE:** (323) 343-0714 **DATE:** 2/12/2012 **TIME:** 00:30

PLACE OF DEATH / PLACE FOUND: HOTEL/MOTEL

ADDRESS OR LOCATION: 9876 WILSHIRE BOULEVARD #434

CITY: BEVERLY HILLS **ZIP:** 90210

PLACE OF INJURY	AT WORK	DATE	TIME	LOCATION OR ADDRESS	ZIP
HOTEL/MOTEL	No	2/11/2012		9876 WILSHIRE BOULEVARD #434, BEVERLY HILLS, CA	90210

DOD: 2/11/2012 **TIME:** 15:55 **FOUND OR PRONOUNCED BY:** PARAMEDICS

OTHER AGENCY INV. OFFICER: BEVERLY HILLS P.D. - DETECTIVE HYON **PHONE:** (310) 285-2156 **REPORT NO:** 12-0806 **NOTIFIED BY:** **NO**

TRANSPORTED BY: JOHN GREEN **TO:** LOS ANGELES FSC **DATE:** 2/11/2012 **TIME:** 01:10

FINGERPRINTS?	Yes	CLOTHING	No	PM RPT	No	MORTUARY
IND EV	Yes	INVEST PHOTO #	75	SEAL TYPE	NOT SEALED	HOSP RPT No
PHYS EV	Yes	EVIDENCE LOG	Yes	PROPERTY?	Yes	HOSP CHART No
SUICIDE NOTE	No	SSR NO		RPT NO	257946	PF NO

SYNOPSIS

ACCORDING TO THE REPORTED INFORMATION, THE DECEDENT IS A 48 YEAR-OLD BLACK FEMALE WITH A MEDICAL HISTORY OF USING NARCOTIC SUBSTANCES. THE DECEDENT WAS LAST SEEN ALIVE ON SATURDAY 02/11/2012 BETWEEN 1445-1500 HOURS BY HER PERSONAL ASSISTANT. THE DECEDENT COMPLAINED OF HAVING A SORE THROAT, BUT SHE HAD BEEN COMPLAINING OF THAT FOR THE PAST FEW DAYS. THE ASSISTANT TOLD THE DECEDENT TO TAKE A BATH, TO START GETTING READY FOR TONIGHT. THE ASSISTANT THEN LEFT THE ROOM TO RUN SOME ERRANDS. AT APPROXIMATELY 1535 HOURS, THE ASSISTANT RETURNED AND USED HER KEY TO ENTER THE LOCKED AND SECURED ROOM. ONCE INSIDE, SHE FOUND THE DECEDENT LYING FACE DOWN IN THE BATHTUB FILLED WITH WATER, UNRESPONSIVE. THE ASSISTANT CALLED FOR HER BODYGUARD, AND TOGETHER THEY PULLED THE DECEDENT OUT OF THE BATHTUB. THE ASSISTANT CALLED DOWNSTAIRS TO CALL 911. 911 WAS CALLED AT 1543 HOURS AND OFFICERS FROM THE BEVERLY HILLS POLICE DEPARTMENT AND PARAMEDICS FROM THE BEVERLY HILLS FIRE DEPARTMENT ARRIVED ON SCENE. ON SATURDAY 02/11/2012 AT 1555 HOURS, PARAMEDICS FROM RESCUE 1 DETERMINED DEATH. THE DECEDENT POSSIBLY OVERDOSED ON A NARCOTIC SUBSTANCE, PRESCRIPTION MEDICATIONS, OVER THE COUNTER MEDICATIONS, AND ALCOHOL. MINOR EXTERNAL TRAUMA WAS NOTED AND THERE ARE NO SIGNS OF FOUL PLAY. DETECTIVE HYON REQUIRES A 2-HOUR NOTIFICATION PRIOR TO THE EXAMINATION. PLEASE SEE CASE NOTES FOT HIS CONTACT INFORMATION.

KRISTY MCCRACKEN 491917 **INVESTIGATOR**

DATE: 2/12/2012 **TIME:** 04:45 **REVIEWED BY:** **DATE:** 2/12/12 **TIME:**

FORM #3 NARRATIVE TO FOLLOW? [✓]

As God is my Witness

In the Body Examination section, it is stated that there were 2 superficial abrasions to the left side of her forehead and one to the left of the bridge of her nose. There was also a abrasion on the top of her right shoulder. She had minor skin slippage to the upper central portion of her chest, to the inner left central portion of her chest, and to the lower central portion of her chest. It was also minor skin slippage to the upper side of her abdomen, and a abrasion to her outer left lower left arm. There were also abrasions to her inner central left arm, as well as to the top of her hand, between the middle and ring fingers. It was also skin slippage to the inner upper right calf and to her outer lower left leg, and finally skin slippage to the central portion of her back!

"DO THESE DESCRIPTIONS SOUND LIKE WHITNEY DID THAT TO HERSELF, BETTER YET, THESE ARE THE CLASSIC SIGNS OF A STRUGGLE" So how was this accidental? Another note is that on Sunday 02/12/2012 at 0005 hours 12:05am the water temperature in the bathtub was 89.0 degrees. Ok why was this important hours later, and secondly you mean to tell me that the water only dropped by 4 degrees 2 hours and 15 minutes later. Lastly how is Whitney's LIVER temperature 96.0 degrees 9 ½ hrs. later.... are you kidding me! WOW!

County of Los Angeles, Department of Coroner
Investigator's Narrative

Case Number: 2012-01022   Decedent: HOUSTON, WHITNEY ELISEBETH

Information Sources:

(1)   Beverly Hills Police Department-Report #12-0806   (310)285-2156
       Detective Hyon

Investigation:

On Saturday 02/11/2012 at 2104 hours, Sergeant Publicker from the Beverly Hills Police Department called the Los Angeles County Coroner's Office to report a natural versus accidental death of a 48 year-old black female that possibly drowned in a bathtub. On Saturday 02/11/2012 at 2120 hours, Lieutenant Brian Elias assigned this case to me. I arrived on-scene at 2220 hours and I cleared the scene on Sunday 02/12/2012 at 0135 hours. Prior to my arrival, the decedent was removed from the bathtub by her personal assistant and bodyguard, and then Paramedics placed the decedent onto the living room floor in order to render First-Aid. Also prior to my arrival, Paramedics moved the couch from out of the living room, and placed it on the patio in order to render First-Aid on the decedent. The decedent's purse was on that couch, and the decedent's California driver's license had been removed from the wallet, which was inside the purse, prior to my arrival. Also prior to my arrival, the majority of the decedent's prescription medication bottles had been removed from a brown bag that was on top of the table in the southeast corner of the living room, and then placed on top of that same table. After completing my investigation, I changed this from a natural versus accident to an accident. The decedent possibly overdosed on a narcotic substance, prescription medications, over the counter medications, and alcohol. Minor trauma was noted and there are no signs of foul play.

Location:

The incident occurred and the decedent died in the bathroom inside her room #434 at the Beverly Hilton Hotel located at 9876 Wilshire Boulevard, Beverly Hills CA, 90210.

Informant/Witness Statements:

I spoke with Detective Hyon at the scene, and he told me the following:

The decedent checked into the Beverly Hilton Hotel on Monday 02/06/2012. She was here for the Grammy award ceremony on Sunday 02/12/2012, and there was a pre-Grammy Party at the hotel on Saturday 02/11/2012. The decedent was last seen alive by her personal assistant on Saturday 02/11/2012 between 1445-1500 hours. The decedent complained of having a sore throat that had been lingering for the past few days. Before she left, she told the decedent to go take a bath, to start getting ready for tonight. The personal assistant then left to go pick up items at Neiman Marcus. The personal assistant left Neiman Marcus at 1525 hours, and per the door key, she entered the decedent's locked hotel room at 1536 hours. She went into the bathroom, and she found the decedent lying face down in the bathtub, unresponsive, with the top of her head facing west. The bathtub was filled with water, and there was water on the bathroom floor, however, the water was not running. She called out to the bodyguard, and they pulled the decedent out of the bathtub. The assistant then called downstairs telling them to call 911. They received the 911 call at 1543 hours, and Paramedics from the Beverly Hills Fire Department arrived on-scene. On Saturday 02/11/2012 at 1546 hours, Paramedics from Rescue 1 determined death. On Saturday 02/11/2012 at 2135 hours, the water temperature in the bathtub was 93.5 degrees. There are no signs of foul play.

Scene Description:

The Beverly Hilton Hotel is located at 9876 Wilshire Boulevard in Beverly Hills. Room #434 was located on the 4th floor in the southwest portion of the hotel. The living room was located in the west side of the room. Located in the northwest corner was a chair and then a computer tower with a Fedora on top of it. Located along the north wall, central portion was a dresser with a

County of Los Angeles, Department of Coroner
Investigator's Narrative

Case Number: 2012-01022   Decedent: HOUSTON, WHITNEY ELISEBETH

mini-bar in it. On top of it was an open bottle of champagne, along with other miscellaneous items. Located in the north wall, northeast portion was the front door to the room. Located in the east wall were doors leading into the bedroom. Located in the southeast corner was a table with multiple bottles of prescription medications, prescribed to the decedent, multiple blister packs, a loose tablet, and other miscellaneous items on top of it. Located in the south wall was a sliding glass door leading onto a balcony. Just south of these sliding glass doors was a couch with a purse on it. Located in the southwest corner was a lamp. Located on the floor in the southwest portion of the room was an empty blister pack. Located along the west wall, central portion were three tables with plates of food, an open can of beer, a single capsule, along with other miscellaneous items on top of it. The decedent was located lying supine on the floor in the central portion of the living room floor.

The bedroom was located in the east side of the room. Located in the north wall, northwest corner was a closet. Just south of the closet were opened suitcases and a lamp. Located in the north wall, central portion was a door leading into the bathroom. Located along the north wall, central portion was a luggage stand. Located in the northeast corner was a table with a bottle of prescription medication, loose tablets, and other miscellaneous items on top of it. Located along the east wall, central portion was a bed. Located along the east wall, southeast portion was a nightstand with a bottle of beer on it. Located in the south wall were sliding glass doors leading onto the same balcony. Located along the south doors, southeast portion was a chaise lounge. Located along the south wall, southwest portion was another luggage stand with an open suitcase on it. Located in the southwest corner was a 3-drawer dresser with a bottle of prescription medication, loose tablets, a bottle of a supplement, and other miscellaneous items on top of it. Located in the west wall were doors leading into the living room. The carpet in the bedroom was soaked with water.

The bathroom was located in the northeast portion of the room. Located along the north wall, central portion was a bathtub. There was approximately 12" of water in the short end and approximately 13" of water in the deep end. In the bathtub was a towel, a bottle of rubbing alcohol, and a pitcher. Located in the north wall, northeast portion was the toilet stall. Located along the east wall was a counter with a sink and drawers below. Located on the counter in front of the sink was an ashtray filled with multiple cigarette butts. Located on the south portion of the counter was a small spoon with a white crystal like substance in it and a rolled up piece of white paper, along with other miscellaneous items. Located on the north portion of the counter was a bottle of prescription medications, and a ripped open small plastic bag, along with other miscellaneous items. Located in the top drawer, in the north side of the counter were remnants of a white powdery substance, and a portable mirror on a base. On the bottom of that base were more remnants of a white powdery substance. Located in the south wall, central portion was the entrance into the bedroom. Located in the southwest portion of the bedroom was a chair with some clothes on it and a blanket on the floor next to it. Located in the west wall, central portion was a door leading into the shower. The bathroom floor was covered with water.

Evidence:

On Saturday 02/11/2012 hours, I collected a plethora of prescription medication bottles, prescribed to the decedent, multiple blister packs, and a loose tablet from off the top of a table in the southeast corner of the living room. I also collected a capsule from off one of the tables in the west central portion of the living room. I also collected an empty blister pack from off the floor in the southwest portion of the living room. I also collected a bottle of prescription medication, prescribed to the decedent from off a table in the northeast corner of the bedroom. I also collected loose tablets from off the same table in the northeast corner of the bedroom. I also collected a bottle of prescription medication, prescribed to the decedent, a bottle of a supplement, and a loose tablet from off a 3-drawer dresser in the southwest corner of the bedroom. I also collected a bottle of prescription medication, prescribed to the decedent, a

As God is my Witness

 **County of Los Angeles, Department of Coroner**
Investigator's Narrative

Case Number: 2012-01022   Decedent: HOUSTON, WHITNEY ELISEBETH

spoon with a white crystal like substance in it, a rolled up piece of white paper from off the top of a counter along the east wall in the bathroom. I also collected remnants of a white powdery substance from out of a drawer and from the bottom of a mirror in the same drawer in the bathroom counter along the east wall of the bathroom. I later booked all of the bottles of prescription medications, the bottle of the supplement, all of the blister packs, all of the loose tablets and capsules, the spoon, and the white powdery substance at the Forensic Services Center as evidence.

On Saturday 02/11/2012 at 2342 hours, Criminalist Mark Schuchardt used a pubic hair kit on the decedent at the scene. On Saturday 02/11/2012 at 2355 hours, Criminalist Mark Schuchardt collected fingernail clippings from the decedent's hands at the scene. On Sunday 02/12/2012 at 0004 hours, Criminalist Mark Schuchardt collected hair standards from the decedent at the scene. On Sunday 02/12/2012 at 0015 hours, Criminalist Mark Schuchardt used a sexual assault kit on the decedent at the scene. Criminalist Mark Schuchardt later booked the pubic hair kit, the fingernail clippings, the hair standards, and the sexual assault kit at the Forensic Services Center as evidence.

Body Examination:

The decedent is a 48 year-old black female with short black hair, brown eyes, and she has all of her natural teeth. There is an old healed vertical scar approximately 2" in length on her inner lower left forearm. No other scars and no tattoos were noted. The decedent was nude, lying supine on the living room floor. The top of her head was facing south. Her right arm was bent at the elbow with her right hand resting on the floor, against the right central portion of her torso. Her left arm was slightly bent at the elbow with her left hand resting on the floor against her outer upper left thigh. Both of her legs were straight with her right foot pointing north and her left foot was pointing northwest. There was a defibrillator patch on the upper right side of her chest and there was another defibrillator patch on the left central portion of her torso. Both of her eyes were congested and there was a bloody purge coming from her nose. There were 2 superficial abrasions to the left side of her forehead and there was a superficial abrasion to the left side of the bridge of her nose. There was a superficial abrasion to the top of her right shoulder. There was minor skin slippage to the upper central portion of her chest, to the inner left central portion of her chest, and to the lower central portion of her chest. There was minor skin slippage to the upper left side of her abdomen. There was a superficial abrasion to her outer lower left arm. There was a possible old puncture wound to her inner left elbow. There was a superficial abrasion to her inner central left forearm and there were minor abrasions to the top of her left hand, between the middle and ring fingers. There was minor skin slippage to the front of both of her knees and to both of the front central portion of her legs. There was minor skin slippage to her inner upper right calf and to her outer lower left leg. There was skin slippage to the lower central portion of her back. On Sunday 02/12/2012 at 0005 hours, the water temperature in the bathtub was 89.0 degrees. On Sunday 02/12/2012 at 0025 hours, the air temperature inside the living room was 67.0 degrees. On Sunday 02/12/2012 at 0031 hours, the decedent's liver temperature was 96.0 degrees.

Identification:

On Sunday 02/12/2012 at 0030 hours, I positively identified the decedent as Whitney Elisebeth Houston with a DOB of 08/09/1963 by the photograph on her California driver's license at the scene.

Next of Kin Notification:

On Saturday 02/11/2012 at an unknown time, friends notified   , the decedent's daughter, of her mother's death. I have not spoken with   at the time of completion of this report. Please see case notes for further information.

502

As God is my Witness

COUNTY OF LOS ANGELES   PRELIMINARY EXAMINATION REPORT - FIELD   DEPARTMENT OF CORONER

6

WAS ORIGINAL SCENE DISTURBED BY OTHERS? Y [X] N [ ]
IF YES, NOTE CHANGES IN NARRATIVE FORM #3

DATE _02/11/12 - 02/12/12_

AMBIENT #1 _64.0_ °F   TIME _0025_

AMBIENT #2 _____ °F   TIME _____

WATER _89.0_ °F   TIME _0005_

LIVER TEMPERATURE #1 _96.0_ °F   TIME _0031_

LIVER TEMPERATURE #2 _____ °F   TIME _____

2012-C1022
HOUSTON,
WHITNEY
ACC-O.D.
THERMOMETER # _____

DATE & TIME FOUND _02/11/12 1536_   LAST KNOWN ALIVE _02/11/12 1445-1500_

APPROX. AGE _48_ SEX _F_ EST. HEIGHT _66_ EST. WEIGHT _151_ CLOTHED? YES ☐ NO ☒ IF YES, DESCRIBE:

_N/A_

DESCRIPTION AS TO WHERE REMAINS FOUND AND CONTACT MATERIAL TO BODY:

Lying supine on the living room floor

SCENE TEMPERATURE REGULATED? YES ☐ NO ☒ IF YES, THERMOSTAT SET AT _____ DEGREES F.

LIVOR MORTIS: TIME OBSERVED _Unk_   RIGOR MORTIS: TIME OBSERVED _Unk_

Fixed

NECK FLEXION:

ANTERIOR _2+_

POSTERIOR _2+_

RT. LATERAL _2+_

LT LATERAL _2+_

JAW _2+_		HIP _2+_	
SHOULDER _2+_		KNEE _2+_	
ELBOW _2+_		ANKLE _2+_	
WRIST _2+_			

R   L   L   R

SCALE

0   ABSENT/NEGATIVE

1   +

2   +

3   +

4   EXTREME DEGREE

USE SCALE TO DESCRIBE INTENSITY OF RIGOR MORTIS

SHADE DIAGRAMS TO ILLUSTRATE THE LOCATION OF LIVOR MORTIS.

DESCRIBE INTENSTIY OF COLORATION AND WHETHER LIVOR MORTIS IS PERMANENT OR BLANCHES UNDER PRESSURE.

K. McCracken #491917

CORONER'S INVESTIGATOR

REVIEWED BY:

70P536 12/93 PS 7-95   NOTE: ALL DATA COLLECTED FOR THIS FORM MUST BE COLLECTED AT SCENE.

COUNTY OF LOS ANGELES

DEPARTMENT OF CORONER

12	# AUTOPSY REPORT	No.

I performed an autopsy on the body of ➡

2012-01022

HOUSTON, WHITNEY E.

at ____ the DEPARTMENT OF CORONER

Los Angeles, California ____ on February 12, 2012 @ 1125 Hours
(Date) (Time)

From the anatomic findings and pertinent history I ascribe the death to:

(A) DROWNING

DUE TO, OR AS A CONSEQUENCE OF

(B) EFFECTS OF ATHEROSCLEROTIC HEART DISEASE AND COCAINE USE

DUE TO, OR AS A CONSEQUENCE OF

(C)

DUE TO, OR AS A CONSEQUENCE OF

(D)

OTHER CONDITIONS CONTRIBUTING BUT NOT RELATED TO THE IMMEDIATE CAUSE OF DEATH

Anatomical Summary:

   I. History of substance abuse.

      A) Perforation of posterior nasal septum.

  II. Atherosclerotic heart disease.

      A) 60% narrowing of right coronary artery.

 III. Pulmonary edema.

  IV. Mild emphysema.

   V. Leiomyomas of uterus.

  VI. Adenomyosis (stroma only).

 VII. Congestion, right colon.

VIII. Perimortem and postmortem scald burns.

  IX. Antemortem injuries:

      A) Contusion and abrasion of left forehead.

      B) Scald burn of sacrum.

      C) Abrasion of left hand.

      D) Abrasion of right lower leg.

      E) Superficial incision of upper lip.

79A000M--Rev 6/84

COUNTY OF LOS ANGELES

DEPARTMENT OF CORONER

12

AUTOPSY REPORT

No.

2012-01022

HOUSTON, WHITNEY E.

Page 2

   X. Resuscitative abrasions of anterior chest.

  XI. Oncocytic microadenoma of adrenal.

 XII. Mild fatty change of liver.

XIII. Fibrous mastopathy.

XIV. See separate radiology, dental, microbiology, criminalistics, and toxicology reports.

CIRCUMSTANCES:

The decedent is a 48 year old woman found submerged in a bathtub that contained extremely hot water (93.5°F at 9:35 PM per detective). She was pronounced dead at the scene by paramedics at 3:55 PM on February 11, 2012.

EXTERNAL EXAMINATION:

The body is identified by toe tags and Coroner's identification band on the left ankle and is that of an unembalmed refrigerated adult Black female who appears the stated age of 48 years. The body weighs 151 pounds, measures 66 inches and is well built, muscular and fairly well nourished.

EVIDENCE OF INJURY:

Note: The word "marking" is used below to describe a circumscribed area of abrasion or scald injury.

Head and neck:

The face shows perimortem skin markings as follows:

1) A 1/4 x 1/16 inch yellow-brown marking in the central forehead.

76A798P—Rev 2/91

505

COUNTY OF LOS ANGELES

DEPARTMENT OF CORONER

12

AUTOPSY REPORT

No.

2012-01022

HOUSTON, WHITNEY E.

Page 3

2) A 1-1/4 x 5/8 inch yellow-brown marking at the lateral edge of the left eyebrow.

3) A 5/8 x 1/2 inch yellow-brown marking on the left side of the nose.

4) A 1/4 x 3/16 inch yellow-brown marking at the lateral left nostril.

The following injuries inflicted during life (premortem) are seen:

1) A 3/4 x 1/4 inch yellow-brown marking of the lateral left forehead with an underlying 5/8 x 1/4 inch contusion.

2) A 3/16 inch very superficial incision of the upper lip.

There is a perforation of the posterior nasal septum.

CHEST AND ABDOMEN:

There are resuscitative markings of the chest as follows:

1) Two roughly round markings measuring 1 to 1-1/2 inch of the right superior chest and left lateral chest (resuscitation marks from defibrillator pads).

2) A 2-1/2 x 1-3/4 inch yellow-brown marking of the central chest (status post cardiopulmonary resuscitation).

76A798P—Rev 2/91

COUNTY OF LOS ANGELES		DEPARTMENT OF CORONER

12 AUTOPSY REPORT

No.

2012-01022

HOUSTON, WHITNEY E.

Page ___4___

The following perimortem skin markings are present:

1) 5/8 inch yellow-brown marks of both clavicular regions and the left upper chest.

2) A 5/8 inch marking of the left breast.

An antemortem 5 x 3-1/4 inch area of yellow-brown skin slippage with erythema of the superior margin located over the sacrum.

A postmortem liver temperature incision is present at the right costal margin.

EXTEMITIES:

In the area of the right elbow are three 3/8 inch yellow-brown abrasions. On the back of the right hand is a 3/8 inch contusion and a 1/16 inch yellow-brown abrasion. There is an additional yellow-brown abrasion of the tip of the right ring finger measuring 1/8 inch.

On the inner surface of the left upper arm there are four contusions measuring 1/4 to 3/8 inch. On the posterior surface of the left arm around the elbow area are two yellow-brown abrasions measuring 3/8 x 1/4 inch and another measuring 3/8 x 1/3 inch. On the back of the left hand at the knuckle of the ring finger is a small yellow-brown abrasion.

On the anterior surface of the right leg is a 1/4 x 3/8 inch yellow-brown abrasion in the area of the knee. There is a 2-1/2 x 1/8 inch hook-shaped red abrasion of the medial surface of the

76A798P—Rev 2/91

COUNTY OF LOS ANGELES

DEPARTMENT OF CORONER

12

AUTOPSY REPORT

No.

2012-01022

HOUSTON, WHITNEY E.

Page ___5___

right lower leg. There is a 2-1/2 inch zone of skin slippage at the right shin. A smaller zone of skin slippage is present at the lateral right ankle.

On the front of the left leg are 3/4 x 1/2 inch yellow-brown abrasions of the knee and shin. Over the dorsum of the left foot is a 3 x 3 inch area of skin slippage.

Tattoos are not present. Rigor mortis is present in the limbs and jaw. Livor mortis is fixed and distributed posteriorly. The head is normocephalic and is covered by black hair. A brown wig is tightly attached to the hair. This is removed and placed in a paper bag to accompany the body. There is no balding and the hair can be described as wavy. The eyebrows are sparse and show irregular hair distribution. Mustache and beard are absent. Examination of the eyes reveals irides that are brown and sclerae that show injection but no jaundice. There are no petechial hemorrhages of the conjunctivae of the lids or the sclerae. The oronasal passages are unobstructed and show bloody purge. The upper teeth have been replaced with a full arch maxillary dental prosthesis supported by dental implants. There are natural lower teeth present (see dental consultant report). There is no removable denture. The neck is unremarkable. There is no chest deformity. There is no increase in the anterior-posterior diameter of the chest. The abdomen is flat. The genitalia are those of an adult female. There is no genital or anal trauma. The extremities show no edema, joint deformity, abnormal mobility or needle tracks. There is evidence of old surgery. The following scars are present:

1) A 3/8 x 1/2 inch scar of the anterior neck near the center.

76A798P—Rev 2/91

COUNTY OF LOS ANGELES   DEPARTMENT OF CORONER

12   **AUTOPSY REPORT**

No.

2012-01022

HOUSTON, WHITNEY E.

Page ___6___

2) Small scars of the inferior margins of the areolae, associated with breast implants.

3) A linear scar of the anterior left forearm.

4) A faint scar at the anterior pelvic brim.

5) A scar at the area of the left hip.

6) Two piercings are present in each ear.

There has not been postmortem intervention for organ procurement.

CLOTHING:

The body was not clothed and we did not see the clothing. The decedent was reportedly found nude in the bathtub.

INITIAL INCISION:

The body cavities are entered through the standard coronal incision and the standard Y-shaped incision. No foreign material is present in the mouth, upper airway or trachea except for bloody purge.

NECK:

The neck organs are removed en bloc with the tongue. No lesions are present nor is trauma of the gingiva or oral mucosa demonstrated. There is no edema of the larynx. Both hyoid bone and larynx are intact and without fractures. No hemorrhage is

76A798P—Rev 2/91

COUNTY OF LOS ANGELES

DEPARTMENT OF CORONER

12

AUTOPSY REPORT

No.

2012-01022

HOUSTON, WHITNEY E.

Page ___7___

present in the adjacent throat organs, investing fascia, strap muscles, thyroid or visceral fascia. There are no prevertebral fascial hemorrhages. The tongue shows no trauma.

CHEST AND ABDOMINAL CAVITIES:

Both pleural cavities contain a small quantity of straw colored fluid. No pneumothorax is demonstrated. The parietal pleurae are intact. The lungs are well expanded. Soft tissues of the thoracic and abdominal walls are well-preserved. Breast tissue is sectioned and shows no abnormality. The organs of the abdominal cavity have a normal arrangement and none are absent.

There is no fluid collection. The peritoneal cavity is without evidence of peritonitis. There are no adhesions.

SYSTEMIC AND ORGAN REVIEW

The following observations are limited to findings other than injuries described above.

MUSCULOSKELETAL SYSTEM:

No abnormalities of the bony framework or muscles are present.

CARDIOVASCULAR SYSTEM:

The aorta is elastic and of even caliber throughout with vessels distributed normally from it. It shows lipid streaking. There is no tortuosity or widening of the thoracic segment. The abdominal aorta has minimal atherosclerosis without calcification. There is

76A766P—Rev 2/91

COUNTY OF LOS ANGELES   DEPARTMENT OF CORONER

12 AUTOPSY REPORT

No.

2012-01022

HOUSTON, WHITNEY E.

Page __8__

no dilatation of the lower abdominal segment. No aneurysm is present. The major branches of the aorta show no abnormality. Within the pericardial sac there is a minimal amount of serous fluid. The heart weighs 340 grams. It has a normal configuration. The chambers are normally developed and are without mural thrombosis. The valves are thin, leafy and competent. There is no endocardial discoloration. There are no focal lesions of the myocardium. There is no abnormality of the apices of the papillary muscles. There are no defects of the septum. The great vessels enter and leave in a normal fashion. The ductus arteriosus is obliterated. The coronary ostia are widely patent. There is segmental coronary atherosclerosis resulting in up to 60% occlusion of the right coronary artery at 4 cm from the ostium, and minimal atherosclerosis of the left anterior descending artery. No focal endocardial, valvular or myocardial lesions are seen. The blood within the heart and large blood vessels is liquid.

RESPIRATORY SYSTEM:

A moderate amount of froth is found in the upper respiratory passages. The mucosa is intact. The lungs are subcrepitant and there is dependent congestion. The left lung weighs 610 grams and the right lung weighs 680 grams. The visceral pleurae are smooth and intact. The parenchyma is moderately edematous. The pulmonary vasculature is without thromboembolism.

GASTROINTESTINAL SYSTEM:

The esophagus is intact. The stomach is not distended. It contains 400 grams of watery fluid with portions of food

76A798P—Rev 2/91

COUNTY OF LOS ANGELES   **FORENSIC CONSULTANT'S REPORT**   DEPARTMENT OF CORONER

13

2012-01022
Houston, Whitney
(Decedent)

Los Angeles County Department of Coroner
Criminalist Report

Investigating Agency: **Beverly Hills Police Department**
Investigating Officer: Publicker; Hyon
Agency File No.: **12-0806**

Page 1 of 2

Also see Coroner Investigator Report for additional information, including scene description, case circumstances, condition of body.

On 10 February 2012 at 1906 hours I was notified by Coroner Investigator B. Elias that the Coroner/Chief Medical Examiner, Dr. L. Sathyavagiswaran, was requesting that a criminalist respond to a death scene. At 2122 hours, Beverly Hills Police Department advised that it was ready for our department to respond to the scene. At that time Coroner Investigator K. McCracken and I responded together, arriving at scene, the Beverly Hilton Hotel, 9876 Wilshire Boulevard, room 434, in Beverly Hills, California, 90210.

At 2236 hours, I entered the hotel room and observed an apparent body lying on the floor of the living room and covered entirely with a white linen sheet, approximately ten feet inside the entrance and several feet west of it. East of this room were the bedroom and bathroom. The bathroom floor was flooded, and water, apparently originating from the bathroom, where reportedly the bath tub had overflowed, had soaked the bedroom carpet, at least along the path to the living room; much of the carpeted area of the living room was moist also, even up to where the body lay. After the sheet was lifted I observed the decedent, an adult black female, lying nude and supine on a tan, patterned, carpeted floor. No clothing was near the body; all that was near the body was an apparent white sheet or table cloth bunched on the floor several feet to the left of the decedent's head.

The body was oriented south to north, with the head to the south. The woman's legs were fully extended and slightly apart. The feet, pointing toward the north wall and entrance, were also extended, the soles somewhat facing each other. The left arm was at the side, slightly flexed, in contact with the floor; the hand was palm down, fingers in a relaxed position, with the lateral aspect of the hand in contact with the lateral hip area. The right arm was more flexed than the left, with the hand raised off the floor, palm down, fingers relaxed, but with the wrist more flexed than the left; the lateral aspect was in contact with the lateral abdomen area. The eyes were closed and the face was oriented straight up toward the ceiling. Two large EKG pads, each with a long white cord, were adhered to the body, one at the upper right breast, the other at the left lateral upper abdomen, below the left breast. A circular area of the skin, approximately several inches in diameter, at the midline of the chest and between the breasts, was entirely devoid of its outer layer. This appeared to have been due to skin slippage from decomposition, and then also perhaps by life-saving efforts by others. Additional apparent skin slippage was noted at the lower

As God is my Witness

13

2012-01022

Page 2 of 2

back and other, smaller areas, were observed in various areas on the body. It should be noted that, per Beverly Hills Police (BHPD) detectives, the body had reportedly been entirely submerged in bath water for what may have been nearly an hour's time, and that the water temperature had reportedly been measured by their personnel to be over 90 degrees Fahrenheit, however long after the body had been removed from the tub.

At the right wrist the woman wore a bracelet made up of a band of numerous small white stones, and attached to the band was a cross made up of similar small white stones. A ring worn on the fourth digit of the right hand had a large white stone, possibly tinged yellow, with small white stones along the band. Each earlobe appeared to be pierced twice. The fingernails and toenails were short, well-kempt, with no colored polish observed. The woman wore a weave of short-length dark brown hair or fibers and some highlighting. The front margin of the weave was in a position slightly back from the front hairline, revealing the woman's natural head hair beneath it; her natural hair was short, dark brown and kinky.

At the time of my examination, the body surfaces were dry, but the head hair and weave appeared to be moist. I collected a Sexual Assault Evidence Kit on the decedent, nothing remarkable being noted. I also collected Fingernail, Hair, and Pubic Hair Kits; I included a clipping from two separate areas of the weave, one representing the highlighted coloring. Investigator McCracken then performed her examination and collected the jewelry items as personal property.

My evidence collection was completed at 0015 hours on 12 February, 2012.
Departure from the scene was at 0041 hours.

EVIDENCE

The following items were collected by me and placed into evidence.

EVIDENCE COLLECTED AT SCENE

Physical Evidence

1. Sexual Assault Evidence Kit.
2. Fingernail Kit.

Reference Item

3. Hair Kit, including weave exemplars.
4. Pubic Hair Kit.

FEB 17 '12
Date report written

FEB 14 '12
Date report signed

Mark S. Schuchardt
Senior Criminalist

cc: Medical File
    Case File

COUNTY OF LOS ANGELES | **MEDICAL REPORT** | DEPARTMENT OF CORONER

15

AUTOPSY CLASS: ☒A ☐B ☐C ☐ Examination Only D

☐ FAMILY OBJECTION TO AUTOPSY

Date: 2-12-12 Time: 1125 Dr. Rogers / Lakshmanan (Print)

FINAL ON: 3-21-2012 By: Lakshmanan (Print)

APPROX-IMATE INTERVAL BETWEEN ONSET AND DEATH

DEATH WAS CAUSED BY: (Enter only one cause per line for A, B, C, and D)

IMMEDIATE CAUSE:

(A) DROWNING — Unknown

DUE TO, OR AS A CONSEQUENCE OF:

(B) EFFECTS OF ATHEROSCLEROTIC HEART DISEASE — Unknown

DUE TO, OR AS A CONSEQUENCE OF: AND COCAINE USE

(C)

DUE TO, OR AS A CONSEQUENCE OF:

(D)

OTHER CONDITIONS CONTRIBUTING BUT NOT RELATED TO THE IMMEDIATE CAUSE OF DEATH:

☐ NATURAL ☐ SUICIDE ☐ HOMICIDE

☒ ACCIDENT ☐ COULD NOT BE DETERMINED

If other than natural causes, HOW DID INJURY OCCUR? 1) FOUND SUBMERGED IN BATHTUB FILLED WITH WATER 2) COCAINE INTAKE

WAS OPERATION PERFORMED FOR ANY CONDITION STATED ABOVE: ☐ YES ☒ NO

TYPE OF SURGERY: _____ DATE: _____

☐ ORGAN PROCUREMENT ☐ TECHNICIAN: Mc Dowell

PREGNANCY IN LAST YEAR ☐ YES ☐ NO ☐ UNK ☐ NOT APPLICABLE

☒ WITNESS TO AUTOPSY ☐ EVIDENCE RECOVERED AT AUTOPSY
Item Description:

Hyon
Publicker, BHPD

31 Autopsy photos 3 in autopsy room 28 in photo lab] Reviewed 2-14-12
1 Intake photos

✔ Viral culture nasophar
✔ Throat culture

Age: 48 Gender: Male / Female

PRIOR EXAMINATION REVIEW BY DME

☒ BODY TAG ☐ CLOTHING
☒ X-RAY (No. CC 29) ☐ FLUORO
☐ SPECIAL PROCESSING TAG ☐ MED. RECORDS
☒ AT SCENE PHOTOS (No. 75 (92/4/2)

CASE CIRCUMSTANCES

☐ EMBALMED
☐ DECOMPOSED
☐ >24 HRS IN HOSPITAL
☐ OTHER: _____ (Reason)

TYPING SPECIMEN

TYPING SPECIMEN TAKEN BY: CR
SOURCE: Heart

TOXICOLOGY SPECIMEN

COLLECTED BY: CR

☒ HEART BLOOD ☒ STOMACH CONTENTS
☒ FEMORAL BLOOD (L) ☒ VITREOUS (2)
TECHNIQUE: External Tracheal air
☒ Femoral BLOOD ☐ SPLEEN
☐ BLOOD ☐ KIDNEY
☒ BILE ☒ Serum (heart)
☒ LIVER ☒ Red cells from
☒ URINE heart (2)

URINE GLUCOSE DIPSTICK RESULT: 4+ 3+ 2+ 1+ 0

TOX SPECIMEN RECONCILIATION BY: ✔

HISTOLOGY

☒ Regular (No. 2) ☐ Oversize (No. _____)
Histopath Cut: ☒ Autopsy ☐ Lab

TOXICOLOGY REQUESTS

FORM 3A: ☒ YES ☐ NO
☐ NO TOXICOLOGY REQUESTED
SCREEN ☒ C ☐ H ☐ T ☐ S ☐ D
☐ ALCOHOL ONLY
☐ CARBON MONOXIDE
☐ OTHER (Specify drug and tissue)
✔ Vitreous glucose, electrolytes, urea
Hemoglobin S' screen
Alprazolam

REQUESTED MATERIAL ON PENDING CASES

☐ POLICE REPORT ☒ MED HISTORY
☒ TOX FOR COD ☒ HISTOLOGY
☐ TOX FOR R/O ☐ INVESTIGATIONS
☒ MICROBIOLOGY ☐ EYE PATH. CONS.
☒ RADIOLOGY CONS.
☐ CONSULT ON: _____
☐ BRAIN SUBMITTED
☐ NEURO CONSULT ☐ DME TO CUT
☐ CRIMINALISTICS
☐ USR ☐ SEXUAL ASSAULT ☐ OTHER

RESIDENT | DME

WHITE - File Copy   CANARY - Forensic Lab   PINK - Certification   GOLDENROD - DME   (Rev 04-09)

As God is my Witness

<u>**Just a few things to think about...ON WHITNEY'S CASE**</u>:

PLEASE DO NOT FORGET THAT WHITNEY HOUSTON HAD CHIPPED FINGERNAILS, FACE/ SWOLLEN JAW, SHE HAD A BUSTED LIP THAT NEEDED SURGERY HAD SHE LIVED, SHE HAD MARKS, LUMPS, SORES, BRUISES AND CONTUSIONS ALL OVER HER HEAD AND BODY! SHE HAD SCARS UP AND DOWN HER ENTIRE BODY FROM HEAD TO TOE! IT WAS BASICALLY AN OVER-KILL! SHE WAS BEATEN AS IF SHE WAS "HATED!"

AND WHY DOES THE MEDIA CONTINUE TO SAY THAT SHE DIED FROM A DRUG OVERDOSE WHEN THE CORONER CLEARLY STATED THAT SHE HAD NO DRUGS IN HER SYSTEM? THE MEDIA KNOWS THIS BUT THEY CONTINUE TO SAY SHE DIED FROM A DRUG OVERDOSE, AND A ACCIDENTAL DROWNING. NO, WHITNEY HOUSTON WAS CLEARLY BEATEN TO DEATH AND SO COLD BLOODEDLY MURDERED IN THAT HOTEL ROOM...

WHY DID PAT AND GARY HOUSTON BOTH RUSH IN, OUT & AROUND THAT HOTEL ROOM TAKING THINGS IN AND TAKING THINGS OUT AND STAGING THAT ROOM WHERE WHITNEY'S BODY LAID. THEY DID IT "TO SITUATE THINGS WHERE THEY WANTED THEM, AND THEN THEY BOTH CLEANED THAT HOTEL ROOM UP BEFORE THOSE OFFICERS GOT THERE?"

WHITNEY'S MANAGER HAD ALREADY TOLD ME AND MY SON THAT THE ROOM LOOK LIKE A TORNADO HIT IT WHEN HE WENT IN THERE AND FOUND WHITNEY DECEASED.

BUT WHERE WAS HE AND WHY WAS HE NOT THERE TO PROTECT WHITNEY? WHY WAS NOT PHONE RECORDS CHECKED ON "THE CORONERS PHONE" AFTER HE WROTE IN HIS REPORT THAT SOMEONE CALLED HIS PHONE AND SAID BE PREPARED TO PICK UP A BODY? WHY DID THEY NOT CHECK WHITNEY'S PHONE, AND WHERE IS HER PHONE? I BET ANY AMOUNT OF MONEY PAT AND GARY TOOK HER PHONE AND IT WAS THE FIRST THING THEY STOLE FROM THAT ROOM...

WHY WASN'T ANYONE WHO WAS AT THAT HOTEL WITH WHITNEY ARRESTED? THOSE OFFICERS KNEW AND WAS FULLY AWARE AND CERTAIN THAT THERE WAS FOUL PLAY DID THE AUTHORITIES QUESTION ANYONE AFTER FINDING WHITNEY'S BODY THEWAY THEY DID? WHY DIDN'T THE AUTHORITIES CHECK HOTEL CAMERAS? DID AUTHORITIES QUESTION ANYONE, AND ESPECIALLY HOTEL SECURITY?

WHY DID WHITNEY'S BODY STAY IN THAT ROOM FOR ALL THOSE HOURS BEFORE BEING PICKED UP? WHOSE IDEA WAS THAT? I BET THAT NEITHER PAT NOR GARY COMPLAINED ABOUT THAT BECAUSE THEY DIDN'T CARE NOT EVEN A LITTLE BIT... WHY WON'T ANYONE WHO WORKED FOR WHITNEY STEP UP TO THE PLATE AND SAY SOMETHING?

As God is my Witness

I AM 100% CERTAIN THAT ANYONE WHO EVER WORKED FOR WHITNEY WHETHER THEY DID HAIR, MAKEUP, SECURITY OR WHATEVER, THEY KNOW THAT PAT HOUSTON IS LYING SO WHY WONT THEY STEP UP TO THE PLATE AN HELP WHITNEY AND TELL THE WORLD THE TRUTH WITH ME? BLOOD IS ON A LOT OF PEOPLE'S HANDS...

ON BOBBI KRISTINA'S CASE:

THE AUTHORITIES CAME INTO KRISSY'S CONDO AND KNEW THERE WAS FOUL PLAY, SO WHY DID THEY NOT ARREST NICK GORDON, MAX LOMAS, AND THE GIRL DANIELLE? COULD IT BE THAT THEY ARE BOTH WHITE AND THAT IS PART OF WHY THEY HAVE REFUSED TO CHARGE THEM? IF IT HAD BEEN THEIR DAUGHTER WHO WAS FOUND THERE, WE ALL KNOW THEY WOULD HAVE ARRESTED PEOPLE IMMEDIATELY!

WHY DID A JUDGE AND/OR AN ATLANTA COURT SYSTEM GRANT A "NON- FAMILY" MEMBER (PAT AND CISSY HOUSTON) AND APPOINT THEM HALF OF MY NIECE'S ESTATE? THEY WERE NOT SUPPOSED TO ALLOW THAT FOR ANYONE BUT HER FATHER, MR. BOBBY BROWN. THAT WAS HIS DAUGHTER'S ESTATE. BUT IT'S OK BECAUSE GOD WILL SOON GRANT US ALL THE JUSTICE WE SO RIGHTFULLY DESERVE. WHY DID THEY GRANT IT SO FAST? DID THEY TAKE THE TIME TO EXAMINE WHITNEY'S WILL BEFORE DOING SO? THE FEDERAL AUTHORITIES NEED TO EXAMINE THAT WILL AND MAKE SURE IT WAS NOT TAMPERED WITH (WHICH I BELIEVE IT WAS).

As God is my Witness

WHERE IS THE PERSON WHO COMMITTED FRAUD AND CRIMES BY IMPERSONATING A NURSE, IS SHE IN JAIL TODAY?... AND IF SO, WHERE IS SHE AT? AND IF NOT... THEN WHY NOT?

WHY DID THEY LET NICK GORDON GO, AND NOT ARREST DANIELLE AND MAX LOMAS, WHO WERE BOTH RIGHT THERE IN MY NIECE'S LIVING ROOM AND HELPED WITH MY NIECE'S BODY BEING PLACED IN THAT BATHTUB? THERE IS NO WAY NICK DID ALL OF THAT BY HIMSELF.

THE FEDERAL AGENTS NEED TO FIND OUT WHO GOT PAID TO KEEP THEIR MOUTHS SHUT BECAUSE 3 MURDERS TOOK PLACE WITH MY FAMILY MEMBERS AND GOD WILL NOT ALLOW ANYONE TO REST UNTIL THERE IS JUSTICE FOR THEM ALL. KNOW AND BE ASSURED THAT EVERYONE WHO KNOWS SOMETHING ... BUT ARE KEEPING QUIET ... WILL NOT BE ABLE TO REST UNTIL THEY COME FORWARD AND DO THE RIGHT THING BY WHITNEY, BOBBI KRISTINA AND BOBBY BROWN JR. THEIR BLOOD IS ON THE HANDS OF THOSE WHO KNOW AND ARE GUILTY....AND UNTIL PEOPLE WHO KNOW ... COME FORWARD AND SAY AND/OR DO SOMETHING....GOD IS ON YOUR HEELS...

GOD IS A 'JUST' GOD ... AND HE SLEEPS ON NO ONE....I AM ASKING THAT "A FEDERAL INVESTIGATION"BE DONE AND RE- OPEN ALL CASES IMMEDIATELY!

PEACE!!!!!!!!!!!!!

As God is my Witness

Chapter 18
KRISSY'S MEDICAL REPORT

Fulton County Medical Examiner

430 Pryor Street SW
Atlanta, GA 30312
404-613-4400

Medical Examiners
Randy Hanzlick, MD
Michael Heninger, MD
Melissa Pasquale, MD
Michele Stauffenberg, MD
Karen Sullivan, MD

Fulton County

Case Number	15-1471
Name (First)	Bobbi
(Last)	Brown
Age, Race, Sex	022 B F

Cause of Death   Lobar pneumonia

   due to Hypoxic ischemic encephalopathy, delayed effects

   due to Immersion of face in water complicating mixed drug intoxication

Other Conditions

Manner of Death   UNDETERMINED

Found in water-filled bathtub. Used opiate,
cocaine, and benzodiazepines.

Medical Examiner(s)   Karen E. Sullivan, MD

Procedure   Autopsy   Monday, July 27, 2015   9:00 AM
                Karen E. Sullivan, MD

Signatures: _Karen E. Sullivan, MD_   _4 March 2016_

Print date: 9/22/2015
Referrals: None

As God is my Witness

REPORT OF
THE MEDICAL EXAMINER

REASON FOR PERFORMING AN EXAMINATION:

This 22 year old black woman was found unresponsive in a bathroom tub in her home with her face reportedly immersed in water. She was transported to North Fulton Hospital where she was diagnosed as having suffered an anoxic brain injury. After approximately a week she was transferred to Emory University Hospital, and then DeKalb Rehabilitation Center before being admitted to Peachtree Christian Hospice. She died on July 26, 2015 approximately six months after her original hospitalization.

SUMMARY OF FINDINGS:

I. Hypoxic ischemic encephalopathy (anoxic brain injury).
    A. Reported finding of decedent in water-filled bathtub and face immersed in water.
    B. Mixed drug intoxication; antemortem testing performed on hospital blood specimen per NMS Labs.
        1. Morphine level 8.9 nanog/ml.
        2. Recent cocaine use; benzoylecgonine level 300 nanog/ml.
        3. Benzodiazepine use.
            a. Clonazepam level 12 nanog/ml.
            b. 7-amino clonazepam level 100 nanog/ml.
            c. Alprazolam level 5.4 nanog/ml.
        4. Marijuana use.
            a. Delta-9-tetrahydrocannabinol (active marijuana ingredient) level 1.9 nanog/ml.
            b. Delta-9-carboxy-9-tetrahydrocannabinol (inactive metabolite) level 11 nanog/ml.
    C. Seizure disorder as a result of hypoxic ischemic encephalopathy.
    D. Bilateral lobar pneumonia.

II. Ancillary Studies.
    A. Postmortem toxicology results per NMS Labs.
        1. Blood acetaminophen level 21 mcg/ml.
        2. Blood phenobarbital level 85 mcg/ml.
        3. Blood clonazepam level 11 nanog/ml.
        4. Blood 7-amino clonazepam level 86 nanog/ml
        5. Blood morphine level 380 nanog/ml.
        6. Blood levetiracetam level 6.1 mcg/ml.
        7. Blood phenytoin level 32 mcg/ml.
        8. Blood topiramate level 13,000 nanog/ml.
        9. Blood lacosamide level 12 mcg/ml.
    B. Laboratory results per Grady Memorial Hospital.
        1. Vitreous fluid glucose level 111 mg/dl (mildly elevated).
        2. Blood hemoglobin A_{1C} level within normal limits.
        3. Vitreous fluid urea nitrogen level 40 mg/dl (mildly elevated).

As God is my Witness

**REPORT OF
THE MEDICAL EXAMINER**

15-1471
BOBBI BROWN
Page 3 of 10
Examiner: Karen E. Sullivan, MD

4. Vitreous fluid creatinine level within normal limits.
5. Hemoglobin phenotype AA.

CAUSE OF DEATH:

Lobar pneumonia.
Due to: Hypoxic ischemic encephalopathy, delayed effects.
Due to: Immersion of face in water complicating mixed drug intoxication.

MANNER OF DEATH:

Undetermined.

OPINION:

It is my opinion that Bobbi Kristina Brown died as a result of lobar pneumonia which was a delayed complication of hypoxic ischemic encephalopathy due to mixed drug intoxication and immersion of her face in water. Hypoxic-ischemic encephalopathy is defined as brain injury due to asphyxia. The primary causes are systemic hypoxemia (low blood oxygen levels) and/or reduced cerebral blood flow.

Pneumonia (infection of the lungs) results in accumulation of protein and white blood cells in the alveolar (air) spaces. The presence of these materials prevents the normal exchange of oxygen and carbon dioxide in the lungs. In pneumonia, bacteria and viruses from the upper airways or, less commonly, from the bloodstream spread to the lung tissue. Once there, a combination of factors (including the type of microorganism and overall health of the person) may lead to pneumonia. Pneumonia may occur in individuals undergoing prolonged mechanical ventilation and in individuals with altered levels of consciousness resulting from seizures, drug intoxication, or head trauma.

Morphine is a drug produced from the metabolism of many opiate compounds including heroin. It depresses the central nervous system and can be fatal by causing respiratory depression and/or coma. Fatality rates are higher in patients who use alcohol and other drugs such as benzodiazepines and/or cocaine. 6-monoacetylmorphine, the demonstrative metabolite of heroin, was not isolated from Ms. Brown's hospital blood sample.

Clonazepam and alprazolam are benzodiazepines. Benzodiazepines are sedatives/hypnotics and prescribed for anxiety relief. All the sedative-hypnotics are general central nervous system depressants. Deaths associated with use of benzodiazepines are caused by respiratory arrest. Alcohol use greatly enhances the activity of benzodiazepines.

Benzoylecgonine, an inactive cocaine metabolite, was identified in Ms. Brown's hospital blood sample, but non-metabolized cocaine was not present. The presence of benzoylecgonine is

As God is my Witness

suggestive of recent cocaine use. Cocaine causes coronary artery spasms in addition to increases in blood pressure and pulse resulting in the development of dysrhythmias (abnormal heart rhythms). Prolonged dysrhythmias may cause an individual's death as blood does not circulate in an efficient manner to the body's internal organs including the brain.

The circumstances under which Ms. Brown entered the bathtub are unknown. Whether her death was due to intentional or accidental causes are unknown. Therefore the manner of Ms. Brown's death is classified as undetermined.

As God is my Witness

REPORT OF
THE MEDICAL EXAMINER

15-1471
BOBBI BROWN
Page 5 of 10
Examiner: Karen E. Sullivan, MD

DATE, TIME, AND PLACE OF EXAMINATION:

Under the provisions of the Georgia Death Investigation Act, an autopsy is performed in the morgue of the Fulton County Medical Examiner's Center on Monday, July 27, 2015 commencing at 0900 hours.

PRESENTATION, CLOTHING, AND PERSONAL EFFECTS:

The body is received supine in a white plastic disaster bag secured with a red plastic seal numbered 0024590. Attached to the plastic seal is a Fulton County Medical Examiner's Center identification tag with the designation "15-1471; Brown, Bobbi K.". The following items of clothing and personal effects are on or accompany the body:

1. White hospital style sheets beneath the decedent's body within the disaster bag.
2. A pink head band and black elastic hairband in the hair.
3. A pink nightgown on the upper extremities and torso.
4. A disposable adult undergarment at the waist.
5. A cloth doll with light brown and gold clothing with a purple yarn magnetic holder containing printed words on a white placard.
6. White metal jewelry in the right cheek.

The disposable undergarment is discarded. The remaining items are released with the body.

DIAGNOSTIC AND THERAPEUTIC DEVICES AND MARKINGS:

1. A tracheotomy tube in the anterior surface of the neck.
2. A percutaneous gastric tube in the left upper quadrant of the abdomen.

POSTMORTEM X-RAYS:

Twenty-five postmortem x-rays of the head, torso, and extremities are obtained. Neither recent nor remote fractures are noted. No foreign objects are identified.

POSTMORTEM CHANGES:

The refrigerated body retains central warmth. Rigor mortis is generalized and mildly to moderately developed. Violet postmortem lividity is posteriorly distributed except in regions of pressure. The corneas are clear. The vermilion borders of the lips are moist. The body is well preserved.

As God is my Witness

REPORT OF
THE MEDICAL EXAMINER

15-1471
BOBBI BROWN
Page 6 of 10
Examiner: Karen E. Sullivan, MD

FEATURES OF IDENTIFICATION:

The unembalmed body is that of an adult black female appearing younger than the reported age of 22 years, measuring 66-1/4" in length and weighing 93 pounds. The decedent has a thin build, is well developed and under-nourished. The brown head hair is 4-3/4" in length. The irides are brown. The natural teeth are in an average state of repair. The left maxillary central and lateral incisors are remotely absent. The left earlobe displays four piercing defects. The right earlobe displays two piercing defect and one full thickness healed vertical defect. Two piercing defects are in the midline of the abdomen just above the umbilicus. The right nostril exhibits a healing/healed piercing defect. The monochromatic tattoo of "222" is on the anterior surface of the left wrist. A monochromatic tattoo of "WEH" on the anterior surface of the right forearm is surrounded by four birds. A monochromatic tattoo of musical notes and scale is on the left lateral torso, extending into the left lower quadrant of the abdomen. A number of well healed scars are on the head and neck, torso, and extremities.

Head and Neck:
1. A 1/16" hypopigmented scar is on the left side of the upper lip.
2. Three scars on the right side of the neck are 1/16" to 3/8" in length and cover an area of 3-1/4 x 1-1/4".
3. A 5/8" scar is on the right side of the neck.
4. Scars on the left side of the neck range from 1/8" to 3/4" and cover an area of 1 x 1/2".

Torso:
1. Two scars on the right side of the upper chest are 1/2" and 1/4" in length.
2. Six scars on the left side of the upper chest range from 1/8" to 1/4" in length.

Extremities:
1. A 1-1/4" oval scar is on the posterior surface of the left shoulder and arm.
2. A 1/4" scar is on the anterior surface of the arm.
3. A 2-1/16" scar is on the posterior surface of the left forearm.
4. A 1/2" scar is on the anterior surface of the left forearm.
5. Four faint horizontal and obliquely oriented scars on the anterior surface of the left forearm are 1/2" to 3/4" in length.
6. Two areas of hyperpigmentation on the anterior surface of the left forearm are 3/4" and 1-1/4" in length.
7. A 1/8" scar is on the posterior surface of the right forearm.
8. A 1-1/2" scar overlies the right lateral malleolus.
9. On the anterior surface of the right foot are two areas of cutaneous hyperpigmentation, measuring 1-3/4" and 1-1/4" in length.

As God is my Witness

EVIDENCE OF ACUTE INJURY:

1. Cutaneous depressions on each mastoid process are associated with dark purple discoloration of the skin.
2. A 3/4" ecchymosis is in the left antecubital fossa.
3. 1/2" and 1/4" ecchymoses are in the right antecubital fossa.
4. 1" and 1-1/4" ecchymoses are on the anterior and medial surfaces of the left thigh.
5. Two ecchymoses associated with remnants of adhesive/tape cover an area of 2-1/2" on the anterior surface of the right thigh.

EXTERNAL EXAMINATION:

The head is normally formed. The soft tissues of the forehead, cheeks, and chin exhibit acne. The facial bones and mandible are free of palpable fractures. Neither ocular nor facial petechiae are present. The sclerae are anicteric. The conjunctivae are pale. The nose is normally formed. The nasal vestibules are clear. The nasal septum is palpated with forceps and is intact. The lips, teeth, tongue, gums, and buccal mucosa are unremarkable. The external meati, pinnae, and mastoid regions are unexceptional.

The trachea is in the midline of the neck. The neck is neither crepitant nor excessively mobile. No palpable masses are present.

The chest and back are symmetrical and well developed. The breasts are free of palpable masses. The flat abdomen is devoid of organomegaly. The spine is straight.

The extremities are symmetrical and well developed. The appendicular skeleton is stable to palpation and manipulation. The hands and feet are normally formed. All of the digits are present. The nails extend to 1/8" beyond the tips of the digits and are covered with light pink, gloss polish.

The external genitalia, perineum, and anorectal areas are normally formed and atraumatic. The inguinal regions and buttocks are unremarkable.

There is no cervical, axillary, or inguinal lymphadenopathy.

INTERNAL EXAMINATION:

Head:

The scalp is reflected using the standard intermastoidal incision. There is no scalp trauma. The calvarium is intact. The dura is intact and free of discoloration and thickening. The base of the skull is examined after stripping the dura and is intact. The leptomeninges are thin and transparent. There is no epidural, subdural, or subarachnoid hemorrhage. The brain weighs 1230

As God is my Witness

REPORT OF
THE MEDICAL EXAMINER

15-1471
BOBBI BROWN
Page 8 of 10
Examiner: Karen E. Sullivan, MD

grams. The gyri are flattened and the sulci are widened suggestive of cerebral atrophy. There are no lesions of the cortical gray ribbon, white matter, or deep gray matter structures indicative of active natural disease processes. Neither brain swelling nor herniation is noted. The normally distributed blood vessels of the circle of Willis are free of atherosclerosis and aneurysms. The substantia nigra is normally pigmented. The cerebellum, brainstem, upper cervical spinal cord, and ventricular system are normally formed. The cerebrospinal fluid is clear.

Neck:

The skin of the neck is dissected to the angle of the mandible. The tongue is atraumatic. There is no trauma of the soft tissues, airway, or vital structures in the neck. No airway mucosal edema is present. The hyoid bone and laryngeal cartilages are free of fractures and deformities. The epiglottis is neither inflamed nor edematous. No foreign objects are in the airway. The carotid vessels are pliable and patent. The anterior cervical spine and atlanto-occipital joint are stable to manipulation.

Chest and Abdomen:

The skin of the chest and abdomen is reflected using the usual Y-shaped incision. The subcutaneous fat is 5/16" in thickness at the level of the umbilicus. The subcutaneous fat and musculature are free of injury. The sternum and chest plate are intact and upon their removal no abnormal fluid collections are in the body cavities. No unusual odors or color changes are present. Examination of the organs in situ reveals normal organ morphology and relationships. The intact diaphragm is normally formed. The organs are removed using the Virchow technique.

Cardiovascular System:

The heart weighs 230 grams and exhibits normal four-chambered anatomy. The ventricles are of normal thickness. The widely patent coronary arteries arise from their usual locations, ramify across their respective ventricles, and demonstrate right dominant distribution. The epicardium, valve leaflets, chordae tendineae, and endocardium are normally formed. The foramen ovale is probe patent. The brown myocardium is free of discrete lesions. The aorta and its normally distributed major branches exhibit minimal atherosclerosis.

Respiratory System:

The trachea, hilar structures, and major vessels are normally formed and atraumatic. The right and left lungs weigh 410 grams and 330 grams respectively. The pleural surfaces are smooth. The parenchyma of the lower lobes is congested with the expression of blood from the cut surfaces upon compression. Neither lung exhibits thrombosis, embolism, infarction, or neoplasia.

As God is my Witness

Autopsyfiles.org - Bobbi Kristina Brown Autopsy Report

**REPORT OF
THE MEDICAL EXAMINER**

15-1471
BOBBI BROWN
Page 9 of 10
Examiner: Karen E. Sullivan, MD

Gastrointestinal System:

The esophagus is lined by unremarkable tan-gray mucosa. The gastroesophageal junction is unremarkable. The gastric mucosa is normally rugated and the stomach contains a scant amount of light green fluid. A percutaneous gastrostomy tube terminates in the fundus. There are no lesions of the mucosa, wall, or serosa of the small bowel, colon, or rectum. No foreign objects are in the gastrointestinal tract. The appendix is in the right lower quadrant of the abdomen.

Hepatobiliary System:

The liver weighs 1890 grams. The intact capsule is of normal thickness. The homogenous, brown parenchyma is free of mass lesions. The gallbladder contains approximately 10 ml of viscous green bile. The mucosa is unremarkable. No gallstones are present. The pancreas is of normal size, has the usual lobular architecture, and free of fibrosis, hemorrhage, and fat necrosis.

Urogenital System:

The right and left kidneys weigh 150 grams and 160 grams respectively. The capsules strip with ease to reveal smooth cortical surfaces. The cut surfaces including the pyramids, pelves, calyces, and vessels are unremarkable. The ureters are of normal caliber. There are no lesions of the mucosa, wall, or serosa of the empty urinary bladder. The nongravid uterus is free of leiomyomata. The endometrium and myometrium are 0.1 cm and 1.2 cm in thickness respectively. No endometrial lesions are present. The ovaries, fallopian tubes, cervix, and vaginal mucosa are unremarkable.

Reticuloendothelial System:

The spleen weighs 130 grams. The intact capsule is of normal thickness. The cut surface is dark red. The red pulp and white pulp are normally distributed. No focal lesions are present. Regional lymph nodes are unremarkable. The thymus gland weighs 20 grams and partially replaced by mature adipose tissue. The residual gray-white parenchyma is free of discrete lesions.

Musculoskeletal System:

The axial skeleton is intact. The lateral aspect of the left 9th rib is slightly irregular by palpation without definitive fracture. The symmetrical skeletal muscles are unremarkable.

Endocrine System:

The symmetrical thyroid gland is of normal size. The golden parenchyma is free of nodules, hemorrhage, and cysts. The adrenal glands are of normal size and free of hemorrhage and nodularity. The grossly unremarkable pituitary gland is of normal size.

As God is my Witness

MICROSCOPIC DESCRIPTION:

Seventeen hematoxylin and eosin stained slides of the heart (including the conduction system), lungs, gastrointestinal tract, liver, pancreas, spleen, lymph nodes, thymus gland, kidneys, uterus, ovaries, thyroid gland, adrenal glands, pituitary gland, and brain are examined.

Cardiovascular System: Sections of the heart reveal focal mild interstitial fibrosis in the region of the atrioventricular node. Neither acute nor chronic inflammation is evident.

Respiratory System: Each lung exhibits lobar pneumonia. Acute intra-alveolar inflammation is evident in one lobe of the right lung and each lobe of the left lung. In addition, the left lung demonstrates interstitial neutrophilic and lymphocytic inflammation. Increased numbers of intra-alveolar pigmented macrophages are present in sections of both lungs.

Brain: Sections of the cerebellum reveal decreased numbers of Purkinje cells.

The remaining histologically unremarkable tissue sections confirm the gross impression.

OTHER PROCEDURES:

1. Blood is submitted to NMS Labs for toxicologic analysis.
2. Vitreous fluid is submitted to Grady Memorial Hospital for electrolyte analysis and beta-hydroxybutyrate quantitation. Blood is submitted for hemoglobin A_{1C} and hemoglobin phenotype evaluation.
3. An air-dried blood spot card is retained in this facility.
4. Documentary and identification photographs are obtained.
5. Representative tissue sections are processed to slides in 17 cassettes.
6. The examined organs are returned to the body cavity.
7. Serum and blood samples are retained in this facility.
8. The clothing and personal effects are handled as described in the text.
9. Records from Emory Johns Creek Hospital, Rural Metro EMS, North Fulton Hospital, Emory University Hospital, DeKalb Medical Long Term Acute, and Homestead Hospice are reviewed.

KES:sm

Dictated: 07/27/2015
Transcribed: 07/28/2015
Finalized: 09/22/2015

www.ingramcontent.com/pod-product-compliance
Lightning Source LLC
Chambersburg PA
CBHW071658120626
46550CB00001B/21